McIntosh and Weatherford,
Creek Indian Leaders

———— · ————

McIntosh and Weatherford, Creek Indian Leaders

————— • —————

Benjamin W. Griffith, Jr.

The University of Alabama Press

TUSCALOOSA AND LONDON

Copyright © 1988 by
The University of Alabama Press
Tuscaloosa, Alabama 35487
All rights reserved
Manufactured in the United States of America

Library of Congress Cataloging-in-Publication Data
Griffith, Benjamin W.
  McIntosh and Weatherford, Creek Indian leaders

  Bibliography: p.
  Includes index.
  1. McIntosh, William, ca. 1775–1825.
2. Weatherford, William, ca. 1780–1824.   3. Creek
Indians—Biography.   4. Creek Indians—History.
5. Creek War, 1813–1814.   6. Indians of North America—
Alabama—History.   7. Indians of North America—
Georgia—History.   I. Title.
E99.C9M333 1988   976.1'04'0922   86-14663
ISBN 0-8173-0340-5

British Library Cataloguing-in-Publication
Data is available.

This book is dedicated to
the memory of my parents,
Ben and Mary Griffith,
and to my wife, daughter, and son,
for their continuing support
and encouragement.

———— • ————

Contents

———— • ————

Illustrations

———— • ————

Preface

———— • ————

It is an audacious act to attempt to write a biography of an American Indian of the early nineteenth century, relying as one must on such historical evidence as has been preserved in the record of white activity along the frontier. The strobe light of such a record illuminates but intermittently, and gaps in the narrative become frustrating. It is even more recklessly bold to attempt a dual biography of two opposing mestizo Creek leaders who, as far as is known, never met, not even in the manner of Lee and Grant at Appomattox. It is almost too presumptuous to admit that in attempting this book I was following Barbara Tuchman's example of using the shadowy figure of Enguerrand de Coucy VII as the spine of her marvelous work on the fourteenth century, *A Distant Mirror.*

Both William McIntosh and William Weatherford are necessary figures if one is to focus on the Creeks in writing a history of Indian-white relations in the Creek Nation from the time of the American Revolution through the Creek War of 1813–14 and the final cessions of Creek lands in Georgia and Alabama. Each is a necessary complement to the other because Weatherford took the side of the Red Sticks in the Creek War, and McIntosh fought alongside the whites and led the friendly Creeks against Weatherford's forces, becoming a major and then a brigadier general in the process.

These two mixed-blood Creeks were to associate closely with some of the most important and interesting men in the early republic. Both knew Andrew Jackson, and one or the other interrelated with Presidents Thomas Jefferson, James Monroe, John Quincy Adams, and James Madison, as well as Tecumseh, Alexander McGillivray, William Augustus Bowles, Benjamin Hawkins, and many other lesser-known figures. In late 1818, when General McIntosh was honored for his military exploits at a public dinner hosted by some citizens of Augusta, he was certainly the most widely known of all Creeks and was the shining example for all those who would Americanize the Indians. A newspaper account of the banquet said of McIntosh: "We have seen him in the bosom of the forest, surrounded by a band of wild and ungovernable savages—we have seen him too, in the drawing room in the civilized walks of life, receiving that meed of approbation which his services so justly merit. In each situation we found him the same, easy and unconstrained in his address, and uniform in his conduct."[1] A few years later McIntosh was to experience a dramatic change of fortune and die disgraced in the eyes of some of his fellow Creeks. Weatherford, once feared and hated as a Red Stick leader, was to die as a south Alabama plantation owner, much respected by his white neighbors.

Thomas L. McKenney, who was superintendent of Indian trade from 1816 to 1822 and who knew McIntosh and other important Indian leaders personally, was among the first to see the mixed-blood offspring of Europeans as forming a class that, despite the Indians' egalitarian nature, came into "the quiet possession of a kind of rank." He wrote that though "bred to the athletic exercises and sports of the Indian, they had a nurture superior to that of the savage." He concluded that "the half-breeds, having the Indian blood on the one hand and the advantage of property and education on the other, became very influential, and had they been permitted to form governments . . . would probably have concentrated in their hands all the property of the Indians. To this class mainly was confined the civilization among the southern tribes so much spoken of a few years ago." One of the most recent to note the importance of this class is Frank Owsley, Jr., who finds it significant that all the Creek prophets were mixed-bloods, "as indeed were most of the battle leaders, like William Weatherford and Peter McQueen."[2] He might have added interpreters, including Paddy Carr, Alexander Cornells, and Samuel Hawkins.

Both William McIntosh (White Warrior) and William Weatherford

(Red Eagle) have become legendary figures, more the subject of yarn-spinning than of serious inquiry. It is hoped that this book will provide a balance by bringing together all that is known about these mixed-blood leaders into a sustained narrative that embraces one of the most colorful and interesting periods of frontier history in the Southeast.

It would be difficult to number all those who have assisted me in writing this book and impossible to name them all. I am especially indebted to Professor C. L. Grant of Georgia State University, Professor Michael D. Green of Dartmouth College, and Professor Frank L. Owsley, Jr., of Auburn University; their careful reading of the original manuscript and their suggestions for improvement have been immensely valuable. Special gratitude goes to Dianne Hannah, Vicky Hannah, and Anita Immele, who typed the manuscript, and to the staff of the Ingram Library at West Georgia College for aid beyond the call of duty.

THE MILIEU OF
MCINTOSH AND WEATHERFORD

(Courtesy of Cartographic Services, Department of Geography, West Georgia College)

McIntosh and Weatherford,
Creek Indian Leaders

1

Introduction

———— • ————

About the time of the American revolutionary war, when the Creek
Indians owned land that is today approximately the lower two-thirds
of Alabama and of Georgia west of the Oconee River, two sons were
born to Indian mothers and Scots fathers in obscure towns in the territory of the Creek Nation, one along the Chattahoochee River and
the other by the Alabama. Both sons were named William, and both
were to become leaders of their mothers' people, opposing each other
in the Creek War of 1813–14. William McIntosh—called Tustunnuggee Hutkee or White Warrior—was commissioned a brigadier general
in the United States Army for his contributions to Andrew Jackson's
forces at the Battle of Horseshoe Bend and for other services to the
country, but he died embroiled in controversy, executed by his fellow
Creeks, who charged that he led in ceding lands to the federal government in violation of the agreed-upon policy of the other chiefs of the
Creek Nation. William Weatherford, called Red Eagle, opposed Jackson's troops but was so noble in his surrender that he won Old
Hickory's respect and pardon. He died a planter and local hero in
southern Alabama, near the site of Fort Mims, against which he had
led a brutal assault during the Creek War.

Racial mixtures that resulted in such remarkable men as these were
not uncommon. French and British traders had begun filtering into
the Creek Nation at a very early date, and it was advantageous for
such men to have Indian wives. It was not always so for farmers, who
found that some Indian women could not easily adapt to the ways of
European housekeeping and husbandry. Precise records are lacking
to indicate the percentage of Caucasians in the Creek Nation, but it
was probably less than 10 percent. Caleb Swan, an army lieutenant
and deputy Indian agent, who knew the Creeks of this period first-

1

hand, set the white population among the Creeks in 1790 at three hundred, a number, he added, "sufficient to contaminate all the natives."[1] Historical accounts of the Creeks are liberally sprinkled with such British and European names as Burgess, Cornell, Galphin, Grizzard, Kennard, McIntosh, McQueen, Milfort, Moniac, Perryman, Sullivan, Walker, and Weatherford.

There is nothing to indicate that the Creeks discriminated against the whites or their mestizo offspring. Since descent was determined through the female line rather than patrilineally as in white society, the father's ethnic background meant little to the Creeks.[2] Moreover, the Indians, as Peter Farb points out, had a well-established system of assimilating new members into the tribes. Often prisoners of war were adopted by Indian families to replace husbands or sons who were battle casualties, and such persons were completely integrated into the new society. When a white settler took an Indian wife, he acquired the support of her entire clan. In an analysis of thirty captive whites, fifteen males and fifteen females, the anthropologist John R. Swanton found among them an unusually high percentage of social success. Three or four men became chiefs, and about the same number of women became wives of chiefs.[3]

It is fortunate that both McIntosh and Weatherford chose to live in the Creek Nation, where their mixture of Indian and Caucasian blood was no handicap. American English has a number of words to describe a person of mixed blood, all with varying degrees of unfavorable connotation: half-breed, half-caste, hybrid, mestizo, miscegenate, and mongrel. Outside the Creek Nation, Red Eagle and White Warrior were to face throughout their lives the common prejudice toward their hybrid heritage, accompanied by the inevitable charges of emotional instability and psychic dualism.

Indian women were attractive to North American settlers from the beginning. Within a few years after Virginia was settled in the early seventeenth century, more than forty male colonists had married Indians. "Indianizing," or adopting the ways of the Indians, became such a threat to the dissolution of the early settlements that the colony of Virginia instituted severe penalties against going to live with the Indians, and Cotton Mather preached against Indianizing. The Creek Indian agent Benjamin Hawkins said of Indian wives that "if the concurrent testimony of the white husbands can be relied upon, the women have much the temper of the mule, except when they are amorous, and then they exhibit all the amiable and generous qualities of the cat."[4]

The Indian lifestyle was also alluring to the early settlers. Michel Guillaume St. Jean de Crevecoeur, in his *Letters from an American Farmer* (1782), wrote that there must be in the Indian's "social bond something singularly captivating, and far superior to be boasted of among us; for thousands of Europeans are Indians, and we have no examples of even one of these Aborigines having from choice become Europeans!" As Peter Farb concludes, "Whites who had lived for a time with Indians almost never wanted to leave. But virtually none of the 'civilized' Indians who had been given the opportunity to sample White society chose to become a part of it."[5]

William McIntosh's paternal grandfather was John McIntosh, a Highlander from Inverness, who came to Georgia in 1736, settled in Savannah, and married a Scotswoman, Margaret McGillivray.[6] He later established a trading post along the Tombigbee River on land granted him for service to the king. William McIntosh's father was Captain William McIntosh, a Tory who commanded a contingent of Creeks who were allied with the British in the revolutionary war, and his mother, said to be called Senoya, was a Creek woman of unmixed blood. Little is known of her except the tradition that she was a member of the most powerful and privileged of all the Creek clans: the Wind clan. Shortly after the Revolution, Captain McIntosh sired another son, Roderick (or Rolly), by another Creek woman, and then he left the Indian country forever. He moved to Savannah and married a cousin, Barbara McIntosh, sister of General John McIntosh.[7] Ironically, General McIntosh's youngest daughter, Catherine, was to become the mother of George M. Troup, who was governor of Georgia at the time that his first cousin William McIntosh met violent death at the hand of some fellow Creeks for ceding land to the federal government, land cessions that had been largely precipitated by Governor Troup.

William Weatherford also sprang from a distinguished family. He was the great-grandson of Captain Marchand, a French officer in command of Fort Toulouse, located on the junction of the Coosa and Tallapoosa rivers, and his Indian wife, Sehoy, a Creek of the noble Wind clan. Before he was assassinated by his men in a mutinous uprising in 1772, Marchand fathered a daughter, also named Sehoy, who first married a Tabacha chieftain, whose name is unkown. From that union came a daughter, called Sehoy III, who was to become the mother of William Weatherford. Sehoy II later took as her second husband a Scots trader, Lachlan McGillivray. As a youth, McGillivray had arrived in Charleston about 1738 with a shilling and a jackknife in his pocket.

He headed for Indian country, where he traded his knife for pelts, and from this meager capital he amassed a fortune by the time of the Revolution—enough to retire on in Scotland and to assuage the pain of having $100,000 worth of real property confiscated by Georgia patriots.[8] Lachlan and Sehoy had four children, a son and three daughters. The son, Alexander McGillivray, became the most influential of all the Creek chiefs, and from 1787 until his death in 1793 he symbolized the Creek Nation to whites. His uncanny diplomatic skill enabled him to play the British, Spanish, and Americans against each other to gain benefits in trade and protection for his people.

Sehoy III, daughter of the Tabacha chieftain, was married in 1768 to John Tate, the last British agent among the Creeks. At the outbreak of the Revolution, Tate was given the rank of colonel in the British army; he recruited a large force of friendly Indians and in the summer of 1780 marched with them toward Augusta to reinforce Colonel James Grierson's army. On the way, however, he became deranged and died.[9] Shortly thereafter, Sehoy married Charles Weatherford, a red-headed Scotsman, who was a friend of her father.[10] From this union came the celebrated Red Eagle, William Weatherford. Less than half Indian, with black eyes and light skin, this handsome young man with the Scots name of Weatherford could have merged into the white man's world without notice, but he chose to live as an Indian, reluctantly siding with the Upper Creeks, who were hostile to the white settlers, in the Creek War of 1813–14. Red Eagle's lifestyle differed greatly from that of his uncle, Alexander McGillivray. Despite his power and influence among the Creeks, McGillivray was culturally more allied with the whites. He lived in a plantation house, owned black slaves, and customarily spoke English, so disdaining the Creek language that he always spoke through an interpreter at public meetings of his people.

The actual date of William McIntosh's birth is obscured by conflicting data, but he was probably born in 1778.[11] His birthplace was the Lower Creek town of Coweta, located on the right bank of the Chattahoochee, at the junction of Broken Arrow Creek, fifteen miles downriver from the present-day Columbus, Georgia, and three miles below the fall line in what is now Russell County, Alabama. Coweta, because it was the seat of the political head of the Creek Nation, was visited often by early travelers. William Bartram, the English naturalist, who visited there in 1777, wrote that Coweta "is called the bloody town, where the Micos, chiefs, and warriors assemble when a general war is proposed; and here captives and state malefactors are put to death." Hawkins, for nearly twenty years an agent to the Creeks, described in 1797 an execution site at Coweta, which McIntosh surely observed as a boy growing up in the town: "I was shown in an old field some stakes to which the Cherokees had been tied in the last war they had with the Creeks about 40 years past when taken prisoners. Three of the stakes remain. Here the captives were tied and here they received their doom, which with the exception of the young lads and a few women was the torture till death."[12]

In 1799 Hawkins described Coweta Old Town, the "public establishment" of the Lower Creeks and the residence of the agent, as good, rich land on a "high flat." The Creeks estimated the number of gunmen in Coweta at one hundred; Hawkins "ascertained by actual enumeration" that they had sixty-six. Hawkins fenced in two hundred acres and tried to "introduce regular husbandry to serve as a model and stimulus for the neighboring towns who crowd the public shops here, at all seasons, when the hunters are not in the woods." Even as he wrote he doubted the success of the project, "from the difficulty of changing the old habits of indolence and sitting daily in the squares, which seem peculiarly riveted on the residenters of the towns." He was no more complimentary to the Indian country white man, whom he described, "with but few exceptions," as "a lazy, cunning, thievish animal, so much degraded in the estimation of the Indians that they are considered a slave of their family and treated accordingly."[13]

LeClerc Milfort, a young French adventurer whose hastily written account of his twenty-year sojourn in the Creek Nation has sometimes been found questionable, claimed to have arrived in the town of Coweta in May 1776, a short time before McIntosh's birth. He wrote of the timber cabins set three to a side in a perfect square in the center of the town, with the grand cabin of the great chief of the nation facing the rising sun. Milfort mentions sleeping on the floor on a bearskin rug and his bounteous meals of roasted meat, bread, and sagamite, a drink made of fermented corn meal.[14]

The year of William Weatherford's birth is given in most sources as "about 1780," but since Sehoy Tate did not become a widow until the late summer of that year, a more likely date is sometime in 1781. He was born near Coosauda, an Upper Creek town situated on the west bank of the Alabama River, three miles below the junction of the Coosa and Tallapoosa rivers.[15] Weatherford's father had set up a trading post on a high bluff near the river and built a race track nearby. He devoted much of his energy to breeding and training fine horses, and the crowds attracted by his races added to the prosperity of his trading business. Benjamin Hawkins visited the Weatherfords in December 1766 and described the experience in his journal: "Mr. Weatherford showed me this morning some fine horses raised by him, on his plantation, they were blooded nearly full, 15 hands high, looked well, their feet somewhat too flat, owing to their being raised in flat swampy lands." Near Weatherford's house, Hawkins noted, were five conic earthern mounds, the largest thirty yards in diameter and seventeen feet high and the others thirty feet in diameter and five feet high. He did not speculate on the purpose for which these obviously ceremonial mounds were raised, but he pointed out a practical use, that of giving cattle and horses a safe place of refuge when the Alabama River overflowed its banks.[16]

The agent met Mrs. Weatherford and remarked, "I am informed [she] lives well in some taste, but expensively. Her negroes do but little, and consume everything in common with their mistress, who is a stranger to economy." He did not mention young William, who would have been about fifteen years old at the time. After leaving the Weatherford plantation, Hawkins paddled his canoe to the site of Fort Toulouse, on the Coosa River one mile above its junction with the Tallapoosa. In his visit on December 20, 1796, Hawkins found five iron cannon with the trunnions broken off and a few bunker beds, all that remained of the old fort that was destroyed by its commandant, Chevalier Lavnoue, at the close of the French and Indian War in 1763.[17] Young Weatherford must also have explored the nearby site of the Old French fort, where his great-grandfather Captain Marchand was killed by his own men.

The Indian ancestors of McIntosh and Weatherford were a remarkable people, the Muskogees, called Creeks by the English traders because of the many streams and rivers in their homeland. Creek legends relate that they came to this rich and abundant land, later to become the envy of cotton-planting white settlers and encroachers, by way of the Red River. When the Creeks first came is not known, but it may have been as early as A.D. 800; then for two centuries Indians from the north continued to pour into the Southwest by way of the eastern Rockies. As they moved eastward, the Muskogees incorporated defeated remains of tribes into a loose confederacy of at least twelve distinguishable ethnic groups. Before Europeans arrived, the Creeks had taken in the Alabama, Koasati, and Hitchiti Indians; later, members of the Apalachee, Shawnee, Yuchi, Natchez, and Chickasaw tribes joined the confederacy. Many of these peoples retained their own languages, and by the eighteenth century, six languages were spoken in the confederacy. By the early part of the nineteenth century, however, the tongue of the Muskogees was the dominant one, and many of the original differences in social organizations and clan relationships had merged into what became generally known as the Creek way of life.[18]

The confederacy was divided along geographical lines, with the Upper Creeks living along the Coosa and Tallapoosa river valleys, in present-day Alabama, and the Lower Creeks in the valleys of the Flint and Chattahoochee, primarily in what is now Georgia. Michael D. Green theorizes that the designations Upper and Lower Creeks were given by the Charleston traders, who traveled west on a road that forked in central Georgia, the left, or lower path leading to the Chattahoochee, and the right, or upper path leading to the Tallapoosa River. In fact, the upper towns lay almost directly west of the lower towns. The thirty-nine upper towns, as reported by Francis Ogilvie in the summer of 1764, were divided into three groups: the Alabamas, the Tallapoosas, and the Abeikas. The most important Upper Creek towns were Tuckabatchee and Coosa, and the principal Lower Creek towns were Coweta, home of McIntosh, and Cusseta. These towns were also divided into two other categories: red towns and white towns. The red towns were associated with war and the white towns with peace, and they were often so designated according to whether the chief of the town was a member of a red or a white clan. Clans had from the earliest times been designated so that the white clans, the *hathagalgi*, supplied the councillors who spoke for peace, and the red clans, the *tcilokogalgi*, supplied the "bearers of the red sticks," traditional Creek war symbols.[19]

Whether they lived in an upper or lower town, the Creeks were blessed with lands well favored by nature. Traveling in Creek country in the middle of the eighteenth century, James Adair wrote: "Most of their towns are very commodiously and pleasantly situated on large beautiful creeks, or rivers where the lands are fertile, the water clean and well tasted, and the air extremely pure."[20]

Creek villages, which had no ceremonial squares, were residential communities, offshoots of nearby towns, which were themselves small, usually with fewer than two thousand persons. Towns consisted of houses located in small square compounds that radiated out from the town square, the seat of government and ceremony, and the nearby chunky yard or playfield. William Bartram described the ingeniously arranged family compounds at length:

The dwellings of the Upper Creeks consist of little square, or rather of four dwelling houses inclosing a square area, exactly on the plan of the public square. Every family, however, has not four of these houses; some have but three, others not more than two, and some but one, according to the circumstances of the individual, or number of his family. Those who have four buildings have a particular use for each building. One serves as a cook room and winter lodging house, another as a summer lodging house and hall for receiving visitors, and a third for a granary or provision house, etc. The last is commonly two stories high, and divided into two apartments, transversely, the lower story of one end being a potato house, for keeping such other roots as require to be kept close and defended from cold in winter. The chamber above it is the council. At the other end of this building, both upper and lower stories are open on their sides; the lower story serves for their shed for their saddles, pack saddles, and gears and other lumber; the loft over it is a very spacious, airy, pleasant pavilion, where the chief of the family reposes in the hot seasons, and receives his guests, etc. The fourth house (which completes the square) is a skin or warehouse, if the proprietor is a wealthy man and engaged in trade or traffic, where he keeps his deerskins, furs, merchandise, etc., and treats his customers. Smaller or less wealthy families make one, two, or three houses serve all their purposes as well as they can.[21]

McIntosh and Weatherford were born to relatively wealthy Creek families, but as privileged members of their society, they did not shirk the causes of their people. They were born in areas already redolent with history and prehistory, but many significant dramas were still to be played out near Coosauda and Coweta, and Red Eagle and White Warrior were to play important roles in these events.

They came to manhood at a time when external pressures were reshaping the Creeks from a loose affiliation of autonomous tribes into a nation. The National Council, which had from ancient times been a means of gathering civil and war leaders in a primarily social annual conference, now became more of a legislative body as the Creeks sought to cope with such pressures as the encroachments of white settlers, the territorial aspirations of Georgia, and the further encirclement caused by the admission of Alabama to statehood in 1819. During this crucial period, some towns and villages clung stubbornly to their autonomy, and others joined political factions formed around such influential leaders as McIntosh, Weatherford, Opothle Yoholo, Little Prince, and Big Warrior. Federal officers, sent to the Creek Nation to negotiate treaties, and Georgia politicians already on the scene sowed dissension among the Creek factions and used bribery and intrigue to set one group against another to achieve the goals of expansionism and the ultimate removal of the Creeks from the Southeast.[22] In these turbulent times, these two mixed-blood Creeks played significant roles in the destinies of their mothers' people.

2

Children of Their Mothers' Clans

——— • ———

It is not surprising that both McIntosh and Weatherford, despite their predominantly Caucasian genes, chose to live as Indians rather than whites. Their mothers were Indians, and in the matrilineal Creek society, the offspring belonged to the clan of the mother, with close relationship to her and her family, not to their biological fathers.[1] Not only to their young children but to their white husbands as well, the Creek women were matriarchs. Benjamin Hawkins observed the system firsthand and wrote to Thomas Jefferson that among the Creeks "the women have invariably the habit of governing absolutely in all cases when connected with a white man." Hawkins wrote that he had considered forming "amorous connexions" with Creek women, but after observing what happened to the agency blacksmith, who took an Indian wife, he decided against it and "prohibited all amorous intercourse between red and white people at the agency." He wrote that the blacksmith's wife and family "first took charge of the provisions, then the house and pay and finally the absolute government of everything at the agency whether connected with the smith or not." It is understandable, then, that the Indian wife and her family took complete charge of rearing and educating their mixed-blood children. Hawkins observed that "the traders, several of whom have amassed considerable fortunes, have almost all of them been as inattentive to their children as the Indians."[2]

As John R. Swanton explains, the Indian father's seeming lack of concern about the education of his children was not the result of an unnatural indifference toward his offspring. The explanation lies partly in the complex Creek system of clans. An Indian woman always married a man of a clan other than her own, not just to guard against the taboo of incest but also in order that her clan and that of her husband could enlarge their spheres of support in times of difficulty. The clans were also matrilocal, and a husband normally lived in his wife's town, the house and fields belonging to her. The sons were instructed, counseled, and protected by their maternal uncles and the clan elders or *pawas*. The elders regularly gathered the children to tell them stories illustrative of clan loyalty, respect to elders, concern for others, and other Creek virtues. They would frequently lecture to them at the annual busk ceremony. Either *pawas* or uncles administered corporal punishment, for women were not allowed to strike their sons at any time. James Adair reports having seen one of the *pawas* in 1766 punish a boy with a thick whip, about four and a half feet long, made of plaited silk grass and the fibers of button snakeroot stalks, tapered to a knotted point. The young fellow was charged with being more effeminate than was seemly for a future warrior. He lived near a wealthy and prissy German trader, whom the *pawa* feared had corrupted the boy. As he applied the lash he said to him quietly, "You are as one who is wicked and almost lost."[3]

McIntosh's mother, a full-blooded Creek, must surely have reared her son in the traditional ways, and although Weatherford's mother was only three-quarters Indian, Red Eagle apparently chose the Indian ways unequivocally. George Cary Eggleston wrote that "in his tastes and instincts this son of a Scotchman was altogether an Indian." He was fortunate to be tutored by his unusually gifted maternal uncle, Alexander McGillivray, whose contributions to Red Eagle's education were primarily linguistic, particularly in oral English. Young Weatherford refused to learn to read and write, and he remained obstinate in this resolve throughout his life, but he worked assiduously to master spoken English. He was aware of the practical usefulness of English in communicating with the Americans, but he also had the interesting theory that command of so complex a tongue as English would add to his force and eloquence in speaking his native Creek language. He aspired to become famous in the Creek councils for his eloquence, and he achieved his ambition fully. Weatherford learned French from another maternal uncle, LeClerc Milfort, and he also picked up enough Spanish for ordinary conversation.[4]

Although the Indians were in some ways permissive parents, allowing the children to nurse as long as they pleased, or until the mother was pregnant again, much of the early training of children was for the purpose of toughening them for the rigors of life as adults and preparing them for their roles as braves or as Indian mothers. The two sexes received different treatment from the instant of birth, the male babies being wrapped in cougar skins and the females in bison hides or deer-skins, perhaps to symbolize the man's role of hunter. The infants spent their first year bound in cradle boards made of light wooden frames, which were uncomfortable and confining, but which, the Indians thought, made them grow up hardy and straight-limbed. They believed that the flattening of the skull and forehead that resulted from being bound to the cradle board postioned the eyes in such a way that it improved the vision and made a man a better hunter.[5] Everyone—men, women, and children–began each day, summer and winter, by going to a stream and plunging under water four times. Jean Bernard Bossu, an eighteenth-century French traveler among the Creeks, observed infants still at the breastfeeding stage being bathed in near-freezing water in the dead of winter.[6]

Children were punished if they failed to take their morning baths; the *pawas* would lightly rake the legs and arms of the disobedient child with snake's teeth. This "dry scratching" was harmless but hu-miliating to the child and proved to be a strong deterrent because it left abrasions and light scars on the skin for several days so that every-one could see them and taunt the child. For more serious offenses the *pawas* would scratch the calves and thighs of the boys with the jaw-bone of a garfish or tooth of a snake until they drew blood. The Creeks believed that this practice served both a physical and emo-tional purpose. It was thought to loosen the skin and give a pliancy to the limbs, enabling the boy to run more swiftly. It also stimulated courage, convincing the child that loss of blood does not necessarily lead to loss of life.[7]

Karsten Petersen, a Moravian missionary to the Creeks, provided a different rationale as well as an interesting account of this punish-ment, which he observed in 1811 in a household very similar in its racial mixture to those of McIntosh and Weatherford. Alexander Cor-nells, a Scots-Indian, and his half-Indian wife paid a visit to the mis-sion, and three of their children sneaked under the peach trees and knocked down some of the green fruit with a stick. Mrs. Cornells "picked up one [child] by its head and then another and called for an Indian to help. He picked up four or five pine sticks and placed them between the fingers of one hand. With the other hand he picked up the child by the foot and scratched him with the sticks from the stom-ach down to the soles of his feet until he was covered with blood. Similar treatment was administered to the rest. In response to my inquiry, I was told they have so much bad blood in them, and if that is gotten out of them they will no longer be bad. After having bled for a while the blood was washed off with cold water. This seems to be the usual way Indian women punish their children."[8]

The children in Creek towns spent most of their time within earshot of their mothers, who were busy providers of all food except the game killed by the men. The children observed and sometimes helped in such stoop-labor tasks as planting and weeding corn, sweet potatoes, pumpkins, beans, peas, melons, gourds, collards, and onions. When not farming, the women sat in groups, with the children as onlookers, manufacturing baskets, sifters, and earthen pots.[9]

In McIntosh's town of Coweta, fishing with scoop nets was a labor for women but an adventure for children. Along the Chattahoochee at Coweta there was a deep, steady current coming from the falls. Islands of rock in the river forced the water into a channel about sixty feet wide along the shore. Here the current was too swift for boats to navigate, but fish, as they attempted to swim upstream, could be caught from the banks in scoop nets. As soon as schools of fish made their periodic appearances, the chiefs shouted for women to come and harvest the abundant shad, trout, perch, and sturgeon, and the children were noisy and appreciative spectators. Fish traps were made out of large stones in the shallow, swift-flowing rivers near the fall line, and remains of such traps can still be found today in some of the streams in the old Creek lands. The Indians would pile tons of rocks into a V-shaped dam pointing upstream. Placing conical traps at the apex of the V, the Indians captured fish that swam upstream, entrapped themselves, and were unable to swim back out.[10]

The more gently flowing Alabama River and its tributaries provided no such natural fishery for Weatherford and his mother, but the boy may have observed the women using the ancient Creek method of fishing with poison. Buckeyes and the root of a plant called devil's shoestring were pounded fine in a mortar and scattered in the pond. When the water was stirred with poles, the fish quickly became intoxicated and rose to the surface, floating with bellies upward; the women then gathered them in baskets. Adair wrote that "fish catched in this manner are not poisoned, but only stupified."[11] The active ingredient of devil's shoestring is an organic poison now called rotenone, which attacks the central nervous system.

Early French visitors among the Creeks wrote admiringly of the ingenious fish traps made of reeds by the women. They were cunningly woven so that a fish entered what appeared to be a natural growth of reeds only to find there was no escape from the labyrinth. As the fish were drawn up in the traps, the watching children squealed with delight. Bartram described a fish lure made of the white hair of a deer's tail, shreds of a red garter, and feathers, which the Indians used with all the skill of modern anglers as they fished from canoes near the shore. Even more exciting for the Creek children was watching their fathers catch the sturgeon, which in those days swam upstream on southern rivers to spawn. When schools of these large, sluggish fish appeared, a young man would throw a lasso over the tail of one of them and hold on to the rope as the fish dragged him into the water and often beneath it. If he could hold on until the fish was exhausted, he could drag the sturgeon ashore and finish it off with a blow to the head.[12]

The gathering of food was a never-ending task for the Creek women, occasionally assisted by the children and old men. In every season of the year in that temperate climate, there were berries, fruits, nuts, seeds, and wild vegetables to be harvested. Lands everywhere in the Creek Nation supported abundant forests of oak and hickory, and acorns and hickory nuts were an important food source. They were picked up, dried, and pounded to bits in a mortar; then the pulverized nutmeats were vigorously fanned to blow away as many of the shells as possible, and water was added to make a paste. The women kneaded the doughlike mass with their hands, and as the oil rose to the surface they separated it for use in cooking and as a seasoning. Hawkins ate some beans cooked in this oil and pronounced it "not inferior to Florence oil," the finest of olive oil. Oil was also made from the red oak acorns in a slightly different process by drying them on a reed mat, beating them fine in a mortar, mixing them with water, and letting them stand for an evening. When the oil rose to the surface, it was skimmed off with a feather. It was said that a bushel of acorns had to be processed to produce one pint of oil. Where there were sugar maples, which Hawkins found to be abundant in Creek lands, the women used small wooden troughs to catch the sap, then boiled it to a constituency that crystallized into maple sugar.[13]

The women instructed the children on the dangers of eating certain foods in forbidden seasons. For example, honey in the Creek territory was poisonous in the month of March, and persons who ate it sometimes became fatally ill. The source of the toxic substance was a plant the whites called wolf's tongue, or fire leaves. In March bees were attracted to the plant's yellow blossoms. Hawkins reported an incident in 1795 in which one person in a family died after eating the honey, and all the rest were "sickened instantaneously" but were saved by drinking milk, the only antidote to the poison. According to Hawkins, those who ate the toxic honey first became giddy, then blind, with accompanying great pain and thirst.[14]

Nature was usually benign in supplying food, however, and children like McIntosh and Weatherford could hunt for the china briar root or the bog potato with a sense of security. The china briar, which the Creeks called red coonte, grew profusely along the margin of streams and was an important food to the Creeks. They dug the large, tuberous roots, pounded them in a mortar, and suspended them in a coarse cloth, washing them repeatedly by pouring water over them. The sediment that passed through with the water was left to thicken, the water poured off, and the sediment baked into cakes sweetened with honey. Only in years of food scarcity did the children hunt the bog potato, a small, not particularly succulent root found in old beaver ponds and thick, boggy places. In times of extreme hardship, the women even cooked the poisonous green berries of the wolf's tongue plant, boiling them three times and pouring off the water to remove the toxic substance. The green berries then tasted like garden peas.[15]

Wild fruits, berries, and nuts presented fewer problems in processing, and the Creek children found the forests bountifully supplied with them. The most important fruit was the persimmon. When green, this small, reddish-brown, tree-borne fruit was inedible because of its astringency, which puckered the mouth violently and raised the gorge. When fully ripe, however, in the late fall, it was an extremely sweet, datelike morsel. In the late summer several varieties of wild grapes, notably muscadines and scuppernongs, grew abundantly along the riverbanks. Other fruits commonly eaten were wild cherries, papaws, tart crab apples, wild plums, prickly pears, and maypops. During the early summer, blackberries, gooseberries, raspberries, and wild strawberries were plentiful, as were the great variety of berries harvested from bushes and trees: huckleberries, black gum berries, mulberries, serviceberries, and palmetto berries. Although following the chestnut blight of 1905 the trees virtually disappeared in the South, chestnuts were an important food for the Creeks, as were chinquapins (a small variety of chestnut), pecans, and black walnuts.

Several kinds of seeds were eaten, primarily because they were easy to store during the winter. The seeds of the cockspurgrass were toasted in stone bowls and ground into meal. One of the largest seeds eaten was that of the nelumbo, a large water lily found in the most southerly areas of the Creek lands. The small black seeds of the chenopodium were also ground into a meal and eaten. One species of this plant, called Mexican tea or worm seed, was mildly toxic and was used by the Indians to deworm themselves.[16] Their understanding of this use for the plant is an indication of the sophisticated knowledge about food gathering the Creeks had accumulated in eons of Archaic and Woodland prehistory.

As children, McIntosh and Weatherford were exposed not only to routine domestic tasks but also to violent aspects of the intermingling of Caucasian and Indian cultures. In 1784, when McIntosh was about six years old, he may have witnessed an informal execution that took place in Coweta in view of a crowd of spectators who had moments before been building a house. The man executed was a young Coweta brave, who was on top of a house helping to roof it when two members of his clan, appointed by the chiefs, arrived to kill him with the rifle that had belonged to the young man he had murdered. One of the executioners fired once and missed, and the brave remarked to a fellow worker that someone must be shooting at turkeys. The rifle was fired again, wounding him; he fell to the ground, where he was shot and wounded still another time. He lived about an hour longer, and before he died he said that he had determined to kill a white man, that he had done it, and that now his heart was straight and he was a man.

He had murdered one William Marshall, a seventeen-year-old Irishman, and Thomas Marshall, the victim's brother, had gone to the chiefs of the town to demand satisfaction. The chiefs immediately promised that justice would be done and, after a consultation in the public square, decided that the murderer should be executed. They appointed two members of the murderer's own clan to carry out the sentence. This incident shows clearly that in the Indian law of blood, a clan was responsible if one of its members committed a homicide, and punishing the crime was a clan function. There was a logical reason behind this practice, for when the clan took action against its own, a series of retaliatory slayings could be avoided.[17]

The white settlers who shared the frontier with the Creeks were for the most part rowdy, extremely violent men, whose bloody fights, in which they gouged out each other's eyes, were frequent public spectacles, witnessed by whites and Indians. Weatherford's uncle LeClerc Milfort, the Frenchman who lived among the Creeks at Coweta from roughly the time of McIntosh's birth through his early manhood, described these men as *Crakeurs* (Crackers) or *Gaugeurs* (Gougers), the former name coming from the cracking of their long bullwhips as they drove teams of horses and the latter from their practice of gouging out opponents' eyeballs in their deadly fights, some of which McIntosh and Weatherford may have watched. Milfort relates that the Crackers allowed their fingernails to grow as long as possible and toughened them by smearing them with tallow and holding them in front of the fire. The melting tallow would penetrate the pores of the nails, stiffening them, so that when completely hardened, the nails were as formidable a weapon as the claws of a panther. Crackers also wore sharp-pointed, spikelike spurs on each heel.

When drunk on a potent whiskey made from potatoes, the Crackers would grow quarrelsome, and often a fight would be arranged for an appointed time. Spectators would gather from miles around, the two combatants would stand in the middle of the circle of shouting, drunken spectators, and the oldest person in the crowd would give the signal for the fight to begin by shouting "Anything is allowed!" The fighters would attack each other furiously with spurs, teeth, and claws, and when one succumbed, the other would tear unmercifully at his flesh and gouge out an eyeball. The crowd would then rush in to stop the fray, sometimes too late to save the remaining eye. The victor would climb upon the stump of a tree and, covered with blood and supercharged with adrenalin, would crow about his victory, insulting the spectators and challenging one and all to fight. According to Milfort, who was prone to exaggerate, these conflicts occurred so often that one met few white men in the area of the Creek Nation who still had both eyes.[18]

As a boy, McIntosh had three grim reminders that his fellow Creeks—even the women, who tenderly cared for their babies—were capable of great cruelty. He saw in an old field near Coweta town the three stakes at which captives in the Cherokee war of more than forty years past were tortured to death. Perhaps to give the Creek women a way of relieving anger at losing sons and husbands in battle, they were allowed to torture captive warriors, which they did, Adair wrote, "to the entire satisfaction of the greedy eyes of the spectators." After the captives were stripped naked, the women would gather long bundles of dry cane and stout sticks of fat pitch-pine, and as the victims were led toward the stakes, the women—and sometimes the children—would beat them viciously with their sticks and canes. When a chief sounded the death signal, the victims' arms were tied securely, and a strong grapevine was tied around their necks and then secured to the top of the pole, allowing them to move within a fifteen-yard circumference. The women set fire to their canes and sticks—after carefully covering the victims' hair with wet clay to avoid burning the much-prized scalps—and began punishing the captives with the flames. The victims would kick and resist with all the fury they could muster, and after a time, when they collapsed from the intense pain and fatigue, cold water was poured on them to revive them for further torture. When they finally lapsed into a merciful coma, the women would immediately scalp and dismember them. Charles Hudson states that torture by fire was used against the Indians by early European colonists, particularly by Hernando de Soto's men, and he suggests that the southeastern Indians may have adopted the practice from the whites and ritualized it.[19]

The life of Creek boys was not always violent, of course, and there was plenty of time for wholesome pastimes. Much of Weatherford's boyhood was spent with horses, and when he was still a child he was already a master at breaking unruly colts and racing over the countryside on his father's mounts. An Indian woman who knew him as a boy talked about his skill, grace, and daring on horseback and added that the women "would quit hoeing corn, and smile and gaze upon him as he rode by the corn-patch." Young Weatherford may have taken part in breaking wild horses in an ingenious way developed by the Creeks. They would walk or run the horses in a marsh until the equines were exhausted, or sometimes they would ride them in a river, letting the currents take their toll on the animals' energy. Then the Creeks could ride the weary and docile horses and accustom them to the bridle.[20]

Raising horses in the Coosauda area was not without problems. When Weatherford was in his early teens, a plague swept through the horses in the area of the Creek Nation and lasted for several years. The disease was called "yellow water," named for the yellow fluid that dripped from the noses of the affected horses. Other symptoms included swollen legs, high fever, and a beating in the chest caused by spasmodic contractions of the diaphragm. At death the animal's entrails showed advanced decay. Those horses that survived the first onslaught of the disease seemed to recover quickly, but they would collapse and die if ridden or exercised. Those left to themselves for a prolonged rest would get well. The disease was most prevalent in the hottest part of the summer; some cases occurred in the fall, but none in winter. The Creeks were never able to effect a cure for the disease, which was in all likelihood the disease known today as infectious equine anemia, transmitted by biting insects.[21] As a lover of horses, the child Weatherford must have been often grieved by the death of his favorite mounts.

The children, both boys and girls, played a part in the annual Grand Council of the Creeks, which was held at McIntosh's birthplace, Coweta, each May. All the chiefs of the Creek Nation attended to consider matters of importance in a closed session held at the Grand Cabin in the town square. At sunset the young people would assemble and dance around the fire in front of the grand cabin. This signaled the end of the day's deliberations, which began again the following sunup at the sound of the drum calling all chiefs to assemble.[22] The shuffling, rhythmic Indian dances, accompanied by the beating of drums, the rubbing together of notched sticks, and the piercing screech of the cane whistles, were eerie and unusual to early travelers among the Creeks. To the children, beginning as early as age eight, the dances must have been one of the most exciting activities in their lives.

Perhaps the most terrifying of experiences to young Creeks was listening to the women's stories of evil spirits and ghosts. Adair wrote that ghosts, witches, and evil spirits were the main subjects of their "incredible and shocking stories" on long winter nights. "They will affirm," he wrote, "that they have seen, and most distinctly, most surprising apparitions, and heard shrieking noises." Adair gave one example of such a ghost story: the Creeks told him that when they camped near the site of the former town of Ocmulgee, a Lower Creek town destroyed in the Yamassee War of 1715, they always heard at dawn the sounds of Indians waking up and singing as they walked down to the river to purify themselves by plunging into the stream. "Whenever I have been there, however," Adair wrote, "all has been silent."[23] The Creek women also believed, and so instructed their children, that dust clouds whirling in the air were ghosts of past Indians.[24] The children were taught that everyone's soul lived on as a ghost after death. When someone died, everyone in the village would shout and make noises to frighten the ghost up to the western sky. They also believed that ghosts sometimes became lonely and returned to their former homes. Mothers taught their children never to eat food that had been left out overnight for fear that ghosts might have touched it. To eat food touched by ghosts would make one ill, they believed.[25]

Unquestionably the high point of the year for the Creeks was the annual Green Corn Ceremony, also called the "busk," or *boosketah*, from the Indian word for fasting, *poskita*. It was a time of thanksgiving for the new corn crop, a time of spiritual renewal and purification, when amnesty was given for all crimes except murder, a time when all quarrels and disputes were settled amicably, and a time of restating the social roles in the tribe to remind each person of his status and duties. The Green Corn Ceremony also had special meaning for couples who were divorced during the year. Divorce among the Creeks was accomplished by either partner's choosing to dissolve the marriage, and although men were free to remarry immediately, divorced women had to wait until the conclusion of the next busk before taking another mate.[26] Although other seasonal ceremonies declined in importance during the eighteenth century, the Green Corn Ceremony continued to be a significant annual event and has survived to the present day among the Creeks in Oklahoma.[27]

As children McIntosh and Weatherford must have watched in wonderment the elaborate preparations for the ceremony, which occurred in July or August, depending on the time of the first full moon after the ripening of the late corn crop. The festival lasted eight days in important Creek towns. On the first day the warriors swept clean the yard of the town square and spread sparkling white river sand over it. As early in the morning as he could, the appointed firemaker used friction to ignite the sacred fire, and the warriors cut and brought to the firemaker four logs, each as long as the tallest brave could cover by extending his two arms. These logs were laid in the center of the square, forming a cross, and in the center the firemaker laid his new fire, which burned the logs in the first four days of the ceremony.

Then the dancing began, while the *possau*, a powerful emetic made of button snakeroot, was being brewed. First the women of the turkey clan did their *pinebungau*, or turkey dance. At noon the braves, who had abstained from food all morning, began drinking the *possau*, continuing to drink it until the middle of the afternoon to purge themselves of impurities. Then the *toccoyulegau*, or tadpole dance, was performed by four men and four women. In the evening a group of warriors began the *enehoubungau*, the dance of the braves who were second in command, which lasted until daylight.

On the second day at about ten o'clock in the morning, the women began the *itshobungau*, or gun dance. Shortly after noon the men went to the sacred fire and rubbed their chins, necks, and stomachs with ashes. Then, running and shouting, they plunged head first into the river. Returning to the square, the men took some of the new corn, which the women had prepared for the feast, and rubbed it between their hands, then on their faces and chests. Only then did they sit down to feast on the new corn, ravenously hungry after their long hours of fasting. On the third day, all the men sat in the square and rested, and on the fourth day the women rose early in the morning to clean out their hearths and sprinkle them with sand in preparation for receiving the new fire. The men finished the burning of the first four logs, rubbed themselves with ashes, and dived into the river. Also on this day the braves ate salt and danced the *obungauchapco*, or long dance.

On the fifth day the warriors cut four new logs, placed them in a cross as they had the first four, and ignited a new sacred fire. The fifth day was distinguished by the drinking of the black drink, a strong tea made from holly leaves. On the sixth and seventh days the men remained at the square, but on the eighth and final day the ritual of purification reached its climax. The physic makers filled two large pots with herbs and medicinal plants, added water, and simmered the mixture slowly. The braves drank the brew and rubbed it on their joints throughout the afternoon. They also collected corn cobs and pine cones and burned them to ashes. Four virgins who had not yet experienced a menstrual period brought ashes from their houses and stirred them into the pots. The warriors again rubbed themselves with clay and ashes and, on a signal from the head chief, all ran to the river and crowded together at the water's edge. Then, giving the death whoop as a signal, each man in turn leaped into the river and stayed submerged until he had gathered four stones from the river bottom. Back on shore, each brave crossed himself on the breast four times, each time throwing a stone in the river and giving a death whoop. That night the Green Corn Ceremony ended with the *Obungau haujo,* the wild and spirited "mad dance."

Agent Hawkins, who witnessed this ceremony as early as 1798 and gave this vivid description, made no effort to interpret the various symbolic actions in the ritual. He stated, however, that "this happy institution of the Boosketah restores man to himself, to his family and to his nation." He added that it "seems to bury guilt itself into oblivion."[28] Although Hawkins was interested in the spectacle of the Green Corn Ceremony and understood that the giving of general amnesty resulted in a relief from guilt feelings, he seems not to have been fully aware of the emphasis on purification through fasting and abstinence, which took some peculiar forms. The men, for example, were not allowed to touch any females, even babies, during the eight days of the ceremony. There was even a rule against using the word that denoted "woman" during those days; instead, they used words such as *tcukoleidji* ("one who has a house") or *hompita haya* ("food pre-parer").[29] The choice of these two terms emphasizes the inconsistent roles of women, who in this matriarchal society owned the houses but also performed the labor of preparing food.

A military aspect of the festival is found in a manuscript by George Stiggins, the Creek Indian agent from 1831 to 1844, who was born in 1788 of a Scots father and a Natchez Indian mother. Stiggins's sister Mary married William Weatherford, and Stiggins also grew up in an Upper Creek village near Tensaw, an area well known to Red Eagle. Stiggins wrote that on the sixth day of the *boosketah*, the Creeks would "exhibit their manner of attack in warfare." They would set up effigies in various places on the square, and certain appointed men would attack them. The chosen warriors showed their skill "in coming on the enemy by stealth." When they got near to the effigies, they would "all at once raise the war scream and charge on them, shoot, tomahawk, and scalp them," and then make an escape as they would in an actual attack.[30] This bellicose exhibition during the Green Corn Ceremony became more significant in the early part of the nineteenth century as tensions mounted with the unrelenting encroachments of white set-tlers.

McIntosh and Weatherford spent their childhood close to the basic realities of life: gathering food, becoming aware of danger, assimilat-ing cultural truths, and making war. Traditions were important, and Indian mothers, as Hawkins discovered, held on inexorably to their ethnic customs, even when married to white men, and carefully passed them on to their mestizo offspring.[31] It was a childhood that brought an early maturity and a readiness to meet the rigors of ado-lescence and the rituals that marked their passage into manhood.

3

Boyhood: Sports, Games, and Rites of Passage

———— • ————

As McIntosh and Weatherford grew older, they became increasingly conscious of the roles they would one day assume as men. Little boys in the Creek Nation learned early to eschew woman's work, and they were careful to avoid even a suggestion of the tasks that occupied little girls, such as maintaining the fires, helping to make baskets and pots, gardening, and housework. Instead, Creek boys began at an early age to learn the skills of the hunter by roving through the forests, shooting at small game or targets with their scaled-down bows and arrows. Each boy dreamed of killing a white-tailed deer, the elusive animal that is estimated to have provided 90 percent of all meat eaten by the Creeks. Strongly ingrained in the boys was the importance of the stoical virtue of withstanding pain without crying out. They would have contests to see which of them could silently endure the most stings by wasps and yellow jackets. The boys were also taught when very young that their advancement in the nation depended on their success as warriors. Other abilities, such as oratory, giving wise counsel, and being stoical in times of trial, were honored by the Creek Nation, but no ability was so esteemed as that exemplified by the brave warrior. Each boy knew that the day would come when he must prove himself by bringing in a scalp. Only then would he gain a council seat in the public square. Until that longed-for day, he would remain in a kind of disgrace, being given the menial tasks of lighting the warrior's pipes, hauling wood for the ceremonial fires, and cooking the black drink, a potion of great ritual importance.[1]

Cooking the black drink was not merely a menial task for the young Creeks, however; it placed them near the seats of power in the council

23

of chiefs, enabling them to overhear the verbal flourishes, oratory, and debate. The black drink was brewed, as William Bartram observed, in an open shed directly opposite the door of the town house where the council meeting was held. This dark-brewed beverage held a central place in the life of the Creeks, and they sometimes drank it in such quantity and strength that it became an emetic, causing vomiting.

LeClerc Milfort, who was introduced to this spectacle almost immediately upon his arrival in the Creek Nation, thought it sickening and disgusting to see the braves retching in the council meetings, sometimes holding their arms across their chests in a cermonial manner and projecting their vomit six or eight feet. He had an interesting theory, however, concerning the practical reason for this ritual, which, he wrote, "appears only ridiculous at first, [but] has nonetheless a very wise basis, and which would not always be out of place in the assemblies of civilized peoples." The purpose, as Milfort understood it, was to assure the chief of the assembly that each member had a stomach free of food and strong liquors and therefore a clear head for the council deliberations.[2] The caffeine in this dark tea made from the dried leaves of a variety of holly called *Ilex vomitoria* was also a factor in keeping the braves alert in the council sessions. When the black drink was consumed in large quantities before battle or a ball game, the caffeine could be a decisive factor in stimulating the braves to superhuman efforts. It was even thought that the black drink was beneficial if a warrior were wounded, and recent evidence indicates that large doses of caffeine do indeed speed up blood clotting.[3]

At the age of fifteen McIntosh and Weatherford were doubtless as impatient as any teenagers to leave adolescence, with its repetitive, menial tasks, and assume the state of manhood. They were ready for the rite of passage into adulthood. Benjamin Hawkins, who knew the towns of Coweta and Coosauda in this period firsthand, described this rite in detail in "A Sketch of the Creek Country in the Years 1798 and 1799." In a part he entitled "The Ceremony of Initiating Youth into Manhood," he wrote that the rites were usually administered to boys between the ages of fifteen and seventeen. Because it involved fasting to achieve purification, this initiation was called *boosketah* (the word also used to denote the Green Corn Ceremony), after the Creek word *poskita*, meaning "to fast."

On the first day, the candidates gathered two handfuls of *sou-watch-cau*, a bitter root, and ate nothing but this throughout the day. Their only drink was a tea made from the leaves of the *sou-watch-cau*, which,

Hawkins wrote, had "the effect of intoxicating and maddening." At dusk they would eat three spoonfuls of gruel made from coarsely ground corn. Remaining isolated from the rest of the community, the candidates would repeat this procedure for four days, after which time they were free to leave their confinement and go into the community, proudly wearing a new pair of moccasins. The ritual continued, however, and they were still restricted in their diets, not being allowed to eat deer meat (except from old bucks), turkey, cocks, fowls, peas, and salt; and for the first four months of the rites, they cooked their own food at separate fires. At the appearance of each new moon for a period of twelve months, they repeated the four-day cycle of fasting and eating *sou-watch-cau,* and on the fifth day following the twelfth cycle, they came out of the house where they had been isolated, gathered corn cobs, burned them to ashes, and rubbed them all over their bodies. At the end of the twelfth moon, the initiates would sweat under blankets and then run shouting into the water, completing the ceremony. When they emerged from the water, they were free from the pollution of juvenility. Hawkins wrote that although the length of the ceremony varied, and was sometimes as short as twelve days, the course was always the same and always under the direction of the "great leader," who, when speaking to Hawkins of a youth being initiated, would say, "I am physicing of him" or "I am teaching him all that it is proper for him to know."[4]

Hawkins, who was intimately associated with the birthplaces of McIntosh and Weatherford in the period of their youth, was perhaps more knowledgeable about the prevailing general practice, but John Swanton has presented another version of the rite of passage, a special rite in which certain boys who wished to become priests or medicine men would go in groups of not more than four to an old priest and request instruction. If he agreed, he would take the youths to an isolated, heavily wooded place near a stream, where they would pile up green boughs to shield themselves so that they would not be disturbed or overheard. First, the candidates located and dug up the red root of the *miko hoyanidja,* a type of willow greatly prized by the Creeks as an instrument of purification as well as a medicine to cure rheumatism, nausea, fever, malaria, swellings, and other maladies. The boys would pound the red root into a pulp and place it in a pot of water; then the priest would breathe into the potion and chant over it. Before noon on the first day of instruction, the boys, who were abstaining from solid food, would drink the liquid four times. A powerful emetic, the red root liquid would cause them to vomit, thus, in the eyes of the Creeks, purifying them for the instruction to come later in the day. At sunset the old priest would return to give instruction in a patterned, structured manner, which the novitiates were expected to memorize verbatim.[5]

It is not surprising that in this warrior society the first body of knowledge the novices mastered concerned the treatment of wounds. Not only were they taught which plants made up their pharmacopoeia, they were taught the correct songs to sing to make the medicines work. The songs, chants, and formulas had to be learned by rote, word for word, and they performed them over and over, being criticized by the old priest until every nuance of the lore had been perfectly mastered. The principal curative agent for wounds was *hilis hatki*, "white medicine," which was ginseng root boiled in water and made into a potion to stop the flow of blood. The novices were also taught herbal treatments for other disorders. After four days of intensive instruction, the boys retired into a tent, where hot stones were placed on the ground and inundated with water, causing clouds of steam and vapor. When they had sweated sufficiently to be purged to the satisfaction of the priest, the boys plunged into the cold waters of a creek and were sent home.[6]

For the next one or two months the novices would perfect their memorization and assimilate what they had learned; then they would request another four-day period of instruction from the priest. In some instances, groups of initiates would have five or six of these four-day instructional periods and then ask for an eight-day, and then a final twelve-day, session. At the conclusion of this last period the priest would place each young man in a hole that had been dug in the earth to resemble a shallow grave. Each was given a hollow cane to breathe through, told to lie down, and covered with earth. The ground was then sprinkled with a thin layer of dry leaves and set afire. After this ritualistic burial, the young man arose from his grave a priest, permitted to wear a horned owl's feather in his headdress.[7]

Such rigorous training required admirable discipline, but for most young Creek boys the principal aim at this stage of life was not to become a priest or medicine man but to perform some warlike exploit that would earn for them a war name and title. As Caleb Swan states, this desire for status "stimulated them to push abroad, and at all hazards obtain a scalp, or as they term it, bring in hair."[8] The Creek war titles that boys like McIntosh and Weatherford so avidly sought were made up of highly descriptive combinations of words. The first word was usually the name of a tribe, town, or totemic animal. The second word was usually one of the following: *hadjo,* which means "mad," "crazy," or "furious in battle"; *fixico,* "heartless or ruthless in battle"; or *yoholo,* the ceremonial, long-drawn-out shout given by the bearers of the black drink while the chiefs and warriors are taking it. There were also four words used to indicate military and political titles: *imala, tustunnuggee, heniha,* or *micco.*[9]

The king, or "micco," as Hawkins wrote it, was a person of great influence in a town, always chosen from the same clan and given the office for life. When he died, one of his nephews, if fit for the office, was chosen to succeed him; the descent was always in the female line. One of the micco's principal responsibilities was to bring young braves to positions of leadership. Hawkins wrote in 1799: "When a young man is trained up and appears well qualified for the fatigues and hardships of war, and is promising, the Micco appoints him a governor, or as the name imports, a leader *(Istepuccauchau)* and if he distinguishes himself, they give him a rise to the center cabin. A man who distinguishes himself repeatedly in warlike enterprises, rises gradually to the rank of the Great Leader *(Istepuccauchau thlucco).* This title is seldom attained as it requires a long course of years, and great and numerous successes in war."[10]

Some examples of Creek war titles are *Itco fixico* ("Heartless Deer"), *Tcito hadjo* ("Crazy Snake"), *Fus hatchi micco* ("Bird Creek Chief"), and *Yufala tustunnuggee* ("Yufala Warrior"). According to George Stiggins, the bestowing of these war names was a colorful adjunct to the annual Green Corn Ceremony. In intervals of rest in the late evening, when the braves and young men were seated about the fire, a micco or tustunnuggee intimated to one of the boys that he was about to be divested of the given name that he had known from infancy and be invested with a war name. The micco or tustunnuggee then whispered the new name to the boy. Later, when the ceremony of naming began, a warrior rose from his seat and called the name in a "shrill, long tone of voice," as Stiggins expressed it. At the call, the young man rose, picked up a war club *(attussa),* and went to the warrior, who told the boy that he was now named as other men and could assume the manners and customs of manhood. He then put a feather on the youth's head, and the newly dubbed man raised the war club above his head, shouted a long whoop, and ran around in a circle to where he had started. When he stopped, he shouted "youh, youh!" and, Stiggins wrote, he "is ever after a man with a name."[11]

William McIntosh's war title was written Tustunnuggee Hutkee (White Warrior), with the title "tustunnuggee" denoting an order of merit and distinction that could not be earned initially by a young brave. Normally, he would earn various titles in sequence, perhaps beginning with a name that included the word *hadjo*, then progressing to *tustunnuggee* or *micco*. The Creeks used an interesting and impressive ceremony to initiate a brave as a war chief or *tustunnuggee*. William McIntosh must have been inducted in much the same manner as that described by LeClerc Milfort, who was ceremoniously initiated as a *tustunnuggee* at an assembly in the Creek town of Tuckabatchee in May 1780. As Milfort described it, he was transported to the grand cabin in the town square on a litter made of bearskin, carried by four lesser chiefs. In front of the litter, several young warriors, each holding an eagle tail fastened to a stick, danced and chanted, accompanied by two men, one shaking a rattle and the other beating a drum. Surrounding the litter were old chiefs, each carrying an eagle tail, half of which was painted red. This suggests that William Weatherford's war title, Red Eagle, must have had special symbolic significance, denoting a high-ranking chieftain. At the rear of the procession were six priests or medicine men who wore deerskins on their shoulders like chasubles. Each of these priests carried a white bird's wing in one hand and the plant used in making war medicine in the other.[12]

When they reached the grand cabin in the town square, the procession halted. Two warriors, carrying the war medicine in large gourds painted red, came to meet the procession, accompanied by a priest, who sprinkled the war medicine on the ground and sang an invocation. Then the highest-ranking war chiefs came out of the cabin, dipped their hands in the war medicine, and wet their faces with it. The six priests who carried the white bird's wings passed the wings over the faces of the chiefs as if to wipe them. Then the whole procession followed the war chiefs into the town square, where they remained for twenty-four hours, taking nothing into their stomachs but war medicine, which was a strong emetic. On the following day everyone disrobed and went into a circular building used as a sweat house. The heat was so intense that Milfort found it almost unendurable. After half an hour, everyone ran out and plunged into a nearby river. After this rite of purification, they dressed and returned to the square, where, as Milfort states, they were served a "magnificent meal." Throughout the three-day ceremony no one was allowed to sleep, and when Milfort became drowsy, cold water was splashed in his face. When the ceremony ended, he was taken back to his house on the litter. There the oldest priest proclaimed Milfort a *tustunnuggee* and told him he must endure cold, heat, and hunger with courage to defend the interests of the Creek Nation.[13]

Benjamin Hawkins, always the pragmatist in attempting to improve frontier conditions for the Indians and settlers, reasoned that the initiation ceremonies should include teaching the importance of good race relations. In the midsummer of 1804 he wrote to Hopoie Micco, the speaker of the Creek Nation: "I am certain if our old Chiefs at the head of our annual festivals, and those appointed to initiate youth into manhood, would make it a cardinal point to instruct them to protect the traveller and strangers in our land, then when the impression is once made on infant minds, the pleasure resulting from such estimable conduct would free us from any apprehensions on this head."[14] In the bloody days that were to follow, Hawkins must have wished many times that his advice had been heeded.

For the Creeks, warfare and the collecting of scalps were means of testing as well as ways of gratifying the egos of young men. The Creeks and the Cherokees, who were ancient enemies, had been engaged in desultory warfare since the Yamassee War in 1715, and the fighting was especially bitter between 1750 and 1752. When the white man entered the Creek Nation in ever larger numbers after the Revolution, however, the Indian war activity increased in intensity, both against the encroaching settlers and against each other as the tensions of forced acculturation mounted. This activity elevated the esteem in which the war chiefs were held. Milfort in 1802 wrote that the *tustunnuggee*, or war chief, "had, at first, no part in the domestic administration. His authority lasted only as long as the war; but, today, he is the head chief of the nation with respect to civil as well as military affairs."[15] Big Warrior's high rank in the early nineteenth century is a good example of this elevation in rank. The English, as they maneuvered the Creeks into position for their role in the War of 1812, began early to commission war chiefs to act as their agents in the towns. The Spanish also tried to win over Creek war chiefs with attention and gifts.[16] McIntosh and Weatherford would soon be attaining manhood in a world in which allegiances were complex and bribery was commonplace.

When in their early teens, McIntosh and Weatherford were able to participate in the sports and games that were an important part of Creek life. Red Eagle was reputed to be the swiftest runner in all the Creek Nation and was so fond of sports that he was involved in all the contests of strength, speed, and skill available to him. One of his favorite sports, and one in which his skills, endurance, and personal daring made him particularly apt, was the game of ball-play, which was called "the little brother of war" by the Creeks and was of such political and ritualistic importance that if a town lost four consecutive games to a rival, it had to assume the rival's white-town or red-town designation.[17]

The Indian ball-play was an ancient sport that had flourished in pre-Columbian times, and accounts of the games—which resembled pitched battles to non-Indians—appear frequently in the writings of Spanish explorers. The object was to catch the ball in midair with a racquet-shaped, webbed stick and then run to the end of the field and hurl the ball through the goal posts for a score. With fifty braves on a side, however, the player with the ball was subject to being pummeled, kicked, or trampled underfoot on his way to the goal, with never a penalty. Although fractured bones were frequent and fatal injuries sometimes occurred, there was apparently a spirit of fair play despite the roughness of the sport. John Pope, who attended a Creek ball-play as a guest of Alexander McGillivray, wrote: "Suffer what they may, you'll never see an angry look or hear a threatening word among them." Adair, who also observed many Creek ball-plays in the era of Weatherford and McIntosh, wrote: "It is a very unusual thing to see them act spitefully in any sort of game, not even in this severe and tempting exercise."[18]

Preparations for a ball game between two Creek towns were long and elaborate, often requiring three or four months. One can imagine the impatience of young players like McIntosh and Weatherford as they waited for their elders to make the arrangements in the slow, traditional process. First, the messenger from one town went to the chief of another and issued the challenge, laying down a ball stick with a feather tied to it, The chief then called his townspeople together to inform them of the challenge and ask what they wanted to do about it. After counting the number of good players available, the people would make a decision. If affirmative, each town would select four contract makers, who would meet at the midpoint between the towns to negotiate the terms of the contest. These eight would decide not only on when and where the contest would be held but also on such complex questions as whether men related by birth and marriage to both towns would be allowed to play and whether men who were born in the towns and were now married and living elsewhere could return and play. At this point the differences among the contract makers might be so great that negotiations would cease and the game would be called off.[19]

If agreement on all points was reached and the game was scheduled, most of the people of both towns would encamp at the appointed place a few days before the selected day. Then the eight contract makers would agree upon the precise plot of ground where the game would be played. The land would be cleared, with people of both towns cutting underbrush and felling trees. The logs would be laid around the camps so that the spectators could sit on them in a semicircle during the pregame dance. Most of the dancing was done by the women, who danced four times to songs sung by the spectators. When the women finished their ritualistic movements and retired to the shadows, the ball players rushed in, brandishing their ball sticks, running about, and shouting, accompanied by the beating of drums. After midnight the women and spectators would retire to sleep, but the players remained awake and alert all night, waiting for daylight, when the game would begin. At the first flush of dawn in the eastern sky, the players would cut down a sapling, twelve to sixteen feet high and about six inches in diameter, and split it in two. They carried the split sapling to their end of the selected ball ground site, dug holes, and erected the poles about three feet apart, with a crosspiece on top. The two goals were usually from 150 to 200 yards apart in the Creek games. The field had no side boundaries, and the spectators on the sides of the field were frequently overrun by the players.[20]

The equipment was simple. The players among the southern tribes used sticks that were much like those used in lacrosse, a present-day game that developed from Indian stickball. The sticks were about two feet long, made of hickory, curved into a circle at the end, and webbed with raccoon or squirrel skin. The ball was made of deerhide and stuffed with animal hair or moss and tied with thongs of buckskin. Just before the game was to begin, the two teams approached the line that marked the median between the goals. Each player threw a stick down opposite those of an adversary, thus establishing an equal number of players on each side.

It was at this time that the final wagers were made. The Creeks loved to gamble, and at every ball-play there were many ponies, articles of clothing, pieces of jewelry, and food items bet on the outcome of the game. Pope wrote that "sometimes their whole Family Stock of Food and Raiment is hazzarded." While waiting for the game to begin, the players would jest with one another across the line of sticks. They were nearly nude, wearing only breechcloths or "flaps," and their bodies and faces were painted in various colors, the most popular combination being spiral streaks of red, white, and blue stripes that resembled snakes intertwined. Some of the players wore the tails of animals sticking out from the backs of their breechcloths in the belief that they would be endowed with the strength, cunning, and endurance of the chosen animal.[21] It is not difficult to imagine the excitement of young players like McIntosh and Weatherford as they waited for the struggle to begin. They, like all other healthy boys in the town, would have been playing the sport in informal games from the age of eight, anticipating the day when they would represent their town in the adult games.

For seven days before the game the players were forbidden to touch a girl or woman, for the ball-play was exclusively a male sport, and a woman's touching a ball stick would render it unfit for use. A man whose wife was pregnant could not play, on the theory that much of his strength had been exhausted in the creation of the infant. Also, throughout the long ball-play season, which began in midsummer and lasted until the winter weather was too severe for games, the players practiced regularly and abstained from eating such foods as rabbit, because the meat might transmit the rabbit's tendency to become frightened and easily confused; frog meat, because the frog's bones are brittle and easily broken; and the sucker fish, because its movements are sluggish and slow. The players waiting for the game to start were bleeding from the ceremonial scratches on their arms, legs, chests, and backs. This ritual scratching was done by a priest's assistant, using a comblike instrument made of seven sharp splinters of turkey leg bone tied to a frame made of turkey feathers. The scratching was believed to make the arms more lithe, freeing the limbs for swifter movements. Also, they believed, the turkey's fierce, warlike spirit was transferred to the players. Each was scratched four times on his upper and lower arms as well as his calves and thighs. Finally, a cross-scratch was etched on his breast and back.[22]

Play began when an old man, whom the Creeks called the "ball-witch," walked onto the field, made a brief speech about fair play, and tossed the ball up into the air between the two teams, shouting, "Here goes up the ball for twenty stakes." The ball could be picked up only with the sticks, not the hands, and in the ensuing melee and clattering of sticks, ten minutes might elapse before any player was able to gain control of the ball. Then suddenly a player with the ball cradled in his stick would emerge from the pack and run toward the goal as far as he could. When stopped by opposing players, he would toss the ball to one of his own men or attempt to hurl it through the goal posts. Each side had a scorekeeper who had ten sticks, and he drove one in the ground each time a goal was made. When all ten sticks were in the ground, he would withdraw them for each subsequent goal.[23]

George Catlin, who willingly rode thirty miles on horseback to see a ball-play, reported that two striking aspects of the game as played in the late eighteenth century were the dust, which often obscured the furious action, and the noise, "with every voice raised to the highest possible key, in shrill yelps and barks." Bleeding noses, broken limbs, and fisticuffs, according to Catlin, brought no stop to the action. When a goal was scored, a medicine man immediately ran to the center of the field and tossed the ball up again. Catlin reported that these games, which began in early morning, often lasted until near sundown. The game was an arduous test of endurance and stamina, but it was also a scene of great beauty to Catlin, who wrote: "And I pronounce such a scene, with its hundreds of Nature's most beautiful models, denuded, and painted of various colors, running and leaping into the air, in all the most extravagant and varied forms, in the desperate struggles for the ball, a school for the painter or sculptor, equal to any of those that ever inspired the hand of the artist in the Olympian games or Roman forum." The game continued into the late nineteenth century in the Indian territory with the violence undiminished. Adam Hodgson, an Englishman who visited the Creeks and observed a ball-play in 1820, was impressed with their attitude toward the rough play. He wrote, "All violence on these occasions is forgiven; and I was informed it is the only case in which life is not generally required for life."[24]

Another favorite game of the Creeks, and one which McIntosh and Weatherford must have played often, was chunkey, a variation of the hoop and pole game played by Indians throughout North America. Everywhere except in the Southeast, the game was played with a hoop of wood, which was rolled along the ground as the two participants jogged along beside it. When the hoop was about to stop, each player threw his pole at it, and the one whose stick was closest when the hoop came to rest was given a point. Two points were awarded if the stick was touching the hoop. The Creeks played the game in the same way except that they used a carefully polished stone disk. Many of these quartz chunkey stones have been excavated, and some are beautifully crafted works of art. They are two to three inches in breadth and eighteen to twenty-four inches in circumference. So valuable were the chunkey stones that they were owned by the towns and carefully preserved.

Each town had a smooth chunkey yard near its square, sometimes covered with packed sand so the stones would roll true. The game and the players made an unfavorable impression on Adair, who described their running at half-speed after a stone disk in the hot sun most of the day as "a task of stupid drudgery." He also described their addiction to gambling on the game, on which they "staked their silver ornaments, their nose, finger, and ear rings; their breast, arm, and wristplates, and even all their wearing apparel, except what barely covers their middle."[25]

Another favorite pastime was the single pole game, which was more social in nature than the chunkey and ball-play and was unique in that both sexes participated. Adjacent to the chunkey yard was a circular area with a pole, twenty-five to thirty feet high, in the middle. The ball used in the single pole game was the same deerhide-covered sphere used in ball-play, and the men used their ball-play sticks. The object of the game was to hurl the ball and hit a cow's or horse's skull at the top of the pole, so accuracy, not strength, was important. The women were given the advantage of picking up and throwing the ball with their hands, but the men, probably to sharpen their skills in ball-play, used only their webbed sticks. Often the men, in uncharacteristic displays of gallantry, contrived to let the women win. The winning score was twenty, and the scorekeeper used the ball-play method of driving ten sticks in the ground as points were scored up to ten and drawing them out again as the score moved toward twenty.[26]

Games of chance, which allowed the Creeks to indulge their love of gambling, were popular. In one game, four eight-inch sticks, made of cane split lengthwise, were used. Each player threw the sticks in the air, and points were scored on the basis of whether the sticks landed with the convex or concave side up. All four landing with the convex side up counted ten, all concave scored five, and combinations of the two were worth fewer points. Another game, involving both skill and chance, was the hidden ball or moccasin game, in which a small, round stone was hidden beneath one of four items of clothing, such as moccasins. The object was to guess where the stone was hidden. The skill of the players lay in their ability to confuse the guesser by using tricks such as special chants or swaying from side to side to lead him to make the wrong choice. The player guessing would also use such tricks as making false moves toward the moccasins to try to make his opponent react and give away the true location of the stone. When white settlers adopted the game, it came to be called the shell game, with a dried pea hidden under one of three small sea shells. The Creeks also played a game of chance in which they tossed up kernels of corn that had light and dark sides; points scored were based on the number of light or dark sides facing up.[27]

McIntosh and Weatherford grew up among fun-loving people who were creative in finding ways to fill their leisure hours. If the ball-play sport was "the little brother of war," it was good training for the times ahead, for both young men would be involved in warfare in the not-too-distant future. Their wits were also sharpened in the games of skill and chance for the tactics of battle and the stratagems of negotiation that would occupy much of their adult lives.

4

The Revolutionary Period: Dissension and Intrigue

———— • ————

The period of the American Revolution was a turbulent time for the Creeks, who sought to remain neutral even though both sides in the conflict pressed them for assistance, and the events of these years set into motion chains of future actions that would alter the lives of McIntosh and Weatherford. During young Weatherford's formative years, his father was involved in the intrigue between the Spanish and Alexander McGillivray, even acting as a double agent, and later he was to become a key figure in negotiations for peace between the Creeks and the United States. McIntosh, in a very real sense, owed his existence to the Revolution. In the fall of 1776, John Stuart, the British superintendent of the southern Indians, appointed Captain William McIntosh as his deputy to the Lower Creeks, who were in a short-lived period of favoring the British. Captain McIntosh had been ordered to the Lower Creek towns to recruit warriors for the British cause, but he was able to persuade only a few Hitchitis, with the warrior Hycut as leader, to go to St. Augustine to be equipped to fight against the Americans.[1] It was during this recruiting journey that the young captain met the Creek woman who was to become Chief McIntosh's mother.

The Creeks at this time were vulnerable to many persuasive spokesmen, who divided them, creating animosities that led to violence in the events surrounding the War of 1812. At the outbreak of the Revolution the two traders who were the Creeks' largest suppliers were also the two most active in the American revolutionary cause: Robert Rae, a trader in the upper towns, and George Galphin, who served the lower towns. Opposing them was David Taitt, sent by the

British to promote the crown's interests. Taitt had negotiated a land cession of more than two million acres in 1773 at Augusta, extending the English frontier on the west bank of the Savannah River to a depth of thirty to forty miles in an area of continual combat between the settlers and the Creeks. This treaty, which had been signed primarily to pay off Creek trading debts, caused widespread dissension in the Creek Nation. Another powerful spokesman, Alexander McGillivray, worked for the British and was involved in intrigue with the Spanish. This mixed-blood uncle of William Weatherford arrived in Coweta in the summer of 1777 as the British superintendent Stuart's newly commissioned deputy. The Creek headmen listened to McGillivray's arguments in favor of the British, but this did not prevent the Cusseta King, several other chiefs, and about five hundred warriors from going to Ogeechee Old Town to meet with Galphin, Rae, and the Georgia Indian commissioners. Galphin promised them guns and ammunition if they would protect his traders and drive out Taitt and Captain McIntosh.[2]

Before and during the Revolution, two factions emerged in the Creek Nation: the majority of headmen argued for peace with the British at any price, but the nativist faction held that the Creeks must ally themselves with the French and Spanish and fight to expel the British. Nativism became an increasingly powerful force when the frontier was broken after the American Revolution and white land-seekers wantonly invaded the Creek lands, accelerating the tension already present from the occasional attempts to acculturate the Upper Creeks, who were generally more nativistic than their lower town brothers. Theron A. Nunez, Jr., contends that it was the unresolved stress of nativism versus acculturation that led to a prophetic movement, a civil war, and a war between the United States and the Creek Nation.[3]

In 1783 the state of Georgia began to defy the wishes of the federal government and move toward a policy of negotiating independent treaties of land cession with the Creeks. Georgians maintained that the law was on their side, for the Union's "sole and exclusive right and power of regulating the trade and managing all affairs with the Indians," as stated in Article IX of the Articles of Confederation, was limited to those Indians who were "not members of any of the States." The United States, Georgia claimed, could not constitutionally intervene in the South, where all Indians were legally state members.[4] According to a Georgia Supreme Court decision in the case of *Harcourt* v. *Gaillard* in 1783, the United States contained no land other than that belonging to individual states. Consequently, in November of that year five commissioners appointed by the state met with a minority of Creek headmen and warriors at Augusta and negotiated a brief treaty running new boundary lines and securing large additions of land for Georgia.

McGillivray was outraged, charging that civil chiefs of Cusseta and Tallassee—called the Fat King and the Tame King—had acted for the entire Creek Nation in ceding to Georgia this land between the Tugaloo and Apalachee rivers. McGillivray claimed that they "were only two chiefs of the second rank and a few followers" and could not speak for the nation. Ironically, a similar charge was made against William McIntosh when he signed away all the then remaining Creek lands to Georgia in February 1825. McGillivray also claimed that the two chiefs and their followers were kept surrounded by armed men for five days until they consented to the demands, a charge denied by Georgians, who claimed that friendly cooperation made coercion unnecessary. It is relevant that the two chiefs had been friendly to the Americans during the Revolution and that they were unhappy over a recent demotion in status given them by McGillivray.[5]

Conditions along the frontier worsened, and in March of 1785 Congress appointed commissioners to seek to conclude a lasting peace with the southern Indians; the commissioners included Benjamin Hawkins of North Carolina, who was later to complete a term in the United States Senate and assume the role of longtime agent to the Creek Indians. Among the other four members appointed to the commission was Lachlan McIntosh, a distant relative of William's. The commissioners planned to meet the Creeks at Galphinton, a famous trading post on the Ogeechee River, on October 24, and the key figure in their plans was McGillivray, who could not attend the meeting but chose two chiefs from the upper towns and two from the lower towns to represent him, giving them instructions "to protest in the warmest manner against the encroachments that had been made" and "to insist upon all the Settlers to be removed." On October 24 the commissioners arrived to begin the meeting, but they had to wait for five days before being joined by Creek chiefs from two towns and a small band of about sixty warriors. The Creeks assured the commissioners that other important chiefs would eventually join the conference, apparently in an effort to trick the commissioners into proffering gifts. More than two weeks passed, and the commissioners withdrew in disgust, explaining that they could not negotiate with so few representatives of the Creek Nation. General Elijah Clarke and John Twiggs, agents of the state of Georgia, were pleased with the departure of the United States commissioners, for they had no scruples about dealing with a minority of Creeks. On the following day they signed a treaty by which Georgia secured all land east of a line running southwest from the junction of the Ocmulgee and Oconee rivers to the St. Marys. The Galphinton treaty also confirmed the land cession of the earlier Treaty of Augusta, to the great jubilation of Georgians.[6]

McGillivray deplored the action at Galphinton, and the following April he called a general convention of the Creek Nation to determine how to circumvent it. McGillivray told the Indians that their only alternative was "war with arms in our hands to force them to abandon their unjust usurpations." He instructed the chiefs to assemble warriors and depart immediately for the disputed lands to drive away the American settlers and destroy their buildings, but he admonished them "to shed no blood on no pretense but where self-defense made it absolutely necessary." On April 2, 1786, the Creek council declared war on Georgia, and, using arms supplied from Pensacola by the Spanish, war parties began attacking settlers on the Oconee lands, at Muscle Shoals, and Cumberland. McGillivray wrote that the Americans of Georgia were removed "without Injury to their persons," but that a "few were killed at Cumberland, which was unavoidable." It was unavoidable, McGillivray explained, because of the "extreme hatred" these people bore to the Indians, who, having sustained many injuries from the settlers at Cumberland, exceeded orders in "satisfying their revenge."[7]

The Cumberland settlers, outnumbered by the belligerent Creeks, made immediate overtures for peace, and the Georgia legislature appointed Daniel McMurphy as "their agent to reside in the Creek nation to preserve peace with their Friends the Creek Indians." McMurphy, called Yellow Hair by the Indians, was not well received by the majority of Creek headmen. He high-handedly demanded that all travelers into the state have passports and that all traders have Georgia licenses. He protested strongly against the actions of Spain in supplying McGillivray's forces within Georgia with arms.[8] McMurphy's efforts at peacemaking ultimately failed, and despite the Treaty of Shoulderbone (1786), the Treaty of New York (1790), and the continued efforts of the Georgia legislature and the United States Congress, there was no sustained peace between the frontier Georgians and the Creek Indians from the revolutionary war until after the War of 1812 and its attendant Creek Indian wars.

Charles Weatherford, William's red-haired Scots father, was deeply involved in the growing tensions between the Creeks and the Americans and in the intrigues between the Spanish and McGillivray. In 1786, when William was no more than five or six, his father was one of the packhorse men who served as letter carriers to and from Pensacola in the Spanish sector. It was apparent that Weatherford was playing a dangerous game. As brother-in-law to Alexander McGillivray, he was privy to most of his plans, and later, when the two men quarreled, he was willing to peddle his secrets to the Spanish.

Matters between McGillivray and Weatherford began to take a bad turn when the latter incurred a debt to John Leslie, a partner in the trading firm of Panton, Leslie, and Company, located at Pensacola. The powerful trading company was headed by William Panton, a Scots Tory who had lost property to Georgia by confiscation in the Revolution. This partnership dealing in the fur and peltry trade had operated under British auspices at St. Augustine and St. Marys and had remained viable and even extended its monopolies to Pensacola and Mobile when the territory became Spanish. The Spaniards, knowing the company was a great ally in making the Creeks loyal to Spain, gave it special favors. It was exempt from the normal requirement that all goods used in trading with the Indians must be Spanish made. The firm was allowed to sell British products, which were greatly preferred by the Indians, and was given the privilege of bringing them into the Floridas at a low rate of duty.[9]

Needless to say, the company exercised great political skill and recognized in McGillivray a powerful ally, making him a junior partner. McGillivray was also well aware of the importance of the company to his political goals, particularly in providing financial support and arms. When he learned of Weatherford's debt to Leslie, McGillivray wrote to the Spanish governor of West Florida, Arturo O'Neill, on December 3, 1786, on behalf of the creditor and against his brother-in-law: "Leslie has requested me to write concerning his affair with Weatherford. I think your Excellency would not judge wrong if you made Weatherfords property answerable for poor Leslie's debt." In a letter the following month to Governor O'Neill he characterized Weatherford and several others as "notorious offenders" and recommended that they be made to "suffer the rigors of the law." In July of 1787, McGillivray, hearing that Weatherford had escaped from jail, wrote to Governor O'Neill: "I wish that Weatherford had been better secured." Learning later that Weatherford had not escaped and was securely incarcerated, causing distress to his wife and children, McGillivray seems to have had a change of heart. He wrote to the Spanish governor of Louisiana, Esteven Miro, asking that he be released.[10]

Considering himself betrayed, Weatherford was resolute in his desire to undermine McGillivray when he had the chance. Governor O'Neill wrote Governor Miro on October 28, 1788: "Within twenty days one of McGillivray's confidants will be here, who, resenting past insults, has promised to inform me secretly what is going on now. If this works out, this individual is the one most to the purpose of cutting short the sinister intentions of McGillivray and his associates, who . . . practice the greatest falsehood." In another letter on the same matter he identified Weatherford by name but asked that his name not be divulged lest it result in "complete ruin" for him. The information given by Weatherford concerned, for example, the general rumor in the Creek Nation that peace would be made with the Americans in the spring or earlier, so that the nimble McGillivray could establish better trade and commercial ties with the English. Governor O'Neill quickly passed this bit of intelligence on to William Panton. Weatherford also told Governor O'Neill that McGillivray had contrived a marriage between his own sister and the mestizo son of James Colbert, the influential Chickasaw trader, with the intention of forming an alliance with that nation.[11]

In the summer of 1792 Weatherford supplied information to James Seagrove, a United States agent of Indian affairs, about the increasing unrest among Georgians which had grown out of the Treaty of New York, signed in 1790. This treaty took away some of the lands ceded to Georgia by the Galphinton treaty, and it also established a boundary line between the Creeks and the Georgians. Weatherford reported a chance meeting on the trail with Colonel Samuel Alexander of Greene County, who told him, "We are determined the boundary line shall not be run." Alexander claimed that a thousand men could be raised in seven days in the northern counties of Georgia to prevent the line's being run. Weatherford wrote that when he "intimated that this conduct would be opposing the United States as well as the Indians," Alexander's reply was that "he did not care, he and his friends were determined it should be so."[12]

In September of 1792 Charles Weatherford was considered so important a source of information for the United States that a schooner was chartered to convey him from Savannah to Philadelphia; a vessel then loading freight for several northern ports was thought to be too slow. The information that called for such quick action concerned an excursion through the Creek Nation by William Panton in the summer of 1792. He visited the principal towns and held conferences with the headmen and chiefs of the nation, urging them not to abide by the Treaty of New York. According to Weatherford, he told them they should not allow their boundaries to be cut and delimited as that treaty had specified and assured them that the king of Spain considered them under his royal protection and would support them in any struggle for their rights. Panton reminded them that the Spanish were more affluent than the American settlers, who could give them no presents of value. He also attempted to persuade the leading Creek chiefs to visit the Spanish governor of New Orleans, who, Panton promised, would give them handsome presents as well as muskets and ammunition with which to defend themselves against the encroaching Georgians. It was generally known at the time that the Spanish gifts to the Creeks represented a cost of $40,000 to $50,000 a year.[13] Weatherford's evidence was so explosive that after he gave testimony before the authorities in Savannah—which "filled up more than twelve sheets of paper," according to McGillivray—he was sent by the swift schooner to testify before the United States Congress in Philadelphia.[14]

When McGillivray died on February 17, 1793, Weatherford's stature among the American and Spanish authorities was increased. On March 9 Weatherford wrote to tell Seagrove about McGillivray's death, which was caused by an acute fever, complicated by gout and a pulmonary problem. In the letter he revealed that as soon as the Creek leader's demise was known, Governor O'Neill had sent for him to come to Pensacola immediately. Apparently Weatherford wanted no part of the Spanish cause. He wrote Seagrove: "I shall always be happy in doing everything in my power to serve you, as I have ever looked upon you as a sincere friend in every respect." Aware of the dangers inherent in his position as a double agent, he added that he was "hoping that every matter of importance will be secret to you and myself alone." But all did not go smoothly in this time of crisis; on March 22 Weatherford reported to Seagrove "a great confusion in the Nation" as a result of McGillivray's death. He predicted that "this will not be ended without some difficulty and trouble."[15]

Despite his pessimism, Charles Weatherford continued to work to promote good relations between the Creeks and the United States. A letter from Alexander Cornells, another Scots-Indian, to Seagrove on April 8, 1793, praised Weatherford's efforts: "If every man would exert himself as well as . . . Mr. Weatherford, we should have everlasting peace with our brothers of the United States." Cornells assured Seagrove that "we don't want to shed no white people's blood, for I have got white people's blood in me." Timothy Barnard, an early settler and interpreter, wrote to Seagrove on April 19: "Charles Weatherford, by what I can learn, is doing all he can for the good of the United States; and I think, was he sure of your protection, would be a very useful man in that quarter against the Spanish commissaries. . . . Weatherford has great influence in that quarter, and wants revenge from the *Dons* for making a prisoner of him." Barnard thought that if Seagrove gave them instructions, he and Cornells would prevent any good talks between the Spaniards and the Creeks.[16]

At the impressionable age of twelve, William Weatherford was surely pleased with his father's growing importance as an instrument of peace between the United States and the Creek Nation. In a letter to Seagrove on June 11, 1793, Charles Weatherford wrote: "I hope now matters are very well settled in behalf of the United States, as I have left nothing unturned, that I thought would be beneficial, or preserve peace in that quarter." Seagrove had asked him to attend a meeting between the Creeks and the Spanish, and he wrote: "It was a singular satisfaction to me, to have your orders to attend in behalf of the States; and I have so fully completed the business, that I hope, for the future, there will be no danger, as the whole of the Upper towns, and a large majority of the Lower, agree to be in peace with the United States." Seagrove was grateful for Weatherford's service. He wrote him on July 29: "Your conduct, in all matters, I highly approve; continue to persevere; firm, determined conduct is every thing, either with red or white." He requested Weatherford to arrange to have the chiefs of the upper and lower towns meet him at Ocmulgee by September 10 with sufficient forces to escort him to the Cussetas. Addressing him as "my dear Weatherford," he added, "I depend upon your utmost exertions, and shall, without fail, expect to meet you at the Rock Landing."[17]

The meeting did not occur precisely as scheduled. Seagrove reported to the secretary of war on October 31: "On the 27th instant, Charles Weatherford, a white man, who lives in the Upper Creeks, came here with letters to me, and orders from the chiefs, to bring me into the Nation, they being desirous to settle all matters, and live in peace with us. Weatherford was accompanied, as far as the Oakmulgee, by some chiefs and warriors as an escort for me." Seagrove was unable to leave immediately, and, fearing the Indians might grow impatient, he "sent off Weatherford on the 29th to keep them easy."

Seagrove believed that the Georgians were more of a problem than
the Indians. He reported to the secretary: "From decided and clear
information, I am enabled to say, that the whole of the Creek Nation is
desirous of peace with the United States. . . . From these repeated
incursions of the people of Georgia into the Creek towns, I fear that
the minds of the savages will be irritated and soured to such degree,
that it will be impossible to convince them of the good intentions of
the President of the United States toward them, and that, if these
things are not speedily stopped, a general Indian war is inevitable."[18]

Constant Freeman, the agent for the Department of War in Georgia,
reported just such an inflammatory incident to the governor on December 28, 1793. White Bird-tail King and eight Cusseta warriors, encouraged by assurances of safety from Seagrove, were hunting
between the Ocmulgee and Oconee rivers when two of their number
were murdered by a party of whites. Three whites, unarmed and ap-
pearing to be hunters, came into the Cussetas' camp and accepted the
Indians' food and hospitality. They left for a time, then returned with
arms and the rest of the party and fired upon and killed two of the
Indians. Bird-tail King and the other six fled immediately and went to
Fort Fidius to demand the reasons why they were so attacked while
under the protection of the United States. Freeman wrote: "They were
also induced to make us this visit, because they knew that Weatherford was at this time here, on business from Mr. Seagrove."[19]

The white frontiersmen saw these tense and frightening times
from a different perspective, of course, and the story can hardly be
told better than in the words of General Sam Dale, who dictated his
recollections of his younger days as an Indian fighter to J. F. H.
Claiborne:

> In 1794, the Indians being restless and discontented by the advance of
> the whites, Captain Foote was authorized by the Governor of Georgia to
> organize a troop of horse for the protection of the frontier. Putting a
> steady old man in my place on the farm, I volunteered for the service.
> Our accoutrements were a 'coonskin cap, bearskin vest, short hunting-
> shirt and trowsers of homespun stuff, buckskin leggins, a blanket tied
> behind our saddles, a wallet for parched corn, coal flour, or other
> chance provision, a long rifle and hunting-knife. After some months'
> scouting we were mustered into the United States service, and ordered
> to Fort Mathews, on the Oconee. The pay I received, and a first-rate
> crop of tobacco made by the children, enabled me to pay more than half
> the price of our land, besides having an abundant supply of provisions.

Next year we extinguished the debt, and our household grew up with thankful hearts to an overruling Providence.

In 1794 the Creek Indians renewed their depredations, burning houses and driving off horses and cattle. Our company was ordered out. We followed them to the Oke-fus-kee village, near the Chattahoochie. Crossing the river before daybreak, we got silently into the town just as the Indians, having taken the alarm, were rushing from their cabin. We killed thirteen warriors, captured ten, and then set fire to the village.

Scouting in front of my company on our return march, I came upon an Indian lodge occupied by two warriors. I shot one dead; the other jumped into the cane-brake. One O'Neal, who came up just then, and myself pursued him. The cane was very thick, and we wormed along slowly, when the Indian fired, and O'Neal fell dead by my side. By this time our troop had come up, and seeing no one, and supposing that Indians were concealed in the thicket, they began a general fire, cutting the cane all about me. I threw myself on the ground, drew up O'Neal's corpse as a shield, and it was riddled with balls, two of them inflicting slight wounds upon me. It was some time before the fire slackened sufficiently for me to apprise them of my position. At the same moment a party began to fire on the opposite side of the thicket, and the Indian, who all this time was not twenty yards off, but invisible, took the bold resolution to advance upon me and escape. Gliding through the cane like a serpent in an almost horizontal posture, he briskly approached me. I cocked my rifle, and the instant I got sight of his head I pulled trigger, but missed fire; before I could re-prime he was upon me (for I was sitting on the ground), with his knife at my throat and his left hand twisted in my hair. At the instant one of our troop (Murray) fired, and, leaping to my feet, I plunged my knife into the Indian's bosom. But he was already dead; Murray had shot him through the heart, and, without a spasm or a groan, he fell heavily into my arms. He was a brave fellow, so we wrapped his blanket around him, broke his gun and laid it across his body, and departed.[20]

In their teenage years, William Weatherford and William McIntosh lived in a world of almost constant friction between the Creeks and the encroaching Georgians, and the violence to come in their manhood was clearly presaged in their youth. Their complex relationship with both parties in the struggle, their ties of blood on both sides, as well as the roles their close relatives played and were to play, complicated the decisions each would have to make in the crisis to come. Weatherford's role was to be different from that of his famous uncle, for McGillivray's talents lay more in advising than commanding.

Benjamin Hawkins (Courtesy of the North Carolina Division of Archives and History)

McGillivray's efforts to maintain the independence of the Creek Nation by strengthening Creek political organizations were to prove useful to the ambitions of McIntosh.[21]

McIntosh's fortunes were enhanced when Benjamin Hawkins became Indian agent to the Creek Nation in 1796 and stepped confidently and somewhat self-righteously into the power vacuum left by McGillivray's death. Hawkins, a product of the Age of Enlightenment and addicted to "that Indian fascination," according to one writer, accepted the challenge of President George Washington "to sacrifice a few years of your life in making the experiment which you have suggested, and try the effects of civilization among them."[22] To bring civilization to the Creek Nation Hawkins envisioned a system of gov-

ernment under his control, and he set about to hand-pick an executive committee of the National Council and to have the full council
meet annually at his residence in the historically important town of
Coweta. Later the meetings were alternated between the two easily
monitored towns of Tuckabatchee and Coweta. Hawkins moved to
reduce the influence of the clans, break down Creek tribalism, and
release a spirit of individuality in the Creek Nation. His actions aggravated ancient dissensions between the lower towns and the more
nativistic upper towns, and Hawkins increasingly leaned for support
on such Lower Creek leaders as Bird-tail King of Cusseta, Little Prince
of Broken Arrow, and William McIntosh of Coweta, who were to become—with Hawkins's help—prime movers in the Creek Nation, in
opposition to Upper Creek chiefs Mad Dog and Big Warrior.[23] Conditions were now favorable to channel McIntosh into the checkered career that lay ahead of him.

5

Weatherford and McIntosh
Become Famous:
Capturing Bowles and
Debating with Jefferson

——— • ———

About the turn of the century the names of William McIntosh and William Weatherford began to appear in the historical record. Benjamin Hawkins noted on May 15, 1798: "Paid William McIntosh, a half-breed, for beef for the public meeting at Cusseta $12.00." Two years later, at the age of about twenty-two, the enterprising McIntosh had become an underling chief among the Cowetas. His name, however, was not among those signing the treaty of June 16, 1803, at Fort Wilkinson on the Oconee. This controversial treaty conference, which was boycotted by most of the Lower Creek towns, gave the white settlers a foothold on the west bank of the Oconee River and was the beginning of the end of Creek landownership in Georgia. While negotiations were in progress at Fort Wilkinson, the Georgia Compact was signed, pledging the United States to acquire all land claimed by Indians within Georgia boundaries that could be acquired "peaceably and on reasonable terms," a caveat that, in effect, gave the Indians the right to refuse. In return, the state gave up its territorial claims to Alabama and Mississippi to the federal government.[1] During the discussions at Fort Wilkinson, the treaty commissioners understandably did not mention the impending Georgia Compact.

Although he was some distance away in Florida, an important figure in the background of the negotiations at Fort Wilkinson was William Augustus Bowles, a bizarre character who was to be associated with William Weatherford's sudden rise to prominence. Bowles, a Maryland Loyalist, had resigned his commission in the army and left Pensacola in a fit of temperament in 1778 to live among the Lower Creeks on the Chattahoochee. After an unsuccessful attempt to return to the white world, Bowles had rejoined the Creeks and in 1791 proclaimed himself director general of the affairs of the Creek Nation. Bowles's chief aim was to undermine Alexander McGillivray's influence and prevent the execution of the Treaty of New York of 1790, which McGillivray had led the Creeks to sign. The treaty ceded part of the disputed land east of the Oconee River, which was already settled by Georgians and almost certainly irretrievably lost to the Creek Nation.

From 1792 to 1798, Bowles was a prisoner of the Spanish, but in October of 1799 he was back in Florida and had reassumed the title of director general of the Creeks. His principal aim at this time was to set up a pro-British state that would thwart Spanish intentions at every opportunity and also protect Creek lands against encroachment. His first act was to call the Creek and Seminole leaders to a conference at Wekiwa, at which he announced that no more Indian lands would be ceded and no dividing line run. He also issued a proclamation directing the Indians to drive out of their territories all persons who held commissions under the United States, an edict aimed primarily at Hawkins. In November Bowles, in a letter to Little Prince, wrote that Hawkins "must go immediately as he is a dangerous man and will cause some mischief to you by staying, I shall seize him if I find him." A newspaper columnist who quoted this letter wrote: "We will soon see which of these men have the most influence among the Indians, as Hawkins must quit the ground or drive Bowles [out]."[2]

Understanding the threat presented by Bowles's return to power, Hawkins denounced him at a meeting of the Creek National Council at Tuckabatchee on November 27, 1799, and demanded that the council go on record as opposing Bowles, which it obediently did. The headmen also agreed to adopt Hawkins's organizational plan, which was to divide the Upper Creek towns into nine districts, each directed by a warrior. Hawkins's plan proposed a system of government by war leaders that was similar to the government structure that McGillivray had employed so well. It is often argued that Hawkins replaced McGillivray as the prime mover of the Creeks, and it is true that both men exercised strong influence over the Creek government in attempting to unify it. Michael D. Green has stated, however, that there was a major difference in purpose between the two. "McGillivray," Green wrote, "tried to strengthen the Creek government in order to preserve the Nation's independence. Hawkins tried to strengthen Creek government in order to control it and thereby destroy the Nation's independence."[3]

On April 5, 1800, in retaliation for the Spanish burning of his headquarters at Wekiwa, Bowles declared that a state of war existed between the Muscogees and Spain. On April 9, he led a force of between two and three hundred Seminoles and Creeks against the Spanish fort at St. Marks and forced its surrender without, he claimed, the loss of a single man. The Spanish governor at Pensacola, Vicente Folch, put a bounty of $4,500 on Bowles's head, but no Indian attempted to win the award, deterred either by the popularity of Bowles or by the strength of his sixty-man team of bodyguards. On October 9, 1801, an informant wrote to Hawkins that Bowles "is down near the Muckesukee, continues to encourage the Indians to annoy the Spanish government, assures them that they will receive assistance from their friends the British."[4]

The high esteem in which Hawkins was held at this time is shown in a position paper written on September 26, 1801, by some Coweta, Cusseta, and other lower town chiefs to Mad Dog and others of the upper towns in anticipation of the negotiations at Fort Wilkinson: "We are informed by some of the Georgians that we are to be called to a meeting at Oconee as soon as our beloved man Col. Hawkins returns at which time the Georgians is to make a demand of all the property taken since the Treaty of New York, and if it cannot be restored they are to be demanded the land as far as the Ockmulgee, but we trust and depend on our beloved man Col. Hawkins to stand our friend and put a stop to so large a demand."[5]

That Bowles was in the background of the treaty negotiations at Fort Wilkinson in 1802 is also evident in the report on the difficulties of the negotiations by the three commissioners, Benjamin Hawkins, Andrew Pickens, and James Wilkinson. "In presenting these views," they reported, "we had to combat, not only the jealousies, distrusts, & fears natural to the Indians, but also to an apprehension serious & alarming to the old chiefs, that if they ceded any part of their country their young warriors might resist the act by joining the partisans of Bowles, divide the nations, wrest the government from those who at present administer it, and by some potent measure involve the country in ruins."[6]

In early 1803 Hawkins began diligently preparing for an Indian council to be convened in May at the Hickory Ground, on the banks of the Coosa River. Secretary of War Henry Dearborn had emphasized the importance of this council in his instructions to Hawkins and the other two commissioners. He particularly desired a strong natural boundary, such as a river, to separate the Creeks and the Georgians. He stressed the need for frugality, for only $30,000 had been appropriated for meeting the demands of several Indian nations; therefore, he warned, the Creeks must be confined to reasonable demands.[7] This council, which was to include delegates from the Upper and Lower Creeks, Seminoles, Cherokees, Chickasaws, and Choctaws, would, Hawkins hoped, approve an extension of the Georgia boundary and endorse the capture of his nemesis, Bowles. Hawkins had heard rumors that Bowles was planning to visit the Hickory Ground.[8]

About the middle of May the Indians began to assemble. First to arrive were the Upper Creeks, followed by delegates from the Lower Creeks and neighboring tribes. The number soon grew to four hundred, despite Secretary Dearborn's warning to Hawkins as to the "impropriety of a very numerous assembly." Among the few white faces in the crowd were those of John Forbes, head of the powerful Panton, Leslie, and Company, and Esteban Folch, son of the Spanish governor. Both expected to arrange for Bowles to be seized and turned over to Spanish authorities or, barring that, to encourage one of the leading chiefs to assassinate him. Forbes and Folch were invited to lodge with Hawkins as proof that the rumors of an American disagreement with Spain were overblown, particularly in regard to the Bowles problem. Although Bowles was well aware of the dangers awaiting him at the Hickory Ground, he resolved to attend the council, confident that he could denounce Spain and the United States with such eloquence that the council would elect him king of all the southern Indians.[9]

On May 24 runners brought the message that Bowles and his entourage were approaching, and on that day the director general swaggered into the council square, proud and disdainful, surrounded by his Seminole warriors. Despite the tension that swept through the assembly grounds, Bowles seemed assured of his safety, perhaps reasoning that by tradition no violence would be done to him in a Creek peace town, or white town. He also took comfort in being surrounded by friendly Seminoles, by some Cherokees he had specially invited, and by a number of partisans from Lower Creek towns. Hawkins reacted quickly. In a letter written on May 24, Dearborn showed that he clearly expected Hawkins to take action: "If he should place himself within your reach, I have no doubt but that you will secure him . . . it would be desirable that the nation should take advantage of the reward offered by the Spanish government . . . the most effective and certain mode of terminating his career."[10] Gaining the approval of most members of the council, Hawkins appointed a group of men to capture Bowles; the party included Sam Moniac, Bob Walton, Mad Dog, Charles Weatherford, and his son William.

Hawkins and John Forbes led the party as it marched into the area where Bowles and the Seminoles were encamped among the Cherokee delegates. When the Indians who supported Bowles discerned the purpose of Hawkins's visit, they began showing signs of resisting the arrest of their leader. Hawkins announced boldly that he had come to arrest Bowles and that they must deliver him up. He then ordered Moniac and young Weatherford to step forward and make the arrest. To the sound of scores of rifles clicking to the cocked position, Moniac and Red Eagle, with reckless courage, seized Bowles and held his wrists to be shackled. One of the benefits of the 1802 Treaty of Fort Wilkinson was the agreement of the United States to furnish the Creek Nation with two sets of blacksmith tools and men to work them; one of these blacksmiths provided a snug-fitting set of handcuffs for Bowles. Folch had the privilege of snapping them shut around the director general's wrists.[11]

It has been charged that the United States violated international law in encouraging the capture of Bowles on American soil and then turning him over to the Spanish. Certainly Hawkins, Forbes, and Folch argued strongly for the capture, but it could never have been accomplished without the consent of the Indians, who considered themselves sovereign on their own soil in their most sacred meeting place.[12] Nevertheless, Bowles was in irons. Hawkins advised the Indians, who were embarrassed at the circumstances of the capture at Hickory Ground, to turn the prisoner over to the Spanish for the $4,500 reward.[13] Moniac, the Weatherfords, and the other Upper Creeks set off for Mobile with the manacled Bowles, rowing down the Alabama River in a pirogue. Along the way groups of Indians gathered on the shore to watch the captive director general glide past. It was warm enough at night to camp comfortably in the open, and on the fourth night, downstream from present-day Salem, the troop camped on an island in the middle of the river. During the night, while his guard slept, Bowles managed to free himself from his bonds, steal the pirogue, and escape, and when the Indians awoke at daylight, they discovered that the prisoner was gone. The abandoned boat was in plain view on the opposite shore, where Bowles in his haste had left it. In a few moments the Indians were on his trail; the pirogue led to the director general's tracks through a thick cane swamp, and by noon he was again a captive. This time no chances were taken, and the Creeks shortly reached Mobile with their famous prisoner. Governor Vicente Folch and a cadre of employees of Panton, Leslie, and Company were on hand to greet them and to hand over the reward money. The governor also had six soldiers waiting to take the prisoner and escort him aboard a ship bound for New Orleans, where he was placed on another ship setting sail for Havana. In less than eighteen months, on December 23, 1805, he lay dead in a military hospital.[14]

Hawkins, who was sometimes given to a near-poetic style in his letters to important personages, summarized the story of Bowles's capture, with emphasis on the hubris and theatricality that finally ended his career, in a letter to President James Madison: "It was inconceivable to me that Bowles who understood a good deal of the Indian language, had been here formerly and visited with General McGillivray, should not have been able to make the necessary distinction between the past and present. He must have seen a material change in the manners of the Indians . . . and yet he goes on reacting his former part of Director General, until he was apprehended in the midst of his guards and adherents and at the eve in imagination of being a king of the four nations, and quits the stage in irons." Bowles's megalomania, though inexplicable, was well known. Andrew Ellicott, who knew the director general, told Hawkins, "He speaks in the style of a King, 'my Nation,' and 'my people' are his common expressions."[15]

In ordering the capture of Bowles, Hawkins had cannily calculated his risks, and he knew the Creek leaders well enough to predict their reaction precisely. He reported to Georgia Governor John Milledge: "As soon as the event took place a general murmur for the day only ran through the chiefs in opposition. With the evening, by the prudent conduct of the Council of the Nation, the whole subsided, and they were brought to take the United States and Spain by the hand in friendship, and to join in a solemn declaration of the National Council that they were resolved 'on eternal peace with all the world.'"[16]

The dramatic capture brought instant fame to Red Eagle. As Thomas Woodward wrote: "I had seen Billy Weatherford before the war, but only knew him from character. The circumstances of him and Moniac aiding Col. Hawkins in the arrest of Bowles made them generally known to the people of Georgia who wished to know anything about Indians."[17] Also, in the capture of Bowles, young William

Weatherford had encountered one of the most colorful figures in the turbulent history of relations between the Indians and the United States. Bowles could never deny himself the grandiose gesture in any dramatic situation, and who can surmise what influence he had on Red Eagle, who was later to ride boldly into the camp of Andrew Jackson to surrender after the Battle of Horseshoe Bend?

In early 1805 the stage was being set for William McIntosh, only about twenty-seven years of age, to achieve national recognition as the spokesman and most important member of a six-man delegation of Creek chiefs selected to renegotiate a treaty with President Thomas Jefferson in Washington. On February 12, 1805, Secretary of War Henry Dearborn informed Benjamin Hawkins that the Senate had disapproved of the treaty Hawkins had negotiated and signed with the Creeks at the agency on November 3, 1804. Under the terms of that treaty, the land in the forks of the Oconee and Ocmulgee rivers, as far north as the High Shoals of the Apalachee, was to be ceded to the United States. In reporting to Dearborn, Hawkins had written: "We have acquired somewhat more than two millions of acres, half of which is unquestionably the best land in this country." The Creeks were to have received $200,000 in stock that paid 6 percent annually, with the interest being paid twice a year. The price, the Senate voted, was too high and the mode of payment objectionable. The refusal of the price Hawkins had negotiated is hardly surprising. In appointing a treaty commissioner to the Wyandotts in April 1805, Dearborn had explained: "The price usually given for Indian cessions, in different parts of the United States has not exceeded one cent per acre. And the United States is, in no case, except for particular favored tracts, inclined to give, at most, more than the rate of two cents per acre." In a message to the Senate, Jefferson said that Hawkins had exceeded a reasonable price limit for the land cession but was "induced to go beyond this limit, due to the strong interest the state of Georgia has in cession" and "by despair of procuring it on more reasonable terms, from a tribe which is one of the most fixed in the policy of holding fast to their lands." Jefferson also objected to the payment scheme involving stock, which, the president said, "may be passed into other hands, and render them the prey of speculators."[18]

Although the previous treaty was not ratified, Dearborn reiterated that the cession of land between the Oconee and the Ocmulgee rivers was so important that President Jefferson had directed him to invite Hawkins to bring the speaker of the Creek Nation "and such other chiefs as you and the Nation think proper to select" to Washington in

William McIntosh, attributed to Washington Allston (Courtesy of the State of Alabama Department of Archives and History)

April, May, or June, if practicable. Dearborn asked Hawkins to assure the chiefs that they "will receive every attention and mark of friendship from their father the President." Dearborn wrote: "The best mode of travelling from Augusta will be by stage. Money will be placed in the hands of our agent at Fort Wilkinson for bearing expenses." Dearborn also wanted to know the sum necessary to pay the debt due by the Creeks to the "House of Panton."[19] The firm of Panton, Leslie and Company still wielded considerable influence in Georgia, Alabama, and Florida.

Frontier altercations continued to worsen in the summer of 1805 as Hawkins prepared for the trip to Washington with his six chiefs. Secretary Dearborn wrote to the agent on June 28 that President Jefferson had learned that settlements were forming on the Creek lands between the headwaters of the Oconee and the Ocmulgee. "It is the express direction of the President," wrote Dearborn, "that any white settlers who may intrude on the Indian lands be removed by military force without delay." He assured Hawkins that the commanding officer at Fort Wilkinson would provide aid "in execution of the law providing for the removal of intruders on Indian lands." He added that he looked forward to seeing Hawkins and the chiefs, "duly authorized and inclined to fix a strong natural boundary between the Creeks and the people of Georgia, and to establish a post road through their country on reasonable terms." Dearborn concluded, "If the Oakmulgee can once be established as the Boundary, I trust I shall not live long enough to hear any contention for any other boundary line between Georgia and the Creek Nation."[20]

During the summer, President Jefferson showed a continuing strong interest in the coming visit of Hawkins and the Creeks. Dearborn wrote to Hawkins in mid-July: "I hope you will be able to prevail on the Speaker to accompany you. The President of the United States will be disappointed and mortified should he not come, and will consider his not coming as a strong indication of want of friendship."[21] Hopoie Micco, the speaker of the Creek Nation, did not accompany Hawkins to Washington because of ill health, thus giving young McIntosh an opportunity to serve as spokesman for the group and make his debut as a leader in Creek public affairs. He was to make the most of his unexpected opportunity, showing a rare eloquence and talent in debate during his lengthy encounter with the intellectual President Jefferson.

On August 4 Hawkins reported to Georgia's Governor John Milledge: "A deputation of Indians are appointed and probably will set out to the seat of Government some time early in the next month." Almost two months later, on October 2, he wrote to Milledge: "I am now on my way to the seat of government with a deputation of the Creeks and expect to be in Augusta on Monday next [the seventh]." On October 4 Hawkins and his chiefs passed through Sparta, Georgia, and three days later, as predicted, they arrived in Augusta. The *Augusta Herald* published an editorial laudatory of Hawkins's good work among the Creeks.[22]

There were no roadways in southwest and central Georgia, only trails, and the Hawkins group had to make its way on horseback to Augusta, which boasted a twice-a-week stagecoach to Savannah, as well as a coach going northward to Washington.[23] By stagecoach the approximately 550-mile trip over the rough and primitive roadways from Augusta to Washington took a minimum of ten days if the journey was uneventful and without problems with either horses or vehicles. Even though the horses were changed at stations 20 to 25 miles apart all along the journey, uneventful trips were rare and problems with spavined horses and broken axles commonplace. Hawkins and his chiefs rode in one of the larger coaches, which could seat fourteen passengers if two rode on top. As the coaches approached the next station, a blast on the post horn would alert the agent there to make ready the fresh horses.[24] Although lacking in comforts either in the bumping, swaying coach or at the crude inns along the way, where guests often slept on the dirt floor in the dining room, long trips were inexpensive. As late as 1848, for example, the 444-mile trip from Knoxville to Richmond cost $28.50.[25] The thousand dollars that had been budgeted to finance the mission to Washington seems to have been more than adequate.[26]

Hawkins and the six Creek chiefs arrived in Washington in the latter part of October and excited a great deal of curiosity as they moved about the city, visiting a session of the House of Representatives and the Navy Yard. The Creeks reached Washington about the same time as a large party of Osage Indians, who had been invited to the seat of government by Meriwether Lewis and William Clark during their western expedition, and the dress and demeanor of the southern Indians contrasted markedly with those from the West. Charles William Janson, a British traveler who observed them with great interest, wrote: "The Creeks are nearly civilized, and, from the dress of the greater number, there was no distinguishing them from the American citizens—some indeed were a little darker than the inhabitants of the Southern States." Sir Augustus Foster, a British diplomat, gave a more precise description of their clothing: "When I went to visit them they all rose from the ground where they had been seated in conversation, gave me their hands and touched their hats; they had the appearance of coachmen, each being dressed in a blue coat, with a red collar and gold lace round the hat. They had also pantaloons on and moccasins." In the full-length portrait of McIntosh by Washington Allston, he is wearing close-fitting pantaloonlike trousers, moccasins, and a long outer garment resembling a toga, trimmed with gold fringe and tied at the waist with a broad sash, brocaded in a diamond design.[27]

Several observers commented on the emotional impassivity and imperturbability of the Creeks. Janson found that "they appeared perfectly indifferent and unmoved at the most curious object presented to them. They were grave and reserved, a conduct always observed among the higher order of savages, who consider it beneath the dignity of a warrior to betray emotions of surprise, fear, or joy." Thomas Jefferson may have been referring in part to McIntosh and the other Creeks when he told a friend that he often experimented with visiting Indians by presenting them with striking and unusual objects in an attempt to elicit some expression of astonishment. They had betrayed their emotions only once, when Jefferson was entertaining some chiefs at dinner. The chiefs displayed no emotion at the unusual food, the table service, or the unfamiliar surroundings of a formal dining room, but they did show expressions of doubt and surprise when the wine coolers filled with ice were placed on the table. An elder chief picked up a piece of ice, was startled when it felt cold to the touch, and handed it to a companion, who seemed equally startled. After being convinced that despite the day's warm temperature, it was really ice, they began talking animatedly among themselves.[28]

The romantic notion of the noble savage, so popular in the early nineteenth century in the writings of Jean Jacques Rousseau, is eloquently stated in the words of Margaret Bayard Smith, a prominent Washington socialite and hostess in the Jeffersonian era, who said of the visiting Indians: "Imperturbable as the rocks of their savage homes, they stood in a kind of dignified and majestic stillness, calmly looking on the gay and bustling scene around them." The Creeks' emotional control caused much comment throughout official and unofficial Washington. When the Indians visited the Navy Yard, the largest guns were fired on several frigates, but the Creeks took little notice of the thunderous din. Instead, they calmly discussed the construction of war vessels among themselves and, according to one observer, "appeared gratified with the idea of their conveying a great

number of people at a time over great waters." The Creeks were observed with interest by Charles Janson when they visited the House
of Representatives, then meeting in temporary quarters while the
south wing of the Capitol was being built. Because the gallery in the
temporary room was small, many "genteel females," already seated,
were sent away to make space for the Indians. The Creeks entered the
room with great dignity and presence and took seats on the opposite
side of the makeshift gallery from the Osage visitors. Janson described the scene as they left: "Having with much apparent attention
listened to the business before the house, the chief whispered to the
next, the purport of which appeared to be instantly understood, as
they rose with one accord, and returned in the order they came, without noticing or even seeming to observe any other person but themselves."[29]

The serious business of treaty making began on November 2, with
President Jefferson addressing the group as "Friend McIntosh and
Chiefs of the Creek Nation." He welcomed the chiefs to Washington
and thanked the Great Spirit for bringing them safely on their long
journey. He reminded them that it was now fifteen years since the
meeting at New York, when the Creeks had negotiated a treaty with
President Washington. Jefferson recalled that he had been present,
along with his friend Alexander Cornells, who was among the six
Creek delegates listening to the president that day. It is perhaps re-
vealing that both the delegates whom the president singled out by
name, McIntosh and Cornells, had as much Caucasian blood as Indian. The president told them that the Treaty of New York had laid a
foundation for peace and friendship which had bound them together
since that time. Digressing slightly, Jefferson urged the Creeks to improve their skills in cultivating the earth, raising stock, and making
clothing. He told them he had learned "with great pleasure from our
beloved man, Colonel Hawkins, the progress you have made in these
arts." He pointed out to the chiefs that the Creek population was declining annually, and he assured them that this new mode of life
would help increase their numbers.[30]

Then President Jefferson turned to the matter that concerned him
most: the land cessions. "We are a growing people," he said,
"therefore whenever you wish to sell lands, we shall be ready to buy,
but only in compliance with your own free will." He reiterated that
the price of the land agreed upon in Hawkins's negotiations the previous year was too high. "Nothing like that price was ever before
asked or given in any of the purchases we have made from your

neighbors." He cited land purchases made by the English from the Creeks and by later American treaties and concluded that none had been bought for half as much as was being demanded. He reminded them that they had agreed to part with the land the previous year and that all that remained to do was to reach an agreement on a reasonable price.[31]

The president told the chiefs that since the Louisiana Purchase, the Indian lands had been surrounded by white settlers and that the United States must have a road through the Creek Nation, from Washington through Georgia to New Orleans. William McIntosh must have listened well when the president remarked that those Creeks who settled on the road to provide provisions and lodging for travelers would soon see the advantages of doing so. Later, McIntosh was to operate a ferry on the Chattahoochee, eighty miles northwest of the road, near his principal residence at Lockchau Talofau, which became a tavern and hostelry for the entertainment of both white and Indian travelers.[32] The president made it clear that those using the federal road would pay only for subsistence, not for the right of passage. The United States could not tolerate tolls being exacted by the Creeks. He also stated his certainty that if "bad Creeks" harmed the travelers, they would be punished by the chiefs. In an attempt to counteract Spanish propaganda, he said: "You have been told that we should not long remain masters of Louisiana. While the sun shines in Heaven, Louisiana will remain united with us. We are too strong for it to be taken from us, we are too wise to give it up."[33]

McIntosh's lengthy reply, set down verbatim in government documents and entitled "Talk of William McIntosh, a Creek Chief, delivered to the President of the United States, November 3, 1805," has a rough-hewn eloquence and a hard core of logic and common sense. With admirable poise and presence, McIntosh told the president that the territory between the Ocmulgee and Oconee rivers was a large and valuable tract of land. Nevertheless, the chiefs of the Creek Nation had agreed to sell the land, he said, and thought that they had sold it, but some of the "Great Men of the American Government" considered the price too high. "They judge perhaps from our forefathers formerly," McIntosh said, "as we find since we have grown up, they partly gave their land away,—we now find they have gave too much of it away, we have but little left to set down on." McIntosh, obviously referring to Creeks such as Alexander Cornells and himself, said that "when it is almost too late, we have young half breed men now grown up among us that have learning, that have been taught the value of land." He also stated that there were full-blooded red men who conversed with white people and had learned the value of land from "the Pine Land to the best River Swamp Land." The tract under discussion, McIntosh told the president, was more than a hundred miles from the upper to the lower boundary and a great distance across in many places. He listed the many valuable features of the acreage: "A number of fine streams of water for saw mills or any other kind of mills—on the River Swamp, a great deal of fine cypress, oak, cedar and other useful wood to the white people." He said that most of the principal chiefs of the Creek Nation were convinced that the price they had agreed upon previously was not half the proper value. "We the chiefs here present consider that if you the white people had such land to dispose of, and that the red people had to buy it of you, you, we are convinced, would not let us have it, without you got the full value for it—It will be destroying our country to part with this land for less than the value, as there is still a little game, bear, deer, and turkey left on it."[34]

After skillfully arguing the Creek point of view about the price, McIntosh turned to another matter which President Jefferson had made much of: the use of the Ocmulgee River as a natural boundary line between the Creeks and the Georgians. McIntosh anticipated that this would bring trouble between the Indians and the whites, much as had occurred when the Oconee River had been made a natural boundary in 1790; even though President Washington had placed troops at Fort Wilkinson to protect Creek interests, numerous encroachments and incidents of violence had taken place. He gave cogent reasons for his pessimism:

> It is a very shoal river in many places; cattle will go into the shoals to feed on the Salt Grass, and, of course, walk up the banks on the Indian side—when some of our Red People see that, they will say it will be the same as the Oconee, and perhaps kill them—this we are sure will be the case—now, how are stocks to be kept from going across the river, more than a marked line? Another matter on the same head is,—our Red People are settled on the Flint River—their cattle range near Ocmulgee, especially in the winter, in this case if the cattle belonging to the whites on the East Side of the Ocmulgee are suffered to come across, their cattle and ours, of course, will mix—and when that happens, the whites will be very apt to drive some of our cattle to their side,—our people, of course, will retaliate, which, we must expect will be productive of bad consequences.[35]

McIntosh argued against Jefferson's proposed federal road through the Creek Nation principally on the grounds that there were some recalcitrant Creeks who would cause trouble. He told him that the chiefs had seriously considered the matter of the road, but "we are fully acquainted with the dispositions of our Bad People—we fear it would be attended with bad consequences to our nation, owing to the hostile acts that might be committed by ungovernable people." He pointed out that the "four Nations have given you a free privilege down the Tennessee River, likewise a Road through the Chickasaw and Choctaw Nation, which we hope will be sufficient for a while, till we can bring our Red People to understand things better." He added that the Indians' "friends and Brothers, the white people, pass daily through our land; we wish them to do so still." He promised that the Creeks would do all they could to accommodate travelers on the existing trails and he hoped this assurance would be sufficient until "we have it in our power to bring the business about of a road through our country."[36]

In closing, McIntosh agreed with President Jefferson's statements about the need for the Creeks to improve their domestic skills: "What you say to us with respect to farming, raising stock, spinning and weaving, we know is right, and we are sensible it will work on for our good." He thanked the people of the United States for the articles with which they had assisted the Indians, adding that "it is pleasing to us to find that the Great White People of the country have such friendly wishes toward the poor red people." He specifically thanked the "good White People called Quakers," who had once sent farming tools to the Creeks. He concluded, "This is all we have to say at present, to our Father, the head of the United States. We point out to them our difficulties in our present situation, and look up to them to put us right. When they have seen this and give us their opinion on the various points we related to them, we hope we shall be able to answer them further."[37]

There is no record of the talks that ensued between November 3 and November 14, the day the treaty was signed by Henry Dearborn, the secretary of war, William McIntosh, and the five other chiefs, all of whom except McIntosh used their Creek names. Apparently there was little need for further discussion after McIntosh's talk, for the United States agreed to sign a treaty almost identical in terms to the one Hawkins had negotiated in 1804. Rather than being paid in interest-bearing stocks, however, the Creeks were to receive $206,000 for the land, to be paid in annual installments over an eighteen-year period, without interest charges. The treaty allowed the United States government to cut a horsepath from the Ocmulgee to the Mobile River in a direction the president considered the most convenient. The treaty included the stipulation that "the Creeks will have boats kept at several rivers for the conveyance of men and horses, and houses of entertainment established at suitable places on said path." Colonel Hawkins or his successor would regulate the prices charged for ferriage and for entertainment.[38] William McIntosh and Big Warrior became the principal profit makers from this system.

On November 15 Secretary Dearborn addressed "Friend McIntosh and the other Creeks associated with you." He told them that now that they had completed the business for which they had journeyed so far, had taken the hand of the president, and were about to depart, he hoped that "the Great Spirit will protect you on your way and that you will find your family and friends in health." He promised that the United States would take all reasonable measures to keep peace and friendship between the Indians and the white people in the vicinity of the newly ceded lands and to prevent any of the settlers or their cattle or horses from trespassing on Creek lands. Dearborn advised them that if any white men should drive or entice cattle on to their land, they should shut the cattle up in a strong place near the fort, where they would be protected by the military, and not release them until all damages were paid. He stated that the president expected them to discipline any bad Creeks in the nation and prevent them from "doing any mischief" to white neighbors or travelers.[39]

McIntosh and the other chiefs had gone on a long journey to the seat of government and had succeeded in holding to the terms of the treaty negotiated and signed the previous year. The horsepath the treaty provided for was to be plagued by delays and not opened until 1807, but McIntosh's admonition to the president that the road would create trouble between the Creeks and the Georgians was to prove to be one of his most prophetic pronouncements.

6

Problems from the Outside:
The Federal Road and Tecumseh

———— • ————

Throughout the first decade of the nineteenth century, minor frontier problems persisted, but the rise of Tecumseh and major outbreaks of violence lay not far ahead. William McIntosh, not always with the blessings of his fellow Creeks, was attempting to work through the political system to solve problems caused by white encroachment, and Weatherford was later to assume a significant role during the visit of Tecumseh to the Creek council. Now that the United States was for a time not engaged in negotiating treaties and boundaries, Benjamin Hawkins made slow but steady progress in his attempt to acculturate the Creeks and to bring commerce, in a small way, to their wilderness. The state of Georgia began consolidating its position on the fourteen million acres of land it had already acquired and at this point seemed reasonably content within its boundaries. In Washington, the national government was primarily concerned with resisting involvement in the Napoleonic wars and in avoiding policies that would alienate the Indians at a time when war with France or England was a ready possibility. Except for his efforts to complete the federal road, Hawkins's work between 1800 and 1810 was mainly routine.

The federal road had a high priority on President Jefferson's agenda, and when nothing was accomplished in December, after Hawkins's return from Washington, Secretary Dearborn ordered him to increase his work force and survey the line without delay. Actual road construction proceeded at an even slower pace. In April 1806, Postmaster General Gideon Granger instructed Hawkins to lay out the horsepath from Athens, Georgia, to Fort Stoddert, just north of Mobile, at a cost not exceeding $6,400. The specifications called for a road four to six feet wide, with causeways across marshy ground, and "trees to be fallen across the water courses so as to enable the mail carrier to pass the waters upon them carrying the mail secure from the water and swimming his horse by his side." Delays persisted, and when Hawkins wrote the postmaster general in July 1806 that illness had kept him from completing the road, Granger wrote to President Jefferson expressing fear that Hawkins would never complete his assignment. Hawkins's health, his age, and his many other duties all contributed to his inability to complete the task, Granger wrote. In August Hawkins was relieved of his road-building assignment and a successor, Colonel Joseph Wheaton, was appointed. In February of 1807, a contract was let for regular express mail service from Athens, Georgia, to Fort Stoddert.[1]

As early as the fall of 1807, the Upper Creeks began to express opposition to the federal road. Hawkins reported on a Creek council at Tuckabatchee that lasted from September 6 to 16 and ended in inflammatory speeches that denounced the United States for its horsepath, which, they said, cut the Creek Nation in two, and for its deliberate plan to get possession of their lands. The headmen also stated that they could not set up accommodations for travelers and post riders. When the council met again about two weeks later in the Lower Creek town of Coweta, McIntosh, who was to benefit by providing accommodations for travelers, reiterated that the treaty called for inns to be erected at various points along the road. Other headmen stated that they had no recollection of accommodations being a part of the treaty and tried to turn McIntosh and Tuskenchau Chapco (called Long Lieutenant) out of the council, but they were outvoted. Hawkins believed that the main reasons for the dismissal attempt were that McIntosh and Long Lieutenant "continued to assert the truth about the treaty" and that the chiefs suspected the two of having designs on a larger share of the annuity stipend than they were rightfully due. Hawkins was convinced, however, that the opposition to the road and to the accommodations would be temporary. He wrote to General David Meriwether, head of the Georgia militia, that "you will find the Indians ready to cooperate with you" by the time an inn is built at the Flint River crossing and "a stable put up at the crossing at Coweta where Mr. McIntosh intends settling." He assured Meriwether that McIntosh "notwithstanding the opposition will aid in your efforts in all things."[2]

As McIntosh had warned President Jefferson, the opening of the federal road brought problems in peacekeeping. On December 21,

1808, Chief Tuskegee Tustunnuggee wrote to Hawkins: "You and I Col. Hawkins are daily occupied in keeping up good neighborhoods between red and white people," but he added that there were still "some untoward people." He told the agent of an incident in which four white travelers on horseback robbed an Indian boy of a new knife he had just bought, stripped him, and beat him. He plunged into the icy river to escape and ran to the agency, naked and shivering. Hawkins, apparently not inclined to accept the story at face value despite the overwhelming odds of four adults to one boy, penned a query on the back of the letter: "Had the young man been drinking?" On the next day, Hawkins wrote to Georgia Governor Jarid Irwin, "Our chiefs are exerting themselves unceasingly to keep their young men within the bounds of good neighborhood, and to protect the traveller passing through our country." No mention was made of the need to protect the Creeks from the travelers. The following spring Hawkins received a letter from the chiefs of the lower towns complaining that their white neighbors were ranging their livestock on Indian lands, contrary to the assurances of the United States government. They told Hawkins that near the mouth of Cedar Creek four whites had each put out more than a hundred head of cattle with bells. The whites had also, the chiefs claimed, placed fish traps in the Ocmulgee River and had hunted on Indian land, killing deer and turkeys.[3]

During the next several years, incidents on the well-traveled federal road became less frequent, but problems with the permanent settlers increased. Hawkins wrote in January 1811 that the road "is now crowded with travellers moving westward, for the safety of whose property at times I have some anxiety; yet I have had but two complaints during the fall and winter; two horses and some bells were stolen." Episodes involving encroaching Georgians, however, were so serious that the Lower Creeks appointed McIntosh, Long Lieutenant, and Little Prince to seek an audience with Governor David B. Mitchell to air their grievances. On June 22, 1811, McIntosh and Little Prince wrote Hawkins to ask the governor to meet with them.[4]

Mitchell replied on July 11, requesting Hawkins to inform the chiefs that he had no objection to seeing them and hearing their complaints. He added that he was "uninformed of any outrage or trespass committed by any of our citizens upon them or their rights." He assured the chiefs that they would be well treated "coming and returning and during their stay."[5] A Milledgeville newspaper recorded the arrival on Saturday, July 19, of "a company of fifty-seven of our red brethren of the Lower Creeks, of whom twenty-two are of distinction." They camped on the banks of Fishing Creek, about a mile from the state-house, and about twenty of them attended the morning service the following day at the Methodist church. The newspaper reporter seemed surprised that at worship "their deportment was such as to evince they were disposed to be orderly and attentive."[6]

On Monday at 10:00 A.M. thirty-eight of the visiting Creeks, along with Colonel Hawkins and "a numerous concourse of ladies and gen-tlemen," gathered in the chamber of the House of Representatives for the conference with Governor Mitchell. The principal speakers for the Creeks were Little Prince, Micco Thlucco of Cusseta, and Tustunnug-gee Hutkee, who was, the newspaper stated, "known by the whites as William McIntosh, who was one of the deputation that made the last treaty at Washington City." The purpose of the meeting was "a reciprocal assurance of amity and friendship, and a desire to cultivate a more close attachment and friendly intercourse between the white and red men—to be of one house and one fire." McIntosh was quoted as saying he "was pleased to see so many white men, because they could hear what they had to say and tell others."[7]

Then, unexpectedly, McIntosh chose to address the gathering about the problems caused by whiskey drinking on the frontier. He said that Indians considered intoxicated persons "beside themselves and took no notice of what they said or did—this was their manner of treating white men, and they expected to receive the same treatment in return." This plea for tolerance may be connected with an incident two months previously, when a Moravian missionary found Mc-Intosh lying on the floor of his home "drunk and speechless." The missionary, Karsten Petersen, had fallen from a ferry boat into the Chattahoochee River when his horse shied. Not being able to swim, he had almost drowned before a young Indian rushed out of the McIntosh home and plunged into the river to rescue him. After giving his rescuer two dollars, "which seemed to satisfy him and meet with the approval of the Colonel [Hawkins]," Petersen went into the house, where he was dismayed to find McIntosh and an acquaintance intoxicated on the floor. Peterson wrote in his journal: "Here I had hoped to find some assistance and an opportunity to dry my clothing, for, when sober, Mr. McIntosh is a friendly person. Now the house was in a state of utter confusion."[8]

McIntosh told the assembly at the statehouse that the old people would soon be gone and that "this talk was intended for the rising generation, and to evince to them that their young men would as anxiously cultivate a good understanding with their white brethren as their fathers had done." The opportunistic McIntosh was already attempting to establish himself among Georgia political leaders as a young Creek chief who would listen to reason and cooperate with the white power structure. The chiefs informed Governor Mitchell that there were other matters to discuss but that they would be related through Colonel Hawkins. After the meeting, Hawkins and about twenty of the chiefs dined with Governor Mitchell. Somewhat condescendingly, the newspaper reported: "It affords us pleasure to state that not the least complaint of irregularity or riotous behavior occurred; and brotherly love and harmony mutually subsisted whenever the white and red men were together. It thus appears that rude and uncultivated minds are susceptible of the finest sensibility, of the warmest attachments, of the most inviolable friendship, and that they sometimes practice virtues which would do credit to a people the most refined and enlightened."[9] These red men were, in short, a credit to their race.

While the Lower Creeks, under the benign influence of Hawkins, were negotiating with the governor, the Upper Creeks, who were less acculturated and who resented Hawkins's attempts to change their way of life, were outraged over the arbitrarily imposed federal road that would cut across their lands and make it easy for interloping frontiersmen to form permanent settlements in the lands along the Tombigbee. As early as 1808, Hawkins had been ordered to obtain consent from the Upper Creeks to allow horse mails to proceed down the Coosa route from Tennessee through Alabama to Mobile and New Orleans, but the Creeks flatly refused. In 1810 the secretary of war ordered an exploration along the Black Warrior River–Coosa River divide to determine a site for a roadway through Upper Coosa country. The Creeks protested vigorously to the president, and in January 1811, Madison assured them that the surveyors were only locating a possible roadway and had no designs on their land. As conditions worsened in 1811 and war seemed imminent, the need for military roads was increasingly apparent to the federal government, and a road along the Coosa River from Tennessee to Fort Stoddert above Mobile became of primary importance. Hawkins was authorized to treat with the Upper Creeks on the matter but was unsuccessful. Hopoithle Micco wrote to President Madison in May, telling him that the chiefs and warriors did not want a road: "It would bring trouble on our country." Secretary Dearborn informed Hawkins in midsummer that the United States would have the Coosa road with or without

Creek consent, and in December Hawkins informed the secretary that the road was completed.[10] There is little doubt that it was the bitter resentment of the road by the Upper Creeks that made them susceptible to Tecumseh's revolutionary rhetoric in the early fall of 1811.

Tecumseh left Vincennes, Indiana, on August 5, 1811, to visit the Creeks and Choctaws; his announced purpose was to unite those two nations with other Indian nations into a league of peace. Governor William Henry Harrison believed at the time, however, that Tecumseh's true purpose was to excite the Indian nations to war against the white man, and recent historians have largely agreed that Tecumseh hoped to enlist the southern Indians as British allies in the impending war. It has also been suggested that Tecumseh was invited south by Big Warrior, the headman of the Upper Creeks, and that Tuskeneah, Big Warrior's eldest son, had taken the message to Tecumseh, urging him to return to the land of his forefathers to help in resisting the forces of the white man's civilization and the constant encroachment of the American settlers by way of the federal roads. Tecumseh's mother was a Creek woman and had grown up in Upper Creek villages in Alabama. She met her husband when some Shawnees sought refuge among the Creeks during the 1750s, and the Shawnee father remained with his wife's people until about 1760, when the family moved to Ohio. Tradition has it that as a young adult Tecumseh had returned to the Creek Nation to live among his brothers for two years, hunting with them and achieving fame for his feats as a hunter.[11]

If Big Warrior did summon Tecumseh, the immediate reason may have been the peremptory seizure of the Coosa road by the United States, but British intrigue may also have been a contributory cause. According to William Weatherford, a mysterious white man appeared among the Upper Creeks shortly before Tuskeneah went north with his message to Tecumseh. Weatherford said that the man—a Scotsman, he thought—had several meetings with Big Warrior, carrying on talks through a Negro interpreter who belonged to that chief. Weatherford reported talking with the man several times and thought he seemed particularly interested in the number of warriors the Creeks could raise. Whatever the primary motivation for his visit, however, Tecumseh did depart from Vincennes by canoe with a party of six Shawnees, six Kickapoos, two Creeks, and six braves of an unknown tribe from the Northwest. The journey, equal to the distance from Berlin to Paris, followed a riparian route until the travelers crossed the Mississippi at Chickasaw Bluffs, where they left their canoes and continued overland. The distance of the journey should not be surprising, for there is evidence of much more frequent long-distance travel among the Indians than had been supposed. There are a number of authenticated cases of Indians visiting distant tribes, traveling one to two thousand miles and remaining away from their homes for two months or more.[12]

Tecumseh and his warriors, according to Hoentubbe, a Choctaw chief, were colorfully outfitted for their propagandizing mission to the South. All were armed, dressed, and painted alike, perhaps to symbolize the unity that had been achieved among the various tribes represented in the group. Each was armed with a rifle and a tomahawk, and each had a scalping knife at his belt. All were closely shaved at the temples, with the rest of their hair hanging down between their shoulders in queues of three plaits. Tecumseh wore two long crane feathers hanging from the crown of his head, a white one symbolizing peace among the Indian tribes and a red one as a threatening emblem of war to their enemies, in this case the Americans. The heads of the other braves were adorned with hawk and eagle feathers. They all wore hunting shirts and leggings made of buckskin, and their moccasins were lavishly fringed and beaded. Silver bands were worn on both arms, at the wrist and above and below the elbow; a few of the warriors also wore elaborately wrought silver gorgets around their necks. A three-inch band of red flannel encircled the forehead of each man, and over this was displayed a silver band. Semicircular streaks of red war paint extended outward from the eyes to the cheekbone on each side of their faces, and a small red spot was painted on each temple, with a large red spot emblazoned like a target at the center of each man's chest.[13]

Tecumseh's first destination was the Chickasaw Nation in present-day Mississippi, where a mixed-blood chief named George Colbert wielded considerable power. Tecumseh visited Colbert's house and advocated the Chickasaws' joining his confederacy so that when the inevitable war with the Americans came, they would be strongly allied on the right side. Colbert, who was a kinsman of William Weatherford's first wife, told the Shawnee chief that the Chickasaws were at peace with the Americans and intended to remain so. The Shawnee entourage, finding little likelihood of making converts, left for a visit with the Choctaws. There they received little notice until they reached the village of the noted warrior Hoentubbe, who invited a number of important Choctaw chiefs to come and hear Tecumseh. The most famous Choctaw chief to accept was Pushmataha, who listened disdainfully as the Shawnee orated about the outrages of the whites who were seizing Indian lands and reducing red men to poverty. Tecumseh urged the Choctaws to join other Indian nations in a general war against their oppressors, emphasizing that the British would fight loyally alongside them. He also urged peace among Indian tribes and spoke with great earnestness against the Indian practice of killing women and children in battle. When Tecumseh finished his talk, Pushmataha rose and told his people not to think of going to war against the white man. He said that the Choctaws had never shed the blood of white men in battle and they must never do so, for the white people were friends of the Choctaws.[14]

In such interchanges, Tecumseh spoke and listened through an unusual interpreter, the prophet Sikaboo, a follower of Tenskwatawa and an accomplished orator and linguist, who spoke fluent English, Shawnee, Choctaw, and Muscogee.[15] Through Sikaboo, Tecumseh spoke to Pushmataha and the Choctaws several more times in subsequent days, but he always failed to convince them of his position. In his reply to Tecumseh's final speech to the Choctaws, Pushmataha warned that if any Choctaw warrior should join the hostiles, he must be put to death when he returned home.[16] After holding a conference to determine what to do about Tecumseh, the Choctaw chiefs informed the Shawnee leader that he would be put to death if he did not leave the nation immediately. A band of Choctaws was commissioned to accompany Tecumseh and his warriors as far as the Tombigbee River, near the present Alabama-Mississippi line.

Near the Tombigbee, where the party camped for the night, a large band of marauding Creeks stole several Choctaw and Shawnee horses, leading to a day-long pitched battle between the two forces. About sunset Tecumseh led an assault up a hill, where the Creeks were well dug in, and put them to flight. Both sides had a considerable number killed and wounded. The Choctaws scalped the slain Creeks, but Tecumseh did not allow his men to take scalps. At the river the two parties separated; Tecumseh's group headed toward Creek country, and the Choctaws, after a brief and violent mission of vengeance in which they burned a number of Creek houses and killed their horses, returned home.[17]

Tecumseh and his party arrived at Tuckabatchee on September 20, just in time for the Grand Council of the Creek Nation, an annual affair always attended by the important chiefs, the United States Indian agent, and many traders. General Sam Dale, who is a source of firsthand knowledge of this particular council, accompanied Ben-

Tenskwatawa, by Charles Bird King (from McKenney and Hall, *History of the Indian Tribes*)

jamin Hawkins to the assembly. Dale said that the rumor that Tecumseh would attend had spread rapidly throughout the area and about five thousand persons were present, including many Cherokees and Choctaws. On the second day of the meeting, Tecumseh and his warriors marched to the center of the town square and stood, erect and still, in the gaze of the assembled chiefs. Dale's description of the dress of the Shawnee party is similar to that passed down through the family of the Choctaw chief Hoentubbe. Dale said they were dressed in tan buckskin hunting shirts and leggings, that "they wore a profusion of silver ornaments," and that their faces were painted red and black. Dale said "they were the most athletic body of men I ever saw." He described Tecumseh as "about six feet high, well put together, not as stout as some of his followers, but of an austere countenance and imperial mien. He was in the prime of life."[18]

The Shawnee party stood without speaking in the midst of the great assembly, looking neither to the left nor right. To break the awkward silence, Big Warrior slowly approached and offered his pipe to the Shawnee chief. It was smoked and passed in turn to each brave. Big Warrior, described by Thomas Woodward as "the largest man I ever saw among the Creeks" and "almost as spotted as a leopard," was the ranking chief among the Upper Creeks and was considered by Woodward to be a man of great cunning, with "but little sincerity in his pretended friendship for the whites." Big Warrior's hospitality to the visitors may also have been influenced by his being descended from the Piankashaw, a tribe closely associated with the Shawnees. After the ceremony of the peace pipe, without a word being spoken, Big Warrior pointed to a large cabin several hundred yards from the town square, and Tecumseh and his men marched to it in single file. The cabin had been furnished with food and with skins to sleep on. That night, in front of the cabin, they danced in the distinctive style of the northern tribes, and the Creeks crowded around to watch; but still no words were exchanged with Tecumseh's party.[19]

According to Dale and Sam Moniac, who was William Weatherford's brother-in-law, Tecumseh played a cat-and-mouse game with the Creeks and Hawkins. Each morning he sent an interpreter to the council house to announce that he would shortly appear and deliver his talk, but near the end of the day's session, another message would be sent that "the sun had travelled too far, and he would talk the next day." It is traditional to suppose that Tecumseh played his delaying game so that Hawkins would eventually depart, leaving the Shawnee free to express his true sentiments. Dale, in recounting his memories of the event, says that he told Hawkins that "the Shawnees intended mischief," that he had "noted much irritation and excitement among the Creeks," and that the agent "would do well to remain." Hawkins laughed and replied that the "Creeks were entirely under his control and could not be seduced, that Tecumseh's visit was merely one of show and ceremony." Dale accompanied Hawkins twelve miles to his encampment at Big Spring and then returned to the council ground.[20]

Precisely at noon on the next day, the last day of September, the Shawnees strode out of their cabin, adorned with black paint and naked except for flaps about their loins. All wore angry scowls, and to Dale "they looked like a procession of devils." Led by Tecumseh, who walked with a limp, the warriors marched in single file around the square; at each right angle turn, Tecumseh took tobacco and sumac from a pouch and sprinkled it on the earth. They walked the perimeter three times and each time repeated the ceremony. Then they approached the flagpole at the center of the square, where a small ceremonial fire was burning. They emptied their pouches of tobacco and sumac on the flames and then marched in the same order to the front of the council house, where Big Warrior and the other principal chiefs were sitting. Here Tecumseh sounded a war whoop, echoed by each of his followers. After presenting Big Warrior with a wampum belt of five different colored strands, he passed a Shawnee pipe to Big Warrior, who smoked it and passed it among the Creek chiefs. It was a strange scene, as Dale describes it, with not a word being spoken: "Every thing was still as death; even the winds slept, and there was only the gentle rustle of the falling leaves."[21]

Then Tecumseh began to speak, slowly and sonorously at first. He looked out over the thousands of braves with a sneer of hatred and defiance; his eyes, Dale remembered, "burned with a supernatural lustre, and his whole frame shook with emotion." Dale said, "I have heard many great orators, but I never saw one with the vocal powers of Tecumseh, or the same command of the muscles of his face. Had I been deaf, the play of his countenance would have told me what he said." The effect on the stern and usually stoical warriors was electric; they "shook with emotion and a thousand tomahawks were brandished in the air." Dale watched Big Warrior, who was "visibly affected," and said that "more than once I saw his huge hand clutch, spasmodically, the handle of his knife." Even though the speech was delivered in a northern dialect and had to be translated by Sikaboo, Tecumseh's powerful delivery made a translation almost unnecessary.[22]

Sam Dale professed to remember Tecumseh's speech verbatim, but it is likely that his memory was colored by subsequent emotions inflamed during the Creek War of 1813 and 1814. With many persons sympathetic to the Americans in the audience, some in the employ of Hawkins and the government, it is improbable that the Shawnee would have delivered such an openly bloodthirsty speech as Dale records: "Let the white race perish. They seize your land; they corrupt your women; they trample on the ashes of your dead! Back, whence they came, upon a trail of blood, they must be driven. Back! back, ay, into the great water whose accursed waves brought them to our shores! Burn their dwellings! Destroy their stock! Slay their wives and children! The Red man owns the country, and the Palefaces must never enjoy it. War now! War forever! War upon the living! War upon the dead!"[23] The bellicose tone of this speech is atypical of Tecumseh, and the exhortation to kill women and children is particularly uncharacteristic. There is ample evidence that in many other speeches he counseled humane treatment of everyone except captured warriors.

Also unverified is his statement that he and his men had killed a number of whites on their journey southward. "No war whoop was sounded," he is supposed to have said, "but there is blood on our knives. The Palefaces felt the blow, but knew not whence it came." Despite the inconsistencies in the record, however, there were rumors along the frontier that the Shawnee and his entourage, influenced by the British, were attempting to promote hostilities between the southern Indians and the United States. In a letter to the secretary of war on September 9, an unnamed informant wrote from Nashville: "There is in this place a very noted chief of the Chickasaws, a man of truth, who wishes the President should be informed that there is a combination of northern Indians, promoted by the English, to unite in falling on the frontier settlements, and are inviting the Southern tribes to join them."[24]

Benjamin Hawkins's account of Tecumseh's speech is quite different from Dale's. He depicts the Shawnee speaking, in duplicity, words of peace, which had the underlying meaning of war. In a letter written to Big Warrior, Little Prince, and other chiefs during the Creek War, Hawkins asked: "What did your father, the British, tell your prophets, at the beginning of the war? Tecumseh, in the square of Tuckabatchee, delivered their talk. They told the Creeks not to do injury to the Americans; to be in peace and friendship with them; not to steal even a bell from anyone of any color." Then Hawkins asked: "What was the actual meaning of this British talk? Your whole nation can answer this question. Kill the old chiefs, friends to peace; kill the cattle, the hogs, and fowls; do not work, destroy the wheels and looms, throw away your ploughs, and everything used by the Americans."[25]

The mystical protection in war offered by Tecumseh and the prophets to the Creeks is found in both versions. Hawkins wrote, with irony, "Shake your war clubs, shake yourselves; you will frighten the Americans, their arms will drop off from their hands, the ground will become a bog, and mire them, and you may knock them on the head with your war clubs." Dale reported Tecumseh as saying: "My prophets shall tarry with you. They will stand between you and the bullets of your enemies. When the white men approach you the yawning earth shall swallow them up." Hawkins asked the chiefs, "Has this proved true? Go to the fields of Talladega and New-yau-cau, and see them whitened with the bones of the Red Clubs. Look to the towns, not a living thing in them; the inhabitants scattered through the woods, dying with hunger, or fed by the Americans." A part of Tecumseh's prophecy, widely reported in contemporary accounts, came true in a questionable way. Tecumseh had somewhere learned that astronomers had calculated that a comet would be visible in North America in the latter part of 1811. He is supposed to have told the assembly at Tuckabatchee: "Soon shall you see my arm of fire stretched athwart the sky."[26]

The authenticity of this incident has been debated through the years. H. S. Halbert and T. H. Ball, citing the opinion of professors at the Harvard Observatory in 1894, wrote that the comet of 1811 was clearly visible to the naked eye by August 26 and continued to increase in brightness during September. They concluded that since the comet had already been seen in the nocturnal skies over the Creek Nation, Tecumseh would not have made such a fatuous statement in late September or early October.[27] A study of this incident by B. E. Powell suggests that Tecumseh's threat legitimately and even convincingly may have been made. He points out that the comet was not visible to the Creeks in the summer months because of its location in the same part of the sky as the sun. As late as September 20 it was located close to the horizon and still not readily visible to the untrained eye, but in October it became larger, brighter, and more favorably located for observation and, Powell writes, could be seen throughout much of the night during the autumn because of its circumpolar location in the sky. In October this comet was unusually large, the head measuring more than one million miles in diameter and the tail one hundred million miles long. Also, as he left the Creek Nation, Tecumseh is reported to have pointed his finger in Big Warrior's face and said: "Tustunnuggee Thlucco, your blood is white. You may have taken my red sticks and my talk, but you do not mean to fight. I know the reason. You do not believe the Great Spirit has sent me. You shall believe it. I will leave directly, and go straight to Detroit. When I get there I will stamp my foot upon the ground and shake down every house in Tuckabatchee." In December, according to tradition, an earthquake shook the area of Tuckabatchee, tottering the houses and sending the Creeks into the public square, shouting that Tecumseh had reached Detroit and that they felt the power of his foot.[28]

Big Warrior, as evidenced by his report on Tecumseh's speech to Hawkins, reported no antiwhite tirades. He professed being puzzled by the talk, saying that he and others had tried to learn from the Shawnee what he meant by his veiled references to conversations with the Great Spirit. They had concluded that Tecumseh was either a madman or a liar. Big Warrior, known more for the size of his physique than his intellect, may have been deceiving Hawkins, but more likely he was genuinely bewildered. Sam Dale reported the Shawnee's speech to Hawkins immediately after the address was completed, but, Dale said, "he appeared to attach little importance to it, relying too much on his own influence over the Indians."[29]

William Weatherford, according to two early accounts, understood the true intent of Tecumseh's speech and spoke against it. As soon as Sikaboo had completed his translation of Tecumseh's talk, Red Eagle stood to speak. Tall and commanding, he drew every eye to him as he told the crowd that the Shawnee's talk was the worst counsel that could be given to the Creek Nation and that to follow it would be their ruin. He pointed out that the Americans, when weak and few in number, had defeated the British; now that they were stronger and greater in number, they would certainly conquer again. He told the crowd that the English cared no more for the Indians than did the Americans, that both nations were white, and that all whites were the enemies of the red man. He told them that the wisest course would be to remain neutral, but if they were determined to go to war they should join the Americans. Another account has Weatherford confronting Tecumseh at a small council, with no white men present, but the content of the rejoinder to the Shawnee is virtually the same: the best policy for the Creeks was to remain neutral and though the English and Americans were equally oppressive, the Creeks should side with the Americans if forced into war.[30] Sam Moniac, Weatherford's brother-in-law, agreed with Red Eagle and also spoke in favor of that position.

George Cary Eggleston, an early biographer of Red Eagle—and also coauthor of a biography of Tecumseh—is one of those responsible for the idea that Weatherford was rabidly antiwhite and a willing accomplice of Tecumseh. Eggleston wrote that Tecumseh was "not long in picking out Red Eagle as the man of all others likely to draw the Creeks into the scheme of hostility." Eggleston believed that Weatherford was proud of his Scottish heritage and had a special hatred for Americans, engendered by his uncle Alexander McGillivray and aggravated by contacts with the British and Spanish in Mobile and Pensacola. "His favorite boast," wrote Eggleston, "was that there was 'no Yankee blood in his veins.'"[31] Eggleston wrote that Red Eagle influenced many young Creek braves to join the war party, or Red Sticks, and that it was he who advised Tecumseh to play upon the superstitions of the Creeks by calling up prophets from their nation to stir up the younger warriors to counteract the influence of the older, more conservative Creeks who opposed war only because it threatened their holdings of horses, lands, and cattle. Weatherford did not, of course, need to advise Tecumseh to call up prophets. The prophetic movement, begun by Tecumseh's brother Tenskwatawa, was an essential ingredient in the Indians' effort to resist the Americans, and, indeed, recent scholarship gives Tenskwatawa a more important role in the movement than Tecumseh.[32] Because Eggleston's biography documents no sources and his view of Weatherford's antiwhite attitudes and support of Tecumseh is not corroborated anywhere else, it is not to be taken seriously.

7

Civil War Erupts:
McIntosh the "Law Mender"
and Weatherford the Reluctant Nativist

———— • ————

At the beginning of the War of 1812, another conflict—a civil war between the Upper and Lower Creeks—was ignited. Although it could be argued that this civil war was instigated by the British, or by Tecumseh, or by the religious movement led by the nativistic prophets, it is increasingly evident that the principal reason was the deep division between those who were acceding to Hawkins's attempts to acculturate them and those who were bitterly resisting. It is also true that the fanaticism inspired by the prophetic movement led to some outrageous murders of whites by the more nativistic Upper Creeks and that this, in turn, led to a structured attempt by Hawkins to punish the malefactors. William McIntosh was selected as head of the "law menders," a kind of national police force established by the Creek National Council under the influence of Hawkins. When McIntosh and his band of Lower Creek law menders executed one of the Upper Creek murderers who was at the time claiming the sanctuary and protection of the Tallassee King (Hopoithle Micco), the incident almost immediately incited a Creek civil war.

Benjamin Hawkins and McIntosh were opposed by such Upper Creek leaders of the reform movement as Peter McQueen, another half-Scottish Creek, and the elderly Tallassee King; but the strong emotional core of the nativist movement came from the prophets, of whom Josiah Francis, a mixed-blood of great cunning and ruthlessness, was the leader. Tecumseh had directed the prophet Sikaboo to remain in the Creek Nation to recruit prophets, and Francis had volunteered. In a classic ceremony of setting apart, Sikaboo shut Francis up alone in an isolated cabin for ten days and chanted and danced around it at frequent intervals. After ten days the new prophet came forth, declaring himself blind, but only temporarily. Francis told his fellow Creeks that his sight would be restored in such a way that he could see clearly into the future. After days of being led hesitantly about the town, Francis declared that his vision had returned, and he began recruiting other prophets, including Sinquista and High-Headed Jim. The prophesying, pleading, and speechmaking of this trio, especially when they promised their hearers that the Great Spirit would protect them against death in battle, made a great impression, particularly on the Upper Creeks who lived along the Alabama River, where Hawkins least expected trouble to arise. "The Alabamas were the most industrious and best behaved of all our Indians," he wrote later. "Their fields were the granary of the upper towns, and furnished considerable supplies by water to Mobile. But this Fanaticism has rendered them quite the reverse."[1]

Alexander Cornells, a mixed-blood Creek who was an assistant to Hawkins and an interpreter for the Upper Creeks, understood well the nativist bias of the prophetic movement. "The prophets are enemies to the plan of civilization," he reported to Hawkins, "and advocates for the wild Indian mode of living." He said the prophets claimed to be able to draw a circle around their abode and "render the earth quaggy and impassable." They threatened that any Indian towns refusing to help the prophets would be sunk by earthquakes or by hills being turned over on them; and they boasted of being able to use lightning against their enemies. Hawkins wrote the secretary of war in July: "A great number of Indians seem to be astonished exceedingly, alarmed and timid at the sudden explosion of this Fanaticism. Its boasted magic powers deters them from obeying the calls of their Chiefs."[2]

In the spring of 1812 several widely reported murders of whites by Indians were grim symptoms of the discord engendered by the prophets. On March 26, Thomas Meredith, Sr., described by Hawkins as "a respectable old man," was murdered on the post road at Kittome Creek as he was traveling with his family to the Mississippi Territory. The incident occurred near Sam Moniac's inn, which he kept for the accommodation of travelers on the post road, and Meredith was buried on the inn grounds. Moniac called the killing an accident, but Meredith's son, an eyewitness, said the murder was committed by Maumouth, an old Autossee chief, and others, while "in liquor."

When Hawkins learned of the Meredith murder, Big Warrior, then speaker of the Creek Nation, and some members of the Executive Council were present at the Creek agency. Hawkins read the message to them and directed them to convene their chiefs and see justice done without delay. It was nearly five months before Hawkins could write to Governor David B. Mitchell that Meredith's murderer had been executed by fellow Creeks.[3]

Meanwhile, another incendiary incident occurred on May 23, when a man named William (or Arthur) Lott, a former Georgia legislator, was killed near his home by four Indians "without the least provocation." This came, Hawkins wrote, "amidst the most solemn assurances" from the chiefs that they would "keep their young people from doing acts of violence." The chiefs held a meeting at Tuckabatchee to hear Hawkins's message of remonstrance and to determine how to bring Lott's killers to justice. Hawkins reported that the "Indians seem much alarmed, those of the Lower Creeks particularly have expressed their fears as well as determination to aid the Upper Creeks in bringing the offenders to justice." Now increasingly evident was the impending estrangement between the nativistic Upper Creeks and the Lower Creeks, who were increasingly swayed by Hawkins's policy of acculturation, his political system, and his argument for the necessity of the law menders to see justice done. With British agents acting behind the scenes amid the rumors of war in those months in 1812, the situation was explosive. Hawkins wrote in June that war "would probably be realized in a month." Thomas Woodward wrote: "I have often heard Sam Moniac say, that if Lott had not been killed at the time he was, it was his belief that the war could have been prevented."[4]

Conditions became even more inflammatory in May, when a band of Creeks from the town of Hillaubee killed a family near the Duck River supposedly because of a false report that whites had murdered an Indian woman. The incident happened at the home of a family named Crawley, where a neighbor named Mrs. Manley was visiting at the time, lying in with her newborn child. When eleven Creeks burst open the door of the cabin, Mrs. Manley and her baby were the first to be killed. Hiding behind the door, Mrs. Martha Crawley was overlooked momentarily while two of her children and two of Mrs. Manley's were being tomahawked.[5] After being discovered, she begged for her life, and the Indians temporarily complied, but they took her from town to town, displaying her naked on the town squares and dancing exultingly around her.[6] A grave was dug for her, but on the

William McIntosh, by David Vandenberg (from the Collection of Mr. and
Mrs. Benjamin Griffith III)

night before her scheduled execution, an Indian woman helped her
escape. She was found by white settlers after wandering aimlessly for
two or three days, half-naked and half-starved.[7]

William McIntosh was an important figure in the organized reaction
that followed the murders. Woodward remembered that as soon as
Hawkins heard that Lott was murdered he sent Christian Limbaugh,

an assistant, to Coweta to see "Billy McIntosh, a half-breed chief."
McIntosh and Limbaugh went to Broken Arrow to see Little Prince,
who sent a mixed-blood chief named George Lovett with the others to
visit Big Warrior for the purpose of organizing a party of Creeks, under the leadership of McIntosh, to find and execute the murderers.[8] A
council of Creek chiefs communicated to Hawkins on June 17 their
intention to see the murderers punished: "We the Kings, Chiefs and
Warriors have assembled in our Council House and taken into consideration the danger which threatens our land; we have unanimously
agreed that satisfaction shall be given without delay for the murders
committed in our land. We have appointed three parties, one party
started last evening, the other two this morning, in pursuit of the
murderers of Thomas Meredith and Arthur Lott, who were murdered
on the post road; the parties have received their special orders not to
stop until they have punished these murderers."[9] It was July 12 before Hawkins received the welcome news that one of these parties
sent out after the murderers of Lott had been successful. Hawkins
reported to William Eustis, the secretary of war, that they had put to
death the leader of the Banditti, who had "fled to the white town of
Hopoithle Micco, a great medal Chief, and sat down on his seat as a
sanctuary. The leader of the armed party [McIntosh], pursued and
shot him on the seat through the head and body." This act by Mc-
Intosh and the other law menders was the major incident in the growing intertribal cultural conflict. By killing a man who was claiming the
sanctuary and protection of a medal chief, the law menders, also acting upon the demands of a white man, had enormously insulted the
Tallassee King, Hopoithle Micco.[10]

Hawkins assured Eustis that the chiefs "are exceedingly alarmed
and seem determined to stand well with us." He also reported that by
July 11 three more of Lott's murderers had been put to death. On
August 21, the leader of the Duck River massacre, Hillaubee Hadjo,
was decoyed to the old Council House at Hickory Ground, where he
was executed by his fellow Creeks and his body thrown in the Coosa
River. Two other members of the party were killed on the Black Warrior River. The leader of the Creek party that avenged the Duck River
massacre was William McIntosh, aided by another mixed-blood chief
called Captain Isaacs. Isaacs, an opportunist who attempted to play
both sides in the conflict, was called by Thomas Woodward "one of
the most cunning, artful scamps I ever saw among the Indians."
Isaacs was later attacked by Upper Creeks in one of the first engagements in the Creek War. Isaacs had been one of the early prophets,

and his exploits had evoked the jealousy of the prophets Josiah Francis and Paddy Walsh (or Walch or Welch), who plotted against him, causing him to defect, along with a few followers and some ammunition, to Big Warrior and the Tuckabatchees. The ammunition later proved very valuable to Big Warrior when Tuckabatchee was under siege by a Red Stick force.[11]

On August 24 Hawkins proudly reported to the secretary of war that "the chiefs had had six murderers put to death for their crimes on the post road and to the northwest and seven cropped and whipped for thefts." He added, "We have not had any complaints recently from the travellers or post-riders and the Indians appear very friendly." By August 29, eight had been executed for murder; but travelers in the Creek Nation during the summer of 1812 were still understandably wary. A letter from an Edgefield, South Carolina, lawyer concerning the travel problems of his brother-in-law reveals the tension as well as the trust the Creeks engendered: "The particular time of his departure from us must necessarily depend upon the company that may offer, and the pacific or hostile disposition of our red neighbors. We are informed that they discover evidence of contrition and deep regret for the late murders which have been committed; and little doubt is entertained of the fate of the perpetrators thereof—several have lately come through the Nation who say the Indians are disposed for peace and condemn the conduct of the ungovernable few." Not everyone had such sanguine confidence in the reasonableness of the Creeks. A writer in the *Augusta Herald* expressed alarm that summer at "the indications of hostility in the Creek Indians toward the citizens of this state," adding, "We are apprehensive that it will be necessary to make the whole Creek nation feel the vengeance of this state, or of the United States, in order to compel them to a proper course of conduct."[12]

A bloody massacre by Little Warrior and a band of Creeks returning from a visit to Shawnee country in late February 1813 was the catalyst that set all the forces into motion. Hawkins first heard of the incident in a communication dated March 5 from James Robertson, agent to the Chickasaws, who reported: "Seven families have been murdered near the mouth of the Ohio, and most cruelly mangled, showing all the savage barbarity that could be invented. One woman cut open, a child taken and stuck on a stake." Robertson said he at first blamed the Chickasaws, but some Creeks were seen passing through Bear Creek settlement on the way south, and they had acknowledged committing the murders. The Creeks said further that they had visited the

Shawnee prophet and were delivering beads and talks from the prophet and the northern tribes to the four southern nations, urging them to take up the hatchet against the United States. Hawkins could hardly believe Robertson's accusation. He told the chiefs of the Upper Creeks: "Of all the murderous acts committed by savages against the people of the United States, this is the most outrageous. It is not done by thoughtless, wild young people, but deliberately, by a party under the command of two Chiefs and what makes it still worse, by Chiefs sent by the Creek Nation on a public mission of peace and friendship to the Chickasaws." He told the chiefs: "You must get together one and all, turn out your warriors, apprehend the two Chiefs and their associates and deliver them to me, or some officer of the United States commanding on the frontiers, to be punished according to the laws of the United States. This you are bound to do, by the eighth article of the Treaty of New York."[13]

What could have caused the sudden and seemingly unprovoked violence along the Ohio by these Creeks? Thomas Woodward, who was in the Creek Nation when the incident occurred, said that Little Warrior was told by the Chickasaws that a Creek-American war had begun. No one knows whether the Chickasaw statement was by design or through misunderstanding, if it indeed was made.[14] Hawkins makes no mention of Little Warrior's misconception as a way of explaining the uncharacteristic action by the Creeks, but this is understandable. Even if the agent had known that the Creeks acted on a Chickasaw rumor, no such explanation could possibly have alleviated the harsh sentence he thought necessary to punish the offenders.

Hawkins was despondent about the situation when he wrote on March 25 to Alexander Cornells: "I have sent a talk to the chiefs of the Lower Creeks to help you if they can. I have stated your difficulties and some which they are under themselves. I do not know what they can do. The love of rum has almost destroyed Cussetah and Uchee: whole families live by stealing from me. They even kill my cattle, to get the skins to buy whiskey." But Hawkins was his positive self again when he reported to Governor Mitchell in late April that the Creeks had succeeded in executing some of the murdering war party. He recapitulated the crisis: "As I was of the opinion, if these murderers were not punished on the first attempt, their adherents would gain strength to their party, I advised the chiefs of the Lower Creeks to send a detachment of warriors not less than 50 nor more than 100 to cooperate with their brethren of the Upper Towns. These were commanded by Mr. Wm. McIntosh, one of our most distinguished war-riors."[15]

McIntosh led the party of Creeks who assembled at the Council House at Tuckabatchee on April 16. He asked Nimrod Doyell, James Cornells, and David Tate to accompany them on the mission and wit-ness their carrying out the orders of the nation. Hearing that Little Warrior and his party were at Hickory Ground, they marched all night and before daybreak surrounded the house in which the mur-derers were barricaded. McIntosh's warriors tried to force open the door but could not, and the besieged braves soon began firing, se-riously wounding a nephew of McIntosh's when a ball broke his left arm and lodged in his side. The gunfire was returned, and soon the Creeks inside the house ran out of ammunition. The Tuskegee war-rior, according to Doyell, an eyewitness, shouted from inside that he had killed and eaten white people and that it was he who had killed and cut open the white woman near the mouth of the Ohio. Mc-Intosh's party set fire to the house, and the Tuskegee warrior, who was wounded, died in the smoke and flames; two others who crawled to the door and begged to be taken out of the fire were pulled out twenty yards from the house and beaten to death with tomahawks. Two others dashed shrieking from the flaming house; one was killed, and the other escaped. Little Warrior, who had remained on the other side of the river, was at large for a short time, but on the following day he was decoyed out of the swamp and killed.[16]

Big Warrior, Alexander Cornells, and William McIntosh wrote to Hawkins to report the success of the operation at Hickory Ground and to explain why they had not taken prisoners, as the laws of the United States required. Indians fight until they are dead, they said. They also set Hawkins's mind at ease about their allegiances: "You think that we lean to the Shawnee tribes, because you saw Tecumseh and his party dance in our square, around our fire, and some of our foolish people believed their foolish talks." They assured Hawkins: "You need not be jealous that we shall take up arms against the United States: we mean to kill all our red people that spill the blood of our white friends." Hawkins replied, "Your conduct does you great credit, and will give your Father, the President, pleasure."[17]

The letter from Big Warrior, Cornells, and McIntosh is also signifi-cant because of the titles accompanying the names at the end of the letter. In April of 1813 Big Warrior is listed as speaker of the upper towns and McIntosh as speaker of the lower towns. To the Creeks, oratorical ability was highly respected, and the headman rarely spoke for himself, deferring to a person with rhetorical ability to introduce council business, report council decisions, deliver the long speeches that opened and closed major ceremonies, and negotiate in diplomatic matters. The reference to McIntosh as speaker of the lower towns suggests that he had attained the highest rank of speaker, *hothlibonaya* (war speaker). There were many reasons why McIntosh should attain a leadership position in Creek affairs. He was a member of the Wind clan, he could converse in English, and he could write. More important, he had white relatives who were well positioned in Georgia politics: William R. McIntosh, a legislator, was a half-brother; John McIntosh, a half-brother, was the Treasury Department collector for the port of Savannah; and George M. Troup, United States senator and Georgia governor, was a cousin. By August of 1814, however, Hawkins wrote to Little Prince, referring to him as the speaker of the lower towns. By that time Major William McIntosh was the agent's most important Indian military leader.[18]

In late June, Cornells reported to Hawkins that the warring faction that had been agitated by the prophets was creating a much deeper division than previously supposed. He wrote that Big Warrior had called the chiefs together at Tuckabatchee, where they agreed to invite the prophets to meet with them and give proof of their special powers. They sent the taunting message: "You are but a few Alabama people. You say that the Great Spirit visits you frequently; that he comes in the sun and speaks to you; that the sun comes down just above your heads. Now we want to see and hear what you say you have seen and heard. Let us have the same proof you have had, and we will believe what we see and hear." This derisive invitation so angered the Alabamas that they instantly killed and scalped the messenger who had brought it. Then they surged up the Alabama River, murdering and burning, preceded by the announcement that they would destroy Tuckabatchee and Coweta and every person in the two towns, including Cornells, Hawkins, Big Warrior, and all the old chiefs who had accepted Hawkins's philosophy of Americanizing and civilizing the Indians. Then, they boasted, they would be ready to combat the white people. The chiefs at Tuckabatchee, who had thought the prophets' messages had been no more than a "sort of madness and amusement for idle people," were shocked. They came to realize that the prophets had kept the growth of their movement a secret from the chiefs while it matured among the opponents of civilization and the wild young men.[19]

Hawkins believed the true purpose of the uprising was vengeance against the Lower Creeks for having executed Little Warrior's party of murderers. By July the warring Upper Creeks had succeeded in putting to death nine of the executioners and had burned several villages allied with Hawkins, killing cattle, horses, sheep, and goats and destroying all vestiges of the white man's civilization. Hawkins also reported that the Autossees, who had been recently converted to the Red Stick movement, had driven off their chiefs. A mixed-blood had told Hawkins that some Autossees had told him, "You think the white people are strong and numerous; we shall soon try their strength." Hawkins also wrote of an incident involving two sons of Hopoie Micco, the late speaker of the Creek Nation. The two men apprehended an Alabama lad and were taking him to Tuckabatchee when a "party of the fanatics saw them, fired on them, killed one, and released the lad." In the fall of 1813 the term "Red Sticks" or "Red Clubs" began to appear in Hawkins's letters. These names given to the Creek revolutionaries derived from the ancient practice of displaying a red war club in the village square to denote a state of war.[20]

In the summer of 1813, if a contemporary account is correct, William Weatherford and his brother-in-law Sam Moniac confronted the prophets' wrath in a scene of high drama. According to Thomas Woodward, who knew both men well, Weatherford and Moniac returned from a cattle-trading expedition in Mississippi Territory to find an astonishing scene taking place on Tallewassee Creek near Red Eagle's plantation. Several Red Stick chiefs and prophets were taking the black drink, and the families of Moniac and Weatherford were assembled, perhaps as hostages. The leaders included Peter McQueen, the part-Scots chief of the Tallassees, and two prophets, High-Headed Jim and Josiah Francis. They told Weatherford and Moniac that unless they agreed to join them in their Red Stick war, the two would be put to death in front of their families. Moniac immediately refused and mounted his horse to ride away. His brother-in-law, the newly made prophet Josiah Francis, seized his bridle, but Moniac snatched Francis's war club and struck him a stunning blow. Then he rode away in a shower of rifle bullets. Weatherford agreed to remain. He told the chiefs and prophets that he did not approve of their course of action and that the war would inevitably destroy them. "But," he said, "you are my people, and I will share your fate." He then advised them to gather the women and children and to take them to safety in the swamps of Florida, leaving the old men and boys to hunt for them. Weatherford told Woodward that there were several reasons for his advice. He thought the principal leaders of the two factions might settle their differences while his people were on their journey to Florida, thus sparing the lives of fellow Creeks as well as many whites along the frontier. He also reasoned that if war did come, it could be carried on with less danger and expense, as well as less worry about the safety of the women and children.[21]

The mixed-blood Creek agent George Stiggins, whose sister Mary became Weatherford's third wife in 1817, has a slightly different version of Red Eagle's entanglement with the Red Sticks. On his return from a trip to Pensacola, Weatherford found that his family and movable possessions had been taken to Othlewallee, considered to be the Red Stick headquarters. Stiggins wrote that Weatherford, knowing he could not leave his family and property to the mercy of a hostile band, decided "to hide his disapprobation" and "patiently await a fit opportunity to run off with his family and property from under the eyes of hostile bands." But it soon became widely believed that Weatherford had joined the Red Stick rebellion, and when the Battle of Burnt Corn occurred, it was, Stiggins wrote, "too late a date for him to retract on either side." Stiggins added that "fate so ordered his fortune at that crisis that he was drawn into the war measures of the hostile party in an unpremeditated way." He wrote that Weatherford "abhorred their wicked proceedings though he afterward participated in a conspicuous manner in their war measures."[22]

Peter McQueen was appointed to lead a Red Stick party to Pensacola to acquire guns and ammunition. Peter, whose father, James McQueen, was said to be the first of a long procession of British and European traders to come to the Creek Nation, was a man of property and great influence among the Creeks. Sam Dale called him "shrewd, sanguinary, and deceitful."[23] On July 10 McQueen and High-Headed Jim (also called Jim Boy) led a band of Creeks—100 by Indian account, 350 according to Hawkins—southward with many packhorses to procure the supplies of war. It was this group of Indians that Moniac met near his property, as he stated in a deposition on July 13, 1813, which reveals firsthand much of the anxiety of these turbulent times. After a brief mention of Tecumseh's visit, Moniac said that it was not until about the previous Christmas that any of his people began to dance the war dance. He added that the war dance before the battle, rather than after, was a northern custom and stated that his brother-in-law Josiah Francis, "who also pretended to be a prophet," was at the head of about forty Creeks who initially began dancing the war dance of the People of the Lakes. "Their number has very much increased since," he said, "and there are probably now more than half of the Creek Nation who have joined them." Moniac said he was "afraid of the consequences of a murder having been committed on the mail route," so he went to his plantation on the river, where he remained for some time. The incident referred to is the murder of Meredith, which took place near Moniac's property. Some time in June, Moniac left to take some steers to Pensacola, and while he was away, Sam's brother John and Sam's son, who had joined the war party, led a band of Red Sticks (including Josiah Francis) who burned his river plantation, stole his horses and cattle, and took away thirty-six black slaves.[24]

About July 11 Moniac returned to his home on the post road and found some Indians camped nearby. He tried to avoid them but could not and was approached by High-Headed Jim. Moniac reported: "He shook hands with me, and immediately began to tremble and jerk in every part of his frame, and the very calves of his legs would be convulsed, and he would get entirely out of breath with the agitation." Moniac said that this practice of violent convulsions had been introduced the previous May or June by the prophet Francis, "who says that he was instructed by the Spirit." Moniac stated that High-Headed Jim told him the Red Sticks had a letter from a British general that would enable them to get ammunition from the Spanish governor, and they would continue to get ammunition until each town in the Creek Nation had five horse loads. Then they would make a general attack on the American settlements. He also told Moniac that the war was to be against the whites and not a civil war among the Indians. He said they only wanted to kill the Indians who had "taken the talk of the whites," and the death list included William McIntosh, Big Warrior, Alexander Cornells, and Captain Isaacs.[25] The first three named, of course, had been key figures in the execution of Little Warrior and his party. Isaacs, a mixed-blood who had accompanied Little Warrior and the others on the ill-fated visit to the Shawnees, had saved his own neck by defecting and testifying against Little Warrior.[26] Moniac immediately sounded the alarm that the Red Sticks were storing up arms and ammunition for the impending war, and soon local militiamen and military leaders, including General Ferdinand L. Claiborne and Andrew Jackson, were reacting swiftly to protect the white settlers in the Creek Nation. "There can be no doubt," Jackson wrote the secretary of war on July 13, "but the Creeks and Lower Choctaws are excited to hostilities by the influence of the British." He added: "My brave volunteers, two thousand strong, stand ready for the call."[27]

Those revolutionaries who remained at home while McQueen and his party went to Pensacola were not idle. While awaiting the return of McQueen and his men, they maintained a siege of the symbolically important town of Tuckabatchee, the capital of the Creek Nation. Unable to attack because they lacked sufficient ammunition, the hostile Creeks surrounded the town and waited. Short of food as well as ammunition, the besieged Creeks sent out cries of help to the Lower Creek towns. The Cusseta King reported to Hawkins on July 10: "They are in great distress at Tuckabatchee." He told the agent that the prophet's men wanted Big Warrior and that they meant to destroy Coweta and Cusseta as well as Tuckabatchee. "Before we lose the Big Warrior," he wrote, "we will all die for him."[28] The chiefs of the friendly Creeks believed that it was their fidelity to the white men's treaty that had brought them to this state of civil war. In avenging the murders on the post road, on the Duck River, and on the Ohio River, as the Treaty of 1790 had stipulated was their duty, they had become the hated objects of an internecine conflict.[29] The Cusseta King finally ordered a force of two hundred well-armed Cusseta and Coweta warriors into Tuckabatchee. Perhaps because the hostile Red Sticks lacked firepower, the rescuers entered the capital without a struggle. By July 26 Hawkins was able to report that the Indians of Tuckabatchee, though in "great distress," were now safe in Cusseta, which now became the official capital of the Creek Nation. Hawkins ordered for the Tuckabatchee braves a supply of one hundred pounds of powder, two hundred pounds of lead, one hundred flints, twenty-five muskets, and ten rifles. Big Warrior wrote to Hawkins from Cusseta on July 26: "I never expected a civil war among us." He told Hawkins that when the Cowetas reached him they gave him a letter from William McIntosh containing a speech from the governor of Georgia, which helped allay his distress.[30]

One of the most inflammatory incidents at this time occurred when Letecau, an eighteen-year-old prophet, went up to Aubecoochee with eight young followers and invited some chiefs to come and witness his magical powers. Many chiefs came, bringing with them a crowd of both sexes. Letecau ranged them in a line on the bank of the Coosa River and made them sit down. In front of them he began the dance of the Indians of the Lakes. After some time of violent dancing he suddenly gave a war whoop and attacked and killed three chiefs and wounded a fourth before the onlookers could recover from shock. Then the crowd took to the river, swam over, and recrossed to their towns, where they hastily gathered their warriors and went after the prophets. They found them still dancing, and when one of the chiefs rushed into the circle of dancers, he was knocked down by war clubs and killed with bows and arrows. The warriors then attacked the dancers and killed them and the prophet. After scalping Letecau, they went to the small village of Ocfuskee, where the people had taken the prophets' talks and were dancing their dance. There they put to death everyone in the village.[31]

The tension was heightened even further, however, when Mc-Queen and his party committed a series of outrageous acts as they went downriver toward Pensacola. They assaulted and drove away all Indians they met who would not agree to join their party. McQueen brutalized a white trader, who had done him no harm, beating him senseless and almost to death. They sacked and plundered the house of James Cornells, a half-blood Creek, who, like most of those of mixed blood, refused to follow the message of the prophets. They severely beat a white man and a black slave and carried away Cornells's wife as a slave; she eventually was traded in Pensacola to a French woman named Baronne for a blanket.[32] A man named Marlowe, who lived at Cornells's house, was also taken to Pensacola as a prisoner. Returning home after a brief absence to find his burned-out home, Cornells mounted a fast gray horse and, like a frontier Paul Revere, warned the other settlers of the latest Creek hostilities. On July 27, when McQueen and his party returned from Florida with packhorses laden with ammunition, Cornells and a large force of mixed-bloods and whites were waiting in ambush at Burnt Corn Creek, where the first battle of the Creek War was fought.[33]

One reason why Weatherford was reluctant to make war against the Americans was that he had adjusted remarkably well to frontier life among the encroaching whites. He had a generally accepted public image as a generous host for fellow Creeks and white travelers in the years immediately preceding the Creek War, as shown by an incident related to H. S. Halbert by one of Weatherford's contemporaries.[34] In about 1811 Weatherford had just turned thirty and was the heir to considerable property, which included a plantation on the Alabama River, along the principal route through the Creek Nation to Mobile. His home was often filled with young Creek braves who enjoyed his stable of well-bred horses and his apparently boundless supply of whiskey. As befitted a young plantation owner with Caucasian blood, he dressed in the latest white fashions, and with his reddish hair and Scottish name, he likely suggested to visiting whites very little of the Indian stereotype they might have expected.

One summer evening a notorious character from Georgia appeared at Weatherford's plantation and asked for accommodations. He was Wild Bill Thurman, a hard-bitten gambler and horse-racer who was well known for his addiction to rough-and-tumble sports and practical jokes. Thurman, hoping to have some sport with the famous Red Eagle, bought a horse that could hardly walk and, thus mounted, rode up to the plantation. Weatherford learned from his other guests that Thurman was known as a practical joker, and he determined to outwit the Georgian. After the guests had finished dinner and were sitting comfortably in the plantation barroom, Weatherford called for his black fiddler to entertain the company. When the lively music reached a feverish pitch, Red Eagle drew his pistol and commanded Thurman to dance. The Georgian, casting a wary eye at the cocked pistol aimed at his heart, began to buck and wing with great vigor. For a long time he continued, growing weary as the color drained from his cheeks and perspiration streamed from his forehead. On he went, slowing to an almost comical parody of the dance as Weatherford stared with a level gaze, the cocked pistol still trained on his heart. At last Weatherford signaled for the dance to stop and invited Thurman to rest and have a drink with him.

While the two were seated with their drinks, Thurman grabbed Weatherford's pistol, which was lying on the table beside him. "Now, Bill Weatherford," he said, "it is your time to dance. Now you dance until I tell you to stop, or I will drive a ball through you instantly." He turned to the frightened fiddler and ordered him to strike up the music. Weatherford, although known for his great courage, was not foolhardy enough to test the resolve of the reckless and angry Thurman. He began to dance, and he continued for a full hour. Knowing the reputation of Thurman, no one in the assembly interfered. When the Georgian was finally satisfied that the score had been evened, he laid aside the pistol and stopped the fiddler. Weatherford seemed to accept Thurman's retaliation with no animosity, and, after further conversation, everyone retired to bed. Red Eagle, however, secretly dispatched a party of Indians to take Thurman's broken-down nag into the woods and kill it.

After breakfast the next morning, Weatherford was intent on establishing his athletic superiority over the visiting Georgian. He suggested a wrestling match, and they had several sessions of intense grappling and struggling, with Thurman pinning Red Eagle's shoulders to the ground in each encounter. Although both were by now bone weary, Weatherford challenged Thurman to a fist fight, with the agreement that no one would interfere and that the fisticuffs would not end until one of the adversaries admitted defeat. The brutal bout began and continued long and violently, but in the end Weatherford was forced to admit that Thurman was the better fighter. They then shook hands and vowed their lasting friendship. Weatherford, who was a hero to his fellow Creeks and had never met his equal in Indian sports, felt a deep admiration for Thurman. He insisted that the Georgian remain several days as his guest so that he could be entertained with an exhibition of some of the sports and amusements the Creeks enjoyed. When after a few days Thurman decided to continue his journey, Weatherford sent a servant to bring from the stable his finest horse, equipped with an expensive bridle and saddle. "Here, Thurman," said Red Eagle, "take this horse and never again ride such a horse as the one you rode here, and which I had killed for humanity's sake, but always ride a horse that is fit for a gentleman to ride. And whenever you pass along this way, be sure and come to see me, and make my house your home." Weatherford also gave the astonished Thurman a hundred dollars in silver. The two met frequently after this, and their friendship continued until Weatherford's death.

It is still debatable in some quarters whether Red Eagle willingly accepted his role in the Creek War, but the few contemporary accounts that exist seem to indicate that he had no strong animosity toward the whites and that he was just as reluctant to take up arms on the Red Stick side as McIntosh was anxious to fight on the opposite side in the days immediately ahead.

8

The Conflagration Spreads: The Battle of Burnt Corn and the Massacre at Fort Mims

————— · —————

By midsummer of 1813, settlers along the Tombigbee and Tensaw rivers in southwestern Alabama were terrorized by the report that the Red Sticks were arming themselves in Pensacola for a war against the whites and the friendly Creeks. Many families abandoned their farms and took refuge in the pine-log forts or stockades that had been hastily erected along the Tombigbee and Alabama rivers. Judge Harry Toulmin, writing from Fort Stoddert on July 23, summarized the anxiety and fear in one sentence: "The people have been fleeing all night."[1] Colonel James Caller, the senior military officer on the frontier, ordered out the militia, and the first contingent departed on July 22 to stamp out the uprising early by attacking McQueen's party as it returned from Pensacola. Caller wrote to Brigadier General Ferdinand L. Claiborne before setting out on the mission that "unless this decisive step is taken, our settlements will be broken up."[2]

Colonel Caller, clad unmilitarily in a calico hunting shirt, top boots, and a high, bell-crowned hat, rode at the head of his company on a large bay horse. They crossed the Tombigbee and continued through the town of Jackson to Fort Glass, where they were joined by a company under the famous Indian fighter Captain Sam Dale. Dale had recruited his company of fifty militiamen at Point Jackson, on the Tombigbee, where they had been building Fort Madison. The troops were all well mounted, but their weapons formed a motley collection, including rifles and shotguns of every description. Dale carried a double-barreled shotgun, a weapon rarely seen in that day. After leaving

Fort Glass, the soldiers bivouacked for the night at Sizemore's Ferry, on the west bank of the Alabama, and then moved on to the cowpens of David Tate, William Weatherford's half-brother, where they were met by a makeshift company from Tensaw, led by a half-blood Creek, Captain Dixon Bailey. Caller's force of whites, mixed-bloods, and friendly Indians now numbered 180, in six small companies. On July 26 the troops camped for the night at the intersection of the Wolf Trail and the Pensacola Road, and on the following morning their scouts found McQueen's party camped a few miles down the Pensacola Road at Burnt Corn Creek.[3]

When the scouts returned to camp about eleven o'clock to report that the enemy was busily occupied with cooking and eating, the officers met in conference and decided to take the Red Sticks by surprise. McQueen's warriors were camped near a spring, now known as Cooper's Spring, with their packhorses grazing about them as Colonel Caller's troops turned left off the road, dismounted, and approached from the brow of a hill to the north and east. Then the militia company made a rapid charge down the hill, firing as they ran at the warriors, who were seated or reclining in scattered groups. Though startled by the sudden appearance of their attackers, the Red Sticks quickly sprang to their rifles and returned the fire. For a few minutes they held their ground, but then they were forced to give way and retreat in confusion into Burnt Corn Creek. A small detachment of the militia pursued, driving the Indians across the narrow stream and into the canebrake beyond. The majority of Caller's men, however, indulged themselves in the spoils of war and began happily leading the packhorses away.[4]

The Red Sticks, realizing that their adversaries were few and preoccupied, rallied quickly and came storming out of the swamp with guns blazing and drove the troops before them in disarray. Colonel Caller gave the order to fall back to a hill to secure a stronger position. The troops who were plundering, hearing the word "retreat" and misunderstanding the order, fled in wild panic, leaving only about eighty men to attempt to make a stand in the open woods at the foot of the hill. With Dale, Bailey, and Captain Benjamin Smoot taking command, the troops fought courageously for more than an hour, while the Red Sticks, though somewhat less accurate marksmen than the militiamen, fired at will from their more sheltered position. Sam Dale was wounded by a rifle ball, which struck him in the side, glanced around the rib cage, and lodged against his backbone. As

Dale told it, "I vomited a good deal of blood, and felt easier, and one of my men reloaded my rifle for me."[5]

Finally, however, realizing that their position was hopeless, Caller's troops began retreating in panic. They had dismounted before the attack, and most of the retreating militiamen could not find their horses. Traveling slowly on foot far into the night, they lined the trail from one end to the other with small squads and sometimes a solitary man. Caller's command never reassembled; the men mustered themselves out of the service and returned to their homes. Colonel Caller and Major Wood lost their way in the forest, and when they did not return, their friends became alarmed. General Claiborne asked Sam Moniac, Dixon Bailey, and David Tate to lead parties in search of the officers or their remains, and after fifteen days in the woods the two men were found, half-starved and delirious. Although only two militiamen were killed in the engagement and fifteen were wounded, the Battle of Burnt Corn was inordinately damaging to American prestige. Participants in the battle endured the ridicule of the populace for many years, and few would willingly admit having been present at Burnt Corn.[6]

The Red Sticks, who may have lost as many as twenty men, lost most of their packhorses and were forced to return to Pensacola for supplies. Thomas Woodward quoted High-Headed Jim as saying that if the whites had continued to pursue them into the canebrake, rather than stopping to plunder the camp, the Indians would have quit and the battle would have ended with the American purpose of intimidating the hostile Creeks having been accomplished.[7] Instead, the result was technically a Red Stick victory. Despite their losses, McQueen's men held their ground and forced the militiamen to beat a hasty and demeaning retreat. The Red Sticks now were confident that they could hold their own in battle against the American militia, and the ambush and attack by the whites gave them a unifying cause. Until the Battle of Burnt Corn the hostilities along the frontier were considered by some authorities to be merely a civil war among the Creeks. Now the warfare had become interracial, despite Hawkins's warning to the Red Stick leaders: "If the white man is in danger in your land, you are in danger; and war with the white people will be your ruin." Descendants of William Weatherford in South Alabama have passed along tales of white atrocities at Burnt Corn, such as stripping skins from the thighs of dead Indians to make horse bridles and making tobacco pouches from scrotum sacs, which, they believe, led to the massacre at Fort Mims that resulted in the burial of 247 men, women, and children of that ill-fated stockade.[8] William Weatherford is mentioned in only one contemporary source as having been involved in the Battle of Burnt Corn. In a set of extracts of occurrences at the Creek agency, Hawkins mentions "Bill Weatherford a half breed" in the "fray at Burnt Corn." Stiggins, a source closer to Weatherford, clearly did not believe he was present at the battle.[9]

Fuel for the flames of war had been prepared earlier in July, when Congress authorized the governors of Tennessee and Georgia to raise fifteen hundred men each to move against the Creeks "as circumstances may direct, either separately or together." The governors of Tennessee, Georgia, and the Mississippi Territory were convinced that Hawkins was wrong in thinking the Creek conflict a civil war. They wished to believe that the entire Creek Nation was unified in a war against the United States. Although concrete evidence was not to appear until a later date, the governors believed that the Creek hostilities were in part the result of British manipulations and material assistance from the Spanish.[10] They were also well aware that the split within the Creek Nation made it vulnerable to smashing military defeat for the first time since Europeans came to North America. More to the point, they knew that such a defeat would open the Creek country to white settlers. The conflict, moreover, was not limited to the Creek Nation; the Choctaws and Cherokees were divided along much the same lines as the Creeks. On August 2, shortly after the Battle of Burnt Corn, Hawkins received word from a runner that two hundred Cherokees had attacked Coweta and burned all the houses north of the one owned by William McIntosh.[11]

McIntosh was at the time assuming an increasingly important leadership role among the friendly Creeks. On August 2 Big Warrior sent McIntosh with a letter to the governor of Georgia, requesting that a company of militia be sent to help him and his warriors at Coweta. Big Warrior wrote that McIntosh would come along with the militia and be their pilot. He was particularly desirous that McIntosh be provided with a horse, which he promised to pay for out of the annual stipend paid to the Creek Nation. Two days later Big Warrior had moved into William McIntosh's house and from there wrote a letter to Hawkins summarizing the latest atrocities by McQueen and the Upper Creeks. He pleaded, "It is our sincere wish for you to come on to our assistance in three or four days, if it is only two hundred men, and let the rest of the army follow as fast as they can." He added that they expected "every moment to be attacked by warring Indians." He told

Hawkins that the war party from twenty-nine towns and villages of the Upper Creeks then numbered at least twenty-five hundred. Such dire statistics led Hawkins to report to the secretary of war: "The Big Warrior dreads the contest and is much under the influence of fear; he lends a willing ear to every frightful tale."[12]

A few days before the Fort Mims massacre William McIntosh was ordered by Hawkins to lead a party of friendly Creeks on a mission against McQueen. Hawkins reported on the successful mission to Governor Mitchell: "The party who went with McIntosh to take and destroy the town of Peter McQueen were 375. They burnt the town, destroyed the corn, took 14 head of cattle and considerable quantity of property." When the McIntosh company reached McQueen's town, Chattucchufaulee, and surrounded it, they found it had been evacuated just a short time before, with all the property, including a great quantity of salt, left in the hasty departure. Another war party went out from Coweta, killed three of the Red Sticks, and brought their scalps to the public square, heightening the war hysteria still further. At the time of the attack on Fort Mims on August 30, McIntosh was sent on a mission to the Cherokees to urge them to intervene on the side of the friendly Creeks. When he returned to Coweta, escorted by the influential Cherokee leader Major Ridge, sometimes called Path Killer, the Creek council was in session to discuss the dire events along the frontier.[13] By then, the massacre at Fort Mims, a bloody slaughter that compared in horror with the massacres in the Virginia colony in 1622 and 1644, had escalated the Creek War well beyond the point at which negotiations were possible. The roles of William McIntosh and William Weatherford as leaders of opposing sides in the war were now firmly established.

Although Weatherford was to become one of the principal leaders in the Fort Mims massacre, he was torn with conflicting desires and interests in the days immediately preceding this bloody event. Less than half Indian and comfortable among whites, he found himself on the side of the hostile Red Sticks, on the opposite side of the conflict from his brother Jack and his half-brother David Tate, as well as many other Tensaw mixed-bloods with whom he had attended dancing parties and other social functions. Weatherford well understood the futility of a Creek war against the United States and had counseled against it in the presence of Tecumseh. But when the conflict became irrevocable, Weatherford pondered his dilemma and reluctantly cast his lot with the Red Sticks. Still convinced that the Creeks could not defeat the Americans alone, Weatherford and a Creek chief named

Ochillie Hadjo held conferences in July with the Choctaw leaders in an attempt to persuade that powerful tribe to join forces with the Creeks against the United States. The Choctaws, under the leadership of the influential chief Pushmataha, were proud of never having shed the blood of white men in warfare, and they steadfastly refused to join the Red Stick cause.[14]

After the Battle of Burnt Corn, the Red Sticks called a general council to discuss how best to exact vengeance upon the whites and mixed-bloods who had warred against them. They decided to go downriver and attack Fort Mims and Fort Pierce, which were about two miles apart. The Red Stick military leaders, as well as the prophets, sought the advice of Weatherford, who now, according to Stiggins, realized that he could not persuade them to lay down their arms. He gave them a plan of attack, which he said he thought might succeed, and they were so favorably impressed, Stiggins wrote, that they agreed to place all future operations under Red Eagle's guidance and control. Paddy Walsh, one of the prophets, was named head leader with the understanding that he would "act under the influence of Weatherford's opinion."[15]

To announce the day the forces would be marshaled at Flat Creek for the attack, the "broken days" were sent to the Upper Creek towns that were sympathetic to the Red Stick cause. The "broken days" were bundles of small twigs, broken to about four inches in length, one to be thrown away each day until the attack as a kind of calendar. According to Stiggins, 726 "effective warriors" gathered at Flat Creek, held a war dance, and moved out toward Fort Mims, taking four days to travel fifty miles. Some white settlers noted the large number of Indians, both mounted and on foot, moving in the direction of the fort, but, Stiggins wrote, no one acquainted with the Indian mode of warfare would believe that the Red Sticks would presume to attack a regular fortification defended by militia. Stiggins wrote that Weatherford knew the precise strength of Fort Mims and Fort Pierce, having received the information from several runaway blacks who had left the forts.[16]

On the afternoon before the attack, Weatherford, Walsh, and their Red Stick forces stopped for a rest about six miles from Fort Mims. A few minutes after they called a halt to the march, they saw two mounted militiamen, deep in conversation, pass by on a road only three hundred yards away. They were headed toward a creek the Red Sticks had just forded, and it was feared that the two scouts might pick up their trail, but in a few minutes the scouts returned, still in deep conversation and unmindful of the nearby warriors. Many of the Indians urged a pursuit of the two scouts, but the leaders agreed that to do so was a mistake. If the scouts were killed, they said, the militia would come searching for them and spread the alarm, but if they were allowed to return and report that no enemy could be seen, the fort would remain careless and vulnerable to a surprise strike. After a rest, the Red Sticks moved to within three-quarters of a mile of Fort Mims to halt for the night and, as Stiggins wrote, "to refresh themselves for tomorrow's work."[17]

After dark, Weatherford chose two men to accompany him in reconnoitering the fort. They were able to approach the wooden pickets without detection, even getting close enough to look through the portholes, which were about four feet from the ground and four feet apart all around, with no protective ditch or bank in front of them. There were very few lights inside the fort, and Red Eagle and his two scouts saw little of the interior, but they could hear the people inside moving carelessly about and "conversing on the common topics of life." Weatherford was now convinced that the scouts had given no alarm and that the fort was being negligently guarded. They returned to their camp, and Weatherford told the others what had been learned. Stiggins wrote that "the leaders of the Bands assisted him in digesting the plan of attack" and "every man painted red or black and stripped to the buff knew the part and place he was to act in."[18]

Weatherford is said to have made a speech at this time, urging his warriors to spare the women and children in the battle the following day. He said they were to fight warriors, not women, and he proposed that the women and children be taken back to the Creek Nation as servants. If tradition is correct, Weatherford had a personal interest in protecting the women in Fort Mims. He had fallen in love with Lucy Cornells, a famous beauty of mixed blood, who had fled with her father, Joseph, to Tensaw country and taken refuge in the fort. Twice a widower, Weatherford as a young man suffered the death of his first wife Mary (or Polly) Moniac, and more recently his second wife, Sapoth Thlaine, noted for her beauty and her lovely singing voice, had died while bearing him a son. Now irreversible forces moved him toward the destruction of Fort Mims and Lucy.[19]

Fort Mims was vulnerable and poorly protected that August night. The large stockade, enclosing about an acre of ground, had been hastily erected by fearful whites and mixed-bloods following the Battle of Burnt Corn. It was built around a large frame house belonging to Samuel Mims, a wealthy early settler in Creek country, a mile east of the Alabama River. As soon as the fort was partially finished, settlers fled there and erected cabins and board shelters within the enclosure.[20] According to General F. L. Claiborne, by mid-August 275 to 300 whites and mixed-bloods had taken refuge there, along with an indeterminate number of black slaves. Stiggins gave the total number at the time of the assault as 340. Claiborne's count included 120 Mississippi volunteers under Major Daniel Beasley, 70 mixed-blood militiamen under Captain Dixon Bailey, and 16 men from Fort Stoddert under Lieutenant Osborne.[21]

Major Beasley, who was to prove to be a poor choice, was given command of the fort. When General Claiborne inspected the stockade on August 7, he told Beasley to strengthen the pickets and build additional blockhouses. Beasley, however, was convinced that he and his people were safe. General Clairborne was to say of Beasley later that "although often warned he turned a deaf ear to all idea of danger." He refused to keep the gates of the fort closed and allowed the inhabitants to wander unrestrained along the bank of the lake. Judge A. B. Meek spoke of fellow lawyer Beasley as "unflinchingly brave" but "vain, rash, inexperienced, and overconfident."[22] Despite warnings of imminent danger, and although the time could have been well spent in drilling the raw troops and making disciplined soldiers out of them, Beasley made no demands on his troops, who responded by filling their days with cards, drinking, and horseplay. About August 20 Weatherford had led a part of his army to the plantation of Zachariah McGirth, where they captured several black slaves. One of them, named Joe, informed Weatherford's party of what he knew of the lax state of defense at Fort Mims and advised them to attack at noon, while the troops were busy with their midday meal. But one of the captured blacks managed to escape to Fort Mims, where he told the commanding officer about the proximity of the Red Stick forces and their impending attack. Beasley sent out scouts, who perhaps expected to find the Indians moving about the countryside in full view. They returned to the fort after failing to find anything to corroborate the black's story, and the tension again abated at Fort Mims.[23]

On Sunday, August 29, with the Red Sticks camped a few miles away, a fresh supply of whiskey was brought into the stockade and liberally consumed. On that same day an express message arrived from General Claiborne, warning Beasley of danger and "enjoining the utmost circumspection." Also on that day two young blacks were sent out of the fort to tend some cattle that were grazing a few miles

PLAN OF FORT MIMS.

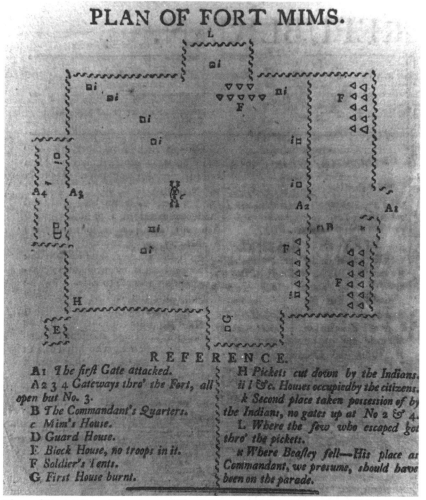

REFERENCE.

A 1 *The first Gate attacked.*
A 2 3 4 *Gateways thro' the Fort, all open but No. 3.*
B *The Commandant's Quarters.*
c *Mim's House.*
D *Guard House.*
E *Block House, no troops in it.*
F *Soldier's Tents.*
G *First House burnt.*

H *Pickets cut down by the Indians.*
ii l *&c. Houses occupied by the citizens.*
k *Second place taken possession of by the Indians, no gates up at No 2 & 4.*
L *Where the few who escaped got thro' the pickets.*
* *Where Beasley fell—His place as Commandant, we presume, should have been on the parade.*

Plan of Fort Mims (Courtesy of the Museum of the City of Mobile)

away. After a short while they appeared back at the stockade, running at full speed and gasping for breath. They reported having seen twenty-four warriors in battle paint. Captain Middleton was dispatched with a detachment of cavalry to the place where the Red Sticks had supposedly been seen but found no evidence of them. The cavalry returned about sunset, and one of the young black men, belonging to John Randon, was tied up and severely whipped for alarming the garrison. The other black belonged to a man named Josiah

Fletcher, who believed the story and refused to allow his servant to be flogged. This defiance so angered Beasley that he ordered Fletcher and his large family to depart from the fort by 10:30 the following morning. To avoid this fate, Fletcher reluctantly submitted his man to the lash, and preparations were made to administer the flogging at noon on the thirtieth. That day Beasley wrote a reply to General Claiborne, which read, "I have improved the fort at this place and made it much stronger than when you were here." He mentioned the report brought in by the two blacks and added: "But the alarm has proved false." Two hours later Beasley wrote a second message to General Claiborne, assuring him of his ability to maintain the fort against any number of Indians.[24]

The Red Sticks, remembering that the unprovoked attack at Burnt Corn Creek had surprised their people as they sat down to eat, chose the noon drumbeat as their signal for attack. As the garrison began the noon meal, the Red Sticks lay poised for attack, obscured by a thick growth of cane, in a ravine four hundred yards from the east gate. While some soldiers were playing cards as they waited their turn to get food, some of the girls and young men were dancing and the children were enjoying their games. A few hundred yards away were more than seven hundred warriors, headed by five prophets with black-painted faces, feathers covering their bodies.[25] Fort Mims had received another unheeded warning before noon on the thirtieth, when the scout James Cornells rode back to the stockade at a fast trot, halted at the gate, and shouted to Major Beasley that the Indians were coming. Beasley, who was drunk, according to eyewitnesses, replied that the scout had seen only a gang of red cattle, and Cornells shouted back that the gang of red cattle would "give him a hell of a kick before night." Others at the gate took Major Beasley's side and said Cornells was no more reliable than Fletcher's black slave, who was then tied up awaiting a whipping. Beasley ordered Cornells arrested, but the scout wheeled his horse and sped away, shouting a final warning to the men at the gate. Weatherford later said that he was near enough to the stockade to recognize Cornells and to watch him ride up to the gate, give his warning, and ride away. When the drumbeat summoned the soldiers of the garrison to dinner, the ravine suddenly came alive with the sound of war whoops. It was a bright, hot day, but the air was soon filled with the dust raised by the running warriors.[26]

When the shouts were heard, Major Beasley, sword in hand, rushed to close the gate, but sand had washed against it, and it could not be moved. One group of onrushing Creeks felled Beasley with

Massacre at Fort Mims, from an early woodcut (Courtesy of the Museum of the City of Mobile)

their war clubs as he stood pushing against the gate, and they leaped over his body into the stockade, storming through the outer gate past the rows of tents where two companies of soldiers were garrisoned and through the old gateway. They were led by four prophets, garish in black paint and feathers, who had been assured by Walsh that their bodies were impervious to the white man's bullets. Although one managed to escape, three prophets were cut down almost immediately by crossfire from the soldiers. Some of the Red Sticks retreated momentarily when they saw that the white man's bullets did not split upon the sacred persons of the prophets and pass off.[27] The confused militiamen valiantly attempted to defend the stockade, but by this time the Indians had nearly surrounded the fort and had taken over three-fourths of the portholes from the outside, firing through them at the soldiers, women, and children within.[28] In some cases an Indian and an American planted their guns across the same porthole to fire at each other. Captain Middleton and his company, stationed to the Red Sticks' right as they entered the east gate, were all killed early in the fighting. Captain Jack and his troops, on the south wing, defended their position bravely and with some success, as did Captain Dixon Bailey, now acting as the commanding officer, who inspired his troops to stiffen and hold the northern pickets against the largest concentration of Red Sticks. He urged them to hold out, assuring them that the Indians seldom fought long at one time.[29]

Susan Hatterway, a survivor of the massacre, claimed that she saw Weatherford as he ran through the gate at full speed at the head of his warriors. She saw him leap over a pile of logs almost as high as his head and, seeing Captain Bailey, who was a bitter enemy, shouted, "Dixon Bailey, today one or both of us must die." After witnessing the first moments of this confrontation, Mrs. Hatterway saw her husband killed, and when she realized that all was lost and that the fort would be reduced to ashes, she took the hands of a white child named Elizabeth Randon and a black child named Lizzie and said, "Let us go out and be killed together." As they walked toward the arena of battle, she was surprised to see one of the warriors, frightening in his war paint and with the blood of slain soldiers on his arms and legs, beckon her to him. When she drew closer she recognized him as an Indian named Dog Warrior, whom she had known when he was a boy. He took her prisoner, along with the two children, and took them to Pensacola, where they remained with some of her friends until the war was over. Captain Bailey, who was a native of Autossee and had been educated in Philadelphia, fought his last battle at Fort Mims. Though severely wounded, he managed to join a party escaping from the stockade; his body was later found in a swamp nearby.[30]

The scene inside the stockade was one of unrelieved horror and bloodshed. One survivor, Dr. Thomas G. Holmes, assistant surgeon at the garrison, said later, "The way that many of the unfortunate women were mangled and cut to pieces is shocking to humanity, for very many of the women who were pregnant had their unborn infants cut from the womb and lay by their bleeding mothers." According to Stiggins, Weatherford became "filled with sorrowful re-

Attack on Fort Mims, by Norman Price (Courtesy of the Museum of the City of Mobile)

flections" over some of his "dearest friends" who were inside the fort
and would soon be victims of the Indians' bloodlust. Stiggins wrote
that Weatherford well knew the "Indian mode of war" and once the
Red Sticks had overpowered their enemy they would spare no one,
despite Weatherford's plea for the lives of the women and children. In
despair, Weatherford mounted a horse and rode to the plantation of
his half-brother David Tate, twelve miles above Fort Mims. He regret-
fully told Tate of the horrible excesses of the scene at Fort Mims, saying he had tried to prevent them, but his excited warriors threatened
his life if he interfered. Those who knew Weatherford in later years
said that he never thought of the terrible scenes at Fort Mims without
the most painful emotions.[31]

With the Red Sticks in control of all the portholes and most of the
houses in the fort ablaze, it was obvious that the desperate resistance
of the militia and settlers was hopeless. Captain Bailey, who was
wounded, assessed the situation and urged all who could to try to
escape. Dr. Holmes cut through several pickets with an ax and led the
wounded Bailey, the captain's black servant Tom (who carried Bailey's
critically ill thirteen-year-old son, Ralph), and a black woman named
Hester through the holes he had cut. A number of Indians stationed
behind a fence fifty yards away began firing immediately at the little
band of escapees, and bullets tore through Holmes's clothing in several places but did not wound him. Bailey and Holmes returned the
fire, but Tom, bewildered and disoriented, ran back into the fort,
where a Red Stick dashed out the boy Ralph's brains with a war club.
Holmes, Bailey, and Hester reached the safety of a swamp, and the
surgeon concealed himself in a large hole left by the roots of a fallen
cypress tree. Bailey died of his wounds in the swamp, but Hester,
though wounded in the breast, was able to reach Fort Stoddert and
give General Claiborne the first account of the massacre.[32]

Holmes lay concealed until midnight, when the flames of the burning fort died down and the fields he must cross were no longer illuminated by the dreadful light. Unable to swim, he was forced to walk
toward the high lands rather than cross the river to safety at Mount
Vernon. Every few hundred yards, he saw Indian fires, around which
bloodstained warriors lay sleeping. Afraid of being discovered, he returned to the swamp, where he lived for five days on water and roots.
On the sixth day he found some horses which he recognized as belonging to friends, and he was so overjoyed he fired his gun. His
friends, thinking the gunshot had come from a war party, fled up the
bayou in a boat, where they hid for two days. Holmes went to the

abandoned house of his friend John Buford and caught a chicken, which he ate raw for fear that the smoke of a cookfire would summon a war party. Three days later he was found by Buford and taken to the safety of Mount Vernon.[33]

No tale that has been handed down from the Fort Mims massacre has as much drama and pathos as the one of Zachariah McGirth, his part-Creek wife, the former Vicey Cornells, and their seven daughters. About ten o'clock on the morning of the attack, McGirth left his wife and children in the fort and went by boat with two of his slaves toward his plantation on the Alabama River for provisions. On the way he heard the sound of gunfire at the fort and surmised that it was under attack by Indians. He and his men hid in a small bayou until late in the evening. Though the firing had ceased by then, the clouds of black smoke and flames rising above the trees told him that the fort was lost and that his wife and children had probably been killed. He determined to go through the swamp to the fort, and when he came within 450 yards of the ruins he left his slaves concealed and went in alone. In the grisly light of dawn he saw a horrible spectacle, with bloody, mutilated, and scalped corpses lying in piles, some half-burned but still sizzling upon the glowing coals. He returned in shock to his slaves, and the three of them went back to search through the blackened bodies as best they could, but none of McGirth's family could be found.[34]

Alone and desperate for revenge, McGirth spent the months of the Creek War riding from the Tombigbee to Georgia with express messages when no one else could be found who was daring enough for the missions. Then one day in Mobile, a friend told him that some people on the wharf had asked to see him. When he went there, he saw a band of wretched Indians who had been captured. From the group a woman and seven children advanced toward him and embraced him. He was speechless with joy, for it was Vicey and his seven daughters. They had a remarkable story to tell, a story that had begun many years earlier, when a small orphan Indian boy, hungry and homeless, had stopped by chance at the McGirth home. The compassionate Vicey took him in, fed and clothed him, and raised him to manhood. His name was Sanota, and he later joined the army of warring Red Sticks. When Vicey next saw him, he was caught up in the bloodlust of war, hewing and hacking women and children at Fort Mims. When he recognized Mrs. McGirth and his foster-sisters, he took them under his protection and the next day led them on horseback toward the Coosa River on the pretense that he had captured them as slaves. He sheltered them at his home, hunted game for them, and protected them from further brutality by his fellow Red Sticks. One day he told his adopted mother that he was going to fight alongside his brother Red Sticks against General Jackson at Horseshoe Bend. He told her that if he should be killed in the battle, she must take her daughters southward to find her husband and friends. Sanota was killed at Horseshoe Bend, and Mrs. McGirth and her daughters started on foot for Fort Claiborne, on the Alabama River north of the site of Fort Mims. After many days of suffering, they were found near the deserted McGirth home by Major Uriah Blue, who took them to Mobile and the eventual reunion with Zachariah, which was marred only by the death of McGirth's only son at Fort Mims.[35]

The facts and folklore concerning the Fort Mims massacre have been handed down primarily from the white man's point of view. Benjamin Hawkins, however, in a letter to the secretary of war, quoted some secondhand comments from Wewocau, a chief of the upper towns, who led his warriors in the battle at Fort Mims. Wewocau said many men were lost in the engagement, and when he and his braves moved in to capture portholes, they saw many Indians shot down. The prophets had told them they would lose at most three men. One of the prophets led the way, rushing into the fort to destroy it with magical powers. From where he was stationed, Wewocau said, he could hear the white people hacking the prophet to pieces with their swords. A contemporary account stated that 202 Red Sticks died in the attack on Fort Mims, but some Creek chiefs estimated to Hawkins immediately after the event that only 40 to 60 had perished.[36] A recent historian has concluded that about half of the hostile Creeks who fought at Fort Mims were killed or wounded.[37] Albert J. Pickett says that the day after the massacre the Indians began burying their dead by laying the bodies in the fields between the potato rows and drawing dirt and vines over them. Because of the great number of dead, however, the project was abandoned. Many of the Red Stick wounded were conveyed upriver in canoes; the walking wounded started home on foot, and some of them died, ironically, at Burnt Corn Spring.[38] The Red Sticks expected that in retaliation the whites would pour into the Creek Nation. To protect themselves and to prepare for the anticipated battles, those who were unhurt went to the almost impenetrable swamps on the north side of Bear Creek. When the onslaught of American forces was slow in coming, Weatherford and several chiefs made the Holy Ground their headquarters.[39]

From his headquarters at Mount Vernon, General Claiborne dispatched Major Joseph P. Kennedy with a strong detachment to bury the dead at Fort Mims. Arriving there ten days after the battle, Major Kennedy found the skies black with vultures and saw hundreds of wild dogs gnawing at the half-burned corpses. The troops, shocked and saddened, dug two large pits and interred 247 bodies. Part of Kennedy's report to General Claiborne read: "Indians, negroes, white men, women and children lay in one promiscuous ruin. All were scalped, and the females of every age, were butchered in a manner which neither decency nor language will permit me to describe. The main building was burned to ashes, which were filled with bones. The plains and the woods around were covered with dead bodies. All the houses were consumed by fire, except the block house and part of the pickets. The soldiers and officers, with one voice, called on Divine Providence to revenge the death of our murdered friends."[40] The best present-day estimates of the grim statistics of Fort Mims indicate that of the 275 to 300 whites, friendly Indians, and mixed-bloods who took refuge there, between 20 and 40 escaped and around 250 to 275 were killed in battle or taken as prisoners.[41] Cries for vengeance spread rapidly, and when the news of the massacre, then exaggerated to 400 to 600 dead, reached Tennessee, a committee on public safety rushed to see Andrew Jackson at the Hermitage to urge the militia commander to act to protect the settlers along the frontier. Though on his sickbed, Jackson agreed at once; he was soon telling his troops: "We must hasten to the frontier, or we shall find it drenched with the blood of our citizens!"[42] It would not be long before the paths of Andrew Jackson, William McIntosh, and William Weatherford would cross.

9

General Jackson Enters the Fray: Retaliation and Countermeasures from Tallushatchee to the Holy Ground

───── • ─────

Tennesseans had been rabid for revenge against the Creeks since the Duck River Massacre of May 1812, and after the tragic events at Fort Mims in August 1813, a writer in the *Nashville Clarion* said the Creeks "have supplied us with a pretext for a dismemberment of their country." At that same time, the Tennessee legislature demanded sufficient troops "to exterminate the Creek Nation."[1] Already at a genocidal frenzy, the Tennesseans had been pleased in July when the federal government authorized the governors of Georgia and Tennessee to raise fifteen hundred men each to move against the Creeks.[2] In a letter to Tennessee's Governor Willie Blount on July 3, 1813, Andrew Jackson threatened to "penetrate the Creek towns" even without authority, adding that he would think himself "justifiable, in laying waste their villages, burning their houses, killing their warriors and leading into Captivity their wives and children." When news of the Fort Mims attack reached Nashville on September 18, a chorus of leading citizens demanded a war "to exterminate the Creek Nation and Abettors," and Governor Blount in a saber-rattling speech to the legislature said that "the employment of a competent force at once would teach those barbarous sons of the woods their inferiority."[3] On September 24 the Tennessee legislature empowered Governor Blount to raise five thousand men for a three-month tour of duty, in addition to the fifteen hundred regular army troops authorized by the federal government. Governor Blount ordered Jackson to call out, "in the shortest possible time," two thousand militiamen "to repel an ap-

112

proaching invasion, and attack, to be made by the Creek Indians on the frontier . . . of this state."[4] Jackson, licking his wounds after a brawl with Thomas Hart Benton two weeks before, had first received the news of Fort Mims when he was in a severely weakened state, his left arm useless from a gunshot wound in the shoulder. On September 24, while still confined to his bed, Jackson wrote reassuringly: "The health of your general is restored. He will command in person."[5] He was not to be denied his encounter with fate and was determined to fight any attempt to replace him with another general. In a little over two weeks he was stooped precariously in the saddle and riding toward the Creek Nation, his six-foot-one-inch body reduced to 145 pounds by a conglomerate of wounds and diseases, courageously embarking on what was to be the most significant and politically profitable eighteen months of his public career.

As forces were being assembled outside the Creek Nation, William Weatherford and William McIntosh were attempting to forge alliances within it. Already mentioned is a tradition that Weatherford and a Creek chief named Ochillie Hadjo met with the Choctaw leader Mingo Moshulitubbe in an attempt to bring the Choctaws into the war on the Red Stick side, but they were unsuccessful. The influence of Pushmataha was too strong for any of his people to take arms against the whites. At the time of the attack on Fort Mims, McIntosh was visiting the Cherokees to urge them to intervene on the side of the friendly Creeks. He was escorted back to Coweta by Major Ridge and several other Cherokees, who met with Big Warrior at the Creek council. Big Warrior's talk, accompanied by a piece of tobacco decorated with colored beads, was taken to the Cherokee council by Ridge, who convinced the other Cherokees of the wisdom of joining with Big Warrior, McIntosh, and the friendly Creeks in their war against the Red Sticks. It was not until September 29, however, that Pushmataha volunteered to bring Choctaw forces into the fray on the side of the friendly Creeks. On that day he went to Captain George Gaines, the factor at Fort St. Stephens, told him he had just heard about Fort Mims, and offered the services of warriors. Gaines, highly pleased at this prospect, rushed Pushmataha to Mobile for a conference with General Thomas Flournoy, who, without giving an explanation, refused to accept the Choctaws as United States troops. Embarrassed by the general's refusal, Gaines and Pushmataha rode back to Fort St. Stephens, but as they were relating Flournoy's refusal to the angry Choctaw warriors, a courier from the general rode up with a message. Flournoy

had reconsidered and was now authorizing Gaines to raise troops in
the Choctaw Nation.[6]

Gaines and Pushmataha left Fort St. Stephens immediately for
Choctaw country, where the chief assembled a council at Kooncheto
village. Speaking to an assembly that was reported to number more
than five thousand braves, Pushmataha left no doubt where his allegiance lay: "You know Tecumseh. He is a bad man. He came through
our nation, but did not turn our heads. He went among the Muscogees and got many of them to join him. You know the Tensaw people. They were our friends. They played ball with us. They sheltered
and fed us whenever we went to Pensacola. Where are they now?
Their bodies rot at Sam Mims' place. The people at St. Stephens are
our friends. The Muscogees intend to kill them too. They want soldiers to defend them." Drawing his sword and brandishing it, he
shouted: "You can all do as you please. You are all freemen. I dictate
to none of you. But I shall join the St. Stephens people. If you have a
mind to follow me, I will lead you to glory and victory!" The response
was immediate. One warrior stood up, slapped his hand upon his
breast, and exclaimed: "I am a man! I am a man! I will follow you!"
Nearly all the other Choctaws then rose up, slapped their breasts, and
joined in a general shout of affirmation, to the great satisfaction of
George Gaines.[7]

In the political machinations that led to the Creek War and the
larger War of 1812, the influence of the Spanish and British was a
factor. The Red Sticks continued to get messages from the Great Lakes
area, assuring them that the British would supply arms to those
Creeks who fought against the United States. The Spanish, convinced
by British emissaries that the Red Stick rebellion redounded to their
advantage, also gave aid and encouragement.[8] A letter from the
Spanish governor of Pensacola, found in William Weatherford's house
at the Holy Ground several months after the Fort Mims massacre,
congratulated the Red Sticks on their victorious attack. Governor Don
Matteo Gonzalez Manrique also assured them of his constant aid, but
he argued against setting fire to Mobile because that place properly
belonged to the king of Spain and would soon, he said, be reoccupied
by the Spanish.[9] This letter may partly explain why Weatherford
chose not to attack the almost defenseless nearby Mobile in the first
flush of his success at Fort Mims, but in all likelihood he never intended to attack the town. The British also continued to be involved in
the war. In September 1813, Governor Charles Cameron of New
Providence Island in the Bahamas dispatched Captain Edward Hand-

Pushmataha, by Charles Bird King (from McKenney and Hall, *History of the Indian Tribes*)

field of the Royal Navy to the Creek Nation to attempt to formalize an alliance. Off the Florida coast Handfield held a meeting on his ship with some Creeks and Seminoles, and he relayed their request for aid to Cameron, who was ordered by Lord Bathurst, secretary of state for war in the colonies, to supply all possible assistance.[10]

Before Jackson was able to travel, his friend John Coffee, who had been promoted to brigadier general on September 24, led thirteen hundred cavalry troops southward across the Tennessee border, arriving at Huntsville on October 4. Jackson took direct command of the infantry and assumed overall command of the troops at Fayetteville, Tennessee, on October 7; four days later he broke camp and headed south to join Coffee. En route he heard that Coffee's mounted troops were in danger of a Red Stick attack, and he marched his men thirty miles in nine hours before a message came through that proved the rumor false.[11] On the following day Jackson's troops reached Coffee's bivouac at Ditto's Landing on the Tennessee River below Huntsville.

One detachment of troops was sent twenty-four miles along the Tennessee to the mouth of Thompson's Creek, where the main supply base, Fort Deposit, was established. The remainder of the men were ordered to cut a road to the south over Raccoon Mountain to where Canoe Creek joined the Coosa River. The fifty-mile-long road was completed in six days through difficult terrain, over mountains, as one provincial infantry-axman naively described them, "more tremendous than the Alps."[12] Fort Strother, the supply base, was built at the end of the road, but neither of the newly built bases held any supplies, and this was a great worry to Jackson, who wrote: "There is an enemy I dread much more than I do the Hostile Creek . . . that meagre monster 'Famine.'" In a letter the following day he wrote, "I am determined to push forward if I live upon acorns."[13] Despite the lack of supplies, which was the result of the inefficient system of employing civilian contractors to provide military provisions, Jackson had a bold plan of action in mind, and he never wavered from his resolve to accomplish it. Jackson's strategy was to move out from Fort Strother, destroying Red Stick towns wherever they were found and driving a wedge through the Creek Nation to create an important military highway to Mobile, linking Tennessee with the Gulf. Then his piece de resistance, a sure avenue to military glory, would be the invasion of Florida to seize Pensacola and stifle the support given to the Creeks by the Spanish, who, Jackson was convinced, were silent partners with the British in the War of 1812.

Jackson's grandiose plan faced some major obstacles, not the least of which was the inefficiency of the Madison administration, which led to a dispute over who would command the armies in the Creek War. The Creek Nation lay partly in the jurisdiction of the Sixth Military District, under the command of Major General Thomas Pinckney, and partly in the seventh, headed by Brigadier General Thomas Flournoy. The secretary of war attempted to solve the problem by placing the entire Creek War operation under General Pinckney, with General Flournoy retaining authority in his district over all matters except those pertaining to the Creeks. This decision led to so much tension between the generals that Flournoy later resigned.[14] There were also three other armies in the field, all commissioned to kill the Red Sticks, to destroy their crops, to divide the Creek Nation with lines of block-houses each a day's march apart, and to meet eventually when the hostiles had been eliminated. The four armies included the one from West Tennessee under Jackson, one from East Tennessee under General John Cocke, one from Georgia under General John Floyd, and a force consisting of a combination of the Third Regiment of U.S. Army regulars and the militiamen of the Mississippi Territory led by Brigadier General Ferdinand L. Claiborne. Jackson's bid to lead his army through the Creek Nation to Mobile and Pensacola had to be reconciled with the wills and egos of the other generals.

In late October William Weatherford sent out a threat to punish all Indians in the area who failed to aid the Red Stick cause. Major Ridge of the Cherokees sent a message to Jackson, telling him of Red Eagle's threat, and Jackson sent back the runners with a reassuring message: "The hostile Creeks will not attack you until they have had a brush with me; and that, I think, will put them out of the notion of fighting for some time."[15] In mid-November, however, the Red Sticks carried out Red Eagle's threatened retribution in the Coweta area. William McIntosh, Big Warrior, Little Prince, and Alexander Cornells sent a letter to General Floyd, begging for his help and informing him that Coweta had been surrounded for four days by the "main body of the hostile Indians," who were "more than double our number." "They are killing everything," the chiefs wrote to Floyd, "and burning all the houses." The chiefs said that they could not "turn out to fight them on account of our women and children."[16] It is likely that this was an act of Red Stick retaliation against William McIntosh, Big Warrior, and Little Prince, who had led a band of friendly Creeks in early October against 150 Uchees, who were on their way to join the Red Stick fac-

tion. After defeating the Uchees in the first battle of the Creek War on
Georgia soil, McIntosh's forces had burned several Red Stick villages
and destroyed their crops over a wide area.[17]

Although General Coffee had doubted the Red Sticks' willingness
to do battle, he was soon to learn that they would stand and fight to
the last man, without asking for quarter. Learning the location of what
was reported to be a considerable body of the enemy, Jackson dispatched Coffee and nine hundred mounted troops on November 2 to
destroy the Upper Creek town of Tallushatchee, on the south side of
the Coosa River, thirteen miles due east of Fort Strother. With the aid
of two Indian pilots, Coffee and his men forded the Coosa and
camped at a place called the Fish Dams. In the predawn hours of the
following morning, Coffee advanced his troops to within a mile of the
village, split them into two divisions, which looped around the village
and met, encircling it. The Red Sticks, when they became aware of the
impending attack, began beating their drums, mingling that throb-
bing sound with yells and war whoops. Two detachments of scouts
entered the village in an attempt to draw the hostiles from their
houses, which triggered a violent charge by the Red Sticks, who soon
reached the ring of soldiers in Coffee's main line, where they were
driven back by a thunderous crossfire.[18] The famous Tennessee frontier hero Davy Crockett was among those firing at the Red Sticks.

Writing of the battle later, Crockett said he counted forty-six warriors running into a house at this climactic point in the fighting. When
he and some others pursued them to the doorway, they found a
woman sitting there with a bow and arrow. Extending the bow fully
with her feet and legs, she let fly an arrow, which killed one of the
soldiers and so enraged the dead man's comrades that they fired at
least twenty rifle balls through her body. Then they turned their attention to the trapped warriors. "We now shot them like dogs; and then
set the house on fire, and burned it up with the forty-six warriors in
it." He saw an Indian boy of about twelve, who had been shot down
near the burning house. With an arm and thigh broken, he was trying
to crawl away from the fire, which was so close "that the grease was
stewing out of him." Crockett was impressed that "not a murmur escaped" the pain-wracked boy. "So sullen is the Indian," Crockett phi-
losophized, "when his dander is up, that he had sooner die than
make a noise, or ask for quarters." On the following day, Crockett and
a detachment went back to the village, where many of the Indian
corpses remained unburied. "They looked very awful," Crockett
wrote, "for the burning had not entirely consumed them, but given

them a terrible appearance." They found a potato cellar under the burned house with a large quantity of potatoes, which the famished Americans ate ravenously. Crockett wrote that "hunger compelled us to eat them, though I had a little rather not, if I could have helped it, for the oil of the Indians we had burned up on the day before had run down on them, and they looked like they had been stewed with fat meat."[19]

The total Indian loss was 186 killed, including some women and children, and 84 women and children were taken prisoner. Forty-one Americans were wounded, and five were killed, two with arrows. The ammunition-short Red Sticks used their bows between reloadings of their rifles. Jackson was ecstatic. "We have retaliated for the destruction of Fort Mims," he wrote Governor Blount. When the prisoners were brought into Fort Strother, Jackson was much taken with a handsome, ten-month-old Creek boy, the same age as his adopted son, Andrew, Jr. Because his parents were dead, the boy was refused help by the Creek women prisoners. "Kill him, too," they told the soldiers. Jackson took the baby on his knee, fed him some brown sugar dissolved in water, and sent him to Huntsville with funds for his care. The child, named Lyncoya, was later taken to the Hermitage and treated as a family member.[20]

The reaction to the victory—despite the embarrassing disproportion in the size of the two forces—was generally euphoric. Coffee wrote to his wife on November 4: "Our men are in excellent spirits— we shall soon finish the work of destruction of those wretches and return home."[21] Colonel William Carroll said: "After Tallushatchee we had the measure of the Creeks. All apprehension was dispelled. Every man in Jackson's army was serenely confident that contact with them meant victory for us, under any conditions. The brightest spot in the history of that campaign is the setting of its pace by John Coffee and his mounted riflemen of Tennessee at Tallushatchee!"[22] The engagement had indeed been unique, for, as General Jackson stated in his report, "Not one of the warriors escaped to carry the news, a circumstance unknown heretofore." The battle had also been noteworthy in that a company of friendly Indians, mostly Cherokees under Richard Brown, had fought under Coffee. To keep them from being confused with the hostiles, they wore white feathers and deertails on their heads.[23]

Not all of Coffee's men were exhilarated by this cold-blooded, systematic slaughter, which was to become the tactical model for subsequent operations against the Red Sticks. Lieutenant Richard Keith

Call found the killing so horrible that it sickened him. "We found as many as eight or ten bodies in a single cabin," he wrote. "Some of the cabins had taken fire, and half-consumed bodies were seen amidst the smoking ruins. In other instances dogs had torn and feasted on the mangled bodies of their masters. Heart sick I turned from the revolting scene." Coffee, in his report of the battle, attempted to explain why women and children were killed in the action: "In consequence of their [the warriors'] flying to their houses and mixing with their families, our men, in killing the males, without intention killed and wounded a few of the squaws and children, which was regretted by every officer and soldier of the detachment, but which could not be avoided."[24]

The decimation of the village of Tallushatchee had the immediate effect of convincing many Creek towns of the wisdom of allying themselves with Jackson's forces. This decision was made despite Weatherford's threat that all Creek villages and towns that sided with the American troops would receive swift and sure retribution from the Red Sticks. The small village of Talladega, which was thirty miles south of Fort Strother, across the Coosa River, decided at once to place its 154 souls under the protection of Jackson, and Red Eagle immediately besieged the town with a thousand braves, who lay in wait to destroy Talladega as an object lesson to all would-be defectors.[25] Red Eagle's warriors laid such a tight siege around the village that no one was able to escape until an innovative chieftain wrapped himself in a hogskin and grunted and rooted along on all fours in the dead of night, thus slipping unnoticed through the enemy encirclement. He ran quickly to Jackson's encampment at Fort Strother, where the general was woefully short of food supplies but spoiling for a fight.[26]

General Jackson, though anxious to attack the force of over a thousand hostiles who were a mere thirty miles away, had a problem to solve. He knew that moving against the Red Sticks immediately was the only hope he had to save the village, thus preventing a setback for American prestige and at the same time administering a punishing defeat to Weatherford's forces. He also knew that he should not leave two hundred sick soldiers, his equipment, and his remaining provisions unprotected at Fort Strother. Jackson had learned that General James White, who commanded the advance forces of General Cocke's Army of East Tennessee, was on his way to Fort Strother, and he dispatched a messenger to White, ordering him to push his men to their limits so they might arrive at the fort the following night. After weighing the risk of leaving Fort Strother vulnerable for a short time against the certainty of Talladega's destruction by the warring Indians, Jackson chose to move at once with a force of twelve hundred infantrymen and eight hundred mounted soldiers. The army was willing but hungry; Davy Crockett reported that in the several days before the battle, all the beef had been eaten and the men had begun eating the beef hides and "continued to eat every scrap we could lay our hands on." Leaving only a token force to guard Fort Strother, Jackson set out shortly after midnight of November 8, his army in the usual three columns. By sunset the following day, the troops, almost famished and thoroughly exhausted, camped six miles from the besieged village. While most of the army slept, Jackson, ill from dysentery and in pain, sat propped against a tree and interrogated his scouts about the topography of Talladega. At midnight he received a message that General Cocke had ordered General White to ignore Jackson's command and rejoin Cocke's forces. Although Fort Strother's wounded men and essential stores were now virtually defenseless, Jackson believed he could not retreat without a battle, for to do so would seriously damage American prestige.[27]

At four o'clock in the morning, after a sleepless night, Jackson ordered his troops roused and readied for marching. At dawn the army was deployed in a crescent-shaped formation, with mounted forces at each of the wingtips so they could ride toward each other, encircling the foe in the same tactic Coffee had successfully used at Tallushatchee. A cavalry unit was placed in reserve behind the main line, and Jackson's strategy, like Coffee's, was to have an advance detachment of riflemen and artillery move forward to provoke the engagement, then fall back, drawing the Red Sticks into the arms of the crescent, where they would be surrounded and would fall an easy prey to the mounted reserve.[28] At about eight o'clock the advance had moved within eighty yards of some of the enemy, who were concealed in thick shrubbery along the edge of a rivulet. According to Davy Crockett's firsthand report, as the soldiers were unknowingly moving into the enemy ambush, friendly Creeks tried to yell a warning from the stockade. Not being understood, two of the Creeks jumped from the top of the fort, ran to the lead horseman, grabbed the bridle, and pointed to the concealed hostiles. The Red Sticks at that moment laid down a heavy barrage, which the advance party returned before following orders and falling back toward the center. At this point, Crockett wrote, the Indians "came rushing forth like a cloud of Egyptian locusts, and screaming like all the young devils had been turned loose." They ran until they came within range of the line of riflemen of which Crockett was a part, where they were met by a hail of bullets that killed a large number of them. Then the Red Sticks turned and ran toward another line, which fired on them. Under a heavy crossfire they ran back and forth from one line to the other, with hundreds falling slain.[29] The Red Sticks fought with bows and arrows as well as guns, and many were fortunate enough to escape through a hole in the encirclement left when a unit made up of drafted militia, either through confusion or fear, suddenly retreated instead of advancing. About seven hundred Red Sticks escaped to fight again because of this blunder, which Jackson called the "*faux pas of the militia*"; he said that were it not for this break the destruction would have been as great as at Tallushatchee.[30]

Jackson reported to General Claiborne that 299 Red Sticks were counted dead on the field, "but this is known to fall considerably short of the number really killed."[31] Jackson's casualties included 15 killed and buried on the battlefield, with 2 of the more than 80 wounded dying on the way back to Fort Strother.[32] In reporting on the battle, Jackson praised his troops highly: "In a word, officers of every grade, as well as privates, realized the high expectations I had formed of them, and merit the gratitude of their country." Jackson himself was praised extravagantly throughout the nation, and one correspondent wrote to him: "The victories gained by you against the Indians will hand your name down to posterity as the first of patriots." General Coffee wrote to his wife: "We only want supplies to enable us to finish the campaign in three weeks."[33] Jackson's men captured a Spanish flag at the Battle of Talladega, which strengthened the General's belief that Spain was involved with his hated enemy England in aiding the hostile Creeks.[34] Jackson did not know then of the letter, found later in William Weatherford's house at the Holy Ground, in which the Spanish governor of Pensacola congratulated Red Eagle on his victory of Fort Mims. General Coffee believed the headquarters at the Holy Ground would be a temporary station for Weatherford and his warriors and that they would soon "move down, no doubt to Pensacola, to their friends and allies, the Spanish and the British." Jackson's letters during the fall of 1813 also make it clear that there was no question in his mind that the Indian problem could be solved only if Spanish and British influence in the area was removed. He wrote of the necessity to invade Spanish Florida and to capture Pensacola, which would "strike at the root of the disease."[35]

Although the two humiliating defeats in six days were damaging to Weatherford and the Red Stick cause, the hostile Creeks were heartened by the knowledge that their policy of destroying cattle and crops had so scorched the earth that it was nearly impossible for invading armies to live off the land. The supply lines were long, and the civilian contractors were not able to provide the promised provisions. It was hunger as much as the lack of protection for the wounded at the fort that forced Jackson to order his men back to Fort Strother rather than pursue the Red Sticks who had fled through his lines at Talladega. He hoped to find on his return that adequate supplies had at last reached Fort Strother, but not a pound of rations had been received. He had directed his surgeons as he left for Talladega to give his own private stores to the wounded if necessary, and all had been consumed except for a few dozen biscuits, which Jackson gave to the hungriest of his men, keeping none for himself. When a soldier approached Jackson later and asked for something to eat, the general told him: "I will divide with you what I have," and drew a handful of acorns from his pocket.[36]

Jackson's difficulties with hungry and mutinous troops were minor compared to a notorious incident on November 18 that aggravated an already serious breach between Jackson's forces and the militiamen of East Tennessee under General John Cocke. Cocke, thinking with some justification that if he linked up with Jackson he would lose his independent command to the intimidating commander, steadfastly ignored Jackson's orders. The result was the Hillabee Massacre, in which General James White, under orders from Cocke, attacked a peaceful village that had already proposed to surrender to Jackson and was awaiting the return of a messenger to confirm the agreement. White and one thousand men attacked the undefended village at dawn, and although they met with no resistance from the Hillabees, killed 60 and captured 250. "We lost not a drop of blood," White reported with pride to Cocke. Jackson was beside himself with anger, and the surviving Hillabees, outraged at what they believed to be Jackson's treachery, spread the word throughout the Creek Nation that the Indians' only recourse was to fight to the end without asking or giving quarter. This massacre was proof to the Red Sticks that they faced a ruthless army, bent on exterminating them, and for the remainder of the war the Creeks fought with a special desperation and a determination not to surrender even against overwhelming odds.[37]

As stated earlier, on November 18 William McIntosh and three other Creek chiefs wrote to General John Floyd, commander of the Georgia militia, appealing for help against the hostile Red Sticks, who had surrounded and besieged Coweta. The chiefs told Floyd that the

Red Sticks were in open pine woods, which would be a "good place to fight them." They added confidently, "We only want 1000 of your men and we could beat them." On November 16 Floyd had written to Georgia Governor Peter Early that runners from Coweta had told of the "state of great alarm" in that place. He told the governor: "It seems that McQueen has expressed his determination to have all our Baggage at the Risk of every man he has, if he persists in this determination, we shall ere long measure strength." The reference to the "baggage" reiterates that both sides in the Creek War were beset by a severe shortage of supplies. In a letter to his sister, written on November 18 as he paused in the march toward Coweta, General Floyd wrote that "the means and risk of regular supplies is my greatest dread." Private foot soldiers, as well as officers, were aware of the cause of the supply shortage. James A. Tait, who was in the ranks of one of Floyd's companies, wrote eloquently in his journal: "Officers in the contracting or victualizing department must give better proofs of their activity and management, or perhaps we shall not in 3 months, move to the object of the expedition."[38]

The Georgia militia did, however, leave Fort Lawrence for Coweta on November 18, led by Floyd, resplendent in a blue frock coat with epaulettes and gold lace on his shoulders.[39] The cold, rainy weather and an assortment of diseases caused 256 men to be declared unfit for travel, but Floyd crossed the Ocmulgee, Flint, and Chattahoochee rivers with an army of 950 militia and, at the latter stage of the journey, 450 friendly Creeks. They advanced to the Tallapoosa River in late November, having traversed about 120 miles of rough country. Included among the leaders of the friendly Creeks was William McIntosh, who was to distinguish himself in the Battle of Autossee. The trail guide for this motley assembly was Abram Mordecai, a Jewish trader who had established a cotton gin near Charles Weatherford's race track in 1802, only to have it destroyed by an irate band of Creeks in retaliation for his seduction of a pretty married Indian woman. Mordecai, who traded with the Creeks for pelts, medicinal roots, and hickory-nut oil, which he sold to the French and Spanish in New Orleans and Mobile, knew the territory of the Creek Nation well, having roamed it extensively since settling in the Autossee area in 1785.[40] Mordecai's abilities as a guide enabled Floyd to move his troops at night through the last few miles of forest toward Autossee, and the Georgians reached the town at daybreak instead of noon, the arrival time the Red Stick scouts had predicted.[41]

It was a calm, clear, and extremely cold morning; frost covered the fields so heavily it appeared like snow when General Floyd and his army reached the outskirts of Autossee on November 29.[42] Floyd's strategy was to deploy his troops, as Coffee and Jackson had done successfully at Tallushatchee and Talladega, into two advancing columns that would surround the town by throwing the right column on Calabee Creek, near the mouth of which the town stood, and resting the left wing on the bank below it. But as daylight increased, Floyd was amazed to discern a second town about five hundred yards below the other. It was now necessary to deploy three companies of infantry, along with mounted troops, to attack the lower town, with the remainder of the army attacking the upper town. The Red Sticks began firing immediately, and as Tait wrote in his journal, "Then, for the first time, was heard to resound on the remote banks of the Tallapoosa the dreadful noise of contending armies." The Red Sticks at first advanced toward the oncoming militia, but artillery fire and a bayonet charge by the infantry drove them back into the thickets at the rear of the town. The old Tallassee King, considered one of the most fanatical of the Red Sticks, then mounted his horse and encouraged his warriors forward by waving a war club. A cannon charge with grape shot was directed at him, and he fell dead at the first shot. The friendly Creeks were directed to cross the river on the west side to cut off the Red Stick retreat, but the cold weather and the difficulty of fording delayed them until the enemy had concealed themselves in caves cut in a bluff along the river. Although some of the friendly Creeks fell back in disarray to the rear of the army at this time, the Cowetas under McIntosh and the Tuckabatchees under the Mad Dog's son fought with great bravery,[43] and the Mad Dog's son was killed in the battle.[44]

Floyd's troops laid down a barrage that swept relentlessly across the bluff, killing a great many of the Indians who were concealed in the reeds and small bushes. Floyd wrote that the Indians, who as a matter of principle never left their dead to the enemy, dragged their slain Red Stick comrades down the bluff to the river's edge, which was "crimsoned with their blood."[45] The fire was heavy on both sides; both of Floyd's aides had horses shot from under them, and the general's kneecap was shattered by a Red Stick bullet. Nine of Floyd's men were killed in the battle, and three of the wounded died later. Estimates of the enemy dead ranged from one hundred to three hundred, with two hundred being a more likely number; among the dead was the Autossee King.[46] Floyd wrote later: "Had we got possession of the lower banks of the river all their women and children would have fallen into our hands, and what to have done with them would have been a question, as we could not have fed them, and I have placed restraints on the friendly Indians from destroying them." Revenge was sweet for the men of Floyd's regiment, who, from the evidence of the scalps of whites and from other articles found at Autossee, believed they had discovered and defeated the murderers of the garrison at Fort Mims. Tait reported that eighteen cannon rounds were fired, "shattering their miserable huts." Pickett's sources gave another value to the houses, however, claiming that the four hundred buildings destroyed included some that were of fine Indian architecture and were filled with valuable articles. Tait wrote in his journal that when "the big guns let loose, they left their huts and scampered like so many wild ants." He was puzzled at the strange conduct of several of the Red Sticks, who "remained in their houses quite passive during the battle, suffering themselves to be slain without resistance." Tait speculated that these passive martyrs might have been under the influence of the fanatical prophets.[47]

When General Floyd was convinced that his mission was accomplished and that the remaining Red Sticks were well ensconced in the caves along the bluff, he ordered his men to collect the dead and wounded and form a line of march. Most of the friendly Indians refused to follow, preferring to remain and pillage the burning town. About a mile from the battle scene the militia halted, formed again, and began burying their dead.[48] As they took up the march again, headed toward Fort Mitchell, and were ascending Heydon's Hill a mile east of the battleground, a large party of Red Sticks attacked the rear of the column. After a few rounds, however, the attackers disappeared.[49]

Two days before Christmas in 1813, the army of General Claiborne opposed Weatherford and an army of hostile Creeks at Ecunchate, a place sacred to the Red Sticks and called the Holy Ground by the Americans. It was a well-defended site of religious rituals, set up by Weatherford after the Battle of Fort Mims on a little peninsula partly surrounded and protected by the Alabama River, marshes, and deep forests. The prophets had confidently declared that no white man had ever trod the paths leading to Ecunchate and, because of their mytical incantations, no white man ever could enter the town.[50] The battle is now chiefly remembered for a much-debated feat of horsemanship by William Weatherford, who is said to have leaped from a high bluff into the Alabama River to escape Claiborne's riflemen.

General Claiborne and his army were camped at Pine Level on November 10, when orders came from General Flournoy for them to proceed to the Alabama River at Weatherford's Bluff, a site named for Red Eagle's father, and set up a supply depot there for General Jackson. Jackson, now convinced that famine was more of a threat to his men than their Indian opposition, wanted to be assured of logistical support as his army moved toward Pensacola.[51] Claiborne and his men, short of supplies but restless for a fight, were in good spirits as they moved out on November 13 toward the bluff. Claiborne wrote to General Flournoy: "My volunteers, half naked, evinced the greatest satisfaction on learning of their destiny. The advance toward the enemy, and the probability of winning distinction on the path to Pensacola, inspired them all."[52] Although the men were sanguinely optimistic that they would soon be in combat, Claiborne was marching under orders that expressly forbade him to move farther into the Creek Nation than Weatherford's Bluff until joined by the Georgia and Tennessee troops. The army included about a thousand whites, a mixed assembly of volunteers, mounted troops, some militia, and 135 Choctaws under Lieutenant Colonel Pushmataha, who was bedecked in a splendid uniform ordered from Mobile by General Claiborne at a cost of $300. The outfit included a suit of regimentals, gold epaulettes, silver spurs, and a hat with a feather. Pushmataha was carefully cultivated by Claiborne even though the small body of warriors he supplied was far short of the number expected from the Choctaw population of about twenty thousand. But with his ranks depleted by the departure of militia men who had served the time specified in their enlistment, Claiborne was grateful for any manpower the Choctaw chief could supply.[53]

On November 17 the army crossed the Alabama River on rafts and halted at Weatherford's Bluff. They began work immediately on a stockade two hundred feet square, protected by three blockhouses and a half-moon battery that had a commanding position overlooking the river. "From this position we cut the savages off from the river," Claiborne wrote Governor Holmes on November 21, "and from their growing crops. We likewise render their communication with Pensacola more hazardous." Before the end of November the stockade was completed and given the name Fort Claiborne, in honor of the commander. About this time, Colonel Gilbert C. Russell, a commander in the regular army, arrived with the Third Regiment of federal troops. Claiborne, determined to lead his men against the Red Sticks, now successfully prevailed upon General Flournoy to allow him to lead a force to attack the enemy at the Holy Ground. Twenty-six of Claiborne's officers petitioned the general to abandon the expedition on the grounds that the army was without winter clothing, shoes, or blankets and that it could not be adequately supplied because of the lack of roads. They also pointed out that a large majority of the soldiers would be entitled to a discharge before the expedition could be completed. The general persisted, however, and every officer who had signed the petition eventually complied. "As soon as the order to march was issued," Claiborne wrote to the *Mississippi Republican*, "each man repaired promptly to his post. Many, whose terms of service had expired, and had not received a dollar of their arrearages, volunteered for the expedition, and with cheerful alacrity, moved to their stations in the line." Sam Dale, who was the captain of one of the volunteer companies, saw the "general shed tears at these demonstrations of patriotism."[54]

On December 13 the army, numbering about a thousand men, moved jauntily out of Fort Claiborne to the tune of "Over the Hills and Far Away" and headed northeastward toward the Holy Ground. After they had marched eighty miles they reached the high lands south of Double Swamp, where Claiborne ordered his men to camp and built another stockade to be used as a supply depot. On the morning of December 22 the task was completed, and Claiborne marched his troops out again, leaving his supply wagons, cannon, baggage, the men who were sick and disabled, and a hundred men to stand guard at the newly built supply depot. In the late afternoon the army camped within ten miles of the Holy Ground. By the following morning the Red Sticks had learned from Weatherford of Claiborne's approaching threat and, despite the prophets' protestations of the invulnerability of the town, Weatherford ordered that women and children be ferried across the river and concealed in the dense forest.[55]

Arriving within two miles of the Holy Ground at about eleven o'clock, Claiborne called a brief halt and gave his battle order. The troops were divided into three columns; the right column, under Colonel Joseph Carson, was to attack the upper town, and the left, under Major Smart, the lower, with the center, commanded by Colonel Russell and Claiborne, remaining in reserve until the forces of battle dictated where they were most needed. Major Cassel's mounted riflemen were deployed on the riverbank west of the town to cut off any Red Sticks who attempted to escape downriver. Carson's column had been ordered to proceed across Holy Ground Creek and march along the higher right bank to the point of the attack, but an impenetrable reedbrake forced them on that chilly day to wade along the swampy left bank in water from six inches to two feet deep. As they left the swamp for firmer ground near the town, the war drums and the horrendous shouts of the Red Stick warriors suddenly assaulted their eardrums.

William Weatherford, who had ridden into Ecunchate to warn of the approach of Claiborne's army, found himself in command when the prophet Josiah Francis suddenly fled.[56] Weatherford posted a large body of warriors with rifles behind the bank of a stream emptying into Holy Ground Creek and a smaller group behind an adjoining fallen tree. When Carson's men came within range, Weatherford's riflemen laid down a withering volley from the ambush. Returning the fire from behind the trees and stumps, Carson's troops slowly moved forward, but Weatherford exhorted his Red Sticks to hold their ground, and he signaled a band of warriors in the rear to send up a shower of arrows toward the American lines. Most of these arrows, shot at too high a trajectory, fell harmlessly behind Carson's men. Amid the group of Red Stick bowmen, one of the prophets, waving a red-tinted cow's tail in each hand, danced wildly and gave out animal-like screams of invective against the invaders. Some of Carson's men finally succeeded in making a flanking movement that enabled them to give the Red Sticks a punishing enfilading volley, which killed or wounded several warriors. Weatherford's men retreated across the branch and continued to resist, wounding some of Carson's men, who had become aggressive and too reckless. A soldier named Gatlin, resting his musket against a tree and taking careful aim, shot and killed the prophet, who was still dancing wildly among the bowmen. As the bullet pierced the breast of the prophet and he stretched lifeless on the ground, the Red Sticks seemed to become demoralized, and many threw down their weapons and left the field, some carrying the wounded. Carson, who had been trying merely to engage the enemy until the encirclement was complete, now released his eager troops. "Boys, you seem keen!" he shouted, "go ahead and drive them!" Carson's troops pressed rapidly forward, driving the retreating Red Sticks through the town to a high bluff near the mouth of Holy Ground Creek, where some crossed the river in boats and others swam.[57]

It was at this point that Weatherford, mounted on his horse Arrow, is said to have made his daring leap from a high bluff into the Alabama River. As the most common version of the story goes, when he found that most of his men had deserted him, Red Eagle began seeking an avenue of escape for himself, but Claiborne's men had cut off all routes on the upper and lower sides of the town. He was riding a horse famous for strength and speed, so he rode swiftly down a long hollow that led to the riverbank and found himself beside a twelve-foot-high bluff, which rose twenty feet above the water on the other side. After assessing the situation and determining that a leap represented his only possibility of avoiding capture and death, he rode back about thirty yards to get space in which to accelerate. Then he turned Arrow's head toward the bluff, drove his spurs into his flanks, and sent the horse dashing up the bluff and over the top into the river. Maintaining his seat even though his horse was submerged when the struck the water, Red Eagle held his rifle high in the air as Arrow broke the surface and swam toward the opposite shore. At a point where he was about thirty yards from safety, the troopers above and below the bluff began firing, and, as Red Eagle told William Hollinger, the bullets splashed around him like hail. As soon as he reached the shore and was well out of range of the troopers' guns, he calmly unsaddled Arrow and inspected the horse for wounds. Arrow was untouched except for a ball that had cut off a lock of mane just in front of the saddle. While the frustrated soldiers looked on, Red Eagle wrung the water from his blanket, resaddled his horse, and, coolly sending back a signal of defiance to Claiborne and his men, rode away.[58]

Thomas S. Woodward, however, who knew Weatherford personally, said that Red Eagle told him he never jumped off the bluff. He told Woodward that his brother-in-law Sam Moniac, who acted as a guide for Claiborne, had recognized him as he appeared on the bluff mounted on Arrow. When he and the horse disappeared suddenly, they assumed he had leaped over the bluff. Weatherford told Woodward that he did not make the leap for fear his horse would be injured, preferring instead to chance a dash down the ravine between the enemy's line, which was more hazardous for himself but safer for Arrow. He told Woodward that after the erroneous report became widely circulated, he "would often own to it for the gratification of some, as they wanted to be deceived anyhow." Halbert and Ball have disputed Woodward's account on the grounds that their study of the topography of the battle site and the deployment of the American troops made an escape in such a ravine impossible. They also quote the manuscript notes of the Reverend John Brown of Mississippi, who in his youth heard James Bankston of Cassel's cavalry tell essentially the same story of the celebrated leap that J. D. Driesback, one of Red

Eagle's relatives, had told. Sam Dale, who was present at the Battle of Holy Ground, recounts the story in great detail, confirming the account by Driesback. The source closest to Weatherford, the narrative written by his brother-in-law George Stiggins, recounts the famous leap at length. He wrote that the bluff from which Weatherford's horse jumped was "between fifty and sixty feet high" and that a neighbor, a Scots-Indian named McPherson, made the same leap immediately after Red Eagle. Both horses and both riders survived. Weatherford's feat has been romanticized and has assumed unrealistic proportions through the accretions of folklore, but it is the consensus that some sort of escape leap occurred, and Woodward's reminiscence, long after the event, is the only dissenting voice among those with contemporary knowledge of the Battle of Holy Ground. Contributing to the longevity of the legend is a bluff at the site of the Holy Ground town, which is more than eight feet high and is still pointed out as the spot from which Red Eagle and Arrow made the prodigious leap.[59]

Most of the fighting at the Holy Ground had been done by Colonel Carson's troops, and when the other columns arrived on the scene, the battle was over. If Major Cassel's detachment had been able to reach its appointed place on the lower side of the town, many more of the Red Sticks would have been captured or killed. Claiborne's count of the slain included twenty-one Indians and twelve black slaves, and no wounded were captured. Only one man from Claiborne's troops, Ensign James Luckett, was killed, and twenty were wounded. This small casualty list was attributed more to the Red Sticks' scarcity of ammunition than to their lack of courage. Claiborne gave all the rights of pillage to Pushmataha and his Choctaw braves, and they sacked the town thoroughly, coming away with clothing, blankets, and silver ornaments; many of the articles were said to have been taken by the Red Sticks at Fort Mims. The Choctaws scalped all the dead, including the blacks, but the latter scalps, it is said, they cast disdainfully aside as trophies unfit for an Indian warrior. Holy Ground, incidentally, is said to be the only battle of the Creek War in which black slaves bore arms for their red owners. In the center of the public square Claiborne's soldiers cut down a tall pine pole, which contained several hundred scalps that were believed to have been taken at Fort Mims. Some of the scalps were from infants and some from gray-haired victims, filling the soldiers, as one account states, "with emotions of horror and revenge." When the Choctaws had completed their pillaging, Claiborne ordered the town burned.[60]

On the morning of Christmas Eve, Claiborne dispatched Major Cassel and some of the cavalry, including Sam Dale, up the river to a home owned by a settler named Ward, and on the way they killed three Shawnees who were retreating from the Holy Ground. Dale stated that he recognized all three as having been at Tuckabatchee with Tecumseh. They had remained in the Creek Nation to inflame the Red Sticks and incite them to war, Dale claimed. On a cold Christmas Eve, Claiborne and his men lay shivering during the night in an ironic location, a cornfield that belonged to William Weatherford and had been owned by his father before him. Christmas dinner for officers and men consisted of boiled acorns and parched corn; General Claiborne ordered the small supply of flour and spirits to be distributed to the sick. During the four days of the return march in wintry weather, parched corn, captured at the Holy Ground, was the only available food. The contracting system had once again failed to get supplies to the troops. On January 14, when he made his report to the secretary of war, Claiborne explained that he and his men wanted to go after McQueen when the battle at the Holy Ground was over but could not because they were "destitute of supplies."[61]

Only about sixty volunteers remained on January 14; the others' terms of service had expired. "My volunteers are returning to their homes," Claiborne wrote to the secretary, "with eight months pay due them and almost literally *naked*. They have served the last three months of an inclement winter, *without shoes or blankets*, and almost without shirts, but are still devoted to their country, and properly impressed with the justices and the necessities of the war." Dale believed the foray into the Holy Ground had been worth the cost. He said: "The moral effect of this bold movement into the heart of the nation, upon ground held sacred and impregnable, was great. It taught the savages that they were neither inaccessible nor invulnerable; it destroyed their confidence in their prophets, and it proved what volunteers, even without shoes, clothing, blankets, or provisions would do for their country."[62] When the good news of the victory reached Fort St. Stephens, the fort was illuminated, and cheers rose up for Claiborne and his men "at the front gate, at the rear gate, and at the grand parade, with appropriate music—an air named by Captain Davis, 'Claiborne's Victory.'"[63] The cheers and general acclamation were well justified, for the Battle of the Holy Ground, for all practical purposes, ended the military career of the Red Sticks in the part of the Mississippi Territory that is now South Alabama.

10

The Demise of the Red Sticks: Horseshoe Bend and Weatherford's Surrender

—————— · ——————

After the Battle of Autossee in late November, General Floyd and his Georgia militia camped for more than six weeks along the Chattahoochee in the vicinity of Coweta. An outbreak of illness had temporarily felled Floyd and 200 of his men, but by Janaury 17 the general was fully recovered, and his force of 1,227 militia and 400 friendly Indians set off toward Tuckabatchee. Arriving at Fort Hull on the twentieth and finding it in need of extensive repairs, Floyd worked his men hard for four days and left the fort on the twenty-fifth, "in good state and fit for defense against any enemy that might be expected to assault it." They marched only three miles in the direction of Tuckabatchee on the twenty-fifth, and just before they made camp, James A. Tait and some others of the enlisted men were convinced by the movement of their leaders that a battle was imminent. "When the line was formed," Tait wrote, "our front had fallen upon a swamp; here we fully expected to hear the rifles of the Red Clubs." The Indians under William McIntosh, now Major McIntosh, began burning lightwood stumps and blackening their faces in anticipation of a battle, but none came. "As it turned out," Tait wrote, "we were all agreeably disappointed; it was all show." On the twenty-sixth the army struck up the line of march early, and when they had marched less than three miles Floyd decided to send back the supply wagons, which were slowing the progress of the march. The army accompanied the wagons for about half a mile and then camped for the night on some high lands bordering a swamp near Calabee Creek.[1]

133

Floyd's army had not marched unnoticed; a Creek scout reported to Paddy Walsh that a large army of Georgians, with cannon in their train, had been observed approaching. Walsh sent runners to summon Weatherford, High-Headed Jim, and a mixed-blood kinsman of Weatherford's named McGillivray to join him in a meeting to plan strategy for the coming battle. He also issued a hurried call for all available warriors to come stripped, painted red, and prepared to fight, and 1,274 fighting men quickly assembled. Walsh told the warriors that the Americans must be dislodged from their position before they became too strong. At about sunset the Red Stick force was marched up to the west side of Calabee Creek, about a mile from the American camp. There an argument ensued concerning the best plan of attack. Paddy Walsh thought that the full force should attack two squares of the camp at about the time Floyd's men were retiring for the night. Walsh wanted the fighting to continue until daylight if the attack met with success but to break off and retreat if the enemy regrouped and began equalizing the engagement. Only High-Headed Jim agreed with this plan.[2]

Weatherford and McGillivray strongly opposed Walsh's tactic; Weatherford proclaimed that a man could not fight hard if limits were placed on him and he was told to run off at the first sign of enemy strength. Weatherford offered a different plan. He knew something of the white man's fashion of camping and said that all the officers would take their place in the center of the square of camps. He recommended that Paddy Walsh take three hundred men, or more if he thought fit, and slyly approach one of the squares, tomahawks in hand. Then they would raise a scream and tomahawk their way through the square to the officers, whom they would kill with knives and tomahawks. After this, the warriors would fight their way out through the same opening by which they had entered. They would be aided by a feinting attack on two other squares, creating confusion. Weatherford stated that it was the manner of white people to fight only as directed by their officers, and with their leaders gone, the common soldiers would be helpless. Walsh and High-Headed Jim shouted down Weatherford's plan, saying it was insane and desperate and would certainly result in the unnecessary sacrifice of three hundred men. They accused Weatherford and McGillivray of trying to get Walsh killed and said that neither of them would do the dangerous job Walsh was being asked to do. Both Weatherford and McGillivray leaped to their feet and offered to lead the three hundred men into the enemy camp, but when a call for volunteers was made, the warriors fearing the power of Walsh's words, only a few agreed to join Weatherford in the special force. Weatherford believed he had been publicly insulted, and he announced to Walsh that he was going home, leaving him to "fight his cautious half fights."[3]

Woodward claimed that Weatherford told him a different version of the strategy he recommended to Walsh. He said that Weatherford was well aware of the short supply of ammunition available to the Red Stick forces, and he believed it would be folly to attack the whites in their camp because they had five cannon and a good supply of ammunition. He proposed that the Red Sticks wait until the army started to cross the creek and, as the advance guard reached the hill on the other side, attack the Georgians from all sides. According to Woodward, Weatherford believed they would be able to capture ammunition even if they did not defeat the whites. But because the chiefs overruled Weatherford, he quit the camp with a few Tuskegees and started home. When he reached Polecat Springs, Weatherford heard the firing commence. Woodward wrote, "It is my belief that had Weatherford's advice been taken, the result of that affair would have been very different; for long before the fight closed, I could understand Indian enough to hear them asking each other to 'give me some bullets—give me some powder.'" He said that many of the Red Sticks had no guns, only war clubs and bows and arrows.[4]

At about twenty minutes past five o'clock, Walsh and the Red Sticks began the attack, running out of the nearby swamp where they had been hiding. In the confusion caused by this furious assault in darkness, Floyd was heard rallying his troops in a loud voice: "Cheer up boys, we will give them hell when daylight comes." The front flanks of the Georgia militia bore the brunt of the attack, and only steady artillery fire held the front line. The enemy rushed to within thirty yards of the cannon, causing considerable casualties among the artillery company. One small detachment under Captain John Broadnax had been assigned as picket guards, but a party of hostile Indians cut off their retreat to the main army. A squad of friendly Uchee Indians, commanded by a mixed-blood, Major Timpoochee Barnard, assisted the Georgians in cutting a path to safety through the Red Stick lines.[5]

General Floyd also proved to be correct when he shouted that his soldiers would give the Red Sticks hell when daylight came. At first light, Floyd ordered his infantry to charge but held the cavalry in reserve in the center. The Red Sticks retreated before the bayonet, and the cavalry rode in and turned the retreat into a rout. Then the

Timpoochee Barnard, by Charles Bird King (from McKenney and Hall, *History of the Indian Tribes*)

friendly Indians joined the rifle companies in pursuing the Red Sticks through Calabee Swamp. Although Stiggins estimated the Red Stick losses at about 40, Floyd judged them to be about 50, based on the number of headdresses and war clubs found scattered among the debris of battle.[6] The American losses were 17 killed and 132 wounded in what was the costliest victory of the Creek War to that date. In addition, 5 friendly Indians were killed and 15 wounded.[7] Tait gave a grisly account of the atrocities committed by the friendly Indians on the corpses of the slain Red Sticks on the morning after the battle. "They ripped them open," he wrote in his journal, "cut their heads to pieces, took out the heart of one, which was borne along in savage triumph by the perpetrators; and strange to tell, cut off the private parts of others. What bestial conduct." They also repeatedly hoisted one Red Stick corpse upon a dead horse, and as he stiffly tumbled off, laughed and shouted, "Whiskey too much."[8]

The Calabee Creek battle left High-Headed Jim dead and Paddy Walsh badly wounded. According to George Stiggins, the defeat at Calabee was devastating to the Red Sticks: "It closed the hostile operations of the Lower Towns . . . it silenced the old and new war dance and whoop of many of the most conspicuous warriors." He wrote that "none of the Lower Towns chiefs ever entered the battlefield after the Calabee affair." This comment seems curious in light of the analysis of Indian factions in the Creek War by Ross Hassig, who states that "the Lower Creeks did not fight against the Americans at all." The answer to this apparent contradiction seems to be that although Hassig found no lower towns among the hostile faction, individual Lower Creeks were on the Red Stick side. Hawkins had written to General Armstrong on July 13, 1813: "The fanatical fright seems to subside a little among the Lower Creeks, and all of them, apparently, are again friendly."[9]

Stiggins believed that Paddy Walsh was a key figure in weakening the Red Stick will. This mixed-blood leader, whom Stiggins described as about five feet two or three inches in height, with a wide mouth that made him look "most inhumanly ugly," was a gifted Indian linguist, speaking the Creek, Alabama, Chickasaw, and Choctaw languages and dialects fluently. Stiggins wrote that Walsh was "a great natural orator, both persuasive and commanding," and that his reasoning was so deep and his eloquence so profound that "no Indians would or could withstand him on any point that he pretended to uphold." Walsh was also widely known for his bravery, and there was no suspicion of cowardice when he told his fellow Alabamas after the defeat at Calabee that "the Indians were unable to fight the white people with any success" and "it was his studied opinion that they had better go to Pensacola and be out of the way of harm until the nation could effect a peace."[10]

This was to be the last battle of the Creek War for Floyd and his Georgia militia. They remained on the Calabee battleground for six days in an entrenched camp, then moved down to Fort Hull on

February 1. They left there for Georgia on February 16, reached the Ocmulgee River on the twenty-sixth, and continued by boat to Milledgeville, the Georgia capital, where Tait's regiment was discharged on March 7 and the other regiment on March 15. At the close of the war, Floyd was in Savannah setting up a defense against a possible British attack. Although the Red Stick war was over for the Georgia militia, Major McIntosh's military career was just beginning, and he was soon to attract the favorable attention of General Andrew Jackson. Although for Floyd and his men the Creek War had been limited to two brief battles, the general remembered the war with fond nostalgia a quarter-century later when he included in his will the item: "To my driver, Ansel, for his faithful service and fidelity during the late war, I give from the proceeds of my estate an extra suit of cheap broadcloth, a hat and a pair of shoes and ten dollars per annum (and his provisions so long as he lives)."[11]

The fighting now shifted to other fronts. On the night of January 21, 1814, Jackson and his motley army camped at Emuckfau Creek. They were now seventy miles from Fort Strother and, although Jackson did not know it, only three miles from the Red Sticks' major fortification at Tohopeka, or Horseshoe Bend. There were fresh trails to be seen, most converging to a point, convincing the general that he was near his enemy. He sent out scouts to make a reconnaissance in the direction of Horseshoe Bend and posted his pickets and sentinels to protect against a surprise attack. The scouts returned about midnight with the news that there was a large encampment of Red Sticks only three miles away at Tohopeka. From the whooping and dancing of the enemy, the scouts surmised that they were already aware of the presence of Jackson's troops in the area.[12] It is extremely unlikely that Weatherford was present at the Battle of Emuckfau Creek, despite the account written in 1893 and based on interviews with old soldiers and Weatherford family members that placed him there. Contemporaneous British records indicate that Peter McQueen and Josiah Francis were the leaders of the Red Sticks who opposed Jackson on January 22, 1814.[13]

Old Hickory believed that he was ready for any attack the Red Sticks might mount, and if no attack came, he was prepared to take the offensive himself. The latter course proved not to be necessary, for just before dawn the signal guns of the sentinels broke the silence, immediately followed by the battle cries of an advancing Red Stick army. Though inexperienced, Jackson's men stood their ground valiantly. Having stood by their guns throughout the night, they were not taken by surprise, and by firing countershots at the flashes from the enemy rifles, they were able to hold off the Red Sticks until daylight. Jackson had placed campfires at strategic points outside the encampment, and his riflemen, concealed in darkness, were able to shoot with great accuracy at the invading light-outlined shadows that moved across their fields of vision. The Red Sticks first attacked the left flank, commanded by Colonel Higgins, and the untried militiamen stood firm. General Coffee, along with Colonel William Carroll and Colonel James Sitler, rushed to aid Higgins at the first sounds of battle. At daybreak Jackson ordered Captain Ferril's company to reinforce the left wing, which charged under General Coffee's command, routing the Red Sticks.[14]

The friendly Indians then pursued the fleeing enemy for about two miles, inflicting considerable losses. At this point in the battle Jackson's casualties were five dead and twenty wounded, but no accurate estimate of enemy dead and wounded was possible. When the friendly Indians returned from their pursuit, General Jackson ordered them to accompany General Coffee and his four hundred militiamen to reconnoiter Tohopeka and destroy the enemy encampment if possible. Finding it too well fortified to risk attack with his small detachment, Coffee returned to camp. In less than half an hour, just as Coffee's men had begun to rest from their march, the Red Sticks attacked again, this time on the right flank. Coffee received Jackson's permission to move his detachment against the enemy's left flank and, at the head of his troops, moved them briskly forward. He was unaware that the militia in the rear had begun dropping off one by one, leaving him with fewer than fifty men. The enemy occupied a pine-forested ridge, with enough low underbrush to conceal them. The horses were useless in this terrain, and despite this tactical disadvantage and his being outnumbered, Coffee ordered his men to dismount and charge.[15]

Almost immediately Coffee sustained a wound in his right side. It was not a mortal injury, but a few minutes later Coffee's brother-in-law (and Jackson's nephew), Alexander Donelson, was fatally shot through the head.[16] Three others of Coffee's men were killed, but the enemy was driven back by the charge to take refuge on the edge of Emuckfau Creek and conceal themselves in the reeds. It soon became evident that the attack on the right flank had been a feint; the Red Sticks made their true purpose known by sending the main force against the left flank, which they hoped to find in disorder. General Jackson had anticipated this strategy, however, and had ordered his left flank to remain firm in its position even if the right flank should show a weakness and seem to require reinforcement. When gunfire was heard on the left flank, Old Hickory rushed to the scene and ordered additional men to strengthen the position. The Red Sticks, gliding from tree to tree, dropping suddenly to the ground behind logs, reloading, and arising again to fire, made elusive targets. Jackson ordered a charge, and the entire line, led by Colonel William Carroll, moved forward briskly and sent the enemy into a confused rout. In the pursuit, many Red Sticks were overtaken and killed, but reports of the battle give no specific number of enemy casualties.[17]

On the right flank, General Coffee, though wounded, continued to attempt to drive the enemy out of the reeds. Realizing that he could not dislodge them from their position without sustaining great losses, he feigned a retreat. The Red Sticks took the bait and left their hiding places to advance quickly toward Coffee and his men, who suddenly turned and began firing. Now on more equal terms, the two armies continued to battle for about an hour, with Coffee's detachment suffering further casualties and becoming increasingly fatigued. But when friendly Indian reinforcements appeared, Coffee immediately ordered a charge, and the enemy, seeing that they were outnumbered, retreated in disorder.[18]

Jackson's troops had been through a day of prolonged battle, and as night began to fall they barely had time to complete the tasks of burying the dead, caring for the wounded, and preparing to guard against a night attack. Jackson ordered trees to be cut so that a breastwork of logs could be placed around the encampment. The green troops, now aware that fighting Indians was dangerous business, had less of their hearty prebattle spirit. During the night it was difficult to keep sentinels at the outposts; at any suspicious sound they would fire a signal shot and run into the encampment. Enemy scouts were in the area all night, but for some reason the Red Sticks chose not to attack. The threat was ever-present, however, and with difficulties mounting, Jackson contemplated returning his troops to Fort Strother. He knew he was unprepared to set up a permanent fortification so near to Horseshoe Bend; his supplies were low, and some of his critically wounded men needed more care than could be provided in the wilderness. He concluded that two tactical advantages could be gained by retiring toward Fort Strother. First, the Red Sticks might consider his movement a retreat and pursue the columns, allowing his troops to counterattack. Second, if the Red Sticks were drawn toward Fort Strother, they would be diverted from General Floyd's expedition.[19]

Jackson ordered litters to be constructed for the sick and wounded, and about ten o'clock the following morning the return march began. It was nearly nightfall before they halted to make camp a quarter of a mile south of Enotachopco Creek. Jackson was aware that the Red Sticks had been pursuing his columns all day, and he ordered log breastworks to be thrown up for defense. Well into the night, when no attack was forthcoming, Jackson concluded that the Red Sticks must be planning to ambush his troops as they forded the creek that lay ahead. He remembered from the outward crossing that near the fording place was a deep ravine, overgrown with underbrush and sedge, which could conceal a large number of enemy warriors. Jackson decided to take a different route from the one the Red Sticks expected. Early the next morning, he covertly sent out scouts, who were able to locate another crossing place about six hundred yards from the one previously used. Jackson then formed his columns with front and rear guards and moved out toward the new fording place.[20]

All went well at first; the guards at the front of the column, as well as the wounded and a part of the front columns, passed through the shallow creek without incident. But just as the artillery had entered the water, an alarm gun was fired. The Red Sticks, discovering that Jackson had outfoxed them, attacked the rear company, which acquitted itself well against superior numbers and gradually retired to join the rear guard. Jackson had previously ordered the rear guard to turn about if attacked and lead the advance charge. The strategy at this point called for the right and left columns to turn and encircle the enemy in a loop, the favorite maneuver employed from the beginning of the Creek War. Jackson was in midstream when the alarm was sounded, and after giving orders for the left column to turn toward the enemy, he rode hard toward the right to rally that column to close with the advancing Red Sticks.[21]

When he reached the right column, Old Hickory was amazed to see both columns unaccountably giving way in panic without firing a shot. They withdrew into the creek, obstructing and confusing any attempt by the rest of the troops to reinforce the front line. One of the officers, Colonel Stump, had scurried fearfully down the bank at the head of his panicked company of soldiers, and Old Hickory was so angered at this dereliction of duty by one of his officers that he tried unsuccessfully to overtake him and cut him down with his sword. The center quickly followed the example of the flanks and gave ground, leaving fewer than twenty men to oppose the Red Sticks' attack. The artillery company, commanded by Lieutenant John Armstrong, hastily dragged its only cannon out of the water and up an adjoining rise of ground. The Red Sticks attacked the position immediately, but the soldiers formed a cordon around the ordnance and defended it with their muskets and bodies. The men fired the six-pounder by using the butt of a musket as a rammer and a musket ramrod to pick the flint. Counting the artillery company, the scouts, and the men remaining with Colonel Carroll at the edge of the creek, one hundred of Jackson's men checked the advance of a foe five times more numerous. When Lieutenant Armstrong fell, wounded in the groin, he told his men, "Some of you will perish, but don't lose the gun."[22]

Jackson and his staff managed to restore a measure of order, and the columns were regrouped and ordered to advance. At this point the Red Sticks, who had been unable to dislodge the smaller fighting force, fled before the increased numbers, leaving behind blankets and other objects that would have slowed their retreat. Again Indian allies were among those detached to pursue the retreating army. In the two-mile chase the enemy army was dispersed and many warriors killed. One of the heroes in turning the tide of battle had been General Coffee, who, because of his wound in the Emuckfau battle, had been carried on a litter the previous day. On the morning of the Enotachopco attack, however, he had mounted his horse in anticipation of a fight, and when it came he met it with "his usual calm and deliberate firmness," according to a firsthand account. Even the hospital surgeon, Dr. Shelby, performed infantry duties courageously in the battle, and Colonel James Sitler, the adjutant-general, rushed across the creek to aid the artillery company, to which he had once been attached.[23]

Old Hickory, of course, was one of the prime movers in rallying the demoralized troops. Major John Reid, Jackson's military secretary, was an active participant in the battle, and he waxed poetic in his description of the general's leadership under fire: "On him all hopes were rested. In that moment of confusion he was the rallying point, even for the spirits of the brave. Cowards forgot their panic and fronted danger when they heard his voice and beheld his manner, and the brave would have formed round his body a rampart with their own." Jackson's charisma saved the day for an army that could have been decimated if its disorder had continued; as it was, Jackson's casualties at the battles of Emuckfau and Enotachopco were 20 killed and 75 wounded. There were 189 bodies of Red Stick warriors found, but this was thought to be less than the total number slain. Red Stick prisoners captured later confirmed that more than 200 of those who went out to battle never returned to Horseshoe Bend.[24]

The enemy made no further attempt to attack Jackson's men on their return march, and on January 26 the troops camped near Fort Strother. The dangerous expedition that had carried them within three miles of the Red Sticks' strongest fortification at Horseshoe Bend was over. The mission had resulted in the immediate benefits Jackson had sought: Fort Armstrong had been relieved, and the diversion had drawn much of the enemy's strength away from General Floyd's path. The skirmishes at Emuckfau and Enotachopco, however, could not be considered unqualified victories or demonstrations of superior military tactics on the part of Jackson's army. Only Jackson's charisma had enabled him to avoid the total annihilation of his forces. Nevertheless, the Red Sticks had been ultimately routed in both battles, and these setbacks seem to have led Weatherford to become less aggressive and to withdraw into the fortress at Horseshoe Bend, setting the stage for a decisive battle later.

Jackson's expedition deep into enemy territory had also proved to be valuable reconnaissance of a route to be used to advantage in later campaigns. Entirely unexpected, however, was the upsurge in voluntary enlistments in Tennessee. Many young men, hearing reports of Jackson's raid into hostile territory, clamored to join Old Hickory's forces and be present in the final glorious days of the defeat of the Red Sticks. After his battered troops returned to Fort Strother, Jackson ordered the sixty-day volunteers to march to Huntsville for honorable discharge. But a much larger army was on its way. Early in February Jackson learned that two thousand militiamen from East Tennessee had been recruited, along with a like number in Middle Tennessee. On the sixth of that month Colonel John Williams marched into Fort Strother with his Thirty-ninth regiment of U.S. Infantry, six hundred strong.[25] Williams, who had led a force of mounted volunteers in a victorious campaign against the Seminoles, was a welcome sight. In 1823 Jackson was to defeat Williams in his bid for reelection to the U.S. Senate in a bitter campaign, but in 1814, on the eve of the battle at Horseshoe Bend, they were close comrades in arms.

While awaiting the buildup of his army, Jackson kept his temporary militia busy constructing flatboats for transporting stores down the Coosa River to support his troops, and he ordered the quartermasters and food contractors to gather sufficient provisions for the campaign.[26] Equally as important as logistics, however, was the need to control the troops. Old Hickory, shaken by the breakdown of discipline in the panic at the Battle of Enotachopco, was determined this time to build a totally obedient, efficient fighting force, with the Thirty-ninth Regiment regulars as the nucleus. No more oratory and rhetoric would be needed to convince summer soldiers to do their duty, no more pleading to keep them at their posts when they wanted to go home. They would obey orders or suffer the supreme penalty for not doing so.

On March 14 Jackson ordered the commencement of the march toward Horseshoe Bend. He was confident that with his iron will in command of a disciplined fighting force, the Red Sticks in their stronghold in the bend of the Tallapoosa River were, to use Jackson's phrase, "penned for slaughter."[27] On the morning of the twenty-first, the army reached the mouth of Cedar Creek, fifty-nine miles below Fort Strother, where he established Fort Williams, named in honor of the commander of the Thirty-ninth Regiment. Here a delay ensued. Because of dry weather, the flatboats, loaded with provisions, were hung on the shoals a mile and a half above the fort site. Learning from the Indians that the stream was even more difficult to navigate farther down, Jackson ordered the stores transferred from flatboats to pirogues.[28]

Before leaving Fort Williams on March 24, Jackson delivered a stirring address to his troops, reminding them first of their glorious opportunity for "avenging the cruelties committed upon our defenseless fellow citizens by the infuriated Creeks" and second that "our borders must no longer be disturbed by the warwhoop of the ruthless savage or the cries of the suffering victims." Much of the address dealt with the importance of discipline. He said, "Your general well knows that the valor of his troops when they are reduced to a proper state of discipline and obedience to orders, never will stoop to disgrace itself by a shameful flight before a savage enemy, when led on by valiant officers." To ensure the validity of this statement, Old Hickory ended his speech with a strongly worded regulation: "Any officer or soldier who flies before the enemy without being compelled to do so by superior force and actual necessity—shall suffer death."[29]

On the morning of the twenty-fourth, Jackson left a detachment to protect Fort Williams and set out, with only eight days' provisions, toward Horseshoe Bend, by way of Emuckfau. The distance between the Coosa and Tallapoosa rivers was fifty-two miles over a terrain of ridges and hollows. Having left strong garrisons at forts along the way, Jackson now had an effective fighting force of nearly three thousand men. On the twenty-sixth he camped six miles from the village of Tohopeka, or Horseshoe Bend. The Red Sticks were well aware of the approach of Jackson's army, and warriors from nearby towns, Ocfuskee, Oakchaya, New Youcka, Hillabee, the Fish Ponds, and Eufaula, had gathered in a force of about a thousand warriors—along with nearly three hundred women and children—in the well-protected loop of the Tallapoosa River. As Jackson described it, "Nature furnishes few situations so eligible for defense; and barbarians have never rendered one more secure by art." The village of Tohopeka was surrounded almost entirely by the river and could be reached only by a narrow neck of land about four hundred yards wide. The Red Sticks had thrown up a huge breastwork of felled timber, five to eight feet high, to cut off the peninsula. A double row of portholes in the breastworks was artfully arranged to give the defenders complete direction to their fire. Jackson wrote that "an army could not approach it without being exposed to a double and a cross fire from the enemy who lay in perfect security behind it."[30]

At 6:30 on the morning of the battle, Jackson deployed General Coffee, seven hundred cavalry and mounted gunmen, and six hundred Indians (five hundred Cherokees and the rest friendly Creeks, led by Major William McIntosh) to cross the river at a little island ford three miles below the bend. They moved into a position across the river from Tohopeka, where they could prevent the Red Sticks from escaping by crossing the river.[31] Jackson moved the remainder of his forces to a position in front of the breastworks, with his artillery—one sixpounder and one three-pounder—set up to his right on a small hill. The artillery pieces were about 80 yards from the near end of the breastworks and 250 yards from the far end. At 10:30 A.M. he opened fire, but the artillery was virtually useless against the heavy log structure, some of the balls whistling through "the works without striking the wall" and others striking noisily but harmlessly against the big timbers.[32] Heavy musket and rifle fire was directed at any Red Stick who showed himself above the breastworks in an attempt to fire at the gun crews. For two hours, with occasional intermissions of silence, punctuated by the derisive yells of the Red Sticks, the firing continued. Red Stick medicine men, shoulders and heads decorated with feathers, danced and shouted incantations to the sun, calling down death and lamentation to the invaders and encouraging the defenders to believe that they were invincible on this sacred ground.[33]

At this point in the battle some of the friendly Indians, apparently on their own initiative, swam across the river and brought back from

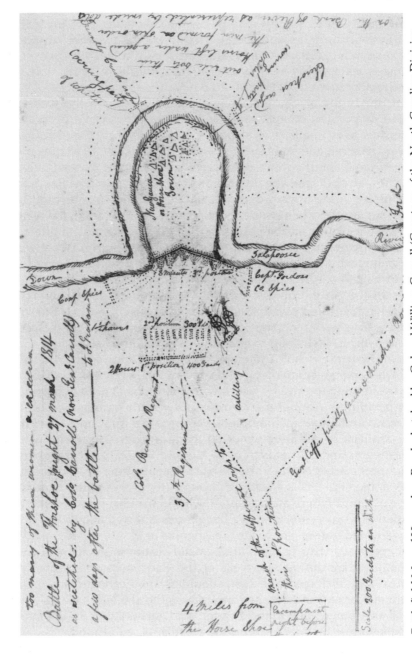

Battlefield Map of Horseshoe Bend, sketched by Colonel William Carroll (Courtesy of the North Carolina Division of Archives and History)

the opposite shore a number of enemy canoes. While their commander, Colonel Gideon Morgan, rode to inform Major Lemuel Montgomery, who commanded the left flank of the Thirty-ninth Regiment, that canoes were available for a crossing, about two hundred of the friendly Indians, probably led by Major McIntosh, had already crossed and were hotly engaged in battle.[34] Colonel Morgan, Major John Walker, and thirty soldiers then crossed to join the fighting and move to the high ground, where the friendly Indians were stubbornly holding against the enemy. Strengthened by these reinforcements, the Indians and Captain Russell's company of scouts began pushing forward toward the defended side of the breastworks, setting fire to huts as they went. Morgan was almost immediately wounded in his right temple, leaving him unconscious until the battle was over, but the detachment continued to move forward until the men were in position to fire at the Red Sticks behind the barricade.[35]

Although Morgan's force was too small to dislodge the enemy from behind the breastworks, its gallant advance provided Jackson with the diversion he needed, and he immediately gave the order to charge. Jackson later wrote: "Never were men more eager to be led to a charge than both regulars and militia. They had been waiting with impatience to receive the order, and hailed it with acclamation." The Thirty-ninth Regiment regulars, led by Colonel Williams and Major Montgomery, as well as the militia under Colonel Bunch, moved forward briskly, ignoring the Red Stick bullets and arrows. They were soon at the barricade, and then ensued what Jackson called "a very obstinate contest, muzzle to muzzle, through the portholes, in which many of the enemy's balls were welded to the bayonets of our muskets."[36] Major Montgomery leaped onto the barricade, scrambled to the top, and called to his men to follow him. Just as he spoke, a bullet struck him in the head and he fell to the ground dead. Others followed on the ramparts, and the Red Sticks fell back in confusion, concealing themselves in the brush and timber.[37]

The concealed enemy kept up a constant fire until Jackson's men mounted a charge and forced them further back toward Coffee's waiting troops. At this point Jackson, now certain that the enemy's further resistance would lead only to their complete destruction, sent a small party, with an interpreter, to propose a surrender. Instead of accepting the terms and surrendering, the Red Sticks fired at and wounded one of the group. They then retreated further into the heavily timbered area, and when thunderous artillery shelling failed to dislodge them, Jackson ordered lighted torches thrown from the hilltop down into the woods. The resulting forest fires drove the Red Sticks from their hiding places, and the carnage continued. Many of the panicked enemy leaped into the river, only to be riddled with bullets from Coffee's brigade.[38] At this point, as Jackson reported, "the event could no longer be doubtful."[39] But many of the Red Sticks continued to fight in a frenzy of desperation. Sam Houston described the scene vividly: "Arrows and spears and balls were flying; swords and tomahawks were gleaming in the sun; and the whole peninsula rang with the yell of savages and the groans of the dying." Houston, who was a young ensign, barely turned twenty-one, suffered a deep puncture wound in the thigh with a barbed arrow as he stormed the barricade, and later that day he was twice struck in the shoulder with rifle balls.[40] Although his wounds were not of the type that are normally mortal, in the wilderness setting of the Creek War, with primitive medical care, they were almost fatal to the heroic young Tennessean. A great warrior-chieftain on the Red Stick side also survived terrible wounds at the Battle of Horseshoe Bend. Menawa, who had been pierced by seven rifle balls, lay unconscious among a heap of dead Red Sticks during the entire afternoon. When he revived after dark, he found his way to the river's edge and escaped in a canoe.[41] Carrying the scars of the battle for the rest of his days, Menawa was later to reenter Creek history as the final adversary of William McIntosh.

Jackson ordered a careful count of the dead following the battle, and, to ensure an accurate tally, his officers had the men cut off and collect the tips of the dead warriors' noses.[42] There were 557 enemy bodies found on the battleground, reported the "officers of great respectability" who counted them, and an estimated 250 to 300 Red Sticks were either killed in the river as they tried to escape or were thrown in by their fellow warriors.[43] Among the dead were found three Red Stick prophets, or medicine men, the most famous of whom was Monahoee, who had been shot in the mouth by a grape shot, "as if," Jackson commented, "Heaven designed to chastise his impostures by an appropriate punishment." Jackson reported to Governor Blount: "I lament that two or three women and children were killed by accident. I do not know the exact number of prisoners taken; but it must exceed three hundred, all women and children except for three or four."[44] The Red Stick warriors chose to fight to the death in their peninsula redoubt, which had become a slaughter pen. Some of the captured women and children were escorted by Major McIntosh to Big Warrior, the principal Creek chief, for whatever purpose he might have. Casualties among Jackson's white sholders were 26 killed and 107 wounded, among the Cherokees 18 killed and 11 wounded, and among the friendly Creeks 5 killed and 11 wounded. The friendly Indians suffered by far the largest number of casualties in proportion to their numbers. The Thirty-ninth Regiment, which led the charge against the breastworks, suffered 17 killed and 55 wounded. Frank Owsley, Jr., has explained that the reason the ratio of Indians killed in the battle was about ten to one, even though the Red Sticks held a fortified position, was not a lack of bravery on the part of the Indians or better training on the part of the whites but the whites' superiority in armament, leadership, and numbers. Probably no more than one-third or one-fourth of the Red Sticks had a gun, however inferior; they fought with war clubs, bows and arrows, and spears against soldiers well armed with rifles and cannon. Owsley stated that "with the exception of Weatherford and a few others" the Creek war chiefs "had no conception of military objectives and were unable to give any direction to their war." They were nearly always on the defensive and were successful only in the few times they took the initiative and had objectives. The Americans nearly always had two or three times more men than the Red Sticks.[45]

Jackson ordered that his dead soldiers be weighted and sunk in the river to prevent their being exhumed from a conventional grave and scalped. The general was convinced that many of his men, killed in previous battles with the Creeks, had later been dug up, stripped, and scalped, and it was reported that many of the dead Red Sticks at Tohopeka were found wearing the clothes of soldiers who had been killed and buried at Emuckfau. Major Reid wrote: "It is true that this could operate no injury to the dead; yet it was wished to be prevented for the future." When the grim task of sinking the corpses was accomplished, Jackson gathered the wounded and marched his army back to Fort Williams, ordering that all Indian villages they passed on the way be burned. "At my approach," Jackson wrote to his wife, "the Indians fled in all directions." Jackson was gloriously victorious in the Battle of Horseshoe Bend, one of the major engagements in the War of 1812. He had killed a large number of hostile Creeks and had crushed their will to make war just at the time the British were preparing to land troops in the South and provide guns and ammunition to their red allies. Had Jackson's decisive victory not come when it did, the Red Sticks could have presented an enormous danger to the southern half of the nation.[46] Despite his victory, however, Jackson was distressed at not having captured William Weatherford, the Red Stick leader at Fort Mims and a hated symbol to all frontiersmen.

After arriving at Fort Williams on April 1, Jackson composed a laudatory speech for his men and the next day delivered his colorful prose to the assembled soldiers: "The fiends of Tallapoosa will no longer murder our women and children, or disturb the quiet of our borders. Their midnight flambeaux will no more illumine their council-house, or shine upon the victim of their infernal orgies." But the task was not yet completed: "A collection of them await our approach and remain to be dispersed." Jackson understood that many Red Sticks were assembled at Hoithlewalee, an ancient Upper Creek town not far from the Hickory Ground.[47] Hoithlewalee was, in fact, the town to which William Weatherford had gone during the Battle of Horseshoe Bend, having for some reason left Tohopeka on March 25. He had apparently not believed that Jackson would attack at that particular time, and it was not until the day after the battle, as he rode toward Tohopeka, that he met some refugees from the defeat at Horseshoe Bend and learned the fate of his warriors.[48]

After giving his men a few days' rest, Jackson marched them out on April 7 in the direction of Hoithlewalee and the Hickory Ground. Along with his principal purpose of killing any remaining Red Sticks, Jackson wanted to effect a linking up of all the southern armies. The North Carolina troops, under General Joseph Graham, and the Central Army, commanded by Colonel Homer Milton, were somewhere south of the Tallapoosa and could not be too great a distance away. The joining of the three armies would prevent the Red Sticks from escaping southward to Pensacola and the Escambia. Jackson had intended to reach Hoithlewalee on April 11, but torrential rains and flood-swollen streams delayed him. On the thirteenth he reached the town of Fushatchee, about three miles below Hoithlewalee, and found it abandoned. He knew by now that the town had been abandoned on the eleventh, the day he had originally planned to attack it.[49]

The Creek War was in effect over, and General Thomas Pinckney, in a letter to Jackson on April 7, was already outlining the government's demands on the Red Sticks when they sued for peace: indemnity for the war by cessions of land, the delivering up of all prophets who were spreading Tecumseh's poisonous gospel, freedom for all U.S. citizens to use the roads and navigate streams through all parts of the territory, and a renunciation of all connections with the Spanish posts.[50] On the eighteenth Jackson moved on to the old Fort Toulouse, where Weatherford's French great-grandfather, Captain Marchand, had been killed by his mutinous troops. He renamed the rebuilt fort Fort Jackson and raised the American flag over it. Chiefs of

various hostile tribes arrived daily with flags of truce, offering to submit to any terms. To test them, Jackson asked the chiefs to show good
faith by capturing Weatherford and bringing him tied as a prisoner to
Fort Jackson, where he could be dealt with as deserved. It rankled Old
Hickory that the principal actor in the slaughter at Fort Mims was still
at large.[51] Red Eagle, however, had other plans; with his sense of high
style and drama, Weatherford had a surprise in store for Jackson.

When Weatherford learned from the other Upper Creek chiefs that
Jackson had demanded his capture, he decided to ride to Fort Jackson
alone and surrender himself, sparing his fellow chiefs the further humiliation of turning their leader over to the white victors. He mounted
the gray horse that had made possible his prodigious leap to freedom
at the Battle of the Holy Ground and rode swiftly toward Fort Jackson.
On his way, a fine deer crossed his path and stopped. Red Eagle killed
it with one shot, hoisted the animal across the rump of his horse, and
continued toward his confrontation with Old Hickory. At an outpost
he politely asked some soldiers for directions to Jackson's quarters,
and they gave him rude and unsatisfactory replies, but a gray-haired
civilian a few steps beyond them pointed the way. Jackson was just
leaving his quarters when Red Eagle rode up. "General Jackson?" he
inquired. Old Hickory looked up into the mild black eyes of the tall,
light-skinned Indian brave, bare to the waist, with buckskin breeches
and badly worn moccasins. "Yes," the astonished general replied. "I
am Bill Weatherford," said the Indian. Jackson fumed: "How dare you
show yourself at my tent after having murdered the women and children at Fort Mims!" "I had directed," the general continued, "that you
should be brought to me confined; had you appeared in this way, I
should have known how to treat you."[52]

They went into Jackson's tent, where the general's aide, young John
Reid, was seated. Reid wrote later in a private letter: "Weatherford was
the greatest of the barbarian world. He possessed all the manliness of
sentiment—all the heroism of soul, all the comprehension of intellect
calculated to make an able commander. . . . You have seen his speech
to Genl Jackson . . . but you could not see his looks & gestures—the
modesty & yet the firmness that were in them."[53] Replying to Jackson's comment that he did not know how to treat a free man who had
walked voluntarily into his camp, Weatherford, according to Reid,
said: "I am in your power—do with me as you please. I am a soldier. I
have done the white people all the harm I could; I have fought them,
and fought them bravely: if I had an army, I would yet fight, and

Weatherford Surrenders to Andrew Jackson (Courtesy of the Museum of the
City of Mobile)

contend to the last: but I have none; my people are all gone. I can do
no more than weep over the misfortunes of my nation."[54]

The Alabama historian Albert James Pickett wrote his account of
Weatherford's speech to Jackson on the evidence of early settlers who
had talked with Red Eagle and purported to quote him directly. In
that version Weatherford is said to have replied:

> General Jackson, I am not afraid of you. I fear no man, for I am a Creek
> warrior. I have nothing to request in behalf of myself; you can kill me if
> you desire. But I come to beg you to send for the women and children
> of the war party, who are now starving in the woods. Their fields and

cribs have been destroyed by your people, who have driven them to the woods without an ear of corn. I hope that you will send out parties, who will safely conduct them here, in order that they may be fed. I exerted myself in vain to prevent the massacre of the women and children at Fort Mims. I am now done fighting. The Red Sticks are nearly all killed. If I could fight you any longer, I would most heartily do so. Send for the women and children. They never did you any harm. But kill me, if the white people want it done.[55]

Reid reported that Jackson was pleased at Weatherford's firmness and told him he would not ask him to lay down his arms and become peaceable. "The terms on which your nation can be saved, and peace restored," Jackson said, "has already been disclosed: in this way, and none other, can you obtain safety." Old Hickory, never one to run from a battle, added that if Red Eagle wanted to continue the fight he was at liberty to leave and rejoin the war party. If later captured in those circumstances, however, he would pay for his crimes with his life. Jackson also offered Weatherford the option of remaining where he was, under the protection of the commanding general.[56]

Weatherford replied that he desired peace and he also wanted relief for the suffering and deprivation of his people. He continued:

But I may well be addressed in such language now. There was a time when I had a choice, and could have answered you: I have none now,— even hope has ended. Once I could animate my warriors to battle; but I cannot animate the dead. My warriors can no longer hear my voice: their bones are at Talladega, Tallushatchee, Emuckfaw, and Tohopeka. I have not surrendered myself thoughtlessly. Whilst there were chances of success, I never left my post, nor supplicated peace. But my people are gone, and I now ask it for my nation, and for myself. On the miseries and misfortunes brought upon my country, I look back with deepest sorrow, and wish to avert still greater calamities. If I had been left to contend with the Georgia army, I would have raised my corn on one bank of the river, and fought them on the other; but your people have destroyed my nation. You are a brave man: I rely upon your generosity. You will exact no terms of a conquered people, but such as they should accede to: whatever they may be, it would now be madness and folly to oppose. If they are opposed, you shall find me among the sternest enforcers of obedience. Those who would still hold out, can be influenced

only by a mean spirit of revenge; and to this they must not, and shall
not sacrifice the last remnant of their country. You have told us where
we might go, and be safe. This is a good talk, and my nation ought to
listen to it. They shall listen to it.[57]

According to Pickett's version, a number of soldiers surrounding
the entrance to Jackson's tent, some of whom had relatives and
friends who were massacred at Fort Mims, began shouting, "Kill him!
Kill him! Kill him!" Jackson commanded them to be silent, saying emphatically: "Any man who would kill as brave a man as this would rob
the dead!" Jackson then invited Weatherford to have a glass of brandy,
Red Eagle gave the deer to the general, and they sat down for a long
and pleasant conversation.[58] All was not serene, however, for not only
was there bad blood between Weatherford and the soldiers, but also a
great enmity was felt by the friendly Creeks. According to one historian, Big Warrior tried to kill Weatherford at Fort Jackson but was restrained by the general.[59] With Jackson's help, peace was negotiated
between Red Eagle and the Creek chiefs, and in a few days Weatherford set out from the camp with a small party to search for his followers and friends who were hidden deep in the woods. Red Eagle
attempted to persuade them to give up the battle and submit to Jackson, thereby avoiding further disasters for the Red Sticks.[60] After this
peace mission, Weatherford returned to his former home on Little
River near the site of Fort Mims, but because of the frightful memories
of the Fort Mims massacre, so strong was the feeling against him that
his life was in constant danger. He turned himself in to Colonel
Gilbert C. Russell at Fort Claiborne, where he was placed in a tent
near the marquee of the commanding officer and kept under the constant guard of a file of soldiers.

One of the guards assigned was James Cornells, who was bitter
toward Weatherford, whom he held responsible for the incident in
which his wife was captured. It was this incident that had led to the
Battle of Burnt Corn, and Cornells had sworn he would kill Weatherford if the opportunity arose. Weatherford heard of Cornells's threats
and asked the man straightforwardly whether he would take advantage of him while under his charge. Cornells answered, "No, I will take
no advantage of you while you are here and I am guarding you. But
when this time is over I intend to kill you." After a pause, Weatherford said: "Well, if you will take no advantage of me on this occasion, I
will trust myself to you." Cornells later learned that Red Eagle had
nothing to do with the indignity suffered by his wife, and the two

later became good friends.[61] It was Peter McQueen, not Weatherford, who had imprisoned Cornells's wife. After ten to fifteen days of anxiety over other threats to kill Red Eagle, Colonel Russell decided to send him back to Fort Jackson secretly. About midnight he sent his aide to accompany Weatherford to the watch station of Captain William Laval, who was officer of the guard. "Captain Laval," the aide reported, "the Commanding Officer says you must take Weatherford to yonder tree, under which you will find a horse tied, and that he must mount the horse and make his escape." Laval escorted Red Eagle past a guard to the horse, and the Creek leader shook him by the hand and with a "Goodbye! God bless you!" leaped into the saddle and rode away.[62]

According to one source, Weatherford remained at Fort Jackson until Old Hickory left in late April to return in triumph to Nashville, and then he traveled as a guest of the hero to his Tennessee home, the Hermitage.[63] Jackson's correspondence and papers, however, do not mention such a visit. Thomas Woodward, who knew both Jackson and Red Eagle and who was at Fort Jackson when Weatherford surrendered, said, "General Jackson, as if by intuition, seemed to know that Weatherford was no savage and much more than an ordinary man by nature, and treated him very kindly indeed." Woodward also said, "I have heard General Jackson say that if he was capable of forming anything like a correct judgement of a man on a short acquaintance, that he pronounced Weatherford to be as high-toned and fearless as any man he had met with—one whose very nature scorned a mean action." That Weatherford was a striking figure there can be no doubt. One early biographer, J. D. Driesback, heard Judge Thomas Tunstall remark that "he had never seen but two men that he could not look straight in the eye, one of them was Daniel Webster and the other was Weatherford the warrior," who, he said, had the eye of an "eagle, and moved with the regal air of a king."[64]

11

The Treaty of Fort Jackson and the Rising Career of William McIntosh

———— · ————

In his farewell address to his troops at Fort Williams on April 24, Jackson was lavish in his praise: "Within a few days you have annihilated the power of a nation that for twenty years has been the disturber of your peace. Your vengeance has been glutted. Whenever these infuriated allies of our arch enemy [England] assembled for battle, you pursued and dispersed them. The rapidity of your movements and the brilliancy of your achievements have corresponded with the valour by which you have been animated."[1] After the army was discharged from further service near Fayetteville, Tennessee, Jackson proceeded to Nashville, where he was hailed as a conquering hero by hundreds of citizens who lined the streets. At the state banquet at the Bell Tavern, Jackson gave another rousing address, again praising his men and demeaning the Creek Indians. "The success which attended our exertions," he said, "has indeed been great. We have laid the foundation of a lasting peace to those frontiers which had been so long and so often infested by the savages. We have conquered."[2] Jackson was lionized throughout his native state, and soon the administration in Washington, gratified by the first American victory since that of Oliver Hazard Perry at Lake Erie, joined the chorus of acclamation. Jackson was offered the rank of brigadier general in the U.S. Army, with the brevet of major general and the post as commander of the Seventh Military District, including Louisiana, Tennessee, the Mississippi Territory, and the Creek Nation,[3] but Jackson was disgruntled by the rank offered. He had expected to be named a major general, which was his rank in the militia, but he accepted the new post on June 8. Old Hickory's luck continued to hold, however; General William Henry Harrison, who had long battled with the administration, resigned his commission, and Jackson was offered a major generalship, which he accepted on June 18.[4] Along with his appointment to the regular army came the information from Secretary of War John Armstrong that the president wished Jackson to proceed without delay to Fort Jackson and conclude a treaty with the Creek Nation.[5]

In establishing the treaty, Jackson was to be guided by the principles given by General Pinckney: the Creeks would give up land equal in value to the expenses incurred by the United States in the Creek War, United States citizens would have the right to travel roads and navigate streams in the Creek country, the Creeks would cut off all relations with any Spanish garrison or town, and the Creek prophets who had ignited the war would be turned over to the United States.[6] The citizens of Tennessee, fearful of the hostile Creeks at their borders and convinced that Benjamin Hawkins would be too lenient to the Red Sticks, had engineered the appointment of Jackson as the sole treaty commissioner. Their assessment of Hawkins's leniency proved correct, for even before the negotiations had begun, he had allowed some Creeks to return to their homes. This angered Jackson, and he wrote to General Pinckney: "I am truly astonished that Colo. Hawkins is permitting the Indians to settle down to their former habitations. I did tell him the territory I had assigned them. I did tell him that no Indians should settle west of the Coosee or north of the Alabama. At this point is the strength of the frontier of the union to be established by . . . wealthy inhabitants, unmixed by Indians."[7] There is also evidence that not all Red Sticks had suddenly become docile and willing to acquiesce to the white man's terms. One of the hostile Creeks, in answer to a demand by the friendly chiefs Big Warrior and Little Prince that he seek peace, replied, "I have now friends and arms; you compelled me to fly and if you attempt to track me up I will spill your blood."[8]

When he arrived at Fort Jackson with a small entourage on July 10, Jackson asked Benjamin Hawkins to call a meeting of all Creek chiefs—friendly and hostile—at the fort on August 1. He invited Hawkins to attend, even though he was no longer a treaty commissioner; the Indian agent would, he hoped, be helpful in influencing the Creeks. Jackson was in no mood for temporizing. "Destruction will attend a failure to comply with these orders," he told Hawkins, and this warning was reinforced in a statement to General Coffee: "If they do not come in and submit, against the day appointed which is the first of next month, a sudden and well-directed stroke may be made that will at once reduce them to unconditional submission."⁹ It was evident that Old Hickory was determined to take a hard line with the Creeks and that he was to make little distinction between the friendly Indians and the Red Sticks. He was convinced that the only logical way to bring civilization to the Indians was to reduce to a minimum the amount of wilderness available to them for hunting grounds; then they would be forced to turn to industry and agriculture for a livelihood.¹⁰

On August 1 some Red Stick chiefs assembled at Fort Jackson, along with a larger number of friendly chiefs, of whom William McIntosh was the most prominent. The friendly chiefs came expecting preferential treatment for their loyalty and their military aid in subduing the Red Sticks. It soon became evident that Jackson would treat them no differently than he had the defeated hostile Creeks. A spacious canopy had been erected for the occasion, and both friendly and hostile chiefs were ranged together on one side of it. Across from them stood Jackson, with his aides and officers and the aged Benjamin Hawkins. Looking on was a large group of Indians, both Creek and Cherokee, along with regimental troops. Jackson opened the first treaty session with a minimal and almost grudging acknowledgment of the help given by McIntosh and the friendly Creeks. Then he turned to the Red Sticks and excoriated them for following evil counsel and committing heinous crimes against the United States, crimes for which the entire Creek Nation would have to pay. As the secretary of war had stipulated, Jackson said the Creeks must cede land equivalent in value to the expenses incurred by the United States in carrying on the war, and he calculated this to be 23 million acres, which was more than half of the old Creek domain and about three-fifths of the present state of Alabama and one-fifth of Georgia.¹¹

Each friendly Creek chief and warrior who owned land in the ceded territory and had aided Jackson's army in the war would be entitled to a reservation of one square mile of land for himself and descendants for as long as they continued to occupy it. Nevertheless, the Creek Nation was to pay an enormous indemnity for the rebellion of the Red Sticks.¹² Although he explained to the Indians that he was merely following the government's instructions in setting the indemnity, it was clear that Jackson, with his frontier Tennessee background, was intent on punishing the Creeks, removing them as threats to Tennesseeans and Georgians, and separating them from the influence of the Spanish in Florida. He intended, in short, to destroy the Creek Nation once and for all and to remove it as an obstacle to the expansion of the United States.[13] The Creek chiefs listened gravely to the interpreter who translated Jackson's words, showing little emotion, and then they gathered in a private council. Jackson, whom they called Sharp Knife or Pointed Arrow, had presented them with an ultimatum that was extremely difficult to accept.

Jackson was answered by Big Warrior, and John Reid, who heard his speech, wrote: "The firm and dignified eloquence of this untutored orator evinced a nerve and force of expression that might not have passed unnoticed before a highly polished assembly."[14] Big Warrior enumerated the causes that led to the war and freely gave credit to Jackson's army for assisting the friendly Creeks in their civil war. He admitted that justice might require a payment to defray the expenses of the war, but he felt that the payment was premature, for the war party was still unconquered and might return from hiding at any time. He tried to acquaint Jackson with the deprivations the Creeks would suffer if they were forced to adopt a way of life other than their ancient one.

Big Warrior's strongest points came with his references to the Treaty of New York, negotiated under the direction of President Washington in 1790, in which the Creeks exchanged two thousand square miles of fine farming and timberland for a royalty of $1,500 a year and "the protection of the United States of America." The first article of the treaty stated: "There shall be perpetual peace and friendship between all citizens of the United States of America, and all the individuals, towns and tribes of the Upper, Middle, and Lower Creeks and Semanolies composing the Creek Nation of Indians."[15] Big Warrior said, "I made this war, which has proved so fatal to my country, that the treaty entered into, a long time ago with father Washington, might not be broken. To his friendly arm I hold fast. I will never break that chain of friendship we made together, and which bound us to stand to the United States." He pointed to Benjamin Hawkins as a symbol of that friendship: "There sits the agent he sent among us. Never has he broken his treaty. He has lived with us a long time. He has seen our children born, who now have children. By his direction cloth was wove and clothes were made and spread throughout our country; but the red sticks came and destroyed it all,—we have none now. Hard is our situation, and you ought to consider it." He spoke about the duplicity of the British, who misled Little Warrior and precipitated the murders leading to civil strife. He regretted Creek involvement in the Revolution on the side of the British. Knowing Jackson's antipathy for the British, he ended his oration with a ringing pronouncement against them: "If the British advise us to do any thing, I will tell you,—not hide it from you. If they say we must fight, I will tell them, No!"[16]

The next speaker was Selocta (or Shelocta), a Lower Creek chief who had joined Jackson's troops at the beginning of the Creek War and had fought in all the battles, according to Reid, gaining the confidence of the commanding general. Selocta spoke of the high regard he had always felt for his white brothers. He told of his efforts to maintain peace; but when war had come, he fought against his own people. Selocta stated that he did not oppose the yielding of the Creek land lying on the Alabama, for doing so would isolate the Indians from Spanish influence. The country west of the Coosa, however, Selocta wished to see preserved for the Creek Nation.[17]

Jackson listened to Selocta politely and then answered unhesitatingly in the negative: "You know that the part you desire to retain is that through which the intruders and mischief makers from the lakes reached you and urged your nation to those acts of violence that have involved your people in wretchedness and your country in ruin. Through it leads the path Tecumseh trod when he came to visit you; that path must be stopped. Until this be done, your nation cannot expect happiness, nor mine security." He gave the chiefs until that evening to make a decision and added: "Your rejecting the treaty will show you to be the enemies of the United States,—enemies even to yourselves." He continued: "Those who are opposed to it shall have leave to retire to Pensacola."[18]

The chiefs were disheartened by Jackson's position and intimidated by his indomitable will, but they found still another card to play. In late April General Pinckney, a benign old Charlestonian, had written to Hawkins, promising indemnity to the friendly Creeks for their losses in fighting the Red Sticks. The chiefs knew of this letter. "You may likewise inform them," Pinckney had written, in reference to the friendly Creeks, "that the United States will not forget their fidelity, but, in the arrangements which may be made of the lands to be retained as indemnity, their claims will be respected; and such of their chiefs as have distinguished themselves, by their exertion and valor in the common cause, will also receive a remuneration in the ceded lands, and in such manner as the Government may direct." The chiefs confronted Jackson with these promises, but Sharp Knife stood firm. He stated correctly that Pinckney's letter was unofficial and that his instructions from the secretary of war had said nothing about indemnity for the friendly Creeks. The chiefs were persistent, however, and continued to argue that this commitment had been made by Pinckney as commanding general and that Hawkins had been instructed to inform the chiefs of the promise. Jackson did not back down, even though, as he later wrote Governor Blount, he had "considerable difficulty in making the arrangement with them in consequence of a letter written by General Pinckney."[19]

The chiefs persisted in trying to change Jackson's mind. As late as August 7 they wrote to Hawkins that they were again in trouble and needed his advice. They told him that Jackson, in disregarding the terms Pinckney had promised, was treating the friendly chiefs more harshly than the hostiles. The friendly chiefs were also disappointed that Jackson had drawn the lines of the lands to be ceded without consulting them. To the credit of the Creek chiefs, their integrity would not permit them to be party to a Cherokee intrigue. The Cherokees asked the Creek chiefs to make the claim to Jackson that some of the land to be ceded had already been given over to the Cherokees, who had been permitted to settle along the Coosa as far south as the mouth of Will's Creek. It would have clouded the issue and perhaps resulted in frustrating delays for Jackson, but, as Reid states, "The only reply obtained from the Creeks was that they could not lie by admitting what did not in reality exist."[20]

When on August 9 the Creek chiefs accepted the inevitable and agreed to sign the treaty, they made one last attempt to assuage their pain and humiliation in a grand, face-saving gesture that may have been intended primarily to embarrass Sharp Knife. The chiefs offered Jackson and Hawkins each a gift of three square miles of their choice of land, and the interpreters, George Mayfield and Alexander Cornells, one square mile each. In offering these gifts, Big Warrior expressed the wish that they would choose land "as near as you can to us, for we want you to live by us and give us your advice." Jackson's reply was calculated to counter the chief's generosity with a suggestion of charity from the government. He would accept the gift if approved by the president, who, he theorized, "would doubtless appropriate its value in aid of your naked women and children."[21] The chiefs were crushed by the general's response and told him that such aid would be unacceptable. The land, they explained, was not given so that he could return it in clothing and provisions. They "wanted him to live on it, and when he is gone his family may have it; and it may always be known what the nation gave it to him for."[22]

Hawkins, however, graciously accepted the gift: "I have been long among you, and grown gray in your service. I shall not much longer be your agent. You all know that when applied to by red, black, or white, I looked not to color, but to the justice of the claim. I shall continue to be friendly and useful to you while I live, and my children, born among you, will be so brought up as to do the same. I accept your present, and esteem it the more highly by the manner of bestowing it, as it resulted from the impulse of your own minds, and not from any intimation from the general or me."[23]

When the treaty was finally placed before them, thirty-six chiefs reluctantly signed it. William McIntosh signed with his rank and village, "Major of Cowetau," and he was also listed at the bottom of the treaty as signing for three other chiefs.[24] Afterward, the chiefs left Fort Jackson to carry the message of the decimation of the Creek Nation to their villages. On the next day Jackson wrote to his wife: "I have just finished the business with the Creeks; the convention was signed yesterday at 2 o'clock P.M. and tomorrow at 12 I embark for Mobile. . . . Could you only see the misery and wretchedness of these creatures perishing from want of food and picking up the grains of corn scattered from the mouths of the horses and trodden in the earth—I know your humanity would feel for them, notwithstanding all the causes you have to feel hatred and revenge against." As one Jackson biographer has pointed out, the engineering of the treaty at Fort Jackson "had the touch of genius. He had ended the war by signing a peace treaty with his allies!"[25] But it was an accomplishment of which Jackson was enormously proud. He sent copies of the treaty to a large number of friends and officials. He wrote to Secretary Armstrong that "the ceded territory contains twenty millions of acres of the first rate within the nation; besides opening a communication from Georgia to the Mississippi Territory, and a rich and extensive settlement from the river Perdido to the county of Madison."[26]

Jackson was aware, however, that the Creeks were in desperate need and that pushing them too far could be dangerous. To prevent the possibility of a rebellion, Jackson favored the federal government's intervention to assist the approximately eighty-two hundred Creeks within the territory. "To clothe the whole number will cost a considerable sum," he wrote to the secretary of war, "but this sum would be very inferior to the value of the territory ceded to the United States: in addition to which I may observe, that the cession . . . will in future effectively prevent their becoming our enemies." In the same letter he recommended that the boundary line be run immediately and the land sold to settlers as soon as possible, further to assure Indian sub-mission. His scheme called for Congress to pass legislation to provide "to each able bodied man who will settle upon this land a section at two dollars per acre, payable in two years with interest—this measure would insure the security of the frontier, and make citizens of the soldiers who effected its conquest."[27]

Another danger Jackson feared was the growing strength of the Spanish in Florida, who openly offered protection to the Red Stick refugees. Although Spain was not at war with the United States as was Britain, Jackson wrote a condescending, threatening letter to the Spanish governor of Pensacola, Don Matteo Gonzalez Manrique. He complained vehemently about the "refugee banditti from the Creek nation," who were "drawing rations from your government and un-der the drill of a British officer." He demanded the arrest, con-finement, and trial of Peter McQueen, the prophet Josiah Francis, and "others forming that matricidal band for whom your Christian bowels seem to sympathize and bleed so freely." He warned the Spanish gov-ernor of his creed: "An eye for an eye, tooth for tooth, and scalp for scalp."[28] It would not be many months before Jackson's frontier code of vengeance would be put into action in Florida against the Semi-noles, who were backed by the Spanish. By his side would be William McIntosh, soon to be promoted from major to brigadier general.

After the signing of the treaty at Fort Jackson, Major William Mc-Intosh began to assume an increasingly prominent role in the affairs of the Creek Nation and to become favored in Jackson's circles for his military leadership and his willingness to assist the American cause. Because of Big Warrior's impassioned speech against the treaty pro-posals at Fort Jackson, however, Old Hickory was doubtful of that leader's allegiance. Governor Claiborne asked Jackson: "Are you cer-tain that the Big Warrior will remain in his friendship for the U. States? I ask this question because it has been stated to me that some of his principal adherents had lately a private audience with Captain Woodbine, the English agent at Pensacola!" A letter written by Big Warrior to Benjamin Hawkins on August 25, however, may have allayed suspicions that the Creek leader was being influenced by the British, who had landed three hundred troops at Apalachicola and were making every effort to incite the Creeks to war against the United States. "The British came on here," he wrote, "and said they were the Indians friend but they came not for that; they came for the Negros. . . . The British who came on shore have plenty of arms and ammunition and our young men want to go and get it from them. We want to know your opinion on the subject. McIntosh will head the party if you will say the word. McIntosh wants to go and see what the British mean by arming the Negros."[29]

Hawkins reacted quickly. He replied to Big Warrior: "Send Major McIntosh with your young warriors to receive all the ammunition and arms landed in your country let them take it peaceably if they can, or forcibly if necessary. I do not wish to see you shed the blood of each other, but attack and take or destroy all the white and black people you find in arms." On September 6 Hawkins was in Milledgeville and told a writer for the *Georgia Journal* that McIntosh had been sent with four or five hundred warriors to seize any arms and ammunition being stored in the American territory. Hawkins later reported to the secretary of war that McIntosh had marched on September 23 "with 196 warriors, 20 rounds of ammunition [surely an error], 20 days provisions." He said that three to four hundred reinforcements were following. "I hope in a few days to hear of Major McIntosh having captured all the stores and negroes on the Apalachicola," Jackson wrote to Hawkins from Mobile on October 19. He added in a postscript: "You will give me the force of your warriors enrolled as soon as possible. If Major McIntosh and two hundred warriors could join me shortly, I would be happy to see him. The Indians engaged on the 15th ran and left their clothing."[30]

McIntosh's military expedition on the Apalachicola was fruitless. When he arrived at Eufaula he was told that the British officers and runaway slaves had left the Seminole country for Pensacola. He continued his march, however, to Perrymans Square, where the Seminole chiefs had convened. McIntosh reported that the chiefs seemed surprised to see him and that they assured him they wanted peace and would hunt up all runaway slaves and return them to their owners. Three unidentified Red Stick chiefs offered to return home if the Upper and Lower Creeks would forgive them. But McIntosh was still disappointed; all the British vessels and munitions had been taken to Pensacola. Jackson wrote to Secretary of War James Monroe: "From the report of Major McIntosh you will have been informed of the friendly declarations of the Seminoles; dependence may be reposed in their fears, but not in their friendship. If I can expell the Indians and British from Pensacola, all the Seminoles and Creeks will be our friends."[31]

It was ironic that McIntosh and other friendly Creeks were willing to be recruited to serve in any capacity a government that had failed to keep several promises, including the payment of annuities promised in the Treaty of 1805. In the same letter that told of McIntosh's departure with his troops, Hawkins wrote to the secretary of war:

> Our chiefs complain much against us. They say, Government has not been just to them in withholding their annuity for 1812, '13, and '14, without assigning any reason for it. They have been faithful to their treaty stipulations with us, yielding whatever was demanded of them. General Jackson is in hopes justice will be done them; but it is still delayed. They are called in for warriors, for runners, and for other purposes, without receiving any pay for the services they have often willingly performed. They are now in a manner naked, their hunting done, their resources destroyed by their civil war, and they are without the means of clothing their helpless people and themselves and winter is approaching.[32]

The situation was no better the following summer, and as negotiations continued concerning the running of the boundary lines agreed to in the Treaty of Fort Jackson, Hawkins wrote to George Graham, chief clerk of the War Department: "From the unceasing efforts made to poison the minds of the Indians by the British agents, who abound in the means of corruption, and the chiefs having already expressed with much warmth that their half of the treaty is lopped off, they may refuse their ratification, which they are advised to do by the British agents; and from the singular manner the capitulation is worded— the parties 'agree to ratify and confirm,' etc.—it appears they have the right to do so."[33]

McIntosh's name next appears in historical records in reference to the surveying of the boundary lines in the summer of 1815. Establishing these lines was a complex task, for the territory ceded in the treaty had extended north and west to Cherokee, Chickasaw, and Choctaw boundaries, which were all disputed by the Creeks and their neighbors. Because of this uncertainty, the commissioners were free to enlarge the Creek claims almost at will, thereby appropriating more land for the United States. The eastern line of the cession, however, which was well defined in the treaty, offered no problems except for a corner of land claimed by both the Creeks and the Cherokees. When the commissioners met on the Upper Coosa in June of 1815, the Cherokee agent, Return Jonathan Meigs, was present to make clear the Cherokee claim, which was to be lopped off the Creek lands. Because of delays in the gathering of the commissioners, the party did not leave Fort Strother until September. Included in the group were McIntosh,

Big Warrior, and Alexander Cornells, who was wearing his wife's Iroquois coat.[34]

An ever-growing crowd of recalcitrant Creeks followed the surveyors downriver, watching disconsolately as a great part of their homeland passed irrevocably from their hands and those of their descendants. They were near starvation, for the United States government had not only withheld the annuity payments but had failed to deliver the supplies promised in the treaty, had not paid for the damages done to Lower Creek towns by the Georgia troops, and had not paid the wages owed to Creek warriors who had fought against the Red Sticks. When they reached the Chattahoochee, the Creeks put up their first formal resistance and declared that the line should go no farther. They were faced at this point by a body of eight hundred regular soldiers, who were headquartered at Fort Mitchell, and the Creek gesture of defiance died aborning without actual conflict.[35]

There is some evidence to support the contention that aid promised by Colonel Edward Nicholls on behalf of the British government provided the impetus for the Creeks' futile stand.[36] Jackson had earlier excoriated Nicholls, an officer in the Royal Marines, in a letter to Hawkins, which also refers to the Cherokee-Creek boundary dispute and McIntosh's part in a phase of it: "Nothing ever surpassed or equaled the bare-faced effrontery of Col. Nichol. If he returns, as he has promised, he must be apprehended and treated by the Indians as they treated Bowles, whom he resembles in his vices without seeming to possess any of his heroism." Then he thundered: "The Creek line *must* be run, and with as little delay as possible"[37]

The controversial part of the boundary, which the commissioners had no authority to survey because of the disputed claims among the various Indian nations, was settled peremptorily and illegally in January of 1816. This settlement was made possible in part by an agreement made earlier between Major McIntosh and Colonel Brown and in part by a change in the personnel of the treaty commissioners. The elderly John Sevier died on September 24, and Benjamin Hawkins resigned because of declining health on the same day.[38] General E. P. Gaines, who replaced Sevier, had previously been authorized by Secretary of War William Crawford to appoint General John Coffee in the event Hawkins's uncertain health led to his resignation or death. There was a power vacuum ready for Coffee to fill, and as a pseudo-commissioner he moved decisively into it at Fort Strother in mid-January. After waiting for a week for the other commissioners, who, he alleged, had promised to meet him there, he collected certain "Creek chiefs and Headmen" to show him where to run the line; then he moved out on his own. There is little doubt that General Jackson instigated Coffee's action and was pleased with the resulting boundary. Coffee incorporated into the treaty cession nearly all the land claimed by the Cherokees and Chickasaws south of the Tennessee River. His line ran from the mouth of Will's Creek on the Coosa River to Coosada Island in the Tennessee River, down that river to Caney Creek, fifteen miles below the shoals, then by Gaines' Trace to Cotton Gin Port on the Tombigbee River,[39] place names redolent of the changing nature of the land—Indian names interspersed with the homey appellations of the frontiersman.

In less than two months, however, the land-grabbing efforts of Jackson and Coffee were thwarted by a decision made by the secretary of war, William H. Crawford. Crawford acceded to the arguments of the Cherokees, who said that Coffee had acted alone and illegally; he also agreed that the United States should return to them four million acres of land that had been claimed under the Treaty of Fort Jackson. The matter was concluded in a treaty signed on March 22, 1816, which also awarded the Cherokees $25,500 in damages for the crops and livestock destroyed by Tennessee militiamen during the Creek War.[40] A committee of five citizens of Davidson County wrote a typical response in a statement entitled "Remonstrance against the Treaty"; they were particularly distressed at the return of the four million acres of land to the Cherokees: "This tract has been settled by a numerous population—by men whose lives and property have been pledged to their Government. We will leave you to imagine the difficulty, distress, and dissatisfaction which will result from dispossessing the population of a country which was considered as a land of promise . . . that the country may remain a wilderness for the refuge of plunderers and murderers." With uncharacteristic steadfastness, Secretary Crawford ignored the outcry and instructed the commissioners to run the Cherokee boundary line precisely as the March 22 treaty had stipulated.[41]

Jackson lashed out at Crawford, all but threatening to disobey any order to restore land to the Cherokees, and he predicted boldly that Tennesseans would never stand by and see disputed territory handed over to "savages." He harped on the humiliation he would suffer in returning land already ceded in a legitimate treaty. "On the principle of right and justice," Jackson continued, browbeating Crawford, "the surrender ought never to have been made." He told the secretary that he believed "the real Indians, the natives of the forest," had no difficulty accepting the Treaty of Fort Jackson. The demand for restoration of the land was a "stratagem" for personal gain by "designing half-breeds and renegade white men." Despite his use of mixed-bloods such as McIntosh to serve his needs, Jackson frequently made them his scapegoats. He said that the government of the United States should stop worrying about "rapacious Indians," who "will claim everything and anything," and try to gain the confidence of its own citizens. He ended his letter to Crawford: "I have now done: political discussion is not the province of a military officer. As a man, I am entitled to my opinion, and have given it freely." The secretary did not seem worried about the distress of the Tennesseans. "The most of these intruders," he answered Jackson a few days later, "have entered upon the land in question since the running of General Coffee's line, and are as liable to be removed as though the act of Congress had never passed." He added that "they had the means of knowing that their intrusion was in violation of the law and the proclamation."[42]

The citizens of Georgia were no more pleased with the Treaty of Fort Jackson than were the Tennesseans. A remonstrance to President Monroe, passed by the Georgia legislature, said: "The citizens of Georgia . . . flattered themselves with the hope that the treaty of General Jackson would have obtained a further cession of territory and established a line with a much greater respect for the interests of Georgia than that treaty has evinced." The Georgians complained about the "sterile and unprofitable land acquired" and said that no new settlers would care to move to such poor land that was located precariously between the Spanish border and the Indian settlements and could cut them off from the rest of Georgia. The Georgia legislators were also disappointed because they felt an ideal opportunity had been lost to extinguish all Indian titles; during the late war "a severe chastisement had been inflicted on the Creeks—their power was broken—their arrogance subdued."[43]

Not only was Jackson having difficulty with the Cherokee boundary to the north, but the Creek land along the Georgia-Florida border—clearly acquired by the United States in the Treaty of Fort Jackson—had not been relinquished. The land was occupied by the fiercely independent Seminoles, some of whom had moved from Lower Creek towns into the area in colonial times to occupy lands vacated by the Apalachees, who were defeated by Colonel James Moore and his South Carolina rangers in 1704. In 1795 a political schism made the Seminoles even more independent of the Creek Nation, but this did not prevent their giving some assistance to the Red Sticks in the Creek

War. After the Battle of Horseshoe Bend they received Red Stick refugees into their villages in such numbers that the newcomers soon had a two-to-one advantage over the Seminoles. With this influx the Seminoles now totaled about five thousand people, scattered among fifteen or so villages located mostly between the Apalachicola and the Suwanee rivers, with Miccosukee the most important town. The name "Seminole," meaning "wild" or "runaway," refers to all Creeks who left the settled towns and migrated to Florida in the eighteenth and early nineteenth centuries.[44]

The independent Seminoles and the assimilated refugee Red Sticks were particularly bothersome to Jackson because he knew they had not been represented at Fort Jackson and did not consider themselves bound by a treaty to cede their land. Also, the British—Old Hickory's prime anathema—were encouraging the Indians in their belief that the boundary lines imposed by the Fort Jackson treaty were illegal. Especially disturbing to Jackson were two officers, Captain George Woodbine and Colonel Edward Nicholls, who worked for the British government during and immediately following the Creek War. Despite having been wounded in the head and leg and blinded in the right eye in a September naval attack on Fort Bowyer at the entrance to Mobile Bay, Colonel Nicholls continued to try to recruit and train a body of Indian and black warriors in the fall of 1814. He gave Woodbine permission to pay his recruits on a declining scale that ranged from two dollars a day for a chief to fifty cents for each black slave furnished by an Indian. Nicholls's grand design of using Seminoles and Creeks to retake parts of Georgia was unsuccessful, partly because of his declining health and the wretched deprivation of his Indian allies. He was convinced that Jackson was inciting Indians to acts of barbarism and that he was paying a bounty for Red Stick and Seminole scalps.[45] He was also repelled by the barbarism of his Indian recruits, who despite his efforts to restrain them, cooked and ate selected parts of Americans who had been killed in battle.[46] If this practice in fact occurred, it likely was as part of a war ritual in which the hearts or other organs of slain enemies were eaten so as to assume the valorous attributes of the dead. Nicholls was able to sway the minds of the more nativistic Creeks, and one of his prize recruits was the flamboyant prophet Josiah Francis.[47] Jackson, in a strong anti-British talk to the Creek chiefs, said: "I hear with sorrow that some of your people has been listening to the wicked talks of Colo Nicholls again."[48]

Not all of Jackson's problems involved Indians. A number of runaway slaves had taken refuge around the Seminole town of Apalachicola near a fort that soon came to be called the Negro Fort. Nicholls claimed to have recruited a fighting force of about five hundred blacks from the Apalachicola area during the Creek War. When he left Florida, a dangerous legacy of several hundred blacks, well armed with thousands of muskets, several cannon, and a large quantity of ammunition, remained behind.[49] This settlement of armed former slaves near the border of the United States caused great alarm among the settlers.

General Jackson had feared the settlement at Apalachicola even before Nicholls had evacuated it, and he had wanted McIntosh and his troops to raid the town as early as the fall of 1814. The conditions were to be right, in the summer of 1816, for McIntosh to embark on yet another difficult assignment for the government of the United States. It was an assignment made even more dangerous because of the bitter animosity the defeated Creeks harbored for McIntosh, leading them to put a price on his head. An address to the king of England, signed by Hopoithle Micco, the young king of the Four Nations, and twenty-nine other chiefs on March 10, 1815, was scathing in its indictment of McIntosh. The primary purpose of this talk, given at a British fort at the confluence of the Chattahoochee and Flint rivers, was to complain that "the U. States, or some part thereof, have thought proper to run a line or wagon road through the Indian nation, from Hartford, in Georgia, to Mobile, in West Florida, without our consent, and to our great hurt and annoyance." As for the Americans, the chiefs added, "we are determined to cease having any communication with them; and we warn all Americans to keep out of this nation."[50]

The chiefs then attacked McIntosh personally:

And whereas that a young chief, called McIntosh, was sent with a message of remonstrance against such a road being run, and of several other encroachments on the Tombigbee, Coosa, and Alabama Rivers, instead of his making such remonstrance, he suffered himself to be tricked by the enemy, and unlawfully sold to them large tracts of land on and about the rivers Oconee and Ocmulgee, which tracts of land we implore our good father to use his endeavor in getting restored, and that the Americans may be obliged to withdraw from them. The above-mentioned McIntosh held a commission as major in the American army, and of the Creek regiment; he has caused much blood to be spilt, for which we denounce him to the whole nation, and will give the usual reward of the brave to any one who may kill him, he having, on a recent occasion, killed and scalped a brother, for no other reason alleged against him than his having British arms about him; and in this, we are told, he has been encouraged by Col. Hawkins, although long after peace was declared and all hostility ordered to cease.[51]

Hawkins wrote to Colonel Nicholls on May 28, 1815, telling him that when he had presented to the Creek Council the statement of Hopoithle Micco, Caupichau Micco, and Hopoie Micco, all carrying the title of king, the council had replied: "We know nothing about them as such. They have nothing to do with our affairs. They reside in Spanish territory."[52] These chiefs in West Florida, encouraged by the British, were primarily seeking to have Article Nine of the Treaty of Ghent respected by the Americans. This article of the peace treaty signed in 1814 after the defeat of the British in New Orleans sought to protect the Indians who had been allied with the British by restoring to them all lands they had possessed in 1811, provided that they desisted from all hostilities against the United States. Jackson insisted that the Treaty of Ghent did not apply to the Red Sticks because they had made a separate treaty earlier at Fort Jackson. This treaty, of course, had been signed only by Jackson's Indian allies and a few Red Stick prisoners, not the true enemy leaders.

Through extensive research in the Public Record Office in London, Frank Owsley, Jr., has pieced together the British reaction to the stubborn refusal by the Americans to apply the Treaty of Ghent to the Indians. Nicholls organized a government for the Creeks in Spanish Florida and then made a treaty between this new government and Britain, which, if ratified, would have established a regular Creek-British military alliance. Nicholls returned to England to attempt to have the treaty ratified, accompanied by the new Creek government's representative, the mixed-blood prophet Josiah Francis, called Hidlis Hadjo by the British. The War Office and Foreign Office in London, unaware of Nicholls's efforts and having, by their inaction, tacitly agreed with the Americans that the Treaty of Ghent did not apply to the Creeks, had no interest in signing Nicholls's treaty or even in meeting with him and a Creek representative. Somewhat guiltily, the British lavished presents on Hidlis Hadjo, and after he had spent a fruitless year in England, they arranged his passage home. "It would appear," Owsley wrote, "that when the British government finally got Hidlis Hadjo out of England, there was no further interest in the Creek Indians."[53] For William McIntosh, however, the world of Creek, Seminole, and American politics and intrigue was no less complicated.

12

"The Gallant Major McIntosh"
Becomes a General in
the Seminole War

———— • ————

In the years 1816–18, McIntosh became widely known through a series of loosely related events that were to affect the course of history in the period. He played a major role in the spectacular destruction of the fortress overlooking the Apalachicola River at Prospect Bluff. He engaged in complex efforts at diplomacy in Washington in an effort to collect old debts and to oppose Jackson's attempts to take from the Cherokees what McIntosh believed to be Creek lands. And he fought in the First Seminole War, being commissioned a brigadier general at the head of a large force of illegally recruited Creek warriors. These were years in which he was called by his superiors "the gallant Major McIntosh" but also years in which he was caught in the crosscurrents between the white and Indian worlds and dealt with callously by Jackson and others in the power structure.

The fort on the lower Apalachicola, about sixty miles below the United States boundary line and fifteen miles from the Gulf Coast, was a matter of grave concern to Andrew Jackson. He wrote to Governor Mauricio de Zuniga of Pensacola on April 23, 1816, that the fort was occupied by upward of 250 Negroes, all well clothed and disciplined, and that the failure of Spain to control this source of danger would "compel us, in self-defense, to destroy them." Captain Vero Amelung, sent to discuss the matter with the Spanish, reported that the governor agreed with Jackson. Amelung wrote that the citizens of Pensacola suffered as much as the Americans from the presence of the Negro Fort but could do nothing about it, for Pensacola itself was poorly defended, with few troops and "not enough gunpowder to fire a salute." The governor told Amelung that if the captain general of Cuba could not send sufficient aid and supplies, he might request support from the United States. When Jackson learned of the inadequacy of Zuniga's forces, he wasted no time in suggesting an American attack on the fort to Secretary of War Crawford; he wrote that "there can be no fear of disturbing the good understanding that exists between us and Spain, by destroying the Negro fort, and restoring to the owners the negroes that may be captured." He then ordered General E. P. Gaines to destroy the fort "regardless of the ground it stands on."[1]

Meanwhile, separate Indian forces, led by McIntosh and Little Prince, were already attempting to solve the problem of the fort. General Gaines wrote to the secretary of war on April 30, enclosing a letter from Little Prince, who was on an expedition to meet with the Seminole chiefs near the Apalachicola "to adopt measures to take the Negro fort." Because Colonel Hawkins was confident that the Indians could effect this object, Gaines sanctioned a requisition to supply them with three hundred bushels of corn to serve as rations. He indicated that he had little faith that they would succeed but encouraged them because of the great benefit a successful expedition would bring to the whites and Indians on the southern frontier. Little Prince feared what would happen if Jackson's forces became involved. "We hope," he wrote the secretary, "you will detain the forces at the places they are at present and wait on the Indians as I am sure they will be able to settle everything."[2]

General Gaines had misgivings about the loyalty of Little Prince and the real intent of the Indians' visit to Apalachicola. He wrote to Lieutenant Colonel Duncan L. Clinch, who was later to lead the forces against the Negro Fort: "The British agent, Hambly, and the Little Prince and others, are acting a part which I have been at a loss for some time past to understand. . . . They must be watched with an eye of vigilance." Clinch left Camp Crawford on July 17 to move toward Apalachicola and was joined that same evening by Major McIntosh and 150 Creek Indians. The following day his troops met with "an old chief, called Captain Isaacs, and the celebrated chief Kotcha-haigo (or Mad Tiger) at the head of a large body of Indians, many of whom were without arms." He added in his official report: "My junction with three chiefs was accidental; their expedition had been long since projected." Clinch said the Indians' object was to capture the Negroes within the fort and restore them to their rightful owners.[3]

The Negro Fort was a structure of earthern walls, which held a strong position atop Prospect Bluff, a steep elevation protected to the rear by a swamp. Because the river was usually too shallow to allow the large gunboats to get close enough to shell it, the fort was more than adequately protected by its artillery pieces: four long twenty-four pound cannons, four long six-pounders, one four-pound fieldpiece, and one brass five-and-one-half-inch howitzer. Within the fort were garrisoned more than three hundred blacks (including women and children), about twenty renegade Choctaws, and a few Seminole warriors from Bowlegs's Town, named for the famous Chief Billy Bowlegs, all under the rigid discipline of Garçon, a black chief whose few encounters with historical record have characterized him as a "lean, intense man, hot-eyed and tight-lipped, cunning, courageous, and cruel."[4]

The strategy Jackson and Gaines hoped to employ was to provoke an attack from the Negro Fort and use this response to justify its destruction. First, Gaines erected a base of operations, which he called Fort Scott, at the confluence of the Chattahoochee and Flint rivers. To take supplies to the isolated new fort, two transport vessels, with ordnance, provisions, and gunboat escorts, were requested from Commodore Daniel T. Patterson of New Orleans. Gaines told Clinch: "Should the boats meet with opposition at what is called the Negro fort, arrangements will immediately be made for its destruction; and for that purpose you will be supplied with two eighteen-pounders and one howitzer, with fixed ammunition, and implements complete, to be sent in a vessel to accompany the provisions."[5]

Two gunboats and two schooners, commanded by Sailingmaster Jairus Loomis of the United States Navy, left New Orleans on June 24 and reached the mouth of the Apalachicola on July 10. There Loomis received a message from General Gaines stating that he had sent Colonel Clinch down the river with troops "to take his station near the fort, and, if the fleet was fired on, to raze the post to the ground." Loomis was ordered not to enter the river until Clinch had taken his position, and he waited without incident until July 15, when a small boat from one of the schooners was fired upon by Negroes from a boat that suddenly appeared from the Apalachicola and quickly withdrew under fire. A more serious incident occurred two days later, when a small crew from one of the gunboats went ashore for fresh water and saw a black man on the bank of the river near a cultivated field. Midshipman Luffborough, who was in charge, assumed the man was a fugitive slave who should be captured and ordered the boat to put in to shore. When it reached the bank, he shouted to the black man, and his call was answered by the clatter of forty muskets in the hands of ambushing blacks. Three men, including Luffborough, fell dead, and the only sailor to escape was John Lopaz, who swam to the opposite bank to report the incident and the clever decoy devised by Garçon. Another survivor was captured, his hands were tied, and he was prodded with a loaded musket along the muddy path to the fort. The other members of the ambushing party quickly stripped and scalped the dead sailors.[6]

On July 18 a party of Creeks captured a messenger from Garçon, who was on his way to the Seminoles carrying one of the sailors' scalps and an appeal for aid to the fort. The messenger told Clinch that the scalp was taken by Garçon and a Choctaw chief, who, with a party of men, had killed several Americans and taken a boat from them. At two o'clock in the morning of the twentieth Clinch and his men landed within a cannon shot of the fort in a protected, wooded area. He sent a message to the commander of the convoy and then communicated his plan of attack to the chiefs. He ordered Major McIntosh and a party of Indians to surround the fort and maintain one-third of his men on the move, keeping up an irregular fire. Clinch reported: "This had the desired effect—as it induced the enemy to amuse us with the incessant roar of artillery, without any other effect than that of striking terror into the souls of most of our red friends." On the evening of the twenty-third Colonel Clinch sent three chiefs— McIntosh, Captain Isaacs, and Mad Tiger—into the fort to demand a surrender, but the three chiefs were "abused and treated with the utmost contempt." Garçon told the chiefs that he would sink any American vessels that tried to pass and would blow up the fort if he could not defend it. The chiefs reported that the blacks had hoisted a Union Jack, accompanied by the red or bloody flag, which signified their intention to fight to the death. This resoluteness impressed Surgeon Marcus C. Buck of the Fourth Infantry, who commented: "We were pleased with their spirited opposition . . . though they were Indians, negroes, and our enemies."[7]

On July 26 Colonel Clinch made his final preparations for attack; he ordered the gun vessels to move up and the transport *Similante*, which had been made ready, to land the artillery under cover of darkness. At daylight the following morning the two gunboats moved upriver "in handsome style," according to Clinch, and as soon as they came within range of the fort received a shot from a thirty-six pounder, which they returned "in a gallant manner."[8] The blacks on

the ramparts of the fort were courageous almost to the point of
foolhardiness, but they were inexperienced artillerists and scurried
confusedly about, attempting to deal with the intricacies of rammer,
linstock, and wiper. Thus far the blacks had suffered no casualties; the
shots from the light guns of the boats were ineffective against the
heavy walls of the fort, and the shots from the ships' heavier cannon
were off target, either passing overhead or falling short of the mark
into the river. Then Sailingmaster James Bassett ordered a shot to be
heated red hot in the galley of gun vessel number 154. It was the first
"hot" shot to be fired, and it soared over the wall and landed in the
magazine, entering through the door, which had carelessly been left
open.[9] According to Peter McQueen, the gunner had been guided to
the magazine by William Hambly, an agent of the Forbes Company,
who ostensibly worked for the British but accompanied the expedition to the Negro Fort.[10]

The explosion that resulted was horrendous, as hundreds of barrels
of gunpowder went up in one roaring, earthshaking instant, with
pieces of human bodies, logs, cannon, and other debris lighted in
flame in the morning sky. The fort was almost completely destroyed.
Clinch reported: "The explosion was awful, and the scene horrible
beyond description. Our first care on arriving at the scene of destruction was to rescue and relieve the unfortunate beings that had survived the explosion." There were about fifty survivors, and two of
them, incredibly, were Garçon and the Choctaw chief, who lived
through the explosion unhurt to face a worse fate. The sailors had
heard that their captured comrade had been "tarred and burned alive."
They turned the two captive chiefs over to the Creeks, who scalped
the Choctaw alive and then fatally stabbed him; Garçon was shot in
execution style.[11]

Clinch's firsthand account of the explosion is interesting both for its
graphic description and its theology: "The war yells of the Indians,
the cries and lamentations of the wounded, compelled the soldier to
pause in the midst of victory, to drop a tear for the sufferings of his
fellow beings, and to acknowledge that the great Ruler of the Universe
must have used us as an instrument in chastising the blood-thirsty
and murderous wretches that defended the fort." Marcus C. Buck,
the surgeon on Clinch's staff, was even more emotional in his response to the death and destruction: "You cannot conceive, nor I describe the horrors of the scene. In an instant, hundreds of lifeless
bodies were stretched upon the plain, buried in sand and rubbish, or
suspended from the tops of surrounding pines. Here lay an innocent

babe, there a helpless mother; on the one side a sturdy warrior, on the other a bleeding squaw. Piles of bodies, large heaps of sand, broken guns, accoutrements, etc. covered the site of the fort. The brave soldier was disarmed of his resentment, and checked his victorious career, to drop a tear on the distressing scene."[12]

On the evening of August 1 Colonel Clinch received the alarming news that a large body of Seminole Indians was descending the Apalachicola and was within a day's march. Clinch believed that his troops, poorly provisioned and greatly outnumbered, could easily be cut off from Camp Crawford. A letter, signed merely "A Soldier," describes dramatically the "gallant bearing of this Spartan band when informed that the whole Seminole tribe had embodied them and their encampment. Without an ounce of food, except the slofky obtained from the Indians, with but a few friendly Indians as allies, and with no means of transportation, they received the news with composure; and with smiles turned their faces to their encampment, determined to cut their way or die in the effort." Colonel Clinch dismissed the incident with a sentence: "I advanced with two hundred Cowetas, under the gallant Major McIntosh, to meet them; but the cowardly wretches dispersed without our being able to get a view of them." Colonel Clinch gave much of the credit for the successful campaign against the fort to his Indian allies: "I must beg leave to recommend to my Government the gallant Major McIntosh, Captains Noble Kennard, George Lovett Blue, and Lieut. Billy Miller (all from Coweta), for their distinguished conduct during the whole expedition." Clinch was also greatly respected by the Indians, and it was reported that both the hostile and friendly Creek chiefs united "and almost unanimously petitioned Col. Clinch to become their Indian Agent."[13]

An anonymous writer in the *Army and Navy Chronicle* has given an insight into the United States Army's opinion of certain prominent Creek chiefs. He writes of "the duplicity, chicanery, and treachery of the Big Warrior, the acuteness, cunning, and hypocrisy of the Little Prince (Chiefs of the Creek Nation whose talents were worthy of more civilized men, who while extending the hand of Friendship to the whites, were secretly encouraging hostilities amongst their tribes, and holding intercourse with the Seminoles)." Colonel Clinch counteracted their plans "in a manner deserving the highest credit; he drew around him the chivalrous and magnanimous McIntosh (Tustinugge Had ke, the White Warrior), the eloquent Mad Tiger (the motion of whose finger alone spoke a language that went to the soul), the sincere, benevolent and hospitable Noble Kennard; and through their influence was enabled to battle all the machinations of those who were their superiors in council." Thomas Woodward, who knew most of these chiefs personally, confirmed, in part, this assessment of their reputations. He said that McIntosh "was the greatest man I ever knew to have been raised entirely among the Indians." "Big Warrior," he stated, "was a man of great cunning, and there is but little sincerity in his pretended friendship for the whites."[14]

Colonel Clinch reported that the 163 barrels of gunpowder found in the ruined fort became "a valuable prize for the Indians." This unexpected comment is made clear when one understands that the colonel had promised his Indian allies all the small arms that were captured in the assault on the fort. It was an agreement casually made, and Clinch did not anticipate that the cache would be so large. The British had left the fort abundantly supplied with arms, however, and 2,500 muskets, 500 carbines, 500 swords in steel scabbards, and 400 pistols fell into the possession of a small number of Creeks. There is little doubt that a large portion of these armaments found their way, by sale and barter, into the hands of the Red Sticks and Seminoles. Still unanswered is the question of why the Seminoles, who once occupied the fort, had allowed the arms to leave their hands in the first place. Nevertheless, the Seminoles could now pursue a course of war against the United States, using this windfall of weapons.[15]

For the remainder of 1816 the Seminoles, still terrified by the awesome display of American power at the Apalachicola fort, were quiet. In the early months of 1817, however, the Seminoles and their Negro allies began to regroup themselves. Their animosity began to rise again as white settlers pressed nearer and nearer to their borders in overwhelming numbers. Atrocities by the white settlers as well as the Indians and blacks kept the caldron boiling, and by February both sides were spoiling for a fight. George Perryman, a Seminole chief, reported from Fowltown, a settlement fifteen miles east of Fort Scott on the Florida line, that the Seminoles and Negroes "say they are in complete fix for fighting and wish an engagement with the Americans, or McIntosh's troops; they would let them know they had something more to do than they had at Apalachicola. They have chosen Bowlegs for their head, and nominated him King, and pay him all kinds of monarchial respect, almost to idolatry, keeping a picket guard at a distance of five miles."[16] McIntosh's fame in the American military establishment and his infamy among rival Indians were growing at the same time, and a confrontation between him and the forces of Billy Bowlegs was moving inexorably closer.

While the Indians in Florida were belligerently calling for a fight with McIntosh's forces, McIntosh himself was in Washington with a deputation of Creeks who were concerned about General Jackson's newest ploy to deprive them of their lands and virtually eliminate tribal control. In January 1817, Jackson began promoting the policy of removing the Indians from their lands in the East and giving them acre for acre in land west of the Mississippi. The idea was not a new one, having been advocated earlier by Thomas Jefferson, who believed that if the Indians could not adjust to the white man's civilization, "we shall be obliged to drive them, with the beasts of the forest, into the Stony [Rocky] mountains." Jackson's first target was the Cherokees, who were the most vulnerable tribe because they had agreed in 1808 to surrender some lands on the eastern side of the Mississippi for lands in Arkansas. In the intervening years several thousand Cherokees had migrated westward and accepted land on the Arkansas River, but none had ceded any lands in the East to complete the trade. Jackson was now given the task of explaining to the remaining eastern Cherokees that they must cede land in compensation for that taken by their Arkansas brethren. As an alternative, they too could move westward, and the United States government would provide money for transportation as well as arms, blankets, and other necessities.[17]

McIntosh was the first signer—and probably the author—of a long letter written in Washington to President Madison on January 15, 1817, arguing against the policy of removal. He addressed the president as "Friend and Father" and told him that the Creeks had heard "much talk" about the Cherokees wishing to exchange lands. "This is a business of their own and with which we have nothing to do," the letter continued, except that "about the time of our late troubles & war the Cherokees attempted to lay claim to a large body of our land . . . and have recently began to settle on it. To this they have no right and we do not admit their claim, nor do we wish you to listen to them on the subject of exchanging any territory . . . until we have councilled with them and understand each other more fully on this subject." The letter continued with an insight into the motivation of two distinct groups of Indians. One, the more influential Cherokees, of mixed blood, were "anxious to swap all their land," McIntosh wrote. The other group was "not so much civilized and live mostly in the woods and do not want to swap but would prefer remaining where they are." The nativistic Cherokees' fear was that the mixed-bloods might swap all their land and leave them "without any land to walk on." The

Creeks feared that the "want of land in their nation might throw them on us." The concluding paragraph reads, "Father, so soon as you can answer our talks now given to you and will let us know what chance we have of obtaining our compensation for losses sustained by our red sticks we will look towards our people and bid you farewell."[18] The latter part of the letter indicates that McIntosh may well have been as interested in his claim for damages, in the amount of $5,212, as he was in the possibility of having further Cherokee land ceded.[19]

McIntosh was still in Washington at Davis's Hotel on March 8, when he wrote a lengthy reply to George Graham, the acting secretary of war. Graham had assured the Creeks that the president had appointed an agent to replace Hawkins (who had died on June 6, 1816) who "will see justice done." The new agent, David B. Mitchell, had resigned as governor of Georgia to take the post and was to have a scandal-besmirched career as agent. The Creeks seemed reassured at learning that the president would have his army protect them from white encroachments but were puzzled that he expected trouble from the strip of land lying between Jackson's line and Georgia, particularly if he intended to post guards to keep out the whites. The Creeks asked that the president let the headmen of the Creek Nation know how he wished the line altered, and "they will conclude among themselves what to do." In his communication through Graham, the president had asked the Creek chiefs to prevent the young warriors from joining the old enemies and bringing trouble into the nation. The chiefs answered that it would be hard for them to prevent it because many people who were hostile during the late war had returned to the Creek Nation, and "some of these might again get crazy and go over into the Spanish line and, joining our old enemies, attempt again to do mischief to your people." The chiefs promised to punish any troublemaking Red Sticks by applying Creek laws, but they did not wish to be held accountable for any hostiles they could not catch. "The little piece of land which you left us," they added, "as your known friends, was left as proof that we are friendly." They reiterated that they had been assured they would be allowed to hold the land reserves forever. Then they commented on the attempts made to mold them into the white man's cultural patterns: "You tell us it would be well to give a farm to different families in the nation, and let them build a good warm house, cultivate the ground and that we would soon become as white people. Brother within the little territory we have left we have our own laws and we must abide by the rules of our people. Many of our people did cultivate and our women have spun their own clothing, but this last war has broken us all up—we have lost all our tools and we are left without any to make use of, but we still try to do the best we can."[20]

In the letter the enterprising McIntosh indicates that he and the other chiefs were fearful that a source of income guaranteed in the Treaty of 1805 might be lost to them. McIntosh had been one of the strongest negotiators with President Jefferson in Washington in 1805, and, in exchange for a horsepath through the Creek Nation, the federal government stipulated that "the Creek chiefs will have boats kept at the several rivers for the conveyance of men and horses, and houses of entertainment established at suitable places on said path for the accommodation of travellers." The letter from the chiefs stated, "You have got a road, a public one, on our land and country on which we do not want the white people to settle or live, for we believe we are able enough to furnish the travellers with corn and provision on that road which leads through our country."[21]

In a letter of March 10 to Graham, McIntosh and the other chiefs again asked for compensation. They pointed out that in the late war one part of the Creek Nation was "your enemy and spilt your blood," and, they said, "we who were friendly to the United States collected our warriors & marched against them and punished them. . . . When the treaty was made with General Jackson he promised to pay all the Friendly Indians during the war and when this was heard by your friends they were in hope of being paid for their services. This is what we wish to understand, if you intend to have us paid we will tell them so—& if not why we can tell them they need not look for pay any more." There follows a paragraph in which McIntosh, the first signer of the letter, speaks in the first person: "Since the annuity has been kept back I have assisted the Nation and furnished them with provisions at their head councils, to the amt. of many dollars for which I have taken the head mans receipt . . . the sum they know to be due me is three thousand seven hundred and forty-five dollars. I wish to know if you can pay us who have true accounts made out before we go away." This letter is signed "William McIntosh," and on the second line the names of three other chiefs, an arrangement that may indicate that McIntosh was the sole author. It seems from this communication that McIntosh's motive in going to Washington was less to act as statesman, arguing for the rights of his people, than as an impatient plaintiff with unpaid debts. On Friday, March 15, another letter was sent to Graham, signed by William McIntosh, with the mark of Yoholo Micco, requesting an answer "to all their talks" by the following Monday so they could begin the long journey home. They also wrote: "We look for your order to our agent to pay the sixty warriors on the muster rolls left with Mr. Brent, Paymaster General. The Drafts for Annuity and Payment of Losses we would be pleased to know had been sent off before we leave you."[22]

If McIntosh and the other Creek chiefs had hoped to deter Andrew Jackson's policy of Indian removal, their visit to Washington was in vain. In a move that was to have implications later for McIntosh and the Creeks, Old Hickory summoned the Cherokee chiefs, including those who had resettled along the Arkansas River, to meet with him and his fellow commissioners on June 20 at the agency at Hiawassee. Jackson arrived at the site of the meeting on June 18, armed with a copy of a convention made with the Cherokees on January 7, 1806, and a talk from the president to a Cherokee deputation in 1809, both indicating that permission was granted to a part of the Cherokee Nation to remove to Arkansas on land the United States would exchange for eastern lands formerly occupied by these emigrants.[23] Jackson was the principal spokesman when the treaty conference began a few days later. He told the Indians that he had been appointed by their father, the president, to receive an exchange of land from the eastern Cherokees to compensate for land being occupied by Cherokees in Arkansas, and he referred to agreements made in 1809 as the basis for the exchange. The chiefs responded that the deputation that visited President Jefferson in 1809 was not authorized to make such agreements. Jackson disputed this claim with testimony from Tuchelee, a chief who had been a part of the deputation, who claimed that they had full power to make the agreements. For this testimony, apparently given out of fear of Jackson, Tuchelee was turned out of the Cherokee council and was no longer considered a chief by his peers.[24]

The Cherokees made a desperate plea at the next session: "Friends and brothers," they addressed the commissioners, "We feel assured that our father the President will not compel us into measures so diametrically against the will and interest of a large majority of our nation. . . . We wish to remain on our land, and to hold it fast. We appeal to our father the President of the United States to do us justice. We look to him for protection in the hour of distress."[25] The chiefs persisted in their contention that the emigration of a small number of Cherokees westward was unauthorized by the headmen of the nation and that no exchange of land was justified. They then presented the tight-lipped, angry Jackson with a statement, signed by sixty-seven Cherokee chiefs, denying Sharp Knife's claims. He bullied the chiefs individually, then, growing livid with rage, delivered a threat. He told them, the Cherokees reported, "to look around us and recollect what had happened to our brothers the Creeks."[26]

A treaty was signed on July 8, ceding two million acres of Cherokee land in Tennessee, Georgia, and Alabama to the United States. In return, the Cherokees would receive an equivalent number of acres west of the Mississippi, with the federal government reserving the right to build roads, military posts, and factories on the Indian land in the West, if needed. More than six thousand Cherokees were removed westward in the next two years, and each was given a rifle and ammunition, a blanket, and either a brass kettle or a beaver trap. Those who remained in the East and who chose "to become citizens of the United States" were granted 640 acres of land, which heads of families could hold in fee simple, but if they later removed, the land would revert to the United States.[27] Although the land cession was large, Jackson was elated that this treaty provided a precedent for the principle of removal, "which will give us the whole country in less than two years."[28]

In the spring and summer of 1817, hostilities continued to grow among the white settlers, the Seminoles, and the blacks along the Florida border. Not surprisingly, one of the major problems was caused by the runaway slaves, from early and recent times, who were harbored by the Seminoles. The Seminoles had long ago welcomed as allies runaway slaves from Georgia and Alabama. These early immigrants, called "maroons" (a Spanish word of West Indian origin meaning "free Negroes"), were thoroughly established among the Seminoles, and though they were held in mild servitude, were regarded as brethren and in a few cases intermarried with the Indians. J. A. Peniere, agent to the Florida Indians, wrote: "These Negroes appeared to me to be far more intelligent than those who are in absolute slavery, and have great influence on the Indians."[29] Many also had great linguistic abilities and were used as interpreters.[30] But the Seminoles' refuge threatened the institution of slavery, and the forays of white slave catchers from across the American border were recurring problems for these Indians and the former slaves.

Border incidents continued into the early fall, and on October 1 Gaines wrote to both Jackson and the secretary of war, summarizing the latest inflammatory acts of the obdurate Seminole chiefs, who stubbornly refused to release known murderers and would not allow American troops to pursue runaway slaves into Indian lands. Chief Emehe Mautby of the village of Fowltown had sent a saber-rattling message to Major David E. Twiggs of the Seventh Infantry warning him "not to cut another stick on the east side of the Flint river, adding the land was his and that he was directed by the powers above to protect and defend it and shall do so."[31] General Gaines paid heed to the warning and immediately began to concentrate forces at Fort Scott.

When Gaines arrived at Fort Scott, he asked the chief of Fowltown, fourteen miles to the east, to visit him. Chief Emehe Mautby flatly refused to come and reiterated the blunt warning he had sent Twiggs. On November 20 Gaines ordered Twiggs to take 250 men to Fowltown and bring back the chief and his warriors, and if they resisted, to treat them as enemies. Gaines ordered Twiggs to return to the fort if the town was reinforced by other villages. The detachment reached Fowltown early on the twenty-first and was immediately fired upon, with the soldiers returning the fire and putting the Indians to flight; four Indians were killed, many wounded. "It is with deep regret," Gaines reported, "I have to add that a woman was accidentally shot." She had a blanket wrapped about her, as did the warriors, and in the early morning mist, she had been mistaken for a man. In the house of the chief Twiggs found a British uniform coat, scarlet with gold epaulettes, along with a certificate signed by a British captain of the marines, Robert White, "in the absence of Col. Nichols," stating that Emehe Mautby had "always been a true and faithful friend to the British." This information confirmed what a Mr. Culloh, a citizen of the area, had written to Gaines the previous spring: "The British agent at Oakelockines sound is giving presents to the Indians. We have among us Indians who have been down, and received powder, lead, tomahawks, knives, and a drum for each town, with the royal coat of arms painted on it. We have at this time at least five hundred Indians skulking in the neighborhood, within three or four miles of us."[32]

Creek agent David Mitchell thought the attack on Fowltown had been a tragic blunder. He wrote to Acting Secretary of War Graham that the friendly Indians at the Creek agency had "unanimously expressed much regret that hostilities should have commenced between the troops under General Gaines and the Fowltown Indians . . . because these Indians, although they did not unite with the friendly ones during the late war, neither did they join the Red Sticks, and had recently expressed a great desire to become decidedly friendly." General Gaines was confident that his action had been right and that the Seminoles would surrender when they came to the realization that the British would not give them the long-term assistance needed to carry on a war against the Americans. He expressed this theory in a letter to Jackson on November 21, but he was soon to learn the error of his prediction.[33] The attack on Fowltown was the first battle of the Seminole War, and for this attack the Seminoles exacted a terrible revenge.

Nine days after the attack on Fowltown, forty soldiers under Lieutenant R. W. Scott, seven soldiers' wives, and four small children were moving cautiously up the Apalachicola River in an open boat when they were attacked by a band of Seminole warriors at a point one mile below the mouth of the Flint River. When the attack occurred, the boat was attempting to navigate a treacherous stretch of white water by staying clear of the swift midstream current and moving slowly alongside a thick canebrake. Lieutenant Scott and most of his men fell dead or wounded in the first withering volley. Six soldiers escaped into the river, but only two made it to Fort Scott to report the event. A Mrs. Stuart, who was uninjured, was taken prisoner, but the other women and children, all struck in the hail of gunfire, were quickly killed and scalped. Wounded children were put to death by grabbing them by the heels and dashing their heads against the sides of the boat.[34]

This atrocity led General Gaines to send another "talk" to the borderland chiefs. The Indians, he told them, "have been at war against women and children; let them now calculate upon fighting men." He warned them bluntly not to expect aid from the British; "The English are not able to help themselves; how should they help the old 'Red Sticks,' whom they have ruined by pretended friendship?" Gaines did not expect an early capitulation. "The Seminole Indians," Gaines wrote to the secretary of war, "entertain a notion that they cannot be beaten by our troops. They confidently assert that we never have beaten them, or any of their people, except when we have been assisted by 'red people.'" Gaines attributed the Seminoles' ignorance of American troop strength to cultural deprivation; they "read neither books nor newspapers; nor have they opportunities of conversing with persons able to inform them."[35]

The Indian agent David Mitchell regretted the outbreak of war. He wrote from the Creek agency to Governor William W. Bibb of the Alabama Territory on December 15: "The General [Gaines] passed this place on Friday last on his way to Fort Hawkins to hasten the march of the troops from Georgia, and on the 11th of next month McIntosh with his friendly warriors are to rendezvous at this place to receive some articles of clothing &c preparatory to their joining Genl. Gaines. I regret that the General should have deemed it necessary to use force against the Fowl Town Indians." Mitchell's regrets about the Seminole War, or perhaps his fears of the legal entanglements in allowing Creeks to invade Spanish territory, may have led him to manipulate the Indian allies and to cause delays when possible in their joining forces with Gaines's troops. Captain Robert Irvin reported to Colonel Matthew Arbuckle, the commandant at Fort Scott, that there was "considerable confusion" among the Indian allies "about marching." He stated that "McIntosh had come as far as Fort Mitchell on his way, and the Agent had sent him home, and told him to meet him at the Agency, for a talk, in thirty days, eighteen of which yet remains; and that he should not move until the General Government should give the order." Mitchell later explained to the secretary of war that he had received a notice from the War Department that General Gaines was prohibited from crossing the Spanish line to attack the Seminoles and that "I declined sending the friendly warriors to join him until that restriction should be removed, or I had the orders of the Government upon that subject." Mitchell attended a meeting of the principal chiefs, called by Little Prince, to discuss the "conduct they should pursue with regard to war with the Seminoles." The agent advised them to send a "trusty chief" to Miccosukee Town, headquarters of the Seminoles and Red Sticks, to propose peace and ask for help in a force to go against the Negro camps.[36]

On December 16 John C. Calhoun, who had assumed his duties as secretary of war six days before, wrote to Gaines, giving him the authority he had hoped to receive, stating that "should the Seminole Indians still refuse to make reparation for their outrages and depredations on the citizens of the United States, it is the wish of your President that you consider yourself at liberty to march across the Florida line and attack them within its limits . . . unless they should shelter themselves under a Spanish post. In the last event, you will immediately notify this Department." Ten days later, Calhoun ordered Andrew Jackson to take command of the assault against the Seminoles. Jackson was to go to Fort Scott and assume command of a force of eight hundred regular soldiers and a thousand Georgia militiamen who had been called into national service. Gaines had estimated the Seminole forces at twenty-seven hundred. Calhoun instructed Jackson: "Should you be of opinion that your numbers are too small to beat the enemy, you will call on the Executives of adjacent States for such an additional militia force as you may deem requisite."[37]

The permission given Jackson to call on executives of adjacent states for additional militia forces, combined with the wholesale recruitment of Creek warriors under McIntosh, led to excesses that were later to be investigated by a congressional committee appointed on December 10, 1820. The investigation was part of a larger political reaction to Jackson's performance in Florida, including his court-martial and execution of two British agents, Alexander Arbuthnot and Robert C. Ambrister, on Spanish soil. The committee was primarily concerned, however, with the specific question of whether monies appropriated by Congress since March 4, 1815, for the support of regular army troops had been used to support any army or detachment raised without the authority of Congress. The committee concluded that the raising of these troops "was in violation of the constitution of the United States and a dangerous infringement on the powers of Congress."[38]

According to the committee report, Colonel David Brearly of the Seventh Regiment of U.S. Infantry was ordered by Major General Gaines "to receive into the service of the United States not exceeding 500 friendly Indians." If such a number should volunteer, the order read, Colonel Brearly should "muster, inspect, and provision them and direct their march to Fort Scott."[39] When Brearly proceeded with his recruitment efforts, he found that because of the desperate poverty of the area, nearly the entire effective force of the Creek Nation would consent to serve. He decided to accept them all and recommended to General Gaines that they be mustered into a regiment of eighteen companies, with William McIntosh ranking as a colonel and two other chiefs, George Lovett and Noble Kennard, being designated majors.[40]

General Gaines approved of Colonel Brearly's recruitment of the Creeks, informing him through a letter from his adjutant on January 29, 1818, that he would "cheerfully accept the services of all the Indians who might be disposed to join him." He made McIntosh a brigadier general instead of a colonel, and a regiment consisting of 1,537 warriors was mustered into the service of the United States on February 24. According to the committee report, "William McIntosh held the rank of brigadier general and received in that capacity $104 per month pay, $72 per month subsistance, $40 per month for forage, and $42.27 per month allowance for servants, having received for two months and fifteen days service from February 24 to May 9, 1818, the sum of $645.72." This was important evidence in the committee's report, for it found a record of General McIntosh's having been paid but no orders from the War Department authorizing mustering of the

Creek forces. The committee report also called into question the legitimacy of McIntosh's commission as a brigadier general: "The appointments of the officers of this corps of Indians and the promotions which took place by order of General Jackson were also, in the opinion of the committee, an infringement on the powers confined to the Executive of the United States and the Senate."[41]

Early in January 1818, General Jackson sent a message to President Monroe which revealed a grandiose design of taking possession of the Floridas by military action. Such action was devoutly wished for by most citizens along the entire southwestern frontier, who perhaps knew little of the delicate negotiations then under way for the purchase of Florida from the Spanish. Jackson wanted only the barest nod of assent from the president to allow him to seize authority and take action. "Let it be signified to me through any channel," he wrote the president, "that the possession of the Floridas would be desirable to the United States, and in sixty days it will be accomplished."[42] On February 6, Secretary of War Calhoun communicated to Jackson "the entire approbation of the President of all the measures which you have adopted to terminate the rupture with the Indians."[43] Jackson took forty-six days to march his troops, numbering about one thousand, from Tennessee to Fort Scott, a distance of 450 miles that seemed longer because heavy rains had made the road impassable for baggage wagons and slow going for the infantry. He reached Fort Scott on March 9 without supplies and found that provisions were almost exhausted at that fort. As in the Creek War, Jackson was at the mercy of an inefficient system of independent private suppliers, who made military logistics an inexact science at best. On the day after his arrival in Fort Scott, Jackson ordered the few available cattle and swine slaughtered, and each man of his combined force of two thousand received three meat rations and one quart of corn, completely exhausting the food supply. General Jackson then marched his troops down the Apalachicola, hoping to meet a returning keelboat that had been sent down to the mouth of the river to bring back supplies from two sloops anchored there. The troops met the keelboat and had their first full meal in three weeks, then were able to reach Prospect Bluff, the site of the ruins of the Negro Fort, in five days' march. There a temporary fort was erected to protect the supplies to be sent from New Orleans.[44]

Meanwhile, McIntosh and his regiment of Indian warriors had already seen limited action. Jackson reported to Calhoun: "General McIntosh, commanding the friendly Creeks, who had been ordered to reconnoitre the right bank of the Apalachicola, reported to me on the 19th that he had captured, without the fire of a gun, one hundred and eighty women and children and fifty-three warriors of the Red Ground Chief's [McQueen's] party, with their cattle and supplies; the chief and thirty warriors making their escape on horseback. Ten of the warriors, attempting to escape after they had surrendered, were killed by the general."[45]

On April 1 General McIntosh and his warriors rejoined the forces of General Jackson, which, six days earlier, had moved out of the fortification at Prospect Bluff (now named Fort Gadsden) toward Seminole country. The troops, though weary and poorly provisioned, were ready for battle and agreed wholeheartedly with their general about their purpose for being in Florida. It was, as General Jackson had written the Spanish, "to chastise a savage foe, who, combined with a lawless band of Negro brigands, have for sometime past been carrying on a cruel and unprovoked war against the citizens of the United States." The first action came about nightfall, when a small party of Seminoles was discovered and, after a brief skirmish, driven quickly through the Miccosukee towns. After a night's rest, detachments were sent in every direction, with orders to "secure all supplies and reduce to ashes the villages." Three hundred houses were burned, and Jackson's troops took a large supply of grain and a herd of cattle, welcome additions to their larder. On the following day the troops came upon a grisly spectacle in the public square at Kenhagee's Town.[46] There was a red pole, described by one officer as "barbarously decorated with human scalps of both sexes." On the pole were fifty scalps, identified as belonging to the unfortunate victims of the Scott massacre. As further proof, one of the Seminoles wore a coat he had taken from a soldier killed there. That same day General McIntosh and a detachment of his warriors routed a small party of savages near Fowltown, killing one black and taking three prisoners.[47] McIntosh rejoined Jackson's forces on April 10, having been temporarily detached, as Jackson had reported, "at Mikasuky, to scour the country around that place."[48]

One of the most dramatic of General McIntosh's military engagements in the First Seminole War occurred on April 12, near Econfanah, or the Natural Bridge. On that morning the officer of the day with Jackson's troops reported that a sentinel had heard cattle lowing and dogs barking during the night. A runner was sent to General McIntosh, who was camped with his warriors a short distance in the rear of Jackson's army, with orders to investigate the area. McIntosh

William McIntosh, by Charles Bird King (from McKenney and Hall, *History of the Indian Tribes*)

sent out Major Kennard with a detachment, but he soon sent back a runner to report that they had discovered a hostile party which out-numbered them. McIntosh then moved in with his entire force of about fifteen hundred warriors, accompanied by about fifty Ten-nessee volunteers. After a spirited engagement the Seminoles were routed, with thirty-seven enemy warriors being killed and six men and ninety-seven women and children taken prisoner. Among the women was Mrs. Stuart, the soldier's wife who had been captured at the Scott massacre.[49]

Thomas Woodward, a veteran of the Creek and Seminole wars and a well-known frontier raconteur, gave a vivid firsthand account in his *Reminiscences* of General McIntosh's actions in this battle. "I shall never, while I live, forget the day we took her [Mrs. Stuart] from the Indians," Woodward wrote. "Shortly after the firing commenced, we could hear a female voice in the English language calling for help, but she was concealed from our view. The hostile Indians, though greatly inferior in number to our whole force, had the advantage of the ground, it being a dense thicket, and kept the party that first attacked it at bay until Gen. McIntosh arrived with the main force. McIntosh, though raised among savages, was a General; yes, he was one of God's make of Generals. I could hear his voice above the din of fire-arms—'Save the white woman! save the Indian women and children!' All this time Mrs. Stuart was between the fires of the combatants." Woodward said that McIntosh ordered him to go with two other soldiers to rescue Mrs. Stuart. "I can see her now," Woodward said, "squatted in the saw palmetto, among a few dwarf cabbage trees, surrounded by a group of Indian women." Some of the friendly Indians, including Major Kennard, joined Woodward, and they were able to "cut off the woman from the warriors" and rescue her. For valor in this engagement, Major Kennard and Major Lovett were promoted to the rank of colonel by order of General Jackson.[50]

Jackson now moved his army toward the town of Chief Billy Bowlegs, located on the Suwannee River. The town was important to Jackson for several reasons: it was the seat of the strong Alachuas and thus a primary power base for the Seminoles; it was the asylum of a large number of runaway slaves; and it held one of the largest concentrations of Seminoles. To defeat Bowlegs's Town would enhance Jackson's military reputation as well as remove a strong rallying point of resistance. There were also in the town a great many blacks who were still smarting from the catastrophe at the Negro Fort. The forage-poor, swampy wilderness which the army passed through to reach the town took its toll on the horses, but Jackson's weary troops reached the vicinity of the town about three o'clock on the afternoon of April 16. Jackson had hoped to reach that point at noon, giving him the entire afternoon to destroy the town, and he would have preferred to camp for the night and wait. His scouts reported seeing six mounted Indians in the distance, however, and he knew he must strike immediately or lose his advantage of surprise.[51]

Jackson divided his force into three divisions, one of them under General McIntosh, and pushed forward. Meanwhile, the mounted Seminoles who had been seen earlier rode into the Negro village, which extended three miles along the west side of the river, to warn them that Jackson was coming. Bowlegs and his mulatto lieutenant, Nero, had followed the advice of British officers and, with the river between them and the oncoming army, began their planned retreat into the swamp. The blacks ferried the women and children across the river, and the operation was almost complete when Jackson's troops appeared from the west, as though coming out of the setting sun. A band of black warriors, joined by a few Seminoles, remained on the west side of the river to attempt to hold the invading armies long enough for the retreat to be completed, but with their British-made smoothbore muskets, the blacks and Seminoles were outranged by the American riflemen as well as being outnumbered almost four to one. The rear-guard action lasted only a few minutes; then, leaving their dead behind, they ran for the river. Nine blacks and two Indians were killed, and seven blacks and nine Indians were captured by the Americans. An anonymous officer gave one theory as to why the enemy casualties were light. He said that "all would have been captured, but for the bad execution of the movement of the left column. The [Creek] Indians, instead of getting above, had thrown themselves between the towns and the centre, thus leaving open the retreat to the river which the enemy readily embraced, after a slight resistance in which they lost 8 or 9 killed, and some prisoners." Disappointed that the capture of Bowlegs's Town had been nearly bloodless and therefore to him indecisive, Jackson ordered, on the morning of the eighteenth, General Gaines and General McIntosh to lead detachments across the Suwannee River in pursuit of the enemy. After advancing six miles, however, it became apparent that the enemy was so widely dispersed in the swamps that capturing them would be impossible.[52]

Despite his willingness to assist Jackson in any way, General McIntosh was soon to be a civilian. On April 24 he was instructed to march his warriors directly to Fort Scott, with an order to the commanding officer to muster the Creek regiment out of service. General McIntosh's military career was over, and the records do not reveal the reason why. Although Jackson may have been dissatisfied with the actions at Bowlegs's Town of McIntosh and his Creek warriors, it is more likely that he feared the consequences of having irregularly mustered them into service. There was still one bitterly ironic incident for McIntosh to endure. He was to learn when he reached Fort Scott that two days before, the friendly village of Chehaw had been attacked in error by a military detachment under Captain Obed Wright. The village had been burned and seven people massacred, including an old chief named Howard and his son, an uncle and a cousin of William McIntosh. Acting on a rumor that Chehaw Indians had been engaged in a skirmish on Big Bend, Wright had obtained authorization from Governor William Rabun to add two companies of United States cavalry, under Captain Bothwell, to his Georgia militia and attack the Chehaws.[53]

General Thomas Glasscock of the Georgia militia reported the incident to Jackson, telling him that although Captain Bothwell had told Wright that he disapproved of the attack and would not accompany him and that "there could be no doubt of the friendship of the Indians in that quarter," Wright would not listen. "This availed nothing," the general wrote, "mock patriotism burned in their breasts; they crossed the river that night and headed for the town." General Glasscock's vivid account continues: "An advance was ordered, the cavalry rushed forward and commenced the massacre. Even after the firing and murder commenced, Major Howard, the old chief who furnished you with corn, came out of his house with a white flag in front of the line. It was not respected. An order was given for a general fire, and nearly four hundred guns were discharged at him before one took effect. He fell and was bayoneted; his son was also killed. These are the circumstances related to the transaction. Seven men were killed, one woman, and two children." He added sadly: "They are at a loss to know the cause of the displeasure of the white people."[54]

Jackson was saddened and outraged by the tragic blunder that had led to the murder of those who had been loyal to him. He wrote to the chiefs and warriors of the Chehaw village that the "news fills my heart with regret and my eyes with tears: when I passed through your village you treated me with friendship and furnished my army with all the supplies you could spare; and your old chiefs sent their young warriors with me to fight and put down our common enemy." He promised that "Captain Wright will be tried and punished for this daring outrage of the treaty and murder of your people." He sent a company of Tennesseans to arrest Wright and transport him in chains to Fort Hawkins, where he was kept confined until Governor William Rabun of Georgia had him transferred to civil authorities. Jackson wrote a blistering letter to Governor Rabun condemning the "cowardly and inhuman attack on the old women and men of the Chehaw village, whilst the Warriors of that *village* were with me fighting the battles of our *country* against the common enemy. . . . You Sir as Governor of a state within my military Division have no right to give a Military order, whilst I am in the field." He closed with an indictment of the state: "This act will to the last ages fix a stain upon the character of Georgia."[55]

Governor Rabun was incensed by Jackson's letter, reporting it to Secretary Calhoun as "a production as inflammatory and indecorous as it is unbecoming a gentleman and a soldier." The governor tried to explain the "unfortunate attack on Chehaw," telling Calhoun that Hopaunee and Philemmees, two chiefs of villages named for them, had committed a number of atrocities against white settlers. The governor had ordered a detachment into service for the sole purpose of destroying the two chiefs who had committed the depredations, and Captain Obed Wright had been placed in command. Wright, while on the march, had heard that Hopaunee had left his own village to reside in Chehaw. The governor told Calhoun that Wright took it upon himself to go to Chehaw with his detachment and attack it, killing several friendly Indians. He told Calhoun that Wright was under arrest, having been released to civil authorities by Jackson's men.[56]

Captain Wright did stand trial and was acquitted by the state of Georgia. An indemnity of $8,000 was awarded to the Indians remaining in Chehaw for the homes and property that had been destroyed, despite Secretary Calhoun's insistence on frugality. He wrote Mitchell, "I have seen it stated that the destruction of the Chehaw village had been estimated at $8,000. The state of the Indian fund requires that the most rigid regard be paid to economy, consistent with the object in view, in the application of the money which has been placed in your hands to satisfy the Indians' claims in this particular instance."[57]

What effect the tragic blunder had on William McIntosh—a former general summarily discharged from the army, long a victim of unpaid debts and unfulfilled promises—can only be conjectured. He is likely to have felt some disagreement with General Jackson's optimistic statement: "The Seminole War may now be considered at a close; tranquility again restored to the Southern frontier of the United States."[58]

13

McIntosh and Mitchell:
An Unholy Alliance

———— • ————

There is a persistent belief among those who have studied William McIntosh's volatile career that the year 1817 marks a watershed in assessing his reputation. "Although there can be no criticism of his conduct before 1817," Antonio J. Waring wrote, "the arrival of David Bridie Mitchell as Agent in that year altered things. Qualities which were hidden in McIntosh the brilliant warrior emerged in McIntosh the trader and tavern keeper, who at the same time was one of the five great chiefs in the Nation. Mitchell, whose motives in accepting the position as Agent were highly questionable, soon found in McIntosh a willing pupil and able partner."[1] The linking of McIntosh and Mitchell as partners in schemes to cheat the Creek Nation is given most of its credence from a statement by Little Prince to General Gaines: "McIntosh and Mitchell used to steal all of our money, because they could write."[2] When Madison appointed Mitchell as agent, William Baldwin, a navy surgeon, wrote of the former governor: "*I know him well* and cannot entertain a doubt that in all his decisions he will lean to the side of Georgia—the state where he is *popular,* and where the *popular* cry is—*exterminate the savages.*"[3]

McIntosh's reputation, deserved or not, is linked with that of Mitchell, whose resignation as governor of Georgia to accept an appointment as Indian agent was viewed with suspicion by such Georgians as Governor John Clarke, a vehement enemy of Mitchell's and thus not an impartial witness. Clarke wrote: "As a man known to be ambitious of political distinction would not probably have made such a change with a view to public honor, it is natural to conclude that some pecuniary inducements must have led to it. And this is ren-

195

dered more probably from the remark of the Agent himself, who was heard to remark that he had 'served the public long enough, and he would be d——d if he did not now serve himself!' "[4] Attorney General William Wirt, however, in reporting to the president and the Senate about Mitchell's alleged slave trading, pointed out that when Mitchell resigned the governorship the $2,000 annual salary was the same as that of the Indian agent. The governor's post was for a term of only two years, but the Indian agent served indefinitely; therefore the latter position had "inferior honor" but "superior tenure." Wirt therefore found nothing in Mitchell's changing of positions "to awaken just suspicion against a character previously fair."[5]

Accusations against Mitchell were reported to Andrew Jackson when he arrived in Georgia early in 1818. He related to Secretary Calhoun on February 14 the particulars on the Indian agent's alleged misconduct, beginning with the previously mentioned delaying of Indian warriors who wished to enlist with General Gaines in the First Seminole War. As Gaines had expressed it, the Creeks under McIntosh "were prevented by the intrigues of the Negro-smuggling agent from joining me."[6] Mitchell's motivation in delaying the troop movement of the Creeks may well have been, as the agent stated, an attempt to clarify the legal implications of his charges' joining an army about to invade Spanish territory.

Jackson's second allegation, that Mitchell had been involved in illegally smuggling black slaves, bought at Amelia Island, into this country, was more difficult to refute. Clarke had accused Mitchell of violating an act of Congress of March 1807, entitled "An Act to Prohibit the Importation of Slaves into any port or place within the United States from or after the first day of January, 1808." Also, the constitution of the state of Georgia had forbidden the importation of slaves after October 1, 1799. Major John Loving testified that he had told Mitchell he would like to purchase Africans in Spanish territory, on Amelia Island or in Florida, provided it could be done safely and legally. Loving stated that Mitchell had replied that "he had been thinking of such a purchase himself and that Loving might bring any African he might purchase through the Indian country, with safety, *to the agency, where he* [the agent] *would protect them.*" Thomas S. Woodward testified that he had been approached by Colonel Joseph Howard, who asked if he would like to go to East Florida or Amelia Island to buy Africans. Woodward had answered that it was illegal and he did not want to do it, but even if it were legal, he would not have the funds to speculate. Howard replied that Mitchell would sup-

David B. Mitchell (Courtesy of the Georgia Department of Archives and History)

ply funds and give him part of the profit. Mitchell also offered his protection of the blacks while at the agency and promised safety in disposing of them through the agency.[7]

The Wirt report pieced together an account, based in large part on testimony by Colonel David Brearly, of an illicit relationship between Captain William Bowen, who had previously been employed by Benjamin Hawkins at the Creek agency, and Mitchell. Bowen bought one hundred blacks at Amelia Island and marched sixty of the most able overland to the Creek agency. They arrived there in the first week of December, while Mitchell was away on a trip; the agent returned on December 8. While the first shipment remained at the agency, Bowen returned to Amelia Island, from where he wrote Mitchell on Christmas Day: "I have just got the balance of the stock that I had left at Amelia and am just starting them under the care of Tobler." He added: "I believe I am narrowly watched, but I think I have evaded discovery as yet." He stated that there was more of a risk than he had encountered in getting the first party through. The cost of the hundred blacks—$250 each for "prime fellows," $175 to $200 for ordinary—must have totaled a considerable sum of money in that era.[8]

Although McIntosh has been accused of being involved in Mitchell's scheme, testimony in the Wirt report seems to deny it. Henry Walker stated that "General McIntosh and Doyle have both informed me that the Agent [Mitchell] solicited them to buy Negroes whilst they were stationed at the Agency; that they refused to do it unless they would make titles; he [Mitchell] said *he* would not do it *himself,* but that *Captain Bowen* would." Nowhere else in the papers relating to the slave-running scheme is McIntosh's name mentioned. Mitchell, however, was incriminated by the evidence. In his report to President Monroe, Wirt was incensed "that General Mitchell should suffer the agency under his command to be a place of rendezvous for smuggled African Negroes; that he should make the government no fair report of the case." He closed his report with the statement: "I am constrained to adopt the conclusion (painful as it is) *that General Mitchell is guilty of having prostituted his power, as Agent for the Indian Affairs at the Creek Agency, to the purpose of aiding and assisting in a conscious breach of the Act of Congress of 1807, in prohibition of the slave trade— and this from mercenary motives."*[9] In February 1821, the secretary of war dismissed Mitchell from the service.[10]

Jackson made other charges of wrongdoing by Mitchell, and McIntosh may have been more heavily involved in these affairs. Jackson wrote to Secretary Calhoun that the Creek Indians complained that Mitchell "has retained in his hands the greater part of the Eighty five thousand dollars, appropriated by Congress to indemnify the friendly part of the Nation for depredations committed on them by the Red Sticks. They further stated that he has paid off the Indians for their military service in goods instead of cash; that he has established a large store and Tavern within the Nation and that he has taken into his possession all the Ferries at which the most extravagant tolls are exacted."[11]

As one suspicious historian has suggested, the Creek indemnity of $85,000, which the Indian agent was privileged to dispense, may well have been the prime motivation for Mitchell's resigning the governorship to become Hawkins's successor as Indian agent. It was this sum of money, in addition to the previously promised Creek annuities, that led Little Prince to accuse McIntosh and Mitchell of stealing from the Creek Nation. Colonel William Hambly later testified at a congressional hearing that McIntosh was opposed to the Indian agent John Crowell because that agent "refused to let him have control of the [annuity] funds, as he was accustomed to have during the agency of General Mitchell."[12]

Jackson's statement that Mitchell paid the Creeks for their military service in goods rather than cash is true by the Indian agent's own admission, and his statement points to possible duplicity by McIntosh: "When I informed the chiefs that the government had directed me to muster the old Creek Regiment and pay them off," Mitchell wrote, "I was especially requested by Mr. McIntosh, in the name and on behalf of the officers and men, to appoint an agent and send him for goods to the amount of their pay, that they preferred goods to money, particularly blankets, homespuns, saddles, etc." Mitchell also told Secretary Calhoun that he had spent $18,000 on goods and that the Indians were pleased, finding the goods of a better quality than ones furnished before and nearly one-half cheaper. It is likely, however, that profit was the real motivation of Mitchell and McIntosh in providing goods rather than cash. Also during this time McIntosh was receiving special favors from the Indian agent; Mitchell reported to Secretary Calhoun on February 3, 1818, that he was making arrangements to send one of McIntosh's sons to a school in Milledgeville, Georgia. A business arrangement soon came to be a family affair when Mitchell's son William married one of McIntosh's daughters.[13]

Although the details of the business venture between McIntosh and his silent partner Mitchell are sketchy, there are several established facts. In 1819, about a year after Mitchell succeeded Hawkins, the federal authorities closed the government trading station, or factory, on the west side of the Chattahoochee near the abandoned Fort Mitchell.[14] McIntosh then enlarged his entrepreneurial interests to include a trading post and store at his son's house near that fort. George Stinson, a white man who had married one of McIntosh's sisters, was hired as a clerk there, furnished with goods by McIntosh and Mitchell, and sent out to sell supplies on credit to the Creeks. The Indian agent then allowed the Creeks to receive their annuities in goods furnished at the McIntosh establishment or in credit against debts owed for purchases through Stinson. This arrangement ceased when Crowell became the Creek agent in 1821, and the repercussions of the ensuing enmity between Crowell and McIntosh were far-reaching. The matter was well summarized by Little Prince, who when asked by General Gaines in a council at Broken Arrow what was the cause of the difference between McIntosh and Crowell, stated that "it was on account of Stinson, who was brought into the Nation, and who traded without a license; and because the Agent would not join with him in cheating the nation out of their annuity, which McIntosh and the former Agent, Mitchell, were in the habit of doing."[15]

There is another side of the story, of course, and there is evidence that the closing of the government factory in 1819 could have been a just action, insisted upon by Mitchell to prevent his red wards from being further bilked by the government factor, Major Daniel Hughes. Mitchell wrote to Secretary Calhoun on June 17, 1818, to report a number of charges which the same disgruntled Little Prince had made against Hughes: "The Prince complains that the Factor extorts exorbitant prices for every Article he Sells; and that the principal part of the goods are sold on his own individual account. That he purchases up all their provision at a cheap rate . . . and at this season of the year when they are almost perishing, & subsisting principally upon roots which they Collect in the woods, he demands for the same Articles 3 and 4 hundred per Cent. And the worst of all is, that in the mean time the money they ought to have received for their provision has been expended in purchasing whiskey. Abject poverty and wretchedness is the result."[16]

Mitchell's compassion concerning the frequent problem with alcohol among the Indians and his attempt at a solution certainly belie the portrait of a calloused mercenary painted by Clarke and others. Mitchell wrote to Calhoun that "all efforts to civilize those people, or to promote habits of economy and industry among them will be wholly fruitless unless the introduction of Spiritous liquors is restrained to some moderate standard, or wholly prohibited." He told of liquor being sold at the government trading station and of seeing "upwards of fifty Indians laying all over the yard so drunk as to be perfectly helpless, and many more rioting and fighting," which prompted him to issue an order, dated June 14, 1818, prohibiting the "introduction of Spirits into the Creek Nation and the Sale thereof to the Indians."[17]

With this lawlessness and chaos as a background, it is ironic that when Mitchell took office as Hawkins's successor, one of his first acts was to receive a copy of the laws of the Creek Nation, signed by Brigadier General William McIntosh, George Lovett, Noble Kennard, and Samuel Hawkins, which had been agreed to at a council at Broken Arrow and published at a general meeting of chiefs and warriors on June 12, 1818. A comment accompanying the laws stated: "To General D. B. Mitchell, Indian Agent; Now you our agent will see the laws we have made for our nation." Antonio J. Waring, who has published an edited version of the Creek laws, believes that "these laws were made in Council, one by one, haphazardly, as individual situations arose. They are laws made in a changing culture, calculated to deal with problems beyond the scope of ancient Creek custom, problems rising out of contact with the white man—cattle raising, slave owning, the use of United States currency, systematic agriculture, trading, and the presence of a stream of passing settlers on the way across the Nation to the Alabama and Mississippi territories." Waring also believed that Hawkins had been a great influence on the Creek laws and that it was only after that agent's death that it seemed necessary to record the laws. There is a manuscript version of the laws, in Chilly McIntosh's hand, set down on January 7, 1825. This copy has special interest because it was written by McIntosh's son and presented to McIntosh's first cousin, Governor George M. Troup of Georgia, whose mother, Catherine, was a sister-in-law of McIntosh's father. The laws reflect the problems caused by Indians who drank alcohol. One law states that if a man kills another "in a rum drinking" and it can be proved that he was out of his senses and was friendly with the victim beforehand, he shall be forgiven. Another law makes it possible to renege on a bargain to swap horses if, within five days, one of the party can prove he was drunk at the time. Law 53 reads: "If a person should get drunk and want to fight it Shall be Rope until he get Sober."[18]

According to Michael D. Green, Mitchell's appointment as the Creek agent had not been an act of innocent error. It had been a cal-

loused political decision, made by Georgia's most powerful political
boss, William Crawford, who had given Mitchell the job of gaining as
much advantage over the Creeks as possible and letting the credit
redound to Crawford. Crawford was a man to be reckoned with on
both the state and federal political scene; he had been Madison's last
secretary of war, the Republican caucus presidential candidate in
1816, and secretary of the treasury in Monroe's cabinet; he had plans
to mount an all-out campaign for the presidency in 1824. Along with
John Milledge, David B. Mitchell, and George M. Troup, all staunch
allies, Crawford led a powerful faction in Georgia. They were opposed by a faction led by Elijah Clarke and his son John, whose sup-
porters were mostly dirt farmers and frontiersmen, whereas the
Crawfordites tended to come from the landed gentry in eastern
Georgia.[19]

As late as November of 1818 McIntosh was still being publicly ac-
claimed. In that month he was the guest of honor at a dinner hosted
by some of the leading citizens of Augusta, at which he was lavishly
praised for his ability to accommodate himself to the world of white
Georgians. His accomplishments in aiding those who wished to acculturate the Creeks were considerable. He had been Benjamin
Hawkins's spy against Tecumseh in 1811 and had led Hawkins's appointed law menders in maintaining order on the frontier. He had
led the military forces that rescued Big Warrior at the siege of
Tuckabatchee, and as a major and then a general he had led the Creek
warriors who accompanied Jackson's forces. He had held the important post of speaker of the lower towns and had been the most important Creek spokesman in negotiations between the Creek Nation and
the federal government. He was also a major trader in the Creek Nation, in a position to operate a large trading store in partnership with
Mitchell. His political talents as well as his political ties by birth gave
him unusual opportunities in a time of great infighting in the state of
Georgia and within the Creek National Council, but at the same time
his life became increasingly complicated and subject to dangerous
turns of events.

Even during the period in which the names of McIntosh and
Mitchell were linked in scandal, the Indian agent was successful in
negotiating land cession treaties, with McIntosh's name always prominent among the signatories. On January 22, 1818, a land treaty was
concluded without difficulty at a meeting of Mitchell and the principal
chiefs at the Creek agency on the Flint River. The treaty ceded two
small tracts, one south of the Altamaha-Ocmulgee and the other be-

tween the Upper Ocmulgee and the Cherokee boundary line. For this land the Creeks were to receive $120,000, with $20,000 as a down payment and $10,000 to be paid annually for ten years. Calhoun later complained that this price was much too high, considering the small amount of land and the quality of the soil,[20] leading one to suspect Mitchell's ethics yet again. If Mitchell was indeed profiting from Creek funds, it would have been to his advantage to pay the highest possible price.

On January 22, 1819, Mitchell wrote to the secretary of war that he wished to visit the city of Washington "with the view principally of settling my Accounts." He added: "I have received a few lines from General McIntosh expressing a great desire on his part to accompany me. It was my intention to have made the trip without being accompanied by any of the Indians, and consequently did not mention to any of them my intention; but McIntosh has by some means heard of it, and upon reflection I am of the opinion that no injury but some good may result from his visit." Mitchell's seemingly casual agreement to allow McIntosh to accompany him is curious if one considers that on that same day Big Warrior wrote to President Monroe to say he was sending McIntosh as the head of a delegation to talk with him: "You will take them by the hand as if you see me yourself. Gen McIntosh will be the head of these others to give you these talks; you will listen to him. I send these men to let you kno everything that is in the Creek nation as if I was telling you my self to the President. I send McIntosh to you he is our head warrior of our nation was pointed by us & the Cherokees he & Gen Jackson went to put & end to all disputes in our nation & now I send him to you so settle buisnes with you & our nation."[21]

McIntosh and his party arrived in Washington on February 14, and he sent a note immediately to "Secketerey of War, Citty Washington. I send Col. [Samuel] Hawkins the publick interpreter of our Nation to let you kno that we have got here today. We was sent here by our Nation to see our father the president. . . . We are at Mr. Shottery tavern." The letter was signed "William McIntosh of the Creek Nation." In his first full letter to Secretary Calhoun, written on February 23, McIntosh began with his strongest point, the incident most calculated to line his own pockets—the unfortunate massacre at Chehaw. He emphasized that though the Creeks had fought with the United States against mutual enemies, "our Brothers of Chehaw have been killed by your people." He stated that the Creeks would "leave this to you to give us satisfaction." He had also been particularly directed to speak about Florida and the Seminoles because at that time the Adams-Onis Treaty was being negotiated for the acquisition of Spanish Florida. "Nobody but the Creeks and head men of our Nation had a right to hold a treaty for that land, if any treaty is to be held for our land in Florida it must be held in our Nation and with our head men," McIntosh told the secretary. He also informed him that his regiment of warriors had been paid only $5 per month for each man, but the white militia had received $8. "Many of the braves had lost their horses, and they want to know whether we'll pay them for those they lost."[22]

In his letter to the secretary of war on March 9, McIntosh showed that he and his fellow Creek chiefs had long memories. He brought up a point that had raised General Jackson's hackles almost five years previously at the negotiations of the Treaty of Fort Jackson. McIntosh referred to a letter, written by General Pinckney to Benjamin Hawkins, promising that the United States would pay for any losses incurred by the friendly Creeks in their war against the Red Sticks and British. McIntosh told the secretary that the $85,000 which was allotted "did not pay us half what we lost." The Adams-Onis Treaty having been concluded, McIntosh further stated, "Now you and the Spaniards have made a treaty for our land in Florida," even though "the friendly Creeks went on our own expense twice to Florida to try to put an end to the war . . . and you are going to take all our land in Florida, & going to throw all these people [the Seminoles] back in our nation."[23] This was a shrewd observation by McIntosh. When on February 22, 1819, the treaty had been signed in Washington by Secretary of State John Quincy Adams and Luis de Onis of Spain, Florida became a part of the United States, and the Seminoles were then under a new and stronger master rather than the loose control of a distant Spanish monarchy. To the settlers along the Florida border, the Adams-Onis Treaty was the first step in removing the Seminoles from the area. To the Creeks it meant the rejoining with the Creek Nation of the recalcitrant, renegade Seminoles, who had warred against their own people, harbored runaway slaves, and sheltered defeated insurrectionist Red Sticks.

When the United States acquired Florida, the Creeks immediately put in a claim for the Seminole lands. The United States government refused to honor the claim and made a counterproposal that the Creeks should receive the Seminoles into their own land in return for compensation from the federal government. As Mitchell reported to Secretary Calhoun in August, William McIntosh played a leading role in discussions concerning compensation for the Florida lands. In a meeting at Broken Arrow, however, McIntosh spoke out strongly for leasing the land to the United States, not selling it. As Mitchell reported, "McIntosh observed that they could lease it for as much for one year as the Government would be willing to give them if they were to sell it." Mitchell believed McIntosh was merely the tool of some frontier entrepreneur: "From my previous knowledge of their opinion upon this subject, I was immediately induced to believe that those statements had been made to them by someone, under an expectation of procuring such a lease." Mitchell told the Creeks that he opposed any lease. He wrote to Calhoun, however, that "if they sold the land to the U States these Indians [Seminoles] would be obliged to remove, of course."[24]

It was becoming increasingly evident that the policy of the United States government was more and more in favor of giving the Indians the choice of either assimilating into the white culture or removing to lands farther west. John C. Calhoun put the matter succinctly in a message to a Cherokee delegation on February 11, 1819; he even used a kind of Indian theology to make his point: "You are becoming like the white people; you can no longer live by hunting, but must work for your subsistence. In your new condition, far less land is necessary for you. Your great object ought to be to hold your land separate among yourselves, as your white neighbors; and to live and bring up your children in the same way as they do, and gradually to adopt their laws and manners. It is thus only that you can be prosperous and happy. Without this, you will find you will have to emigrate, or become extinct as a people. You see that the Great Spirit has made our form of society stronger than yours, and you must submit to adopt ours, if you wish to be happy by pleasing him."[25]

In late November 1819 Big Warrior wrote to Secretary Calhoun to tell him he was again sending a delegation consisting of Hawkins and eleven chiefs and headmen, including General McIntosh, to Washington. The purpose of the visit was "to talk with you upon the affairs of our nation and we have given them full power to transact all business." On December 31 McIntosh wrote to Calhoun, signing the letter "William McIntosh, for self & deputation." "Brother," he wrote, "we have come to see you again. Last year when we were here, we gave you an account of the losses sustained by the friendly part of our nation, from the hostiles, and you told us Congress was about to break up. Our Father would lay a bill before this Congress and try to recover payment for us. We wish to know if this has been done." He also stated that the delegation had been sent to learn whether the Creeks would be paid for the lands lost to them through the treaty with Spain. Plaintively, McIntosh added: "We have been coming to see you every year, and we begin to think that you think hard of us for coming. . . . We wish to know from you whether you intend to give us justice or not."[26]

Although there is no record that McIntosh and his deputation received the payments they sought at this time, a conference was to begin less than a year later that would result in the Treaty of Indian Springs, the terms of which repaid the Creeks handsomely—in their minds—with cash, annuities, and land reserves. The treaty negotiations were marred from the beginning by disagreements between the United States commissioners, who were given the power and the financial backing to conclude a treaty, and the treaty commissioners appointed by the state of Georgia, who had no power to negotiate and whose principal interest was in forcing the Creeks to return fugitive slaves to their Georgia owners, as stipulated in earlier treaty agreements made at Augusta, Galphinton, Shoulderbone, New York, and Colerain—treaties approved by only a part of the Creek Nation and by none of the Seminole chiefs. In appointing Colonel Andrew Pickens and General Thomas Flournoy as U.S. treaty commissioners in August, Secretary Calhoun had told them that the state of Georgia would be sending its own commissioners; he had urged Pickens and Flournoy to correspond with them, inform them of the time and place of the treaty conference, and render them every aid.[27] By mid-September, however, Pickens and Flournoy had both resigned because of the difficulties of dealing with the Georgians, and Daniel M. Forney and General David Meriwether had been appointed to replace them.

The treaty council was held at McIntosh's tavern at Indian Springs in cold and rainy late December weather, with so few Indians present that only sixteen hundred food rations were issued during the two-week period of the council.[28] No important upper town chiefs were present. The United States commissioners opened the meeting on December 27 with strong statements of support for the Georgians' position. Forney and Meriwether told the assembled Creeks that the people of Georgia had complained to the president that the Creeks had not returned their property as they had promised to do in the earlier treaties. "Your father President is very sorry," they told the assembly, "to hear of any differences between his white and red children; he loves them both and wishes them to love each other." They concluded with the admonition: "Listen to the talk of your brothers from Georgia, think on it and make your answers." The Georgia commissioners were unctuous in their opening comments: "Brothers: In order that the chain of friendship may remain bright between the white people and red people, it is necessary that they should do justice to each other. This the white people are always willing to do, and expect to meet the same friendly disposition amongst the red people, their brethren." Then they spoke in general about the claim of loss of property by Georgians. The Creek chiefs asked for a specific statement of claims, which the commissioners brought the following day, with the comments: "Look at these accounts; they are proved according to the laws of our country, and we wish to hear what you have to say about them."[29]

The Creek chiefs chose McIntosh, who hosted the meeting, to make a reply. He began with the usual rites of friendship, saying he was glad to hear of the friendly disposition of the Georgia commissioners and he returned the same friendly feeling. He pointed out that he had not known until the previous day that the chiefs would be called upon to answer the claims of the state of Georgia. He had looked over the statement of claims exhibited by the commissioners and knew nothing about many of the items. He gave the commissioners a summary of Creek efforts to recover the fugitive slaves and abide by the earlier agreements; he then quoted Alexander McGillivray to clarify a crucial point. He said that after the Treaty of New York, General McGillivray informed the people that he had promised to deliver all the prisoners and Negroes belonging to the whites who were then in the nation, but that they would not "be so liable for any that were dead or removed." General McGillivray had collected a number of white and black prisoners, principally in the upper towns, and delivered them to Major Seagrove, then the Indian agent. He told the commissioners that at the Treaty of Colerain a similar statement of claims to the one then being exhibited was presented, but the Creeks refused to acknowledge any claims except those covered by the Treaty of New York, which called only for the restoration of property in the form of Negroes and prisoners. McIntosh stated that in conformity with that treaty, he and other Creek chiefs had delivered a number of Negro prisoners to Colonel Hawkins. He also said that Colonel Hawkins had once told him that he had received a statement of claims made by the people of Georgia but that he had never laid it before the nation. McIntosh told the commissioners that he himself had fought in the Florida campaign under Colonel Duncan Clinch, when the Negro Fort had been destroyed and most of its occupants killed. Those blacks taken alive had been turned over to Colonel Clinch to be returned to their owners. Then he made a telling point that placed the commissioners in a dilemma: "If the President admits that country [Florida] to belong to the Creek Nation, I will go down with my warriors and bring back all the Negroes I can get, and deliver them up." He concluded by saying that when both sides of the argument were fully examined, he did not believe there would be much difference of opinion between the Georgians and the Creeks: "I will not say there is no property in the Nation belonging to Georgians, but I do not know of any. If there is any I am willing to restore it or pay its value."[30]

On December 29 the Georgia commissioners delivered their answer:

> We have heard your talk yesterday, and considered it over. . . . We are sorry, however, to find that you do not consider yourselves bound to restore to us the property as well as the Negroes taken or destroyed by your nation before the Treaty of New York. Brothers: Knowing that some bad men live on our frontiers, who are disposed to do mischief, we are not surprised to hear that you have claims against the white people which have not been exhibited. Brothers: As to the Negroes now remaining among the Seminoles, belonging to the white people, we consider these people [the Seminoles] a part of the Creek Nation; and we look to the chiefs of the Creek Nation to cause the people there, as well as the people of the Upper Towns, to do justice.

Apparently McIntosh's attempt was in vain to make a fine legal distinction concerning the Creek responsibility for fugitive slaves removed from the nation or to clarify the point of whether Florida—and not merely the Seminole people—belonged to the Creek Nation, but he did receive one concession. The commissioners stated: "We agree to your proposition to submit all our claims on both sides to our common father, the President, whose decision we will conform to on our part, and hope there may never more be any cause for difference between us."[31]

The treaty negotiations slowly dragged along past the beginning of the new year. The United States commissioners offered the Creeks an exchange of land, acre for acre, for their eastern lands so that their hunting style of life could continue. There is ample evidence that the Creeks no longer relied much on hunting to supplement their food supply, and so the chiefs responded to the commissioners that they would rather remain where they were and gradually turn their attention to husbandry than to cross the Mississippi River in search of game. They told the commissioners that they had made a law depriving those who abandoned their land in the pursuit of game of their rights in the Creek Nation. Then the chiefs made a legal point that would be important in assessing McIntosh's later actions. They stated that "in the event of any town or towns wishing to cross the Mississippi, the Nation would be willing to give up *their* land to the United States for lands there."[32] Much of the controversy accompanying the treaty in 1825 rested on whether a part of the Creek Nation had a right to cede lands in exchange for lands in the West. Even at this 1821 conference, however, the chief of Tuckabatchee signaled trouble ahead when he arose and said: "McIntosh knows that we are bound by our laws, and that what is not done in the public square in general council is not binding on our people." He turned to the commissioners: "That is the only talk I have for you, and I shall return home." He then withdrew from the treaty negotiations, followed by thirty-five other chiefs. The commissioners told McIntosh they would consider his signature and those of his followers binding upon the Creek Nation.[33]

On January 8 the treaty was signed, ceding 6,748 square miles, or 4,318,720 acres, of Creek lands to the United States.[34] The treaty commissioners reported to Calhoun that "no tract of land within the Indian boundary is as fertile or desirable as the land now ceded." In the first article of the treaty two tracts of land are excepted, the title and possession being reserved to the Creek Nation: "one thousand acres, to be laid off in a square, so as to include the Indian Springs in the centre thereof; as, also, six hundred and forty acres on the western bank of the Oakmulgee river, so as to include the improvements at present in the possession of the Indian Chief General M'Intosh." For the land cession the Creeks were to receive $10,000 immediately and $190,000 to be paid over a fourteen-year period, "in money or goods and implements of husbandry, at the option of the Creek nation."[35]

The treaty also stipulated that the United States government would pay all claims of damages held against the Creek Nation by the citizens of Georgia, up to $250,000. Although this amount was included in the total cost of the land cession—$450,000 for 4,318,720 acres of land—it was an admittedly inflated figure, which duped the Creeks into believing they had received a little over ten cents an acre for their land instead of less than seven cents. In referring to the $250,000 set aside for paying the Georgians their damage claims, Forney and Meriwether told Calhoun that they "cannot believe these claims, on a fair settlement, will exceed $100,000."[36] Their estimate was uncannily close; the total amount of the claims paid was $100,589, making the total purchase price $300,589.[37] The Creeks were charged for all black slaves carried off by the British in the War of 1812 as well as all who had taken refuge with the Seminoles, and the hearings on the depredation claims were held in the interior of Georgia, with the Creeks having no opportunity to attend and present their arguments. The difference remaining between the $100,589 actually paid and the $250,000 set aside in the treaty remained in the federal treasury, and nothing was said about returning this money to the Creeks.[38] In such an atmosphere of duplicity, it is not surprising that an entrepreneur like McIntosh would have become involved, seemingly for his own profit, in the scheming and bribery that led to the ceding of all the remaining Creek lands to the United States in 1825.

William McIntosh and many other Creeks were victims of profound change in their lifestyles, a change caused by forces beyond themselves. Thomas L. McKenney, superintendent of Indian trade, in a somewhat romanticized picture of the noble savage—for this was the romantic period, and in England Byron and Shelley were exalting the image of Rousseau's concept of the primitive hero—states the case well in a communication to the Senate entitled "Trade and Intercourse," which he wrote on December 27, 1821:

> Before the quiet of the aboriginal solitude was disturbed, and the habits with which nature had invested its natives were torn off by the hands of a more enlightened, but, perhaps, less humane race of men, there were no demands to satisfy other than the forests furnished; and no necessity existed, therefore, for commerce, save only that which was implied in the exchange of bows and arrows, and stone axes; and these, again, for skins and meat, which might have been taken in extra quantities by some more fortunate hunter. But the advance of civilization upon this simple state has changed these easily adjusted relations; and its blessings, however highly to be appreciated, have, in reference to our Indians, been less numerous than its curses. New wants have been originated by it, but the corresponding supplies have not been furnished. Disease, physical and moral, has been communicated, without being accompanied by the appropriate remedies.

His conclusion is that "however consistent the extinction of the aboriginal race may be with the designs of Providence, in peopling this new world with a more enlightened and polished society, it is not so clear that some additional efforts were not required of the first settlers, and the generations which had succeeded them, to meliorate the conditions and recover from barbarism those whose domain they invaded, and in the occupancy of which we have so completely succeeded."[39]

There is another side to the coin, however, and Michael D. Green has cogently reasoned that the Creeks may well have received the better of the deal in the Treaty of 1821. The area ceded was primarily hunting land between the Ocmulgee and Flint rivers, where few Creeks lived, and because of the frequent encroachments of hunters, cattlemen, and squatters from Georgia, the game population in the area had severely declined. The value of the land for subsistence had, therefore, already been virtually lost to the Creeks, and it may have been much more practical to accept the long-term annuity income from its sale than to rely on the scant hunting prospects remaining. At the same time, this sale of the last "disposable" land made most of the Creeks even more determined to sign no further land cessions. The remaining ten million acres, which contained rich farmland as well as ancient sites of towns and burial grounds, were absolutely necessary to the Creeks if they were to continue living in the Southeast. For this reason the National Council was prepared to enforce with a death penalty the resolve that no one should sign away any more land.[40]

As speaker of the Creek National Council, McIntosh had been the first to proclaim publicly the law forbidding further land sales, and, ironically, he was later to become the first to be executed under its terms. According to Waring, this law had been formulated as early as July 1817, but it did not appear in the 1818 code presented to Mitchell.[41] As the commander of the law menders, McIntosh also had the major responsibility of enforcing all of the laws of the National Council, but in 1821 he successfully argued that this law should be suspended so that the land could be relinquished and the Creeks' debt to Georgia be paid. The headmen had reluctantly agreed, but according to a white eyewitness to the negotiations, "after the treaty of 1821, much dissatisfaction prevailed among the Indians, and threats were made against McIntosh." Another witness said that Hopoie Hadjo and Little Prince agreed that "since the treaty of 1821, the Indians have been jealous of McIntosh, and looked on him with distrust, and it was with considerable difficulty that he was forgiven for participating in that act; but McIntosh was forgiven for that act in consequence of saying that the Nation was in debt to Georgia." The headmen also agreed that "any man should die who should thereafter offer to sell."[42]

14

McIntosh and Crowell:
Foes in the
Deadly Game of Land Cessions

————— • —————

John Crowell, who had been the first congressional delegate from the Alabama Territory, was appointed in February 1821 to replace the Indian agent David B. Mitchell, who had been dismissed from the service for his slave-smuggling activities. Crowell took some unpopular stands in championing Creek rights against those of the United States and was later to be in the center of the controversy surrounding the final ceding of all Creek lands at a council at Indian Springs in 1825. He ran counter to McIntosh on many occasions. Although the enmity between the two reached a kindling point in 1823, the beginning of the conflict may have occurred immediately after Crowell took office and made it clear that he would not allow McIntosh to be involved in the receiving and paying of Creek annuities, which Mitchell had permitted. The new agent willingly tried to assist the Creeks with their claims for damages in the late summer of 1821. He wrote to Calhoun: "A number of Indians who lost property last war has not been paid any part of their claims . . . some others are entitled to a reserve of land under Jackson's Treaty, whose claims has not been confirmed."[1] Supporting the Creeks with apparent sincerity, Crowell had already begun to play the role of gadfly to the government.

McIntosh was also demonstrating civic responsibility in early September 1821, when he met with the Reverend William Capers, a newly arrived Methodist missionary. Reverend Capers brought an introductory letter from John McIntosh, William's half-brother, pronouncing him "a minister of the gospel, who visited the Indians for a religious and charitable end only." McIntosh made an agreement that allowed Capers to establish two schools in the Creek Nation, one near Coweta and the other near Tuckabatchee, and later he petitioned Capers to open still another school, in the upper part of the nation. Capers, who was then angry with Crowell for having urged Big Warrior to forbid public preaching in the Creek Nation, welcomed McIntosh's pious comment: "Some of the old men would not have preaching, but I think Missionaries ought to preach to the children, as well as teach them to read and write."[2]

Also during this time, McIntosh was deeply involved with political machinations among the Creeks, the Seminoles, and the United States government. On September 18 Andrew Jackson, newly named governor of the new Territory of Florida, received into his executive chambers three prominent Seminole chiefs who had heard some inflammatory information from McIntosh and wanted to get the truth from Jackson. The leader of the three chiefs was Neamathla, the most influential of the Creeks who came to Florida after the Red Stick War. They wanted to know what their father, the president, intended to do with them. They were concerned because Neamathla had been to see the headmen of the Creek Nation, and McIntosh had told him that Jackson would deprive them of all their lands and give each chief only 640 acres for himself and his family to live on. Jackson said: "I give you a plain, straight talk, and do not speak with a forked tongue. It is necessary that you be brought together, either within the bounds of your old nation, or at some other point, where your father the President may be enabled to extend to you his fatherly care and assistance." He concluded, "Your former disobedience is forgotten, and he again receives you as his children."[3]

In December of 1821 McIntosh was involved in a treaty council that attempted to make an agreement concerning a boundary line between the Creek and Cherokee lands. The council was held in the Creek Nation "at General McIntoshes," and the resulting treaty— which was never ratified by the federal government—was signed by both McIntosh and Big Warrior, as well as Cherokee chiefs, on December 11. The line of the boundary was to be run from Buzzard Roost on the Chattahoochee River in a direct line to strike the Coosa River opposite Fort Strother. All land north of that line was to be Cherokee; all south, Creek.[4]

This line caused some problems of political allegiance, which the Indians in council attempted to solve in unusual ways. For example, all Creeks who lived north of the line were to become subjects of the

Neamathla, by Charles Bird King (from McKenney and Hall, *History of the Indian Tribes*)

Cherokee Nation, and likewise all Cherokees south of it were to become Creek subjects. Chiefs of either nation who lived in redesignated territories would become chiefs of their newly adopted nation. If a murder was committed in one nation and the murderer took refuge in the other, the nation where the offense occurred would make application to the nation of refuge to have the murderer killed, and when the deed was done, the offended nation would pay the man who executed the murderer $200. If a Creek or Cherokee crossed the boundary to commit murder or theft and then returned to his own nation, the offended nation could demand satisfaction. Although McIntosh and a number of prominent Cherokees signed this treaty, when the two nations met in council again on October 30, 1822, to repeal certain of these articles—particularly the one making Creek or Cherokee chiefs headmen in their opposite nations—McIntosh was not present to sign.[5]

Apparently the Cherokees were not very confident of McIntosh's integrity at this time. Charles R. Hicks, one of the principal chiefs of the Cherokee Nation, wrote to the secretary of war on January 10, 1822, to say that "if the Creeks has made any promises to the state of Georgia through their warrior William McIntosh for making further cessions of land to them, we have no control over their councils, nor are we governed by them in our councils. . . . I am confident you would not give a countenance to any cessions of lands they might make which did not properly lie within the line of which yourself has believed as the landmarks of the two nations."[6]

McIntosh was to become more deeply involved in 1823 in attempting to persuade the Cherokees to cede their land to the United States, leading to an incident in which he was shamefully ordered out of the Cherokee Nation and excluded forever from its councils. George M. Troup, McIntosh's cousin, was the newly elected governor of Georgia, and the Georgia legislature in 1823 required him to "use his exertions" to urge the federal government to abide by the terms of the Georgia Compact of 1802. In this agreement the state of Georgia had relinquished all claims to territory from the Chattahoochee to the Mississippi in return for the United States government's undertaking to extinguish, by peaceable methods, the Indian titles to land in Georgia. Since the commitments to Georgia had not been honored after more than two decades, President Monroe, at Governor Troup's insistence, sent treaty commissioners to New Echota, or Newtown, in the Cherokee Nation in July 1823 to attempt to secure land cessions.

The Cherokees were adamant in their refusal to cede further land, and the commissioners employed McIntosh to go to New Echota for the purpose of bribing some key Cherokee officials. In late October, soon after the beginning of the council, McIntosh arrived with seven other Creeks, including his son Chilly and an interpreter. The Cherokees received them as friends and brothers, even appropriating money for the foraging of their horses. "After having shewed them every friendship," the Cherokee chiefs wrote to Big Warrior and Little Prince, "we did not expect that Wm. McIntosh had any ungenerous disposition toward the interests of this nation; but we were mistaken." McIntosh approached John Ross, president of the Cherokee National Committee and an Indian who, like himself, had Scots blood in his veins, with an attempted bribe, and Ross insisted that the offer be put in writing. On October 21 McIntosh wrote to Ross:

> My friend I am going to inform you a few lines as friend, I want you to give me your opinion of the treaty, whether the chiefs will be willing or not. If the Chiefs feel disposed to let the United States have the land, part of it, I want you to let me know. I will make the United States commissioners give you two thousand dollars, A McKoy the same and Charles Hicks $3,000, for present, and nobody shall know it; and if you think the land woulden sold, I will be satisfied. If the lands should be sold I will get you the amount before the treaty *sign*, and If you get any friend you want him to *received* they shall receive. Nothing more to inform you at present. N. B. The whole amount is $12,000. You can divide among your friends, exclusive $7,000.

At the bottom of the letter Ross wrote ominously, "Read and exposed in open council in the presence of Wm. McIntosh. 24th Oct., 1823."[7]

When the incriminating letter was read aloud—as McIntosh squirmed with embarrassment—Ross said: "The author has mistaken my character and my sense of honor." Major Ridge (Chief Pathkiller) rose at the conclusion of the reading of the letter and said of McIntosh, "Set him aside." Ridge was emotional as he denounced McIntosh: "As speaker for the Cherokee Nation I cast him behind my back. . . . We are not to be purchased with money." The council, now thoroughly disrupted, ended at once, and McIntosh was reported to have been last seen riding south at such a fast pace that his horse collapsed on the trail.[8] This scene in the council prompted the Cherokee chiefs to write to Big Warrior and Little Prince that "we have this day went through a painful and unpleasant ceremony." They added that McIntosh had that day been "discharged from ever having any *voice* in our *councils*, hereafter, as a Chief connected with this Nation." About McIntosh they wrote: "Brothers, we are astonished at our brother's conduct at this place; and we have lost all confidence of his fidelity towards the interests of the red brethren East of the Mississippi River; therefore, we advise you, as brothers, to keep a strict watch over his conduct; or, if you do not, he will ruin your nation."[9]

Although the entire affair was embarrassing to McIntosh, the attempted bribery at New Echota had further convinced the treaty commissioners that he was a valuable ally. Colonel Duncan Campbell, one of the treaty commissioners present at the scene, reported to the secretary of war: "Upon the subject of a cession the Creeks hold a very different language. From information derived from McIntosh, and since confirmed by the Creek Agent, the prospect (as to getting land) in that quarter is much more favorable." Campbell may have heard McIntosh boastfully tell some chiefs at New Echota that he had offered his whole country to the United States commissioners for two dollars an acre. This was pure fantasizing, for the government was accustomed to paying only ten cents an acre or less for ceded land. He had also made the grandiose suggestion at that council that the Cherokees, Creeks, Choctaws, and Chickasaws all surrender up their country and emigrate west of the Mississippi, to settle under one government.[10]

During 1823 the long-smoldering conflict between Crowell and McIntosh erupted when an incident that occurred at the payment of the annuities at Broken Arrow enraged the agent. Captain Thomas Triplett, who was present, reported that after Crowell had paid the chiefs, they went out of the square to divide the money. McIntosh then went among them and took a large amount of the money from them by violence, claiming that they owed it to him. Triplett said that witnesses heard him afterward say he had taken $8,000. The payment of the annuities, of course, had long been a source of trouble between the two adversaries. Triplett claimed to have been present at the payment of three annuities, which Crowell "uniformly paid the chiefs in cash,"[11] in contrast to the practice of Mitchell and McIntosh, who paid them in goods.

Chicanery was also involved in the cash payments by Crowell, however, if the questionable testimony of Samuel Hawkins, a relative of McIntosh's, can be believed. On April 12, 1825, Hawkins wrote to Governor Troup that in 1821 Crowell had paid off the annuities to the principal chiefs in fifty and one hundred dollar bills. No small bills were made available so that the chiefs could make a fair division among the towns in money; they were forced to buy goods from the trading store of Thomas Crowell, brother of the agent, and divide the goods. Hawkins told Troup that they had to pay Crowell fifty cents a yard for domestic homespun of the same description McIntosh had charged only twenty-five cents a yard for a few months earlier. There was some improvement when the annuities were paid in 1822. Again the agent had paid the annuities in fifty and one hundred dollar bills, but he had told the chiefs that his brother had change for the bills. Thomas Crowell, however, would give them only $5 in cash and the rest in merchandise; at that time he charged thirty-seven and a half cents a yard for domestic homespun. Hawkins also told the governor that the agent had deducted $60 to $100 from each year's payment for the expense of sending a man to the bank in Savannah to transmit the money. Hawkins's testimony may have been prejudiced in favor of McIntosh. When in the course of the congressional investigation of the Indian controversy, Little Prince was asked: "Has the Agent [Crowell] always paid your annuities in money, and to your satisfaction?" he answered: "He does so perfectly to their [the chiefs'] satisfaction: has always paid them in money."[12]

When McIntosh took $8,000 of the annuity payments from his fellow Creeks by violence in 1823, agent John Crowell acted quickly. To retaliate, he ordered George Stinson, McIntosh's brother-in-law and business associate, arrested on the charge of selling goods in the Creek Nation without a license. McIntosh, standing on his rights as a Creek chief of the fifth rank, would not permit Crowell's men to arrest Stinson, but the agent attempted to go over McIntosh's head by appealing to Little Prince. He told Colonel William Hambly, his messenger: "I wish you to state in plain and positive terms to the Prince that I call upon him as the head man of this nation, to have Stinson taken and brought to me, at all hazards; if six men is not enough, send six hundred, and take him by force if he has to destroy McIntosh and his whole establishment to effect it. Tell him it will reflect disgrace on him as the head man of the nation, to suffer one chief to prevent his orders from being put into execution; and this conduct of McIntosh is quite sufficient to break him as a chief." He asked Hambly to warn Little Prince that if he protected Stinson "the Nation must suffer for it." Then follows an astounding set of statements by Crowell, indicating that he was so desperate to have vengeance on McIntosh by arresting Stinson that he would misappropriate Creek funds: "If, however, he [Little Prince] will not have this man [Stinson] taken, I shall adopt such steps as will ensure his arrest, and pay the expenses of it out of the annuity, even should it take the whole of it. I can get men from Georgia that will take him, by paying enough for it, and rather than not have him, I will pay every dollar of the annuity for him."[13]

John Crowell (Courtesy of the State of Alabama Department of Archives and History)

Stinson was eventually delivered into the agent's custody and was tried in a federal court in Savannah. Mitchell and McIntosh were the principal witnesses for the defense, and Stinson was acquitted of the charge of selling goods in the Creek Nation without a license. The defense was based on his being represented as a clerk, not a partner, in McIntosh's trading establishment. As a lesser employee, he apparently would have needed no license. Judge Cuyler, who heard the case, wrote to a disappointed Crowell after the acquittal: "I can only add that I was perfectly satisfied of the guilt of Stinson, and that his defense was not sufficient to authorize his acquittal, and I so charged the jury." T. P. Andrews, the special agent later sent to investigate the controversy between Crowell and McIntosh, reported to Secretary of War James Barbour that the "Agent was right in prosecuting him [Stinson], and he ought to have been convicted." In summarizing his findings concerning the conflict between Crowell and McIntosh, Andrews stated that "it arose from the integrity and firmness of the Agent, chiefly in refusing to permit McIntosh, who was of an avaricious, unjust, and oppressive disposition towards his own people, to defraud them of the money coming from the Government, through the hands of the Agent; a practice which had been tolerated by the predecessor of the Agent, D. B. Mitchell." Andrews also commented on an incident reported by Chilly McIntosh in which Crowell drew a knife and threatened to cut the throat of a man called Srells, or Cells, who had been adopted by the Creek Nation. According to Andrews, Crowell admitted having a quarrel with the man but denied the interference of General McIntosh, who, he said, was present and took no action. Andrews wrote that the "Agent admits having threatened him personally from the impulse of the moment."[14] It is obvious that there is much conflicting and confusing testimony concerning the characters and personalities of both Crowell and McIntosh.

In May of 1824 Big Warrior called a meeting of the Upper Creek chiefs at Tuckabatchee. According to a report by Duncan Campbell, this meeting grew out of a communication from John Ross, a Cherokee chief, to Big Warrior the previous spring advising the Creeks to keep a strict watch over McIntosh's conduct to keep him from ruining the Creek Nation.[15] Campbell believed the principal purposes of the meeting at Tuckabatchee were to provide for concerted action between the Cherokees and Creeks, to plan resistance to government policy, and "to depreciate McIntosh and to destroy his standing and influence." Campbell understood the difference between the chiefs of the upper and lower towns. The former, who lived mostly in Alabama, along the Tallapoosa River, were under Big Warrior; the latter, living along the Chattahoochee in Georgia, were under the control of McIntosh. "The former were stubborn and unyielding," Campbell reported, "while the latter considered our proposition as reasonable, and were disposed to its acceptance. A treaty could have been obtained, signed by a large majority of the chiefs within the Georgia limits, ceding the territory which they occupy, and we doubt not but that there would have been a striking unanimity on the part of the population, but for the threats and intimidating language which had been industriously circulated." At Tuckabatchee the Upper Creek chiefs, along with Little Prince, chief of the lower towns, passed a resolution to follow the Cherokees and not "sell one foot of land." They also began to discuss in a threatening manner the punishment to be handed out to any Creek chief who signed a land cession treaty: "We have a great many chiefs and headmen but, be they ever so great, they must all abide by the laws. We have guns and ropes: and if any of our people break these laws, those guns and ropes are to be their end."[16]

In July 1824, a council was held at Broken Arrow, which McIntosh allegedly attended, to spread the message of resisting further land cessions and frustrating treaty negotiations. According to Elijah M. Amos, an eyewitness, the chiefs were inclined to be secretive. Amos testified in a congressional hearing:

> It was announced by some person in the square where the council was held that something was to be read or communicated that they did not wish the white people to hear. Accordingly, all the white people retired from the square, among the rest Col. Crowell and the witness, leaving no white person in the square but Hambly, the interpreter, and Walker, the subagent. Afterwards, the witness behind the cabin, in front of which the council was held, heard Walker read part of a long paper which was translated by Hambly into the Indian language. The following was, in substance, contained in what witness heard: "We speak this to you in council; we wish you to live like the Cherokees, and not sell your lands, or a foot of them."[17]

Another meeting of the Upper Creek chiefs was planned for November 1824, at a place called Polecat Springs, and the intervening months were spent, according to a report by treaty commissioner Campbell, in "confirming the decisions of the Upper Town chiefs and in exciting and cherishing the fears and alarms of McIntosh and his adherents." The Upper Creek chiefs circulated copies of a letter Campbell had written to the secretary of war in November 1823, telling of a visit from a deputation of Creeks, led by McIntosh, who had suggested that the Creeks were interested in ceding land. The letter, Campbell wrote, "has been used as an instrument in the hands of his enemies, for the purpose of lessening his influence and of bringing him into contempt amongst his own people." Campbell also reported the involvement of Crowell and his subagent Walker in these machinations. The meeting at Polecat Springs was held at Walker's house, and the subagent put the proceedings of both councils in writing and had them published in the Alabama newspapers. "The commissioners," Campbell stated, "derived no aid from the principal agent [Crowell] and encountered their perfidious opposition of his assistant." Captain Walker, he added, "prostituted the duties of his office and wantonly intermeddled."[18] The overreacting Campbell, fearful for his scheme to use McIntosh to persuade the Creeks to cede land, was angry and willing to blast anyone who had a different point of view even though he knew that Crowell was pledged to represent the Indians and that Walker's duties included being the Indians' scribe.

At the time of this meeting at Walker's house, McIntosh was on his way to Indian Springs and the handsome inn he had built on property acquired through the 1821 treaty. There Joel Bailey showed him a newspaper with the account of the Polecat Springs death decree, and McIntosh remarked that it was the first he had seen of the account but that the law was not valid for the entire nation because it had not been made in a full National Council. Then he drew a square on the ground and divided it into four equal parts. He said that one of these parts could not make laws for the other three. Then he told Bailey that though the Polecat Law was not a general law, it might cause the majority of Creeks to be afraid to state their true feelings about ceding land and moving west. McIntosh told Bailey at the treaty conference at Broken Arrow in December that "the Indians were more afraid of the pole cat law than he had expected." During the treaty negotiations at Broken Arrow in December, Campbell answered a letter from Governor Troup, who had been disturbed by newspaper accounts of the proceedings at Tuckabatchee and Polecat Springs. Campbell said the publications "were evidently intended to forestal us. They have, in a great measure, had the effect of spreading alarm throughout the nation, by the miserable farrago of threats which they contain. For some time past, the Cherokees have exerted a steady and officious interference in the affairs of this tribe." He added that they were "now encountering a daily interference, most active and insidious."[19]

In anticipation of the meeting of the treaty council at Broken Arrow on December 1, however, McIntosh seems in his November talk with Bailey to have reversed his position on the validity of the Polecat Law for all Creeks. Previously he had been all too aware of this law and had very nearly suffered the penalty for it in 1821. The Creek general was described by one witness as he stood on a wagon in August 1824 and addressed a crowd assembled to watch a ball-play near Mr. Smith's missionary school. He spread his feet apart as he stood and proclaimed that any man who should offer to sell the first bit of land, no larger than that between his feet, should die by the law. He added that the National Council had made the law. Another witness to this incident reported that McIntosh said "the very first men who should sell land should die by the law" and that "such a law had been made in council."[20] Now, influenced by Campbell and perhaps by greed, he was vainly attempting to find a loophole in a law he knew to be binding.

In the face of this local turmoil, President Monroe, Secretary of War Calhoun, and Governor Troup continued to place a high priority on securing cessions of Georgia lands and removing the Indians to land in the West. Calhoun had appointed Duncan Campbell, who had met with no success with the Cherokees the year before, and David Meriwether as commissioners to call the Creeks to council in an attempt to negotiate a treaty. At a minimum, the commissioners were to acquire all the Creek lands in Georgia, but the government would accept any Creek lands in Alabama as well. In late September, agent Crowell wrote to Campbell to report that he had interviewed the head chiefs of the Creeks and had told them that commissioners had been appointed to treat with them for the purchase of lands in Georgia. He set the date of the council for November 25, but the chiefs opposed it on the grounds that some of them were indisposed. They said December 6 was their earliest possible beginning date. Campbell replied that he wanted the council to begin on December 1, and the compromise was accepted by the Creek chiefs.[21]

Campbell contracted with John H. Broadnax to provide twenty thousand rations for the Indians in the assembly. The ration, to be provided once a day, would consist of a hearty twenty ounces of beef, twenty ounces of sifted corn meal, and "the army quantity of salt." A modest price of nine cents a ration (five cents for the meat, four cents for the meal and salt) was agreed upon, and the full price of $1,800 was advanced to Broadnax for the rations. Campbell and Meriwether arrived on November 30, and the Indians—who had been desperately short of food for years—were already at the council site at Broken Arrow in such great numbers that Campbell contracted for an additional twenty thousand rations.[22] The Creeks, many of whom were more interested in filling their stomachs than discussing treaties of cession, lined up in long queues when the issuing of rations began the following morning.

All such meetings between Indians and treaty commissioners began slowly and with careful attention to traditional ritual. On December 4 the commissioners met with the Creek chiefs around the great council fire and received the peace pipe and the right hand of friendship, and on December 7 Campbell presented his opening arguments. He told them that more than twenty years earlier a bargain was made between the United States and Georgia in which the United States government had agreed to purchase for the state all lands lying within certain limits. He explained to them that Georgia had made several requests of the United States to have the agreement put into effect and that the United States had appointed commissioners, who stood before them to try to make such a treaty. He said, "The President finds you entirely surrounded by white people. He sees that there are frequent interruptions by encroachments on both sides." The president, Campbell told the chiefs, "has extensive tracts of country under his dominion beyond the Mississippi, which he is willing to give you in exchange for the country you now occupy. We make you an offer, not only for your territory within the limits of Georgia, but for your whole country."[23]

As speaker of the Creek Nation, William McIntosh gave the reply of the Creek chiefs on December 8. He stated that the chiefs did not know anything about the talks between Georgia and the United States twenty years before, but he could not believe the president would sign an agreement that would alienate some of his children from the others and result in "aggrandizing the one by the downfall and ruin of the other. That ruin is the almost inevitable consequence of removal beyond the Mississippi, we are convinced. It is true, very true," McIntosh stated, "that we are 'surrounded by white people,' and that there are encroachments made. What assurances have we that similar ones will not be made on us, should we deem it proper to accept your offer and remove beyond the Mississippi? And how do we know we would not be encroaching on the people of other nations?"[24] Though cleverly couching his words negatively and in the form of a question, McIntosh implied that the Creeks might accept removal.

The commissioners were as wily as their Creek adversaries were cunning, and on December 9 they replied: "We ask you, how did the Muscogee Nation come by this country? You came from the west, and took the country from another people, who were in possession."

Campbell reminded them that fifty years before, the Creeks had taken part in the revolutionary war and had been conquered along with the British, with whom they were allied. "All the land which was conquered belonged to the conquerors. The British were all driven off, and you would have shared the same fate, but for the humanity and goodness of the new Government which was established after the war." The commissioners added: "It was not your fault that your forefathers fought against this country, yet you have to be the sufferers by their rashness. Since this time, some of you have shown yourselves to be worthy of being the President's children, by fighting by the side of the white man against the foes of liberty." The commissioners said the "most earnest wish of the president's heart is that you should live and prosper, that you should advance in civilization, that you should have good laws and obey them." The way to achieve such good ends, they advised, was to move beyond the Mississippi.[25]

As the treaty negotiations continued, Campbell argued that the talks signed by some of the chiefs in the councils at Tuckabatchee and Polecat Springs were invalid as well as misguided. When some of them signed a talk to "follow the pattern of the Cherokees and never sell another foot of land," they were "misled" and reached a "hasty conclusion," which they were "unable to support." These two "rash and premature" agreements, he reasoned, "are not binding even upon those who signed them, much less are they binding upon the Nation. This is the place where laws are made—in full council; not at Tuckabatchee or Pole Cat Springs, where a mere handful are gathered together, not, perhaps, so much by their own consent as by designing individuals. This Nation," he reminded them, "was once led into a dreadful war by bad advisors and false prophets."[26] The two designing individuals in Campbell's mind were, of course, Crowell and the subagent Walker, and the bad advisers and false prophets were the nativistic Upper Creeks, who now opposed the policy of removal.

Returning to the main theme of his argument, Campbell told the Creek chiefs: "This is not the first country that has been sold by its proprietors. The United States has lately bought Florida from Spain and the Spaniards are gone." He reminded the Creeks that some years earlier the United States "bought Louisiana from France and many of its inhabitants removed thousands of miles from the place of their birth and where their fathers were buried." The commissioners told them that the United States had lately made a treaty with the Seminoles and marked out land for them and had also exchanged lands with the Choctaws. Now he was offering the Creeks a safe and permanent resting place beyond the Mississippi. They had only two choices, Campbell said: they must either come under the laws of the white man, or they must remove to western lands.[27] There is some indication that whiskey was introduced into the proceedings, perhaps in an effort to soften the Creeks' resolve. On December 9 Little Prince, McIntosh, and two other chiefs signed a brief statement: "This day, we, the chiefs, head men, and warriors, in council, agreed that no person shall sell spirit to any person or persons before the treaty discharge. If found, any person or persons selling spirit shall lose all the spirit and forfeit all the money received this day."[28]

McIntosh spoke for the Creek chiefs in reply to Campbell's arguments on December 11. They professed not to know that the Muscogees were not the original inhabitants of their soil, saying that the tradition had been handed down from their forefathers that they were the original settlers. The chiefs reaffirmed the soundness of the Treaty of 1802, but, McIntosh correctly pointed out, a "stipulation in that agreement declares that the United States will extinguish for Georgia the Indian title to the lands within the ceded limits, so soon only as it can be done on peaceable and reasonable terms. This certainly admits the claim of the Muscogees," McIntosh asserted, using the old name for the nation, "to the right of an occupancy, until they are willing to dispose of that occupancy." He admitted that in the revolutionary war "many of our people were deluded by the British and persuaded to take the side against the colonies." But he cited an article from the Treaty of New York (1790), which read: "The United States solemnly guarantees to the Creek Nation all their lands within the limits of the United States to the westward and southward of the boundary line described by the preceding article."[29]

Like a skilled lawyer arguing his case before a high court, McIntosh continued. He cited the second article of the Treaty of Fort Jackson, in 1814: "The United States will guarantee to the Creek nation the integrity of all their territory eastwardly and northwardly of the said line to be run and described as mentioned in the first article." He added that the guarantees stated in writing in these two treaties had been repeated verbally at Indian Springs in January 1821. Then he came to the powerful conclusion of his argument: "Brothers, we have already parted with various tracts of our land, until we find our limits quite circumscribed. We have barely a sufficiency left us. The proposal to remove beyond the Mississippi we cannot for a moment listen to. Brothers, we have among us aged and infirm men and women, and helpless children, who cannot bear the fatigue of a single day's journey. Shall we, can we, leave them behind us? Shall we desert, in their old age, the parents that fostered us? The answer is in your own hearts. No! Again: we feel an affection for the land in which we were born. We wish our bones to rest by the side of our fathers." In conclusion, he said, "We must positively decline the proposal of a removal beyond the Mississippi, or the sale of any more of our territory."[30]

Despite this ringing rhetoric against removal, it was shortly after delivering this talk of December 11 that McIntosh was "broken" as speaker of the Creek Nation. Perhaps, as speaker, he orated the thoughts of the other chiefs, not his own. Perhaps he merely wanted to get the price for removal increased. Testimony given later in a congressional hearing indicated that McIntosh was so much in the company of Campbell that "it became subject of remark" and "created much distrust and suspicion among the chiefs." Nimrod Doyell testified that the chiefs removed McIntosh as speaker because they were suspicious of him and because he was holding secret talks and meetings with the treaty commissioners. Solomon Belton said that the chiefs were so wary of McIntosh that they kept watch over him and even passed a law in council that no chief could hold conversation secretly with a white man. Belton also testified that when this law was passed, McIntosh continued to meet with the commissioners late at night in the woods, with a Colonel Williamson as intermediary to tell Campbell and Meriwether where McIntosh was hidden. He alleged that the commissioners told McIntosh what to say the next day. Conditions worsened, and McIntosh, now alarmed for his safety, ran away one night to Coweta and did not return to the council. For whatever reason, McIntosh's name does not appear in any further proceedings of the Broken Arrow council. The story of his complicity is given more credence in a letter Campbell later wrote to John C. Calhoun: "He is the only Indian with whom I have ever conversed, who seemed to comprehend rightly the connexion between the Indian tribes and the Government of the United States. . . . He seems to appreciate, very feelingly . . . the very humane and advantageous policy . . . of concentrating all the tribes in compact settlements beyond the Mississippi."[31] This letter strangely belies McIntosh's statements before the council.

After the breaking of McIntosh as speaker, a number of chiefs addressed the council. In one mid-December session, it was reported, "eight or ten chiefs delivered their opinions at considerable length and some with great earnestness and vehemence." The commissioners continued to reiterate their principal arguments: that they must implement the Georgia Compact and extinguish Indian claims in Georgia, that they must remove the Creeks from these lands for the defense of Georgia, and that the Creeks would be safer and happier on the lands in the West. Campbell and Meriwether read a number of documents in an attempt to prove their points, but the Creeks were adamant. As the meetings deteriorated, the commissioners proposed that negotiations be continued with a limited number of chiefs, selected by the council, and that the others, who were "standing around, and occasioning great expense in rations, should be discharged." The commissioners, chilled to the bone by the prolonged meetings in the open, also suggested that they meet in the comfort of a room. The chiefs answered that they would discharge none of the people from the council and that they would meet nowhere but in the square.[32]

When the commissioners met with the chiefs again on December 16, they first attempted to argue that the treaties of Augusta, Galphinton, and Shoulderbone gave the Indians no title to the lands but merely reserved them to the Creeks as hunting grounds. Then they proposed that the United States give the Creek Nation, acre for acre, land in the West in exchange for the entire possession of the nation; indemnify the nation for improvements on the property and the expense of removal; and pay the Indians the sum of $500,000. If the nation wished to exchange only the land within the limits of Georgia, the United States would exchange an equal amount of western land and give $300,000. Little Prince, the aging head chief of the Creek Nation, then spoke, saying they had no land for sale and he would listen to no more old treaties. After the Creeks relinquished some of their land in the Treaty of New York, Little Prince said, General Washington gave the Creeks the balance and told them it was theirs. He said emphatically that he intended never to spare another foot. Two days later, when the commissioners met with the council again, they asked if the chiefs persisted in their determination to cede no more land. Big Warrior, speaking through a deputy, said that he would not take a house full of money for his interest in the land and that the commissioners should take this for a final answer.[33]

On the evening of December 18, Campbell and Meriwether were at last willing to concede that the Upper Creeks of Alabama, led primarily by Big Warrior, were unwavering in their resolve not to give up any more land. They were certain that a treaty could be obtained, however, from the chiefs within the limits of Georgia. Through an exchange of territory, the terms of the Georgia Compact could be met and ten thousand Creeks—one-half of the nation—removed to lands in the West. But because the commissioners had commenced treaty negotiations with the full National Council, they were not certain that a valid treaty could be signed by a divided council. Also, they were fearful of exposing the Georgia Creeks to the wrath of the rest of the nation if a separate treaty was signed. The commissioners agreed that the best course was to declare a temporary adjournment to obtain further instructions from the government. They agreed that Campbell should go to Washington to confer with Calhoun and the president, and the council was adjourned on December 18. Campbell set out for the capital the following day.[34]

There was no doubt that William McIntosh was to be a key figure in future negotiations. In outlining to Secretary Calhoun his proposal for reconvening the council within the Georgia limits and negotiating a separate treaty for removing the Lower Creeks, Campbell wrote that "much conversation was held with General McIntosh concerning the details and consequences of such an arrangement." He said of McIntosh:

In effecting this design he will have it in his power to be eminently useful. Himself and his followers (ten thousand in number) would form the largest tribe in the West; and, by example and invitation, induce others to join them. It is sanguinely believed that even at the outset, if such arrangements were about to occur, that the Nation would not permit itself to be divided, but that the whole would come in and that the removal would be general and entire. But if this desirable end could not be produced at once, the emigrating party would very speedily drain from our limits those who might remain. For considerations like these, I view it a matter of great moment to maintain McIntosh in his authority and influence, and in his estimation of himself. I beg to be pardoned for suggesting that I consider this much his due from the important military services which he has rendered the United States. He stands very differently, in point of merit, from his principal opposer, (the Big Warrior); and the like difference would be found in a comparison of the followers of the one with those of the other. He [McIntosh] has been to the West himself and has the judgment to discover and the candor to acknowledge the superior advantages of a location in that quarter.[35]

James C. Bonner believes it was the removal of McIntosh as speaker of the nation and the humiliation and shame of being deprived of this office in public, before two thousand warriors and chiefs, that caused the radical turn in his career.[36] McIntosh would never again appear in the Council Square of the nation, and his next public act, the signing of the land cession treaty at Indian Springs, was a blatantly defiant one. Convinced that he had been stripped of the office of speaker by Crowell's complicity with Big Warrior and Little Prince, McIntosh began to regroup at Lockchau Talofau, guarded by Coweta warriors.[37] His military exploits and his influence with the Coweta headmen enabled him to remain a Coweta chief even though he was no longer speaker. Now he sought to gather the McIntosh party around him, and he managed to form political ties with about forty Creeks of some influence but little rank from the Lower Creek towns of Coweta, Cusseta, Talladega, Broken Arrow, and Hitchita.

At the time of his furtive retreat to Lockchau Talofau (Acorn Bluff), his plantation at the upper ferry on the Chattahoochee River, McIntosh was a rich man, easily the most affluent of the Creek chiefs. Joel Bailey, who spent five days that spring evaluating the worth of the plantation before making an offer to buy it, observed a number of assets, including a house worth $1,500; 150 acres of "good river land," worth about five hundred bushels of corn annually; one hundred black slaves, many of them "young and very likely"; and two ferries controlled by McIntosh, each worth about $1,000 a year in tolls. He also saw eight hundred head of cattle, mostly large steers; six horses worth an average of $75 each; blacksmith tools "of a very high quality"; a quantity of bacon, salt, groceries, and dry goods; and "a considerable quantity of silver in trunks."[38]

McIntosh also had another profitable enterprise, the two-story inn, which he and a relative Joel Bailey had financed and built at Indian Springs in the years 1819–23. Advertisements in Georgia newspapers brought guests to this handsome, thirty-four-room hostelry, which had a long porch on the front, etchings on the walls, and a piano in the dining room, where meals were served to guests for $1.25 a day, the same price as a day's lodging. Even at these modest prices, McIntosh made money; a local grocer recorded that he supplied the general's inn with $1,650 worth of vegetables the first year it was open for business. Records show that in one season eight hundred persons came to Indian Springs for the medicinal waters and to enjoy the amenities of McIntosh's inn.[39]

In a time when cash was extremely scarce and land was being sold at public auction for fifteen cents an acre,[40] McIntosh had wealth and the power that accrues from it. Thus the question becomes complex whether McIntosh was the manipulator or the manipulated, the money-hungry entrepreneur or the realist who wished the best for his people in a situation that was inevitably to worsen. One might suppose that McIntosh, being offered continued wealth and prestige as headman of the most powerful tribe in the West—as opposed to a position of dwindling rank and increasing white encroachment in the East—would not find it difficult to rationalize a decision to remove, no matter what his logic or his instinct for survival dictated.

15

Betrayal at Indian Springs and the Deaths of McIntosh and Weatherford

——— • ———

Duncan Campbell was in Washington on January 8, having survived an arduous winter journey by stagecoach. In his hotel room he wrote a long and detailed report of the failed Broken Arrow council to Secretary John C. Calhoun, and in it he praised General McIntosh as a Creek leader who understood that the best alternative for his people was to cede the Creek lands in the East and accept the federal government's offer of land in the West, where they could live without fear of white encroachment. He was convinced that the Lower Creeks, under the leadership of McIntosh, were ready to cede their lands in Georgia and that if the president would allow the commissioners to negotiate separately with them, the treaty cession could be agreed upon expeditiously. Then Campbell gave the major point of his dubious argument: "The fact is that McIntosh maintains the right of the Coweta town alone to dispose of the whole country. It would seem that the Upper Towns conceded this authority, and dreaded its exercise; for the utmost consternation was discoverable whenever it was known that the commissioners and Coweta chiefs had an interview." The chiefs' consternation may well have come from a knowledge of McIntosh's vulnerability, not his special power to negotiate singly. Campbell argued that Coweta was the most extensive and numerous town in the nation, extending on both sides of the Chattahoochee from Broken Arrow to the Cherokee boundary. Coweta claimed to be the original town of the Creek tribe, he said, and Cowetans believed that all the other towns were its branches. Campbell cited an example of an incident during the Broken Arrow negotiations in which Little Prince denied the authenticity of an old treaty because "no Coweta chief had signed it." Campbell suggested that other treaties had not been widely approved by the National Council; the Treaty of 1821 at Indian Springs, he stated, was signed by only two chiefs of the upper towns.[1] He might also have cited the Treaty of Fort Jackson in 1814, a document approved almost exclusively by Lower Creeks.

Campbell pressed for an answer without delay: "I would add, very respectfully, that an early decision is desirable. It is in contemplation to return to the Creek country, reassemble the chiefs by the 5th of February and transmit the treaty in time for the adjudication of the present Senate." He told Calhoun that the Creeks of the "emigrating party are desirous that as little time should be lost as possible. They would send out an exploring committee and wish to avail themselves of the spring and summer of this year for that purpose. They are desirous also that the period of their removal should not go beyond the next fall. Such promptness and expedition cannot be otherwise than acceptable to the Government." Having received a verbal negative answer from the War Department, Campbell wrote to Calhoun again on January 11, this time requesting permission to call a national council of Creeks with the intent of persuading all the chiefs to follow McIntosh's lead. He was so confident that this would be allowed that he wrote to agent Crowell the following day calling for a convention of Creek chiefs at Indian Springs on February 7. "We are desirous," he wrote, "that all the chiefs of the Nation should attend who are in the habit of transacting public business and signing treaties." On that same day he sent the chiefs of the Creek Nation an announcement of the meeting to be held on February 7, by "the authority of the President of the United States."[2]

Calhoun wrote a letter on January 18 which reaffirmed to Campbell the president's position that he could not, "with propriety, authorize the treating with General McIntosh alone, as proposed by the commissioners." He stated President Monroe's opinion that "it is not in the power of General McIntosh to cede any portion of the land belonging to the Creek Nation, without the assent of the Nation itself." But the secretary then grasped at the straw offered in Campbell's second letter, which had asked for a reconvention of Upper and Lower Creek chiefs: "Yet the President can see no objection to a renewal of the negotiations, as proposed by your letter of the 11th instant, in order to obtain an arrangement with General McIntosh, with the consent of the Creek Nation, for the cession of the country in question;

and you are accordingly, in conjunction with Major Merriwether, as commissioners, authorized to renew the negotiation." It is odd that Campbell received this authorization six days after he had announced the meeting. Calhoun ended the letter with the president's warning that "whatever arrangement may be made with General McIntosh for a cession of territory must be made by the Creek Nation in the usual form, and upon ordinary principles with which treaties are held with the Indian tribes."[3]

Also on January 18 Calhoun wrote to agent Crowell to upbraid him for his actions at Broken Arrow, instruct him bluntly where his allegiance should lie, and demand appropriate action at the upcoming treaty council at Indian Springs. The president, he told Crowell, "does not approve of your conduct in relation to the late treaty. Though it is the duty of the Agent to protect and cherish the Indians confided to his care, yet that duty never can be in conflict with the paramount one which he owes the government, and which, in all occasions, obligates him to give his hearty cooperation in effecting its views. . . . The treaty is about to be renewed, and the president, feeling much interest in its successful termination, looks with confidence to your hearty cooperation with the commissioners. You will spare no pains in preparing the Indians for the meeting."[4]

McIntosh's key position in the treaty negotiations and his troubles with Crowell were widely known. Georgia's seven-man congressional delegation wrote to General John Cocke, the chairman of the Committee on Indian Affairs, on February 4 telling him that Campbell had come to Washington to seek authority to treat separately with McIntosh and the Lower Creeks. The congressmen told Cocke that such authority had been withheld, and they described the plight McIntosh would be in if he signed a further land cession at Indian Springs: "Colonel Campbell thinks McIntosh and his party are in great danger. A quarrel is existing between himself and Big Warrior, and no good understanding exists between him and the Agent. Unless sustained by the Government, McIntosh will be deprived of his power in the Nation and probably of his life. This is greatly to be regretted, as he enters fully into the views of the Government upon the removal of the Indians over the Mississippi. Colonel Campbell has been furnished with new instructions . . . and has gone to make another effort to procure a cession of land. Success is hardly probable, inasmuch as all the Alabama Indians are opposed to it, and as the commissioners will again have to encounter the intrigues of those who have heretofore interposed their influence to prevent it." The congressmen made it clear that they were referring to the subagent Walker, removed from office but still in the nation, and agent Crowell.[5]

Earlier, on January 25 a group of Creek chiefs, including McIntosh, supposedly wrote a letter to President Monroe, calling for the protection of General McIntosh. "We are informed," they wrote, "that the Big Warrior and his chiefs are now in council, and we suspect are passing such decrees as are derogatory to the safety of McIntosh and the rest of his chiefs." William Barnard's testimony in a later congressional investigation painted a grim picture of the danger McIntosh faced at this time. Barnard said that he had been present at agent John Crowell's house about three weeks after the failure of negotiations at Broken Arrow. Crowell informed the brothers Michee and Timpoochee Barnard that another treaty council would be held at Indian Springs and that he believed McIntosh would sell the lands. According to the testimony, "Michee Barnard, showing much irritation, said that if the lands were sold, McIntosh would be killed. Colonel Crowell then observed that if McIntosh was to be killed, it should be done before the lands were sold."[6]

The same group of Lower Creek chiefs that had asked for McIntosh's protection purportedly wrote a second letter on January 25, endorsing McIntosh as their leader in future treaty negotiations. Referring to themselves as the principal chiefs of Coweta, Talladega, Broken Arrow, and Hitchita town, they acknowledged General William McIntosh to be "our principal protector and chief, having full confidence in his patriotism, integrity, and great regard for his people whom he represents." McIntosh and seven others of the National Council were appointed "to make such arrangements as will be most conducive to the welfare of our people, and to receive such advice as our father the President may think proper to give; and should our father the President give it as his opinion that the claim of the state of Georgia to the land within her limits would prevent a fee-simple title from vesting in our people, then, in that event, General William McIntosh, with the other delegates of our chiefs, are duly authorized, in behalf of our people, to make such arrangements with our father the President, or his commissioners for that purpose, in an exchange for lands west of the Mississippi," adding that "any thing which the said delegates may do on the occasion will meet with the approbation of the National Council in general." The letter was signed by twenty Coweta chiefs, five Talladega chiefs, seven Broken Arrow chiefs, and one Hitchita chief. Despite previous statements that he had been broken as speaker at Broken Arrow, McIntosh was listed as "Speaker of the National Council" and his son Chilly named as clerk.[7]

This document, giving McIntosh power of attorney to negotiate as well as extravagantly praising his integrity and loyalty, is considered suspect. Of the group of about forty followers McIntosh organized among the Lower Creeks and persuaded to sign the document, the majority were not chiefs, and some could not even be classified as warriors. About one-half of the group were of mixed blood, and a few were related to McIntosh. Major John H. Broadnax, a contractor who supplied rations to the Indians in the councils, provided interesting testimony concerning the two letters of January 25. He told a congressional investigator that during the latter part of January, General McIntosh came by and asked Broadnax to go to Chief Joseph Marshall's in the Creek Nation "to do some writing for him." Broadnax testified that he did go and that he drew up two documents for McIntosh dated January 25.[8] If Broadnax told the truth, the prime mover of these documents giving broad powers to McIntosh was McIntosh himself. The legal phrase "prevent a fee-simple title from vesting in our people" indicates the kind of knowledge only McIntosh seems to have possessed among the chiefs.

Nevertheless, McIntosh and a small party of the delegates set off for Milledgeville, Georgia, to see the governor. They then planned to go to Washington, bearing this questionable authorization, to negotiate a treaty, similar to the Indian Springs one, with the president. There is some reason to believe they wanted to discuss the matter with John Quincy Adams, who would assume office in March, rather than James Monroe, who had shown strong reservations about treating separately with the Lower Creeks. According to Broadnax, McIntosh was prepared to make some pretentious promises to the government. Broadnax testified that he heard McIntosh say that "if he could get $2000, he would put his country in pledge for its repayment and that no further expense would attend the making of the treaty; if it was not made, they would refund the money." When McIntosh's party stopped at the state capital in Milledgeville to pay a visit to McIntosh's kinsman, Governor Troup, they learned that Colonel Campbell was already in Washington and that the governor understood that Campbell was—or soon would be—"clothed in the necessary power to make a treaty." McIntosh and his party returned to Indian Springs to be there on February 7 for the opening of the treaty council, but few other chiefs had arrived, and the negotiations did not formally begin. Agent Crowell was present, and on that same day he wrote a note to

Campbell and Meriwether, assuring them that "being instructed to obey your orders in relation to the negotiation, I now have the honor to inform you that I will, in compliance with my instructions, obey such instructions as I may receive from you in the fulfillment of your duties under the instructions of the War Department, and cheerfully co-operate with you in bringing to a successful termination the present negotiation."[9]

Nearly four hundred chiefs and headmen had arrived by February 10, enough for the meeting to begin. The Tuckabatchee chiefs, however, sent a message "that they were not ready, and were not disposed to meet in the room prepared for the council, but were disposed to hold meetings at their own camp."[10] When the speeches began, the commissioners repeated all the arguments they had used ineffectively at Broken Arrow, but this time the audience, largely because of McIntosh's powers of persuasion, was much more receptive. The exception was a chief named Opothle Yoholo, who mounted a boulder near McIntosh's tavern on February 11 and gave a powerful denunciation of McIntosh and any other Creek who would cede further lands. "General McIntosh knows that we are bound by our laws," he said, "and that what is not done in the public square, in general council, is not binding on the nation." He said that he knew there were but few from the upper towns there and that many were absent from the lower towns. He repeated the statement that General McIntosh knew that no land could be sold without the consent of the entire nation. Unexpectedly, he seemed somewhat tempted by the commissioners' arguments. "From what you told us yesterday," the chief said, "I am induced to believe that it may be best for us to remove, but we must have time to think of it." He said that "dissension and ill blood" would result "if the chiefs who are here sell the land now."[11] Some of the chiefs heeded the warning, and that night a part of the influential Cusseta and Sawokli lower town delegations left camp and fled to the Flint River.[12]

On the following day the commissioners had a treaty prepared to be read to the Creek council. The commissioners told the assembly that the departure of certain groups of Indians the preceding night would not "defeat the objects of the government." All the chiefs of the nation had been notified and invited to attend, and their participation was voluntary. Now, the treaty was to be read and interpreted to them, and then they could vote. The treaty was read aloud, article by article, and interpreted by William Hambly. At the end of each article the chiefs gave assent by an exclamatory grunt "after the manner of

Indians." The commissioners told the assembly that as many might sign as chose to do so; the commissioners signed and the chiefs followed, most making a mark and having the clerk write in their names.[13] As McIntosh stepped forward to sign, Opothle Yoholo met him at the table and muttered in Muskogean, "My friend, you are about to sell our country; now I warn you of your danger." Opothle Yoholo then shook hands with the commissioners and left the room.[14] Campbell testified later that perhaps the reason that all the chiefs present did not sign was the lateness of the hour, but, he added, the number that did sign was deemed sufficient by the commissioners. The document was then handed to agent Crowell, who attested it, "without hesitation or remark," Campbell recollected.[15]

The treaty was signed, ceding all the Creek lands in Georgia between the Flint and Chattahoochee rivers and much of the land on the Coosa and Tallapoosa rivers occupied by the Upper Creeks. These lands were to be exchanged for an equal number of acres on the Arkansas River, and to compensate the Creeks for improvements on their ceded lands, the United States was to pay "$400,000 to the nation emigrating." Of this sum, $200,000 was to be paid "as soon as practicable" after the ratification of the treaty, $100,000 at the time of removal, and the remaining $100,000 after the Creeks had settled in the West in installments over a twelve-year period. They were given until September 1826 to leave the ceded lands.[16]

The fifth article of the treaty, which, it is claimed, was never interpreted to the Indians, stipulated that the treaty commissioners pay the first $200,000 directly to the McIntosh party "at the particular request of the party of the second part." One observer noted a shocked expression of disbelief on the face of John Crowell when the article was read in English and he learned that he would have no part in the disbursal of the funds. Even though he signed the treaty as a witness, he immediately wrote to Secretary Calhoun to denounce it:

> Yesterday a treaty was signed by McIntosh, and his adherents, alone. Being fully convinced that this treaty is in direct opposition to the letter and spirit of the instructions, which I have a copy of, I feel it to be my bounden duty, as the agent of the government, to apprise you of it, that you may adopt such measures as you may deem expedient, as to the ratification; for, if ratified, it may produce a horrid state of things among these unfortunate Indians. It is proper to remark that, with the exception of McIntosh, and perhaps two others, the signatures to this treaty are either chiefs of low grade, or not chiefs at all; which you can perceive, by comparing them to those to other treaties, and to the receipts

Opothle Yoholo, by Charles Bird King (from McKenney and Hall, *History of the Indian Tribes*)

for the annuity, and these signers are from eight towns only, when there are fifty-six in the nation.[17]

T. P. Andrews, the special agent who prepared the congressional report on the controversial treaty, agreed with Crowell's assessment of the signatories. He ranked McIntosh as the fifth highest chief in the

Creek Nation but found five others to be underling chiefs, also from Coweta, and twenty-six "executors of laws," eighteen Indians, "fourteen of which were broken or dismissed chiefs," and two "not known at all."[18]

A final article of the treaty, hastily added as a supplementary clause on February 14, was the most controversial of all. This article gave McIntosh $25,000 for two reservations of land that had been awarded in the Treaty of 1821: a 1,000-acre plot on which McIntosh had built his tavern at Indian Springs and 640 acres on the west bank of the Ocmulgee. This article was signed by McIntosh and eight other Creeks, four of whom were of mixed blood. Most curious is the paragraph that precedes the supplementary article in the official document of the treaty. Signed by Big Warrior, Little Prince, John Crowell, and four Creek chiefs, it reads, "Whereas, by a stipulation in the Treaty of the Indian Springs, in 1821, there was a reserve of land made to include the said Indian Springs for the use of General William M'Intosh, be it therefore known to all whom it may concern, that we, the undersigned chiefs and head men of the Creek nation, do hereby agree to relinquish all the right, title, and control of the Creek nation to the said reserve, unto him the said William M'Intosh and his heirs, forever, in as full and ample a manner as we are authorized to do."[19] This statement, giving clear title to McIntosh, is inexplicably dated July 25, 1825, more than five months after the treaty was signed. The document must have been written earlier, for Big Warrior died in mid-February, but it would be difficult to explain why Crowell, known to be unfriendly to McIntosh, would have signed away the reserves to him at any time.

The statement is all the more curious when one compares it to a letter written to President Monroe on February 21 by several Creek chiefs, with Little Prince as the first signatory: "Father and Friend: in justice to our own consciences, and solicitude for the welfare of our people, we are urged to the very unpleasant necessity of troubling you concerning the late transactions at the Indian Springs, which the base treachery of one of our chiefs, General William McIntosh, has made somewhat alarming. This man, McIntosh, we placed confidence in, and we are mortified when we are obliged to say that he has abused it." The chiefs recalled that at Broken Arrow in December, McIntosh, as speaker of the nation, had delivered the chiefs' sentiments in public council while in private he was using his influence "against the known wish of our people and our Nation." They wrote of several secret meetings McIntosh held with the commissioners at which he "fully succeeded in his nefarious scheme." They concluded: "We think $200,000 the price of McIntosh's treachery. After deducting such an amount from the whole sum promised to take us away, it leaves but a small pittance to defray expenses."[20]

Considering the whirlwind that the treaty commissioners had sown, the final entry in the journal of the treaty proceedings is ironic: "The Commissioners then convened the chiefs, distributed some presents, ordered them furnished with rations to take them home, advised them to temperance and unanimity, took final leave, and adjourned." The beleaguered McIntosh certainly did not expect unanimity. He and Etome Tustunnuggee, along with some other Creek chiefs, left Indian Springs hastily for Milledgeville, where they told Governor Troup their fears of reprisal by the Upper Creeks and asked for protection from the state of Georgia. Governor Troup willingly gave his protection and wrote to the Georgia congressional delegation on February 17 that "those of the tribe who refused their assent to the treaty threaten injury to McIntosh and his Chiefs. Should the execution of these threats be attempted (the treaty having been ratified), I will feel it to be my duty to punish, in the most summary manner, and with the utmost severity, every such attempt, as an act of hostility committed within the actual territory and acknowledged jurisdiction of Georgia."[21]

When Campbell and Meriwether wrote to Troup on February 13 to inform him that the treaty had been signed, they reported: "We are happy to inform you that the 'long agony is over.'" For McIntosh, it was just beginning. Still ringing in his ears was the admonition muttered by Opothle Yoholo: "I now warn you of your danger."[22] McIntosh, however, was not entirely without friends among the Creeks. A group of Coweta chiefs met with Governor Troup on February 17 to praise the general and to remind the governor that when the Red Sticks revolted in 1813 "General McIntosh was the first red man who joined the United States and spilt his blood in her defense." They told the governor that they had been warriors under McIntosh and had fought for their country; they emphasized that "we love said McIntosh until death and will hold fast to his talks because we know he acts agreeable to our father's talks, and by him we gain our protection from our father the President. Looking back to 1813," they added, "we believe that but for the relations which McIntosh sustained to the United States, we should have lost our lands without getting a penny for them." They told the governor that many of the Upper Creeks had objected to the treaty at Indian Springs, and they expressed a hope that the governor would protect them if the former Red Sticks should "attempt to breed a disturbance with the friendly Indians." They were more specific three days later, when they again met with the governor to remind him of the law that had been passed by a few chiefs at Polecat Springs to the effect that "if any person should sell or offer land for sale, guns and rope should be their end." These chiefs contended that the law could not be considered a national law because it had not been read before the national chiefs. They had heard, however, that those who had signed the law were determined to enforce it; they told the governor that they would defend themselves, and "with your assistance, they will find a great difference in numbers."[23]

The Executive Journal of February 19 indicates that several Creek chiefs, McIntosh among them, visited Governor Troup on that date. They told Troup that because they had consented to give up their lands and move westward, they expected to encounter "difficulties and privations" before leaving. They referred to the "bad white men" who were endeavoring to stir up trouble, and they referred to agent Crowell specifically as "among their worst enemies"; therefore they "could expect no protection or support from him." The governor promised support, and a week later he had dispatched Colonel Henry G. Lamar, one of his aides, with a strongly worded message to the chiefs of Tuckabatchee and Cusseta. It was typically condescending, in the tone of a firm father to a recalcitrant child:

I hear bad things of you. You threaten McIntosh and his people, because they listened to their father, the President, and ceded the lands to the Georgians. They acted like good and dutiful children. You opposed yourselves to the wishes of your great father, who was doing the best for the interest of his red people, and would not sign the treaty. But this you did, as I believe, under the influence of bad men, who pretended to be your friends, but who cared nothing about you. Now I tell you, take care and walk straight. McIntosh and his people are under my protection, as well as under the protection of the United States. If any harm is done by you, or any of your people, to McIntosh or his people, I will treat you in the same way as if you were to come into our white settlements and do the like. I will pursue you until I have full satisfaction. Do not let bad men persuade you that because you live in and near to Alabama, you will be safe. If you commit one act of hostility on this side of the line, I will follow and punish you. But I hope there will be no occasion for this, and that you will take counsel of wise and good men, and so conduct yourselves for the future, as to receive the approbation and protection of your father, the President, and that I also may look upon you as friends and treat you accordingly. This message will be delivered to you by my Aid-de-camp, Col. Lamar.[24]

In his instructions to Colonel Lamar, Governor Troup urged him to meet the Indians "with friendly dispositions" and, believing the Creeks to be naturally docile and tractable in the face of proven authority, told Lamar to emphasize that "it is the settled opinion of all the wise and good men of the United States that the Indians, looking to nothing but their own interest, present and future, ought to move without delay beyond the Mississippi. They already know this to be the advice of their great father. They will soon know it to be the advice of his great council, the Congress."[25] Governor Troup was correct on this last point. The treaty was approved, despite the protests of agent Crowell, by the Senate on March 3 and was signed on March 7 by President John Quincy Adams, who had been sworn into office only four days before.

In his report to the governor on March 10, Colonel Lamar gave the opinion that the Indians would conform to the wishes of the president. "Their conclusion is," Lamar wrote, "that the powers of the President are absolute, and that he has an unquestionable right to coerce obedience." Lamar believed this to be true despite the efforts of some white men in the Creek Nation whose fortunes lay in preserving the status quo and who were secretly attempting to excite discontent. Lamar discovered that the Creeks as they contemplated moving westward feared perpetual warfare with the tribes already inhabiting the lands along the Arkansas River. Not knowing that the treaty had already been ratified, Lamar assured the governor that the Creeks would be compliant when the treaty was ratified and signed by the president.[26] Lamar also stated that Opothle Yoholo and Little Prince, two principal chiefs, denied any hostility to McIntosh and the other chiefs who had signed the treaty.[27]

Despite Lamar's optimism, McIntosh and his followers were in great peril. On March 3 Chilly McIntosh dashed off a hurried letter to Governor Troup from Newnan, while a runner waited to deliver it. Referring to those who opposed land cession as "hostiles," he told Troup that he and his party had not yet reached home because of these hostiles and that two friends he had met at Flint River told him that the anti-McIntosh forces had run them off, threatening to cut their throats and to "set up their heads by the road for a show." He told the governor that men had been appointed to kill seven chiefs: "General McIntosh, myself, Joseph Marshall, Samuel Hawkins, James

Island, Etome Tustuggee and Colonel Miller." He added that he had parted from his father at Indian Springs and that when he learned of the threats he had dispatched a runner to his father to urge him to leave his home and meet him in Newnan. On March 5 Troup replied to Chilly: "I am sorry to hear that the hostiles continue to be such fools and madmen. They will soon be taught better. If they do not listen to my talks sent by Col. Lamar, I will send a military force to the line to keep them in order and punish offenders."[28]

John Crowell, who was in Washington in March when the treaty was ratified, did not give up his campaign to undermine the treaty. He wrote to James Barbour, the secretary of war, on March 12 that because the treaty had been signed by Indians who—with the exception of McIntosh—were not headmen of the nation, the Creeks "have just grounds of complaint." He admitted, however, that since the government had ratified the treaty, the Creeks would have to submit and that he, as the agent, must carry it into effect, which he would do "with cheerfulness." He could not resist a parting shot at McIntosh. He called Barbour's attention to Article V of the treaty, which stipulated that monies should be paid and disbursed by the commissioners negotiating the treaty and not by the Indian agent, "a new stipulation in the history of Indian treaties." He thought there "must have been some secret motive for it, and my mind is drawn irresistibly to the conclusion that it was with the view of placing funds at the disposal of McIntosh—and perhaps to cover some promises; in such an event, from my knowledge of McIntosh's character, I have no hesitation in saying the funds would not be honestly and fairly distributed."[29]

When McIntosh wrote to Governor Troup on March 29, he made special mention of Crowell and the danger he and the other friendly Creeks anticipated upon the agent's return from Washington. He also requested funds:

> Sir: I take the liberty of sending Samuel Hawkins to you, seeing in the newspapers your proclamation stating that the treaty was ratified by the President and Senate. We see in the papers, also, where Crowell had wrote to the Department that Chiefs of the lowest grade had signed the treaty, and we see where he says there will be hostilities with us if the United States sign the treaty. We are not any ways in danger until he comes home and commences hostility, and urges it himself on us. If the treaty is ratified, if you can let Samuel Hawkins have two thousand dollars, or stand his security in the bank to that amount, we will send men on now to look at the country to try to move away this fall; the

George M. Troup (from Harden, *Life of George M. Troup*)

money, if loaned to us, will be paid back as soon as the money comes on
to pay the first payment of the treaty.

Any information that you can give him will be satisfactory to us.[30]

In replying, Governor Troup assured McIntosh: "There will be no
danger of any hostility in consequence of the ratification of the treaty."

Citing the report of his agent, Colonel Lamar, Troup wrote "that the Indians opposed to the treaty are quite friendly; that they think of no mischief; that they love you and will do whatever their father the President advises." He stated that he had written to the treaty commissioners to request that funds be made available so that McIntosh and his party could explore some lands west of the Mississippi. He also repeated an earlier request that McIntosh give his assent to the surveying of the newly acquired lands.[31]

McIntosh wrote to Governor Troup on April 12, "in behalf of the nation that signed the treaty," to give consent to having the land surveyed. He said he did so with misgivings because in previous times he had always consulted with the Indian agent appointed by the president. "Some differences existing between the present Agent of the Creek nation and myself, and not having any confidence in his advice, I have determined to act according to the dictates of my best judgment," he wrote the governor. Ever the entrepreneur, he urged Troup to publish a notice in the newspapers, stating that all persons who wished to purchase Creek property "must first attend at my house and enroll their names."[32] On that same day McIntosh sent via the governor a lengthy memorial statement, signed by McIntosh and fifteen other friendly chiefs, to the legislature, with the request that it be read before the General Assembly. It was a poetic statement, which the chiefs referred to as their "last and farewell address" before they emigrated to the West. The following excerpt is typical of the effusively humble sentiment throughout the document:

> The country which you now possess, and that which we now remain on, was by the Great Spirit originally given to his red children. Our brothers, the white men, visited us when we were like the trees of the forest. Our forefathers smoked the pipe of peace and friendship with the forefathers of the white man, and when the white man said, we wish to live with the red man and inhabit the same country, we received their presents, and said, welcome; we will give you land for yourselves and for your children. We took the white man by the hand, and held fast to it. We became neighbors, and the children of the white man grew up, and the children of the red man grew up in the same country, and we were brothers. The white men became numerous as the trees of the forest, and the red men became like the buffalo. *Friends and Brothers:* You are like the mighty storm; we are like the tender and bending tree; we must bow before you; you have torn us up by the roots, but still you are our brothers and friends. You have promised to replant us in a better soil, and to watch over us and nurse us. . . . The

day is come when we surrender the country of our forefathers—the
land of our nativity; our homes, the places of our youthful diversions.
We surrender it to our brothers and friends, and our hearts are glad that
we are not forced to do so by our enemies. We go; our people will seek
new lands; our hearts remain with you.[33]

Along with the memorial, McIntosh wrote to Governor Troup: "In
giving, voluntarily, our consent for the survey of the land in the late
treaty, we were actuated by motives of friendship purely toward you
and toward your people. No consideration of a mercenary nature
could be permitted to enter our breasts when a favor was asked of us,
particularly by your Excellency, and in behalf of your people."[34]

McIntosh received a message on April 12 from Little Prince, inviting him and the chiefs from Coweta to attend a meeting of the Creek
Nation at Broken Arrow on April 19. This would seem to indicate that
Lamar had been correct in stating that Little Prince held no malice for
McIntosh. "My own health will not permit me, probably, to attend the
meeting in person," he wrote, "but all my Chiefs will go."[35] Troup
wrote McIntosh, "I hope that you will meet the Little Prince and council in good friendship. I wish to see you all united in brotherly affection before you move and am convinced the President desires the
same."[36] The letter concerning Little Prince helps to explain a statement made by John Crowell at his brother's store on April 20. A settler
named Jesse Cox swore in an affidavit to a congressional committee
that he heard the agent say: "Any people that would suffer one man
to·sell their nation ought to die and go to hell. I once put that fellow
(meaning McIntosh) down, where he ought to remain; but the Big
Warrior and Little Prince reinstated him. I hope the Big Warrior is
gone to hell for it, and that the Little Prince may soon follow him."[37]

Crowell wrote to Secretary Barbour on April 27 to relate an incident
that had occurred when the chiefs had gathered in general council to
receive their annuity payments. While the council was in session, a
messenger arrived with a proclamation from Governor Troup, calling
for a special session of the General Assembly to authorize the surveying of the lands ceded by the Indian Springs treaty. Along with the
proclamation was a copy of a letter from McIntosh to Troup, agreeing
to have the lands surveyed. Crowell reported to Barbour that when he
read the documents to the assembled chiefs, "it seemed to add to
their melancholy and distress"; the chiefs declared that they had not
been consulted in relation to the treaty and "supposed that the Governor had acted upon the authority of McIntosh and (to use their own

words) such other names as he could steal." Crowell wrote that the chiefs objected to the "surveying of lands until they can remove from them." They believed, and they were later proved correct, that once the survey was decided upon, white settlers would begin to encroach and stake claims. Crowell pleaded: "Justice and humanity require that the protecting arm of the government should be extended to these now helpless and dejected people."[38]

It was also on April 27 that a man named Abram Miles allegedly heard Crowell say that "General McIntosh was at that time in his residence, with a guard around him, and that he would be killed by the party opposed to the treaty."[39] McIntosh was, at this time, still at his residence, Lockchau Talofau, beside the upper ferry of the Chattahoochee in present-day Carroll County, Georgia. He had apparently been lulled into a sense of complacency by Governor Troup's assurances that he was beloved by his fellow Creeks and that if unforeseen dangers arose, he had the full protection of the state and federal governments. He did not reckon, however, with the inflammatory effect of the symbol of the surveyor's chain. Three times since the Creek War, surveyors had irrevocably marked lands for the white man's possession, and the chiefs, already feeling dispossessed and dejected, acted quickly. Less than two days after Crowell's letter was written, an execution party of nearly two hundred warriors was sent out from Tuckabatchee and Ocfuskee, under the command of Menawa, one of the few Red Stick leaders who had survived the Creek War. Their destination was Lockchau Talofau.

Menawa and his Upper Creek warriors arrived at the plantation on the afternoon of April 29 and concealed themselves in the woods surrounding McIntosh's home. The house was also a tavern and hostelry for travelers along the federal road, and that night it lodged several white men, including an itinerant peddler and sometime religious teacher named Francis Flournoy, one of the eyewitnesses who later gave an extended account of the tragedy that was to occur the following morning. The Chattahoochee was swollen out of its banks from unusually heavy rains, and some of the travelers had remained long at the tavern waiting for the weather to abate and the floodwaters to recede.[40]

The concealed warriors watched the activities of the house until dark, observing McIntosh ride out with his son Chilly to pen up some stray cattle and later in the day ride as far as a road fork with Sam Hawkins, his son-in-law, who was returning to his house twenty-four miles away on the eastern branch of the Tallapoosa. Hawkins's wife,

Menawa, by Charles Bird King (from McKenney and Hall, *History of the Indian Tribes*)

Jane, remained at her father's house, for McIntosh and Hawkins had planned to leave on the following morning to look at land along the Arkansas River that had been promised in exchange for Creek lands in Georgia.[41]

Just before daybreak the concealed Indians quietly bestirred themselves and set fire to an outbuilding near the main house, with the object of lighting up the yard and preventing any of the occupants from escaping. They shouted that the white guests and the women should come out at once, without fear of harm, and McIntosh's Cherokee wife, Peggy, his daughter Jane, and the guests came out immediately. Then the main house was ignited. Chilly McIntosh and a mixed-blood named Mooty Kennard, who were sleeping in a small building used to house extra guests, were awakened by the clamor and escaped through a back window into the woods.[42]

McIntosh and the aged Coweta chief Etome Tustunnuggee were seen for an instant at the front door of the main house, and the Red Stick warriors quickly opened fire, killing the old chief and wounding McIntosh. The general pulled himself upstairs, where he began shooting at his assailants from a window. When the flames reached the upper story, he was forced to attempt to leave the house and was shot several times as he staggered down the stairs. He was dragged by his feet some distance from the burning house, where he raised himself painfully to one elbow, gave his enemies a withering, defiant look, and died as the point of a long knife pierced his heart. Flournoy testified that the executioners continued to fire at the two men after they were dead; he estimated that more than fifty shots were fired into each corpse. Peggy McIntosh begged the hostiles to let her have a white suit to bury the general in, but they denied her request. Flournoy said he assisted two other white men in burying the bodies. An aged Red Stick, whose nephew was in the raiding party, told Albert Pickett that McIntosh was scalped and his body thrown in the river.[43]

They continued until late in the morning, according to Flournoy, "plundering and destroying everything valuable, tearing the frock off a young Indian female, carrying off a great many negroes, horses, cattle and said they were ordered to destroy what they could not carry off. I saw them shoot many hogs, which they left on the ground." After observing that one of the older Indians understood English, Flournoy asked him: "Old gentlemen, is this the way your people do? Go to a man's house, and shoot him, and burn his house, and take away everything he has, and carry it away, or are these [indicating the corpses] bad men? What have they done?" Flournoy testified before a Senate hearing that the old Indian replied that he did not love to kill them, but heads of the nation said to do so. The old Indian said that Little Prince and Opothle Yoholo were the heads of the nation now that Big Warrior was dead. Flournoy asked if these two were not the ones who had assured Governor Troup that the chiefs who signed the Indian Springs treaty would not be hurt. He said that this was "true at first," but that the agent had told the council that "the only way to get their land back, and keep it, was to kill all that had a hand in selling it, and burn and destroy all they had . . . and after that other chiefs never would attempt to sell their land, for fear of being treated in the same way."[44]

Although the testimony of Flournoy, Peggy McIntosh, and Jane Hawkins was later considered suspect by Major T. P. Andrews, who evaluated the evidence for the Senate investigation of the Creek Indian controversy, their accounts of the attack at Lockchau Talofau did corroborate each other as well as place much of the blame for the affair upon Crowell. On the morning of the murders, Peggy McIntosh allegedly told Flournoy that she talked with some of the attackers and they told her they were ordered to do what they had done by those who ruled the nation after Big Warrior's death and that they were "supported and encouraged by the Agent." Flournoy said he told her he did not believe that, and she replied that these Indians "would not tell a lie on the Agent, for they must know it would come to his ears, and they would have to answer for it."[45]

Evidence contradicting this statement, however, is found in a certificate, signed by Little Prince and thirty-six others on May 14, which reads in part: "We the undersigned chiefs and head-men of the Creek Nation do certify and declare that we determined of our own free will to put to death the Chief McIntosh and that neither the Agent John Crowell or any other white man were the instigators or abbettors— nor do we know or believe that he the Agent knew that we had any such design—nor did we communicate it to any but a few old and head-men. We determined to put him to death for a violation of a law first proposed by him [McIntosh] and sanctioned by the Big Warrior and Little Prince." The certificate also stated that when the chief who commanded the party that executed McIntosh was asked if he had told McIntosh's wife, or any person, that the agent had directed him to do so, he replied, "No, and that he did not believe his men had done so."[46]

Jane Hawkins gave a graphic account of that tragic day in a letter to treaty commissioners Campbell and Meriwether. "I send you this paper," she wrote, "which will not tell you a lie; but, if it had ten tongues, it could not tell all the truth." Her husband, Sam Hawkins, was captured in the morning and kept tied up until about three o'clock, when he was executed by Menawa's order. Jane was not allowed to bury her husband, and she was devastated by the thought, as she told the commissioners, that he would "remain unburied, to be devoured by the birds and beasts." She wrote: "After I was stripped of my last frock but one, humanity and duty called on me to pull it off and spread it over the body of my dead husband (which was allowed no other covering), which I did as a farewell witness of my affection." Her nakedness did not make her unique among the survivors. She wrote that the attackers "took all the money and property they could carry, destroyed the rest, leaving the family no clothes (some not one rag)."[47]

William Weatherford's last years and his death in 1824 were tranquil in comparison with McIntosh's stormy confrontations and his execution. After the war Weatherford settled down on a farm in the lower part of Monroe County, Alabama. He owned about three hundred black slaves[48] and became known, as the Weatherfords had long been known, for fine horses. Even though he lived near the site of the massacre at Fort Mims, Red Eagle became much respected for his "bravery, honor, and strong native sense." One incident that certainly must have improved his status in the community had occurred in 1820. A number of citizens had gathered at a sale of the property of the late Duncan Henderson, and at the sale an old man named Bradberry was attacked by "two powerful and desperate men named C____ and F____." In the manner of some early historical accounts, only the initials were used to designate felons and others whose full names might be an embarrassment to their descendants. While F____ broke a pitcher over Bradberry's head and pursued him, C____ plunged a long hunting knife in the back of the old man's neck. While the victim lay bleeding at their feet, the two assailants brandished knives and threatened to kill anyone who might attempt to seize them. Justice Henderson called in vain for some of the bystanders to do their duty and overpower the murderers, and Weatherford finally stepped forward and spoke in a loud voice so that all could hear: "These, I suppose, are white men's laws. You stand aside and see a man, an OLD man, killed, and not one of you will avenge his blood. If he had one drop of Indian blood mixed with that which runs upon the ground there, I would instantly kill the murderers at the risk of my life." Henderson assured him that the white man's law would not hurt him, but that he would instead be commended for a citizen's arrest of the two villains, and he again implored Weatherford to act. Then Red Eagle drew a long silver-handled dirk (which had been presented to him by the Spanish in Pensacola) and advanced toward the murderers. He seized C____ by the throat and told him he would kill him if he moved. Then he turned to the crowd and asked that they tie up the prisoner. He then grasped F____, who surrendered without a struggle, saying: "Bill Weatherford, I am not man enough for you." In Pickett's version, he said: "I will not resist *you*, Billy Weatherford."[49]

Another interesting anecdote is found in a letter from Weatherford's grandson Charles to the historian T. H. Ball, repeating a story told him by the mother of the late Colonel William Boyles of Mobile. The prose has a flavor of its own and is worth quoting at length:

> Mrs. Boyles was a widow and lived near Bill Weatherford in Monroe County. She kept what was called at that time a wayside tavern. Weatherford, in going to and from his plantation, passed right by her door. They were warm friends and she frequently invited him to eat a meal with her. On this particular day she invited him to eat dinner. Just before the meal was ready four strangers rode up and asked for dinner. All were seated at table, and discussion commenced, in the course of which the strangers wanted to know where that bloody-handed savage, Billy Weatherford, lived. Mrs. Boyles said Weatherford's eyes sparkled. She shook her head at him to say nothing. The talk went on. Three of the strangers expressed a wish to meet Weatherford, assuring Mrs. Boyles they would kill the red-skin, bloody-handed savage on sight. (Weatherford was fair, with light brown hair and mild black eyes.) Dinner being over, the gentlemen walked out on the gallery. To the surprise of the strangers, the man with whom they sat at table stepped into the midst of the crowd and said: "Some of you gentlemen expressed a wish while at table to meet Billy Weatherford. Gentlemen, I am Billy Weatherford, at your service!" But Mrs. Boyles said she never saw men more frightened than were the three belligerently disposed gentlemen. Not one of the trio was entitled to a raven black or a milk white steed. They quailed under the glance of the Red Eagle's eye. The fourth gentleman, who said but little, stepped forward and shook hands with Weatherford, and introduced himself as Colonel David Panthon.[50]

On February 29, 1824, William Weatherford made a strange prophecy which, as J. D. Driesback stated it, was "illustrative of the poetic superstitions of the untutored savage." Red Eagle was one of a party hunting deer and bear on Lovett's Creek in Monroe County, Alabama. On the hunt an albino deer was killed, making a deep impression on Weatherford, who immediately left the hunt and returned home. He told the others that some one of the party would soon be called to the hunting ground of the spirit land and that the white deer was a "token." The next day Weatherford became severely ill and died three days later on March 4. While ill he said he saw a vision of his former wife, Sapoth Thlaine, also called Sofoth-Kaney. She was reputed to have been the most beautiful maiden of the tribe, noted for her musical voice. She had died a few days after the birth of their only child. In the vision she was standing by his bed, waiting for him to go with her to the hunting grounds of the spirit land.[51]

Weatherford had married three times, twice under Indian law to Mary Moniac and to Sapoth Thlaine. His third and last wife was Mary Stiggins, whom he married under white law in 1817. Red Eagle fathered three children—Charles, William, and Polly—by his first wife, one son, William, by his second, and five children—Alexander, Washington, Major, John, and Levitia—by his third. He still has many descendants in southern Alabama. One of his best-known relatives was a nephew, David Moniac, who became the first minority graduate of the United States Military Academy at West Point.[52]

William Weatherford, though more than half white, was an Indian to the end, and perhaps for this reason, as well as for other attributes, he was perhaps the Creek Indian most admired by whites. Sam Dale, who knew Red Eagle well, said that although he did not have as much education as Alexander McGillivray, "nature had endowed him with a noble person, a brilliant intellect, and a commanding eloquence." Dale believed that Weatherford was in every respect the peer of Tecumseh. Dale also quoted an ironic comment made by Weatherford after he settled in Monroe County following the Creek War: "He said that his old comrades, the hostiles, ate his cattle from starvation; the peace party ate them from revenge; and the squatters because he was a damned Red skin. 'So,' said he, 'I have come to live among gentlemen.'"[53] His grave stands near the town of Little River, off Highway 59, in a lonely area of bushy oak and saplings. Only a few miles away is the old Weatherford plantation along the Alabama River. A cairn of native rocks covers the grave mound and rises to a chimneylike monument about four and a half feet high. On a pink marble slab insert is the simple inscription: "William Weatherford, Red Eagle, 1765–1824." Nearby is the grave of his mother, with a stone slab insert reading "Sehoy Tate Weatherford, Creek Nation Princess, Wind Clan, Mother of William Weatherford."[54]

16

The Bitter Aftermath

———— • ————

The execution at Lockchau Talofau immediately spread alarm along the frontier. General Alexander Ware wrote to Governor Troup on May 1, reporting that several neighbors who lived along the Chattahoochee near McIntosh's plantation had heard the war whoop and rifle fire and had seen the glow of the flaming buildings before dawn the previous morning. There was a general fear that the event presaged another civil war, for an Indian named Miller, who had taken refuge at Ware's plantation with about 150 other friendly Indians, said that the "hostiles" now numbered about 4,000, the friendly Indians 500, and that the Red Sticks intended to march on the white settlements within three days. Ware reported that Major Finley Stewart was recruiting volunteers to reconnoiter the country and that he would set out with them as soon as practicable.[1]

Governor Troup wrote the president on May 3 that Chilly McIntosh had brought him an account of the death of his father. "The crime of McIntosh," the governor wrote, "is to be sought in the wise and magnanimous conduct which, at Indian Springs, produced the treaty of the 12th of February, and which, in making a concession of their whole country, satisfied the just claims of Georgia, reconciled the State to the Federal Government, and made happy, at least in prospect, the condition of the Creeks." It was by "the last of his generous actions"—agreeing to the surveying of the appropriated land—that he "met the stroke of the assassin, and the bravest of his race fell by the hands of the most treacherous and cowardly." Governor Troup laid the burden of punishing the malefactors on the president, and he warned that keeping the peace would be an almost impossible task unless the government exacted atonement promptly for the murder of McIntosh. He wrote that same day to Joseph Marshall, who had been named chief of the Cowetas: "Friend, I heard, with sorrow, yesterday, of the death of our common friend, McIntosh. All good hearts among the whites deplore it as much as you. Satisfaction will be demanded, and satisfaction shall be had; but we must not be hasty about it." In a carefully worded statement—which, he told the president, would "be taken as an order" by the surviving chiefs—he wrote: "You be peaceable and quiet until you hear from me, in the same manner as if nothing had happened to McIntosh or Tustunnuggee; but depend on it, my revenge I will have."[2]

It now seems clear that it was Governor Troup's plan to discredit agent John Crowell in the chaotic and tension-filled period following McIntosh's execution and that his motive was to replace Crowell with a more tractable political ally. Georgians who talked with Chilly McIntosh when he arrived in Milledgeville on May 2 with the tragic news heard him say that his father had been executed in accord with the law of the National Council. After conferring with the governor, however, Chilly's story changed, and Crowell was put forward as the instigator of the execution.[3] Probably at the governor's suggestion, Chilly, his uncle, and two others of the McIntosh party went to Washington to tell President John Quincy Adams the grim news. They took with them the May 3 letter from Governor Troup to the president, broadly intimating a conspiracy: "The guilty authors of this massacre it will be for you to detect and punish. I have done my duty." In Washington, Chilly and the other Cowetans told Secretary Barbour that Crowell had always been opposed to McIntosh and that if "Colonel Crowell is continued as agent, we fear that the friends of General McIntosh will be sacrificed."[4]

Because of "the existence among the Creeks of the most frightful anarchy and disorder" the governor, through his aide-de-camp Seaborn Jones, on May 5 ordered Major-Generals Ezekiel Wimberly II, Reuben Shorter, and Andrew Miller to hold their divisions in readiness "to march at a moment's warning, either to repel invasion, suppress insurrection among the Indians within our own territory, or give protection to the friendly Creeks, and avenge the death of McIntosh, who, always a firm friend of Georgia, fell a sacrifice to her cause." Duncan Campbell, however, did not believe there was much danger in the situation. In a letter to Secretary Barbour on May 4, written to discuss a hasty distribution of the funds promised in the recent treaty, he said the chiefs would "readily receive their respective portions. Accounts of their discontent, if not wholly unfounded, have, at least, been greatly exaggerated."[5]

The "atrocious murders" of McIntosh and the two others was the subject of a special presentment by the Grand Jury of the U.S. Sixth Circuit Court at Milledgeville on May 10. Although the name of agent John Crowell is nowhere mentioned in the document, his presence can be easily inferred: "The Grand Jury deem it necessary to the character of the government of this country that the authors, perpetrators, aiders, and abettors of the crimes lately committed, should be sought for, and, when ascertained, prosecuted and severely punished. They have no language strong enough to mark their abhorrence of the white persons, if any, who have seduced or irritated the unhappy Indians to perpetrate this tragedy."[6]

In the meantime Crowell, assisted by his foster son and interpreter Paddy Carr, could not refrain from taking part in the controversy. He wrote to Secretary Barbour on May 8 that "the [Little] Prince wishes me to inform the Government that this party of warriors [who killed McIntosh] acted under the orders of the proper authorities of the Nation." He added that "intelligence reached the Prince two days ago that the friends of McIntosh intended to put him to death and had likewise threatened me."[7] The full letter was published in the *Macon* (Georgia) *Messenger* on May 11, prompting a letter of denial, written for publication by Rolly McIntosh, Chief Joseph Marshall, and other members of the McIntosh party. They said that the claim of threats on the lives of Little Prince and Crowell was a lie. They also said that the statement that McIntosh was killed to carry out a law prohibiting further land cessions, which McIntosh himself had signed at Broken Arrow, was "positively false" and "only made use of as a pretext for the cruel murders which have been committed." They reasoned, "It certainly would have been very inconsistent of General McIntosh, or any of us, to have signed the treaty at the Mineral Springs, had such a law as that come within our knowledge; and it is very droll, too, that such a law as that should exist, and that the national clerk [Chilly McIntosh] and none of us should have any knowledge of it. . . . If such a law had been made, we should have known it." They admitted having heard of such a law being read at Polecat Springs, but this was not at a National Council, and therefore a law passed there "could only subject those who were present," and McIntosh had not been there. As to whether Crowell's life was in danger, the chiefs may have been incorrect in their denial. Brigadier General Charles McDonald had written to Governor Troup on May 6 to tell him that the Indians were friendly to whites, except for the agent, Crowell. "On his destruction," he said, "both parties seem determined."[8]

Paddy Carr, by Charles Bird King (from McKenney and Hall, *History of the Indian Tribes*)

Although Crowell's name is not mentioned, Governor Troup leaves little doubt that he is referring to him in a message to the Georgia General Assembly on May 23. He said that the difficulties that had embarrassed the treaty commissioners from the beginning and "were well nigh producing a rupture" of the Indian Springs treaty "proceeded from a quarter the least of all to be expected—from the officers in the pay and confidence of the Federal Government, who, instead of rendering the commissioners the most cordial co-operation, had organized an opposition." He added: "I verily believe that but for the insidious practice of evil-minded white men, the entire nation would have moved harmoniously across the Mississippi." Troup was still smarting from a letter he had received from Secretary Barbour on May 18; Barbour had written that Crowell blamed the governor for triggering McIntosh's death by prematurely issuing a proclamation relating to the surveying of the newly acquired lands.[9]

Meanwhile, Chilly McIntosh had gone to Washington to ask the protection of the federal government and the assistance of the president in bringing his father's slayers to justice. Also, the clamor against Crowell became so widespread and the controversy concerning the treaty so heated that President Adams appointed Major T. P. Andrews as a special agent to "examine into certain implied charges against Col. Crowell, the Indian Agent." Andrews presented himself to the governor on May 31 with a request that Troup furnish him with charges, specifications, and evidence. On that same day, Troup put his charges against Crowell in writing: "1st. Predetermined resolution to prevent the Indians, by all the means in his power, from making any cession of their lands in favor of the Georgians, and this from the most unworthy and injustifiable of all motives. 2dly. With advising and instigating, in chief, the death of McIntosh and his friends."[10] Troup included no evidence along with his charges, and on June 8, having heard that Andrews had said in a conversation that "the evidence submitted to him did not furnish even probable cause to suspect the Indian agent as guilty under the charges exhibited against him in the Governor's letter of 31st May," wrote to Andrews about this statement. Andrews replied that he recalled that in that conversation he said that "until he was furnished with the documents and evidence referred to in the Governor's letter of 31st May, he did not consider himself at liberty to form any opinion, even as to the propriety of suspending the Agent."[11]

In his frequent reports to Secretary Barbour during this time, Andrews placed much of the blame for the brewing controversy on the Georgians. On June 2 he stated his belief that the system, peculiar to Georgia, of allocating land lots by lottery was "the first cause of all the anxiety on the part of the authorities of Georgia to acquire possession of the Indian lands within their limits; for most, if not all, public men in Georgia seek to recommend themselves to their fellow citizens by a display of zeal in procuring land to be thus disposed of among the people." He said he saw no reason why the land would have to be surveyed before the scheduled Indian removal in September of 1826, "but the authorities of this State appear to me to have acted so precipitately, and have committed themselves so far, and now show so much temper on the subject, that I doubt if they forego their intentions." He concluded this letter with the opinion that the Indians had been "harshly dealt with" in the recent treaty.[12]

In his reports to Secretary Barbour Andrews made frequent reference to Governor Troup's role in the controversy. On June 7 he wrote that the governor's correspondence generally shows "that if the killing of McIntosh was not in strict compliance with the laws of his people (which it is, as yet, impossible to determine,) it was at least apprehended by himself and friends, and anticipated by the Governor of Georgia." He told Barbour on June 12: "From three to four hundred stand of arms have been sent off by the Governor to the Indian Springs, but whether for the military or McIntosh's Indians, I am unable to determine." In this same letter in which he used conjecture to damage Troup's reputation with the secretary, he wrote that the evidence against Crowell was "weak" and "contradictory."[13]

On June 10 the Senate and House of Representatives of the state of Georgia passed a resolution calling for the dismissal of Crowell and stating, in part, "that his continuance in office hitherto has been, and hereafter will be, greatly to the injury of the state, and that the confidence of a large part of the Creek nation is now so irrevocably alienated from him that it would hereafter be impossible for him to administer and superintend their affairs to their advantage and comfort, even if he was disposed so to do." The report of the senatorial investigation referred to the long-standing enmity between Crowell and McIntosh and cataloged the threats and statements of ill will allegedly made by Crowell concerning McIntosh (which have been earlier cited on this work). "On the whole," the report read, "your committee does not see in the evidence sufficient proof to justify them in presuming that the Agent ordered, contrived, or instigated the murder of General McIntosh; but until the contrary shall be made to appear, they must fully believe that he knew of the approaching event and could have prevented it. . . . It is believed that if the Agent had been removed from office last January, General McIntosh would have now been in life."[14]

Governor Troup continued to urge Andrews to suspend Crowell from his duties as agent, but Andrews was able to resist until the latter part of June by calling for evidence and specifications of the governor's charges. On June 21, however, Andrews wrote a polite letter to Crowell, suspending him "until all the testimony to be collected in the Indian nation has been obtained and examined" and directing him to turn over the agency to his subagent, Captain Triplett. "Your suspension," Andrews explained to Crowell, "is made from courtesy to the authorities of Georgia, who have repeatedly and urgently demanded it—on the ground that it would be impossible to elicit unbiased testimony in the Indian Nation whilst you are in the exercise of your functions." He was careful to point out that "this determination does not proceed from any present impressions unfavorable to your innocence." Andrews also stated that "it could not but give me pain . . . to find that in taking testimony against you, all the usual prerequisites were lost sight of by the authorities of Georgia. You were neither *'informed of the nature and cause of the accusation,'* or *'confronted with witnesses against you,'* nor had you *'compulsory process for obtaining witnesses in your favor!'* " Crowell gave the letter to the *Milledgeville Patriot,* which published it on June 28; and he stated, making the letter public, "Indeed the untiring zeal manifested by Gov. Troup in the accomplishment of his purpose, has rarely been equaled and never surpassed—it stands without parallel in the annals of persecution." He also spoke of "the inquisitorial proceedings of the Governor and Legislature of Georgia." Governor Troup angrily fired off a letter to Andrews: "If this letter be authentic, you will consider all intercourse between yourself and this government suspended from the moment of the receipt of this." Andrews wrote a long letter in answer to Troup's outburst; he avowed authorship of the letter to Crowell, "with the exception of a few typographical errors," and sent the governor a corrected copy. He also praised Crowell's "inflexible integrity and firmness in stemming a torrent of corruption, disgraceful, in my opinion, to the national character."[15]

It would not be long before Governor Troup also locked horns with General Edmund P. Gaines, the hero of the Creek and Seminole wars, who had been sent by the federal government both to preserve the peace and to aid in the investigation of the controversy over the Indian Springs treaty. On July 1 Gaines wrote to the governor to report on the council at Broken Arrow, a meeting called as part of the investigation as well as an attempt to settle the differences between factions of the Creek Nation. He was dealing primarily with the Upper Creeks, also called the "hostiles," and Gaines reported that they were adamant and even willing to make a show of passive resistance to make their point:

They refuse to receive any part of the consideration money, or to give any other evidence of their acquiescence in the treaty. But they have, in the strongest terms, deliberately declared that they will not raise an arm against the United States, even should an army come to take from them the whole of their country; that they will make no sort of resistance; but will sit down quietly and be put to death where the bones of their ancestors are deposited; that the world shall know that the Muscogee nation so loved their country that they were willing to die in it, rather than sell it or leave it.

Troup was cynical in his reply: "I much fear this ardent love of country is of recent origin; we can scarcely believe that the *amor patrioe* is all upon the one side, and that side the hostile one." He reminded Gaines, in closing, that the followers of McIntosh were willing to remove to the West and that he expected from the general his best efforts "to accomplish this most desirable and holy end; holy, I say, because it is the only one that can consist with their peace, safety and happiness."[16] Troup clearly believed it was Gaines's Christian duty to effect the Indian removal as soon as possible.

Gaines wrote a letter to Governor Troup on July 10 that drove the governor's anger instantly to the kindling point. After he had conferred with chiefs in both McIntosh's party and the so-called "hostile" party, Gaines concluded: "The reputed hostile party consists of all the principal Chiefs and of nearly *forty-nine-fiftieths* of the whole of the Chiefs, Head-men, and Warriors of the Nation: among whom I recognize many who were in our service during the late war, and who, to my certain knowledge, have been for twenty years past, (and I think they have been at all times), friendly to the United States as any of our Indian neighbors could have been known to be." He concluded: "I could not, therefore, but view the supposed hostile party as in fact and in truth the *Creek Nation*." As if this were not enough, Gaines then presented a certificate from William Edwards and Joseph Marshall, who stated that they were present when Governor Troup's message came to McIntosh, requesting that the survey of the ceded lands be begun immediately. Edwards and Marshall testified that "General McIntosh replied that he could not grant the request, but would call the Chiefs together and lay it before them—which was never done." This, Gaines continued, "proves that your Excellency has been greatly deceived in supposing that the McIntosh party ever consented to the survey of the ceded territory being commenced before the time set forth in the treaty for their removal."[17]

Governor Troup's livid anger in reply lent a heightened eloquence to his pen: "The certificate of Marshall, no matter how procured, is one of the most daring efforts that ever was attempted by malignant villainy to palm a falsehood upon credulity. Now, sir, that you may be at once undeceived with regard to this trick, which has been played off by somebody, I have to assure you that, independently of the assent three times given by McIntosh, under his own hand, which I have in my possession, this same man, Marshall, has repeatedly declared to me that there was not a dissentient voice from the survey among the friendly chiefs."[18]

Gaines, also a proud man who had been long accustomed to having deference paid to his rank, was incensed by the governor's letter, and he kept it on his table a week in the "expectation that a little reflection would suggest" to the governor "the propriety of correcting some expressions, apparently hasty and calculated to call forth an answer partaking of the climate and heated atmosphere in which I find myself." But because he had been handed a copy of this letter from the governor, as published in a newspaper, he could no longer withhold a reply. "You say," he reminded the governor on July 28, " 'the certificate of Marshall, no matter how procured, is one of the most daring efforts that ever was attempted by malignant villainy to palm a falsehood on innocent credulity.'—'*No matter how procured!*' " He stated that the certificate was given voluntarily, and he defended Chiefs Edwards and Marshall as honest and upright citizens whose statements were "simple and apparently unprejudiced and unimpassioned." He told the governor that all his duties with the Indians were performed in "*open day*" and that he "had no secret project to promote, nor any '*secret griefs*' to remedy, or secret hopes to gratify." Warming to his task, Gaines wrote that "it is apparent from McIntosh's letters, 'no matter how procured,' (I will offer no apology for making use of your Excellency's pregnant phrase,) or by whom written, that he himself considered the permission to survey as merely conditional. But I contend that neither General McIntosh nor his *vassal Chiefs* had any right to give such permission: for the treaty, 'no matter how procured,' had become *law of the land:* its provisions could not therefore be changed." He assured the governor that the "tongue and pen of calumny can never move me from the path of duty," and he added, "I have seen, of late, with regret, that it is scarcely possible for an officer of the General Government to differ with you in opinion without incurring your incourteous animadversion or your acrimonious censure; neither of which shall ever induce me to forget what is due to myself or the venerated station you fill."[19]

It was apparently this bitter exchange that led Gaines to report to Secretary Barbour the chaotic nature of the situation in Georgia and to conclude that Congress should reconsider the Indian Springs treaty. Barbour wrote to Governor Troup on July 21 that the United States government had hoped that the entire Creek Nation could reach agreement on the treaty but that "communications from General Gaines, recently received here, have entirely destroyed that hope." Barbour stated that "a large majority of their Chiefs and Headmen of the tribe have denounced the treaty as tainted alike with intrigue and treachery and as an act of a very small portion of the tribe against the express determination of a very large majority; a determination known to the Commissioners." The question presented by these allegations "necessarily refers itself to Congress, whose attention will be called to it at an early day after the next annual meeting." Barbour also pointed out that the president, "acting on the treaty as though its validity had not been impeached," believed that the eighth article would protect the Creeks from surveys or other encroachment until their removal in September 1826. It is not known on what date Governor Troup received this letter, but he answered it on August 15: "It may be otherwise," he wrote to Barbour, "but I do sincerely believe that no Indian treaty has ever been negotiated and concluded in better faith than the one which is the subject of this letter." Then he became defiant, claiming that the treaty was still valid: "The legislature of Georgia will, therefore, on its first meeting, be advised to resist any effort which may be made to wrest from the State the territory acquired by the treaty, and no matter by what authority that effort be made."[20]

The Georgia legislature convened on November 7, and on the following day Governor Troup transmitted a long message to that body, recapitulating the relationships between the federal government and the state of Georgia, with particular reference to the Indian problems. Referring to the Georgia Compact of 1802, Troup stated that the territorial claims of the state "had been so long neglected that time seemed to be running against them. The Indians were acquiring a permanency of foothold, under the direct encouragement of the United States, which would rivet them, like their fixtures, to the soil forever." He lambasted the Indian agent Crowell as well as Major Andrews and General Gaines, the special agents sent by the federal government. The unvarnished references to the character and integrity of the three representatives of the federal government are remarkable for their candor in a public message given by a governor of a state. As to the president's referring the Indian Springs treaty back to Congress for reconsideration, Troup said that "the treaty was as untainted with fraud as most other Indian treaties."[21] Before the legislature adjourned on December 22 it had passed a resolution in both houses expressing full reliance in the Indian Springs treaty, to the effect "that the title of the territory obtained by said treaty, within the limits of Georgia, is considered as an absolute, vested interest, and that nothing short of the whole territory thus acquired will be satisfactory." The General Assembly also passed an act "to organize the territory lately acquired from the Creek Indians, lying between the Flint and Chattahoochee Rivers, and west of the Chattahoochee River" into four new Georgia counties, Muscogee, Troup, Coweta, and Carroll, the first named "in honor of McIntosh, and to perpetuate the memory of the Creek people."[22] This premature action was part of a classic confrontation between the rights of a state and the rights of the federal government.

Governor Troup's stormy rhetoric was to avail him nothing, however; on the first Monday of December 1825, the Senate assembled to discuss the abrogation of the Indian Springs treaty. The lengthy reports from Major Andrews and General Gaines, both damaging to the validity of the treaty, were in hand, and President John Quincy Adams questioned whether the treaty had been negotiated in good faith. Adams told the Senate: "I have been anxiously desirous of carrying it into execution; but, like other treaties, its fulfillment depends upon the will not of one, but of both parties to it." He said it had been expected that the treaty would be concluded with a large majority of the Creek Nation. "This expectation has not merely been disappointed," he said. "The first measures for carrying the treaty into execution had scarcely been taken when the two principal chiefs who had signed it fell victims to the exasperation of the great mass of the nation."[23]

Andrews's report consists largely of an examination of the evidence for and against agent Crowell, with the anti-Crowell testimony almost entirely ruled by Andrews to be false and the pro-Crowell testimony almost all considered valid. So one-sided is the evaluation of the evidence that Governor Troup's statement about the federal government's protectiveness of the agent seems almost reasonable. Troup told the legislature on November 8: "No evil report of him [Crowell] would be listened to; the word of no man taken against him; all testimony in his favor eagerly received, all against him promptly discredited." The testimony of Flournoy, for example, was disallowed because he had been found guilty of frauds and perjury and had been disfranchised for twenty years by the legislature. Therefore, even though he was an eyewitness to McIntosh's murder, "his oath is worthless." Andrews also reported that Peggy McIntosh and Jane Hawkins could not write and that the letters allegedly written by them and entered as testimony were written by Flournoy. Because they were related to McIntosh, the testimony of Samuel Hawkins and Chilly McIntosh was not acceptable. Andrews claimed to have found only one witness, Adam Miles, whose anti-Crowell testimony could not be "directly disproved." Persons who worked with Crowell, such as the acting agent Thomas Triplett or the interpreter William Hambly, gave testimony favorable to Crowell and were considered unbiased. In a letter to the president, Troup had singled out Hambly for giving biased testimony because he was a friend of Crowell's. In the same letter Troup tried to discount testimony given by several missionaries to General Gaines: "Now that they are in danger of being ousted of their living, if the treaty is carried into effect, they make a common cause with the Agent to rupture the treaty and will swear or affirm to nothing against him."[24] Both sides, it seems, were not above poisoning the wells of testimony in this controversy.

After listing the principal points in the case, that only eight of the fifty-six Creek towns were represented, that thirty of the fifty-two signers were from one town, Coweta, and that McIntosh, the fifth-ranking Creek chief, could not speak for the nation, Andrews stated:

> These are the facts with which persons at all acquainted in the Creek Nation are conversant. But, from McIntosh's being a half-breed, and conversant with our language, his former gallant conduct as a warrior, his intercourse with the whites, and his anxiety on all occasions to be conspicuous: a different opinion measurably has prevailed with the public. It is also proved that McIntosh was induced to sign the treaty, and to induce or compel his adherents to sign with him, from large douceurs or bribes offered or given to him by the Commissioners, at the same time remarking that he forfeited his life in doing so, under the laws of his Nation. . . . No unprejudiced person, after reading the mass of testimony now submitted, can withhold the belief, that the treaty made at Indian Springs, in February last, was in fact agreed on in private in the nocturnal interviews between the commissioners and McIntosh at Broken Arrow in the preceding December.

He also concluded that Crowell "has fully succeeded in establishing his entire innocence of the charges preferred against him."[25]

After reading this report and hearing President Adams's reservations about the Indian Springs treaty, Congress quickly abrogated that tainted agreement, and on January 24 Secretary of War Barbour, by the president's authority, concluded a new treaty in Washington with a small number of Creek chiefs who were called, in the heading of the treaty, "Chiefs and Head-men of the Creek Nation of Indians who have received full power from the said Nation to conclude and arrange for all matters herein provided for." There were only fourteen signatories, but these included Opothle Yoholo, who had spoken out eloquently against McIntosh and the treaty at Indian Springs; Menawa, who led the executioners of McIntosh; and Selocta, who had long before spoken out for Indian rights, even against the Sharp Knife, Andrew Jackson. Witnessing the treaty signing was John Crowell, agent for Indian affairs.[26] In one historian's opinion, this treaty was obtained by "using a form of persuasion only a little less hypocritical than that used by the federal commissioners at Indian Springs the previous year."[27] The treaty was signed, extinguishing the claims of virtually all Creek lands in Georgia, despite the impassioned question raised by Opothle Yoholo in the preliminary discussions: "Why cannot we be allowed to have land, and homes, and live like our white brothers and learn of them how to be comfortable?"[28]

In communicating the new treaty to the Senate, President Adams outlined the "troubles" that "had ensued" from the former treaty, including the deaths of McIntosh and the others. He also told the Senate that the families and dependents of McIntosh, led by Chilly, had come to Washington to advance "pretensions to receive, exclusively to themselves, the whole of the sums stipulated . . . in payment *for all* the lands of the Creek Nation which were ceded by the terms of the treaty."[29] This avaricious ploy, of course, was denied, but the treaty did award to the McIntosh party, in "consideration of the exertions used . . . to procure a cession at the Indian Springs, and of their past difficulties and comtemplated removal" the sum of $100,000 if there were three thousand persons in the McIntosh party removing to the West "and in the proportion for any smaller number." The sum of $15,000 would be paid immediately after the ratification of the treaty and the remainder upon their arrival in the country west of the Mississippi. Besides this incentive to swell the number of persons already committed to removal, the treaty promised the McIntosh party reparation for damages. Possession of the ceded land was to be yielded on or before January 1, 1827.[30] Governor Troup's style was at its most ironic when he wrote the president about the new treaty, which was negotiated "at Washington, [where] we are to presume the existence of perfect freedom of will, uncontrolled and unconstrained, united to the romantic love of country, dictating every article and paragraph of the new treaty; whilst in the woods of Georgia, the same freedom has been corrupted by gold and the will misdirected to the ruin of Indian rights and interest."[31]

Despite the efforts of Senators John M. Berrien and Thomas W. Cobb from Georgia, the Senate ratified the new treaty on April 22, 1826. "Defeated in these particulars," Senator Berrien wrote to Governor Troup, "I still thought it an act of duty to the friends of McIntosh, and interesting to Georgia, to attempt something for their relief and for the encouragement of their emigration."[32] The Georgia delegation had been particularly disturbed that the 1826 treaty did not include about a million acres of land lying between the western bank of the Chattahoochee and the Alabama territory and including parts of present-day Carroll, Troup, Heard, and Haralson counties in Georgia. This narrow strip in northwestern Georgia was ceded by the Creeks in a final treaty signed November 15, 1827.

From the time of the ratification of the treaty on April 22, the McIntosh Creeks became a separate entity in the Creek Nation. Colonel David Brearly, who had been an agent to the Arkansas Cherokees, was appointed on May 13 as agent to the McIntosh Creeks. In May the following year, Brearly and an exploring party of five Creeks arrived in Arkansas and found the land that was to be their new home. In August the McIntosh Creeks, now under the leadership of Chilly, parted peacefully with their fellow Creeks, Chilly exchanging speeches of friendship with Little Prince and Mad Tiger. By November, 739 members of the emigrating McIntosh party, far short of the hoped-for 3,000, reached Tuscumbia on the Tennessee River to embark on boats that would carry them west. Along the way they were harassed by persons with fake legal attachments, laying claim to property they had in their possession. Not until they reached Tuscumbia were they treated hospitably. "Here we have remained several days," Chilly stated, "and have received all kind of hospitality and good treatment. The citizens of Tuscumbia have treated us like brothers and our old helpless women were furnished by the good women of the town with clothing."[33] It was a sad reversal of fortunes for the proud McIntosh party.

In 1826, a chief named Mushulatubbe was deposed as headman of one of the Choctaw districts. According to his successor, David Folsom, the former chief had been addicted to drunkenness, too tyrannical, and too likely to yield Choctaw lands to the United States. "We do not want a General McIntosh in our tribe," Folsom wrote.[34] But was William McIntosh really a villain, and was it fair for Folsom to use his name as an anathema to the Choctaws? A good case could be made to the effect that McIntosh, who had been honored as a military leader when he espoused the white man's cause and fought against the Red Sticks, had merely been too easily swayed by the treaty commissioners, who themselves were under pressure from the highest officials in the state and federal governments. Who can argue against the possibility that McIntosh, who had early been made aware of the power of the United States by his confrontation with President Jefferson, may have genuinely believed that it was hopeless for the Creek Indians to attempt to maintain their old lifestyle in the East, where white settlers were daily encroaching? Always the pragmatist, he may well have reasoned that the time was right to take the government's offer of equal lands in the West—plus cash and annuities—and emigrate.

Thomas L. McKenney, the superintendent of Indian trade, knew McIntosh from his frequent trips to Washington and was inclined to take a charitable view toward his actions:

> It is not difficult to imagine the inducements which led McIntosh to enter upon this treaty in defiance of the law of his nation, and its bloody penalty. He probably foresaw that his people would have no rest within the limits of Georgia, and perhaps acted with an honest view to their interests. The intercourse he had enjoyed with the army of the United States, and the triumph of their arms over the desperate valour of the Indians, which he had witnessed at Autossee, the Horseshoe, and in Florida, induced him to believe he would be safe under the shadow of their protection, even from the vengeance of his tribe. But there were, besides, strong appeals to his cupidity, in the provisions of the treaty of the Indian Springs, and in its supplements. By one of these, the Indian Spring reservation was secured to him; and by another it was agreed to pay him for it twenty-five thousand dollars. Moreover, the second article of the treaty provided for the payment to the Creek nation of four hundred thousand dollars. Of this sum he would of course have received his share. Such inducements might have been sufficiently powerful to shake a virtue based upon a surer foundation than the education of a heathen Indian could afford. Besides this, he was flattered

and caressed by the commissioners, who were extremely eager to complete the treaty, and taught to believe that he was consulting the ultimate advantage of the nation. These considerations, in some measure, remove the odium from his memory. But it must still bear the stain which Indian justice affixes to the reputation of the chief who sells, under such circumstances, the graves of his fathers.[35]

Peggy McIntosh, the general's Cherokee widow, believed McIntosh's actions were motivated by such pressures. Two decades after her husband's murder, she was seen at the office of Pierce M. Butler, agent for the Cherokee Indians in the West, and the incident was described in the *Cherokee Advocate:*

Some one casually observed she could not entertain a very friendly or partial feeling for those who had thus deprived him [McIntosh] of his existence—the remark was repeated before she appeared to notice it; suddenly however, the shawl, which covered her shoulders and held together by her arm partially enveloped her form, was loosed, and with a sparkling eye, and a voice full of tremulous emotion, she broke out into an indignant rebuke of that government, which had beggared her children and left her portionless and a widow to the cold, heartless, and uncertain charity of the world. "No," she exclaimed, "no, I do not blame these people for these things—I do not blame the Creeks, the Creeks treat me well, the Cherokees treat me well—it was the Government caused me to suffer, it was by Government my husband lost his life—Government say to my husband 'Go to Arkansas, go to Arkansas, and you will be better off.' My husband wished to please the Government—my home is burned, myself and children run—my children naked—no bread—one blanket, is all—like some stray dog, I suffer; with one blanket I cover my three children and myself—the Government say 'Go!' The Indians kill him; between two fires my husband dies; I wander—Government does not feed me—Creek does not feed me—no home, no bread, nothing! nothing! Till Gen. Ware gives me a home, I suffer like some stray Indian dog."[36]

If McIntosh is considered culpable, the white settlers also must share some of the blame. Adam Hodgson, who traveled in the Creek Nation in 1820 and who knew McIntosh personally, came to understand the changes in the Indians' ethics and sense of values that occurred with the encroachments of the whites. Hodgson reported a chance meeting near the Chattahoochee with a white man who had married a Lower Creek woman and who regretted "the injury which the morals of the Indians have sustained from intercourse with the

Tustunnuggee Emathla, by Charles Bird King (from McKenney and Hall, *History of the Indian Tribes*)

whites." He told Hodgson that he remembered when stealing was almost unheard-of among the Creeks and they would leave silver trinkets and ornaments hanging in open huts while they were absent. He said: "Confidence and generosity were then their characteristic virtues. A desire for gain, caught from the whites, has chilled their liberality." One of the Creeks who had caught this desire for gain was McIntosh, whom Hodgson had met in Washington as one of a Creek deputation in 1820. Hodgson spoke of McIntosh as "the most popular and influential person" in the Creek Nation, "who is consulted on every occasion, and who, in a great measure, directs the affairs of the country." After arriving among the Lower Creeks in the same year of 1820, Hodgson concluded that "the more reflecting of the Creeks . . . see plainly that it is a question of civilization or extinction." One of these more thoughtful Creek chiefs was Tustunnuggee Emathla, who joined the pro-McIntosh forces and spoke at numerous councils in favor of exchanging Creek land for western land.[37] That this chief was able to espouse removal without being condemned by the Upper Creeks leads one to conclude that McIntosh's case was unusual.

One difference in McIntosh's case was the long-standing enmity between him and the Upper Creeks, incurred during his activities as a law mender and heightened by his heroics in the War of 1813–14. McIntosh, of course, signed the land treaty at Indian Springs in defiance of laws passed at Broken Arrow and Polecat Springs, but other Lower Creeks signed and yet went unharmed. It is true that McIntosh's blood ties with the white power structure made him particularly susceptible to influences from that quarter, resulting in his accepting money for achieving the materialistic ends of the Georgians and his own entrepreneurial goals. McIntosh was also a mixed-blood, who was able to break with the nativistic tradition that did not allow the concept of individual ownership of land, believing it was to be held by the Creek Nation as a whole for those who would come after them. As young McIntosh had told President Jefferson in 1805, "we have young half breed men now grown up among us that have learning, that have been taught the value of land."[38] He could well have believed sincerely that the Creeks' best alternative was to remove to the West, but in acting upon this belief he seems to have badly miscalculated the ingrained intransigence of the nativistic Upper Creeks.

Notes

———— • ————

Preface

1. *Niles' Weekly Register*, November 7, 1818.
2. Thomas L. McKenney and James Hall, *The Indian Tribes of North America*, ed. Frederick Webb Hodge, 2 vols. (Edinburgh, 1933), 2:50–51; Frank L. Owsley, Jr., "Prophet of War: Josiah Francis and the Creek War," *American Indian Quarterly* 11 (1985): 273.

1: Introduction

1. Henry R. Schoolcraft, ed., *Historical and Statistical Information, Respecting the History, Conditions and Prospects of the Indian Tribes of the United States*, 6 vols. (Philadelphia, 1851–57), 5:263.
2. John Walton Caughey, *McGillivray of the Creeks* (Norman, Okla., 1938), p. 6.
3. Peter Farb, *Man's Rise to Civilization: The Cultural Ascent of the Indians of North America*, 2d ed., rev. (New York, 1978), p. 250; John R. Swanton, "Notes on the Mental Assimilation of Races," *Journal of the Washington Academy of Sciences* 16 (1926): 501.
4. Farb, *Man's Rise to Civilization*, p. 249; Benjamin Hawkins, *A Sketch of the Creek Country in the Years 1798 and 1799*, in *Collections of the Georgia Historical Society*, 3, pt. 2; (1848; rpt. Spartanburg, S.C., 1974), p. 8.
5. Michel Guillaume St. Jean de Crevecoeur, *Letters from an American Farmer* (London, 1782), pp. 294–95; Farb, *Man's Rise to Civilization*, p. 249.
6. E. Merton Coulter and Albert B. Saye, *A List of Early Settlers in Georgia* (Athens, Ga., 1949), p. 86; James C. Bonner, "William McIntosh," in Horace Montgomery, ed., *Georgians in Profile: Historical Essays in Honor of Ellis Merton Coulter* (Athens, Ga., 1958), p. 116.
7. Harriet Turner (Porter) Corbin, *A History and Genealogy of Chief William McIntosh, Jr.* (Long Beach, Calif., 1967), pp. 15 and 83; Bonner, "William McIntosh," p. 116.

8. Marie Bankhead Owen, "Indian Chiefs," *Alabama Historical Quarterly* 13 (1951): 81–83; Caughey, *McGillivray of the Creeks,* p. 9.

9. J. D. Driesback, "Weatherford—'The Red Eagle,'" *Alabama Historical Reporter* 2 (1884): no page number.

10. Tom Tate Tunstall, "Tom Tate Tunstall Defends the Name of Weatherford," *Arrow Points* 9 (1924): 6; see also Tunstall Bryars, "Chart of the Family of Sehoy and Col. Marchand," *Baldwin County Historical Society Quarterly* 6 (1979): 50.

11. Bonner, "William McIntosh," p. 117.

12. William Bartram, *Travels through North and South Carolina, Georgia, East and West Florida,* facsimile of 1792 ed. (Savannah, Ga., 1973), p. 387; Hawkins, Journal, January 23, 1797, C. L. Grant, ed., *Letters, Journals and Writings of Benjamin Hawkins,* 2 vols. (Savannah, Ga., 1980), 1: 38; hereinafter Grant, ed., *Hawkins Papers.*

13. Hawkins, "A Sketch of the Creek Country," ibid., p. 309; Hawkins to unknown, n.d., ibid., 2: 457.

14. Louis LeClerc Milfort, *Memoirs, or a Quick Glance at My Various Travels and My Sojourn in the Creek Nation* (1802), trans. and ed. Ben C. McCary (Savannah, Ga., 1959), pp. 26, 92–93, 96.

15. George Cary Eggleston, *Red Eagle and the Wars with the Creek Indians of Alabama* (New York, 1878), p. 41.

16. Hawkins, Journal, December 20, 1796, Grant, ed., *Hawkins Papers,* 1: 23.

17. Ibid., pp. 24–25; W. Stuart Harris, *Dead Towns of Alabama* (University, Ala., 1977), p. 54.

18. David H. Corkran, *The Creek Frontier, 1540–1783* (Norman, Okla., 1967), pp. 3–5.

19. Michael D. Green, *The Politics of Indian Removal: Creek Government and Society in Crisis* (Lincoln, Neb., 1982), p. 11; Corkran, *Creek Frontier,* p. 607.

20. James Adair, *History of the American Indians* (1775), rpt. ed. Samuel Cole Williams (New York, 1930), p. 274.

21. William Bartram, "Observations on the Creek and Cherokee Indians" (1789), *Transactions of the American Ethnological Society* 3 (1953): 55–56.

22. Green's *Politics of Indian Removal* is the most complete study in print of the political struggles surrounding the Creek land cessions following the Creek War of 1813–14.

2: Children of Their Mothers' Clans

1. John R. Swanton, *Social Organizations and Social Usages of the Indians of the Creek Confederacy* (1928; rpt. New York, 1970), p. 363; Green, *Politics of Indian Removal,* pp. 4–6.

2. Hawkins to Jefferson, July 11, 1803, Grant, ed., *Hawkins Papers,* 2: 455–56; Hawkins to James McHenry, January 6, 1797, ibid., 1: 63.

3. Swanton, *Social Organizations*, p. 365; Adair, *History of the American Indians*, p. 163.

4. Eggleston, *Red Eagle*, pp. 42–43.

5. Charles M. Hudson, *The Southeastern Indians* (Knoxville, 1976), pp. 322, 31.

6. Jean Bernard Bossu, *Travels in the Interior of North America*, 1751–62 (1768; rpt. trans. Seymour Feiler, Norman, Okla., 1962), p. 100.

7. Adair, *History of the American Indians*, p. 126; Hudson, *Southeastern Indians*, p. 324; Swanton, *Social Organizations*, p. 363.

8. Carl Mauelshagen and Gerald H. Davis, ed. and trans., *Partners in the Lord's Work: The Diary of Two Moravian Missionaries in the Creek Indian Country, 1807–1813*, Research Paper 21 (Atlanta: Georgia State College, 1969), pp. 51–52.

9. Hawkins, Journal, December 3, 1796, Grant, ed., *Hawkins Papers*, 1: 7.

10. Hawkins, "A Sketch of the Creek Country," ibid., p. 307; Hudson, *Southeastern Indians*, p. 282.

11. Adair, *History of the American Indians*, p. 432.

12. Benjamin Franklin French, *Historical Collections of Louisiana and Florida*, 2d ser. (New York, 1875), p. 172; Bartram, *Travels*, p. 106; Hudson, *Southeastern Indians*, p. 284.

13. Hawkins, Journal, December 16, 1796, Grant, ed., *Hawkins Papers*, 1: 20; December 10, 1796, pp. 14–15; December 4, 1796, p. 9.

14. Ibid., December 23, 1796, p. 27.

15. Hawkins, "A Sketch of the Creek Country," ibid., p. 286; Hawkins, Journal, December 23, 1796, p. 27.

16. Hudson, *Southeastern Indians*, p. 287.

17. Hawkins, Journal, January 21, 1797, Grant, ed., *Hawkins Papers*, 1: 37; John Phillip Reid, *A Law of Blood: The Primitive Law of the Cherokee Nation* (New York, 1970), p. 78.

18. Milfort, *Memoirs*, pp. 86–88.

19. Hawkins, Journal, January 23, 1797, Grant, ed., *Hawkins Papers*, 1: 38; Adair, *History of the American Indians*, pp. 418–19; Hudson, *Southeastern Indians*, pp. 255–57.

20. Eggleston, *Red Eagle*, p. 44; Milfort, *Memoirs*, p. 52.

21. Hawkins, Journal, December 23, 1796, Grant, ed., *Hawkins Papers*, 1: 26–27. I am grateful to Dennard Davis, D.V.M., Carrollton, Georgia, for identifying this disease.

22. Milfort, *Memoirs*, p. 95.

23. Adair, *History of the American Indians*, pp. 38–39.

24. Gloria Jahoda, *The Trail of Tears: The Story of the American Indian Removal, 1813–1855* (New York, 1975), pp. 149 and 318, n. 8.

25. Hudson, *Southeastern Indians*, pp. 171–72.

26. Hawkins, "A Sketch of the Creek Country," Grant, ed., *Hawkins Papers*, 1: 321.

27. Hudson, *Southeastern Indians*, p. 366.

28. Hawkins, "A Sketch of the Creek Country," Grant, ed., *Hawkins Papers*, 1: 323–24.

29. Hudson, *Southeastern Indians*, pp. 368–69.

30. George Stiggins, "A Historical Narration of the Genealogy, Traditions, and Downfall of the Ispocaga or Creek Tribe of Indians, Written by One of the Tribe," Manuscript in Lyman Draper Papers, Wisconsin Historical Society, Madison, ed. Theron A. Nunez, Jr., *Ethnohistory* 5 (1958): 131–32; hereinafter, Stiggins, Narrative.

31. For example, Mrs. Bailey, an Indian woman married to a white farmer, insisted that her family continue the Indian custom of bathing each morning in a cold stream, summer or winter; see Hawkins, Journal, December 18, 1796, Grant, ed., *Hawkins Papers*, 1: 22.

3: Boyhood: Sports, Games, and Rites of Passage

1. Hudson, *Southeastern Indians*, p. 324; Green, *Politics of Indian Removal*, p. 3; Swanton, *Social Organizations*, p. 366.

2. Milfort, *Memoirs*, pp. 91–92.

3. Hudson, *Southeastern Indians*, p. 228.

4. Hawkins, "A Sketch of the Creek Country," Grant, ed., *Hawkins Papers*, 1: 324.

5. Hudson, *Southeastern Indians*, pp. 338–39.

6. Ibid., p. 339.

7. Ibid., p. 340.

8. In Swanton, *Social Organizations*, p. 366.

9. Hudson, *Southeastern Indians*, p. 325.

10. Hawkins, "A Sketch of the Creek Country," Grant, ed., *Hawkins Papers*, 1: 319.

11. Stiggins, Narrative, p. 132.

12. Hudson, *Southeastern Indians*, p. 325; Milfort, *Memoirs*, pp. 99–100.

13. Milfort, *Memoirs*, pp. 99–100.

14. Hawkins, Journal, July 28, 1804, Grant, ed., *Hawkins Papers*, 2: 479.

15. Milfort, *Memoirs*, p. 104n.

16. Corkran, *Creek Frontier*, p. 27.

17. Hudson, *Southeastern Indians*, p. 236.

18. Swanton, *Social Organizations*, p. 459; Adair, *History of the American Indians*, p. 429.

19. Swanton, *Social Organizations*, p. 460.

20. Ibid., p. 461.

21. Ibid., pp. 458, 460.

22. Hudson, *Southeastern Indians*, pp. 411–12.

23. Swanton, *Social Organizations*, pp. 461–62.

24. George Catlin, *North American Indians*, 2 vols. (Edinburgh, 1926), 2: 140; Adam Hodgson, *Remarks during a Journey through North America in the Years 1819, 1820, and 1821* (New York, 1823), p. 271.

25. Hodgson, *Remarks*, p. 423; Adair, *History of the American Indians*, p. 431.

26. Swanton, *Social Organizations*, p. 467.

27. Hudson, *Southeastern Indians*, p. 426.

4: The Revolutionary Period: Dissension and Intrigue

1. Corkran, *Creek Frontier*, p. 301.

2. Ibid., pp. 281, 304–305.

3. Theron A. Nunez, Jr., "Creek Nativism and the Creek War of 1813–1814," *Ethnohistory* 5 (1958): 3.

4. Robert S. Cotterill, *The Southern Indians: The Story of the Civilized Tribes before Removal* (Norman, Okla., 1954), pp. 58, 64.

5. McGillivray to Miro, May 1, 1786, Caughey, *McGillivray of the Creeks*, pp. 106–107; Cotterill, *Southern Indians*, p. 58.

6. McGillivray to Miro, May 1, 1786, p. 107; Treaty commissioners to Congress, November 17, 1785, *American State Papers, Indian Affairs* (Washington, D.C., 1834), 1: 16; hereinafter *ASP, IA*.

7. McGillivray to Miro, May 1, 1786, pp. 108–10; Cotterill, *Southern Indians*, p. 70.

8. Cotterill, *Southern Indians*, p. 71; McMurphy to Governor O'Neill, July 11, 1786, Caughey, *McGillivray of the Creeks*, pp. 119–20.

9. Caughey, *McGillivray of the Creeks*, p. 24 and p. 78, n. 25.

10. McGillivray to O'Neill, December 3, 1786, ibid., p. 141; January 6, 1787, p. 141, n. 78; ibid., July 12, 1787, p. 158; McGillivray to Miro, January 10, 1788, p. 167.

11. O'Neill to Miro, October 28, 1788, ibid., p. 205; December 22, 1788, p. 212.

12. Weatherford to Seagrove, July 10, 1792, *ASP, IA*, 1: 307.

13. Frederick Merk, *History of the Western Movement* (New York, 1978), p. 139.

14. Leslie to Quesada, October 2, 1792, Caughey, *McGillivray of the Creeks*, pp. 339–40.

15. Weatherford to Seagrove, March 9, 22, 1793, *ASP, IA*, 1: 385–86.

16. Cornells to Seagrove, April 8, 1793, ibid., pp. 384–85; Barnard to Seagrove, April 19, 1793, ibid., p. 387.

17. Weatherford to Seagrove, June 11, 1793, ibid., p. 395; Seagrove to Weatherford, July 29, 1793, ibid., p. 405.

18. Seagrove to secretary of war, October 31, 1793, ibid., p. 469.

19. Freeman to governor of Georgia, January 1, 1794, ibid., p. 473.

20. John Francis Hamtramck Claiborne, *Life and Times of Gen. Sam Dale, the Mississippi Partisan* (New York, 1860), pp. 36–43.

21. Green, *Politics of Indian Removal*, p. 36.

22. Grant, "Introduction," *Hawkins Papers*, 1: xvii.

23. Hawkins to James McHenry, January 6, 1797, Grant, ed., *Hawkins Papers*, 1: 62–64; Green, *Politics of Indian Removal*, pp. 36–38.

5: Weatherford and McIntosh Become Famous: Capturing Bowles and Debating with Jefferson

1. "The United States in Account with the Indian Department," *Letters of Benjamin Hawkins, 1796–1806* . . . , *Collections of the Historical Society* (1916; rpt. Spartanburg, S.C., 1974), p. 342; Bonner, "William McIntosh," p. 117; Cotterill, *Southern Indians*, p. 135.

2. Cotterill, *Southern Indians*, pp. 127–28; *Columbian Museum & Savannah Advertiser,* January 21, 1800.

3. Cotterill, *Southern Indians*, p. 128; Hawkins, "A Sketch of the Creek Country," Grant, ed., *Hawkins Papers*, 1: 306; Green, *Politics of Indian Removal*, p. 36.

4. Cotterill, *Southern Indians*, pp. 129–30; William Hill to Hawkins, October 9, 1801, Records of the Bureau of Indian Affairs, Letters Received by the Office of the Secretary of War Relating to Indian Affairs, 1800–1823, National Archives Microfilm M-271, reel 1, 50; hereinafter NA Microfilm M-271.

5. Report of the lower town chiefs to Mad Dog, September 26, 1801, NA Microfilm M-271, reel 1, 46–47.

6. Commissioners' report to Secretary Dearborn, June 17, 1802, Records of the Bureau of Indian Affairs, Documents Relating to the Negotiation of Ratified and Unratified Treaties with Various Tribes of Indians, 1801–69, National Archives Microfilm T-494, reel 1, 3; hereinafter NA Microfilm T-494.

7. Secretary of war to commissioners, May 5, 1803, Records of the Bureau of Indian Affairs, Letters Sent by the Secretary of War Relating to Indian Affairs, 1800–1824, NA Microfilm M-15, reel 1, 151; hereinafter NA Microfilm M-15.

8. J. Leitch Wright, Jr., *William Augustus Bowles: Director General of the Creek Nation* (Athens, Ga., 1967), pp. 162–63.

9. Dearborn to Hawkins, May 5, 1803, NA Microfilm M-15, reel 1, 152; Wright, *Bowles*, pp. 163–64.

10. Cotterill, *Southern Indians*, p. 142; secretary of war to Hawkins, May 24, 1803, NA Microfilm M-15, reel 1, 154.

11. Driesback, "Weatherford," n.p.; Wright, *Bowles*, p. 166.

12. Wright, *Bowles*, pp. 166–67.

13. John Forbes, "A Journal of John Forbes, May, 1803: The Seizure of William Augustus Bowles," transcribed by Mrs. J. W. Greenslade, *Florida Historical Society Quarterly* 9 (1931): 282.

14. Wright, *Bowles*, pp. 167–68, 171; Albert J. Pickett, *History of Alabama* (1851; rpt. Birmingham, 1962), p. 471.

15. Hawkins to James Madison, July 11, 1803, Grant, ed., *Hawkins Papers*, 2: 458; Andrew Ellicott, *The Journal of Andrew Ellicott* (Philadelphia, 1803), p. 232.

16. Hawkins to Governor Milledge, June 8, 1803, Louise Frederick Hays, ed., "Letters of Benjamin Hawkins, 1797–1815," p. 67, typescript; 1939, Georgia Department of Archives and History, Atlanta.

17. Thomas S. Woodward, *Reminiscences of the Creek, or Muscogee Indians, Contained in Letters to Friends in Georgia and Alabama* (1859; rpt. Tuscaloosa, Ala., 1939), p. 89.

18. Dearborn to Hawkins, February 12, 1805, NA Microfilm M-15, reel 2, 27; Hawkins to Dearborn, November 3, 1804, *ASP, IA*, 1: 692; Dearborn to Jouett, April 2, 1805, ibid., p. 703; Jefferson to Senate, December 13, 1804, ibid., pp. 690–91.

19. Dearborn to Hawkins, February 12, 1805, NA Microfilm M-15, reel 2, 27.

20. Dearborn to Hawkins, June 28, 1805, ibid., reel 2, 46.

21. Dearborn to Hawkins, July 15, 1805, ibid., reel 2, 47.

22. Hawkins to Milledge, August 4, 1805, Grant. ed., *Hawkins Papers*, 2: 496; Hawkins to Milledge, October 2, 1805, Hays, ed., "Letters of Hawkins," p. 116; *Augusta Chronicle*, October 12, 1805; Merritt Pound, *Benjamin Hawkins: Indian Agent* (Athens, Ga., 1951), p. 186.

23. Caroline E. MacGill et al., *History of Transportation in the United States before 1860* (New York, 1948), p. 258.

24. John L. Ringwalt, *Development of Transportation Systems in the United States* (Philadelphia, 1888), p. 62.

25. Seymour Dunbar, *A History of Travel in America* (New York, 1937), p. 1119.

26. Dearborn to Hawkins, July 15, 1805, NA Microfilm M-15, reel 2, 47.

27. Charles William Janson, *The Stranger in America: Containing Observations Made during a Long Residence in That Country* (London, 1807), pp. 220–22; Sir Augustus Foster, *Jeffersonian America: Notes on the United States of America, Collected in the Years 1805–6–7 and 11–12*, ed. Richard Beale Davis (San Marino, Calif., 1954), p. 23; Emma Lila Fundaburk, ed., *Southeastern Indians: Life Portraits* (Metuchen, N.J., 1969), p. 143; the painting hangs in Alabama Department of Archives and History, Montgomery.

28. Janson, *Stranger in America*, p. 220; Mrs. Margaret (Bayard) Smith, *The First Forty Years of Washington Society*, ed. Gaillard Hunt (New York, 1906), pp. 402–403.

29. Smith, *First Forty Years*, p. 402; Janson, *Stranger in America*, p. 222.

30. Jefferson to Friend McIntosh, NA Microfilm M-15, reel 2, 74–75.

31. Ibid.

32. Ibid.; Bonner, "William McIntosh," p. 119.

33. Talk of President Jefferson and Creek Indians, November 3, 1805, NA Microfilm M-15, reel 2, 75–76.

34. Ibid.

35. Ibid.

36. Ibid.

37. Ibid.

38. Charles J. Kappler, *Indian Affairs: Laws and Treaties*, 3 vols. (Washington, D.C., 1892–1913), 2: 85–86.

39. Dearborn to Friend McIntosh and other Creek chiefs, November 15, 1805, NA Microfilm M-15, reel 2, 66.

6: Problems from the Outside: The Federal Road and Tecumseh

1. Granger to Hawkins, April 24, 1806, Clarence E. Carter, ed., *Territorial Papers of the United States: Territory South of the River Ohio, and Mississippi Territory*, 22 vols. (Washington, D.C., 1934), 5: 459–60; Granger to President Jefferson, August 4, 1806, ibid., p. 474; Granger to Hawkins, August 15, 1806, ibid., p. 478; Granger to Denison Darling, February 16, 1807, ibid., p. 512.

2. Hawkins to Meriwether, October 1, 1807, Grant, ed., *Hawkins Papers*, 2: 526–27.

3. Tuskegee Tustunnuggee to Hawkins, December 21, 1808, Hays, ed., "Letters of Hawkins," pp. 121–23; Hawkins to Irwin, December 22, 1808, ibid., p. 125; Chiefs of the lower towns to Hawkins, March 14, 1809, Louise Frederick Hays, ed., "Unpublished Letters of Timothy Barnard," pp. 296–97, typescript, 1939, Georgia Department of Archives and History, Atlanta.

4. Hawkins to Eustis, January 6, 1811, Grant, ed., *Hawkins Papers*, 2: 581; McIntosh and Little Prince to Hawkins, June 22, 1811, Hays, ed., "Letters of Hawkins," p. 144.

5. Mitchell to Hawkins, July 11, 1811, Governor's Letterbook, November 28, 1809, to May 18, 1814, Georgia Department of Archives and History, Atlanta.

6. George White, *Historical Collections of Georgia* (New York, 1854), p. 268.

7. Ibid., pp. 268–69.

8. Ibid.; Mauelshagen and Davis, eds., *Partners in the Lord's Work*, pp. 45–46.

9. White, *Historical Collections*, p. 269.

10. Hopoithle Micco to president, May 15, 1811, NA Microfilm M-271, reel 1, 555; secretary of war to Hawkins, June 27, 1811, and July 20, 1811, NA Microfilm M-15, reel 3, 56–57, 59; extract of letter from Hawkins to secretary of war, December 14, 1811, ibid., reel 3, 65.

11. Cotterill, *Southern Indians*, p. 166; Woodward, *Reminiscences*, pp. 94–95; R. David Edmunds, *Tecumseh and the Quest for Indian Leadership* (Boston, 1984), p. 19; Eggleston, *Red Eagle*, p. 51.

12. Woodward, *Reminiscences*, p. 94; extracts of letters to War Department, August 6, September 10, 1811, *ASP, IA,* 1: 800–801; William E. Myer, *Indian Trails of the Southeast,* U.S. Bureau of Ethnology, Annual Report 42 (Washington, D.C., 1924–25), p. 735.

13. H. S. Halbert and T. H. Ball, *The Creek War of 1813 and 1814* (1895; rpt. ed. Frank L. Owsley, Jr., University, Ala., 1969), pp. 42–43.

14. Ibid., pp. 41–45.

15. Ibid., p. 40; see also Edmunds, *Tecumseh,* pp. 150–51.

16. Halbert and Ball, *Creek War,* p. 51.

17. Ibid., pp. 51–55.

18. Cotterill, *Southern Indians,* p. 172; Claiborne, *Sam Dale,* pp. 50–51.

19. Claiborne, *Sam Dale,* p. 52; Woodward, *Reminiscences,* p. 116.

20. Claiborne, *Sam Dale,* pp. 52–53; Eggleston, *Red Eagle,* p. 53.

21. Claiborne, *Sam Dale,* pp. 53–55.

22. Ibid., pp. 55–59.

23. Ibid., p. 59.

24. Ibid.; extracts of letter to War Department, September 9, 1811, *ASP, IA,* 1: 801.

25. Hawkins to Big Warrior, Little Prince, and other chiefs, June 16, 1814, *ASP, IA,* 1: 845.

26. Ibid.; Claiborne, *Sam Dale,* p. 61; Hawkins to chiefs, June 16, 1814, *ASP, IA,* 1: 845.

27. Halbert and Ball, *Creek War,* p. 72.

28. Pickett, *History of Alabama,* pp. 514–15; B. E. Powell, "Was Tecumseh's 'Arm of Fire' the Comet of 1811?" *Georgia Journal of Science* 39 (1981): 87.

29. Cotterill, *Southern Indians,* pp. 172–73; Claiborne, *Sam Dale,* p. 62.

30. Driesback, "Weatherford," n.p.; Woodward, *Reminiscences,* p. 95.

31. Eggleston, *Red Eagle,* pp. 59–60.

32. R. David Edmunds, *The Shawnee Prophet* (Lincoln, Neb., 1983), pp. ix, x, 190.

7: Civil War Erupts: McIntosh the "Law Mender" and Weatherford the Reluctant Nativist

1. Eggleston, *Red Eagle,* pp. 61–62; Hawkins to Armstrong, June 28, 1813, Grant, ed., *Hawkins Papers,* 2: 643.

2. Cornells to Hawkins, June 22, 1813, *ASP, IA,* 1: 845–46; Hawkins to Armstrong, July 6, 1813, Grant, ed., *Hawkins Papers,* 2: 644.

3. Hawkins to Eustis, April 6, 1812, Grant, ed., *Hawkins Papers,* 2: 605; Hawkins to Mitchell, September 7, 1812, ibid., p. 617.

4. Hawkins to Eustis, May 25, June 9, 1812, ibid., pp. 609–10; Woodward, *Reminiscences,* p. 37.

5. William Henry to John J. Henry, June 26, 1812, *ASP, IA,* 1: 814; Hawkins to Eustis, May 25, 1812, Grant, ed., *Hawkins Papers,* 2: 609.

6. Governor Blount to Eustis, *ASP, IA,* 1: 813.

7. W. Henry to J. Henry, June 26, 1813, ibid., p. 814.

8. Woodward, *Reminiscences,* pp. 35–36.

9. *Augusta Herald,* July 9, 1812.

10. Hawkins to Eustis, July 13, 1812, Grant, ed., *Hawkins Papers,* 2: 612.

11. Ibid., pp. 612–13; Hawkins to Mitchell, August 31, 1812, ibid., p. 616; Woodward, *Reminiscences,* p. 37; Stiggins, Narrative, 152–53.

12. Hawkins to Eustis, August 24, 1812, Grant, ed., *Hawkins Papers,* 2: 615–16; Hawkins to secretary of war, September 7, 1812, *ASP, IA,* 1: 812–13; Edmund Bacon to Mrs. A. Pannill, July 19, 1812, Edmund Bacon Letters, Department of Archives and Manuscripts, Louisiana State University, Baton Rouge; *Augusta Herald,* August 27, 1812.

13. Hawkins to Upper Creek chiefs, March 25, 1813, Grant, ed., *Hawkins Papers,* 2: 631–32.

14. Woodward, *Reminiscences,* p. 36.

15. Hawkins to Alexander Cornells, March 25, 1813, Grant, ed., *Hawkins Papers,* 2: 631; Hawkins to Governor Mitchell, April 26, 1813, ibid., pp. 633–34.

16. Report of Nimrod Doyell to Hawkins, May 3, 1813, *ASP, IA,* 1: 843.

17. Three chiefs to Hawkins, April 20, 1813, ibid., p. 841 (misdated April 26); Hawkins to three chiefs, April 24, 1813, ibid., p. 842.

18. Green, *Politics of Indian Removal,* pp. 9, 54; Hawkins to Jackson (enclosure), August 30, 1814, Grant, ed., *Hawkins Papers,* 2: 694.

19. Alexander Cornells to Hawkins, June 22, 1813, *ASP, IA,* 1: 846.

20. Hawkins to Armstrong, June 22, 28, 1813, ibid., p. 847; Hawkins to Floyd, November 19, 1813, Grant, ed., *Hawkins Papers,* 2: 675.

21. Woodward, *Reminiscences,* pp. 95–97.

22. Stiggins, Narrative, pp. 159–60.

23. Claiborne, *Sam Dale,* p. 67.

24. Halbert and Ball, *Creek War,* p. 91; see also Hawkins to Armstrong, June 28, 1813, *ASP, IA,* 1: 847, in which the name Sam Moniac is transcribed incorrectly as "some maniac"; also Hawkins to secretary of war, July 28, 1813, ibid., p. 850.

25. Halbert and Ball, *Creek War,* pp. 92–93.

26. Woodward, *Reminiscences,* p. 37.

27. Jackson to Governor Blount, July 13, 1813, *ASP, IA,* 1: 850.

28. Cusseta king to Hawkins, July 10, 1813, ibid., p. 849.

29. Talassee Fixico to Hawkins, July 5, 1813, ibid., p. 847.

30. Hawkins to Armstrong, July 26, 1813, ibid., p. 849; Big Warrior to Hawkins, July 26, 1813, Hays, ed., "Letters of Hawkins," pp. 223–24.

31. Hawkins to secretary of war, July 28, 1813, *ASP, IA,* 1: 849–50.

32. Woodward, *Reminiscences,* pp. 97–98; Big Warrior to Hawkins, August 4, 1813, *ASP, IA,* 1: 851.

33. Halbert and Ball, *Creek War,* p. 126; Cotterill, *Southern Indians,* p. 180.

34. Mrs. Dunbar Rowland, *Andrew Jackson's Campaign against the British, or the Mississippi Territory in the War of 1812* (New York, 1926), pp. 112–16. Rowland cites a manuscript signed by Halbert, which is among the Claiborne Papers in the Mississippi State Historical Department, Jackson.

8: The Conflagration Spreads: The Battle of Burnt Corn and the Massacre at Fort Mims

1. Halbert and Ball, *Creek War,* p. 129.
2. Claiborne, *Sam Dale,* p. 72; Caller wrote that they were to set out on a Thursday, which would have been July 22.
3. Halbert and Ball, *Creek War,* pp. 129–31.
4. Ibid., pp. 132–35.
5. Ibid., p. 136; Claiborne, *Sam Dale,* p. 74.
6. Pickett, *History of Alabama,* pp. 524–25; Halbert and Ball, *Creek War,* p. 141.
7. A. J. Pickett Papers, Department of Archives and History, Montgomery, Ala., reprinted in Lucille Griffith, *Alabama: A Documentary History to 1900,* rev. ed. (University, Ala., 1972), p. 107; Eggleston, *Red Eagle,* p. 76; Woodward, *Reminiscences,* p. 98.
8. Hawkins's demand on the fanatical chiefs, July 6, 1813, *ASP, IA,* 1: 848; letter from Weatherford descendant to author, July 7, 1980; Frank L. Owsley, Jr., *Struggle for the Gulf Borderlands: The Creek War and the Battle of New Orleans, 1812–1815* (Gainesville, Fla., 1981), p. 39.
9. Hays, ed., "Letters of Hawkins," p. 241; Stiggins, Narrative, pp. 156–59.
10. Blount to Flournoy, October 15, 1813, *ASP, IA,* 1: 855.
11. Henry Wigginton to Hawkins, August 2, 1813, Hays, ed., "Letters of Hawkins," p. 231.
12. Big Warrior to Robert Walton, August 2, 1813, ibid., p. 229; Big Warrior to Hawkins, August 4, 1813 (two letters), *ASP, IA,* 1: 851; Hawkins to Armstrong, August 23, 1813, Grant, ed., *Hawkins Papers,* 2: 659.
13. Hawkins to Mitchell, August 28, 1813, Grant, ed., *Hawkins Papers,* 2: 659; Hawkins to secretary of war, August 23, 1813, *ASP, IA,* 1: 852; Cotterill, *Southern Indians,* p. 182n.; see McKenney and Hall, *Indian Tribes of North America,* 2: 390.
14. Halbert and Ball, *Creek War,* pp. 120–21.
15. Stiggins, Narrative, pp. 161–62.
16. Ibid.
17. Ibid., pp. 163–64.
18. Ibid., p. 164.
19. Driesback, "Weatherford," n.p.; Eggleston, *Red Eagle,* p. 81.
20. Pickett, *History of Alabama,* pp. 528–29.

21. Halbert and Ball, *Creek War,* p. 148, wrote that 553 people were in the fort; F. L. Claiborne to the editors, *Mississippi Republican,* March 25, 1813, gives the lower number of 275 to 300.

22. Halbert and Ball, *Creek War,* pp. 148–50.

23. Eggleston, *Red Eagle,* pp. 97–98; Pickett, *History of Alabama,* p. 531.

24. Halbert and Ball, *Creek War,* pp. 150–53.

25. Pickett, *History of Alabama,* p. 532, gave the number of warriors as one thousand.

26. Woodward, *Reminiscences,* p. 98; Pickett, *History of Alabama,* p. 532.

27. Pickett, *History of Alabama,* p. 533; Stiggins, Narrative, p. 164.

28. Interview with Dr. Thomas G. Holmes, survivor of Fort Mims, June 3, 1847, in Griffith, *Alabama,* p. 107; Stiggins, Narrative, p. 165.

29. Pickett, *History of Alabama,* p. 534.

30. Halbert and Ball, *Creek War,* pp. 174–75.

31. Holmes interview, Griffith, *Alabama,* p. 109; Stiggins, Narrative, pp. 166–67; letter from Charles Weatherford to T. H. Ball, October 17, 1890, Halbert and Ball, *Creek War,* pp. 173–74; Pickett, *History of Alabama,* p. 537.

32. Pickett, *History of Alabama,* pp. 535–36.

33. Ibid., pp. 537–38.

34. Ibid., pp. 539–50.

35. Ibid., pp. 541–42. Woodward said in his *Reminiscences,* p. 99, that McGirth's family was saved by High-Headed Jim (also called Jim Boy), but Pickett's account seems more reliable because it came from an interview with Zachariah McGirth in 1834. It is also unlikely that the volatile prophet Jim would have acted in such a benign fashion.

36. Hawkins to secretary of war, October 11, 1813, *ASP, IA,* 1: 852–53; Stiggins, Narrative, p. 166.

37. Frank L. Owsley, Jr., "Prophet of War: Josiah Francis and the Creek War," *American Indian Quarterly* 11 (1985): 281.

38. Pickett, *History of Alabama,* p. 539.

39. Woodward, *Reminiscences,* p. 100.

40. Pickett, *History of Alabama,* p. 542; in June 1968, excavations at the Fort Mims site indicated that some of the bodies were thrown into the main well (*Baldwin* [Alabama] *Times,* June 25, 1968).

41. Owsley, *Struggle for the Gulf Borderlands,* pp. 38–39.

42. John Reid and John Henry Eaton, *The Life of Andrew Jackson* (1817; rpt. ed. Frank L. Owsley, Jr., University, Ala., 1974), p. 33.

9: General Jackson Enters the Fray: Retaliation and Countermeasures from Tallushatchee to the Holy Ground

1. Quoted in Michael Paul Rogin, *Fathers and Children: Andrew Jackson and the Subjugation of the American Indian* (New York, 1975), p. 147.

2. Cotterill, *Southern Indians,* p. 181.

3. Rogin, *Fathers and Children,* pp. 147–48.

4. John Brannan, ed., *Official Letters of the Military and Naval Officers of the United States during the War with Great Britain in the Years 1812, '13, '14, and '15* (Washington, D.C., 1823), p. 215.

5. Reid and Eaton, *Life of Jackson,* p. 33.

6. Halbert and Ball, *Creek War,* pp. 121, 212–13; Cotterill, *Southern Indians,* pp. 182n., 183; McKenney and Hall, *Indian Tribes of North America,* 2: 96–97.

7. Pickett, *History of Alabama,* p. 548.

8. John K. Mahon, *The War of 1812* (Gainesville, Fla., 1972), p. 232.

9. This letter, which was among the manuscript papers of General Ferdinand L. Claiborne, is paraphrased in Pickett, *History of Alabama,* p. 548n.

10. Frank L. Owsley, Jr., "British and Indian Activities in Spanish West Florida during the War of 1812," *Florida Historical Quarterly* 46 (1967): 114–15.

11. Jackson to Blount, October 13, 1813, John Spencer Bassett, ed., *Correspondence of Andrew Jackson,* 7 vols. (Washington, D.C., 1926–35), 1: 332; Reid and Eaton, *Life of Jackson,* p. 37, say the troops marched thirty-two miles from 9:00 A.M. until about 8:00 P.M.

12. Marquis James, *The Life of Andrew Jackson* (New York, 1938), p. 158.

13. Jackson to Pope and others, October 23, 1813, Bassett, ed., *Correspondence of Jackson,* 1: 335; to W. B. Lewis, October 24, 1813, ibid., p. 336.

14. Robert V. Remini, *Andrew Jackson and the Course of American Empire, 1767–1821* (New York, 1977), p. 192.

15. Reid and Eaton, *Life of Jackson,* p. 45.

16. Friendly chiefs to General John Floyd, November 18, 1813, Floyd Papers, Georgia Department of Archives and History.

17. Hawkins to Floyd, October 12, 1813, Grant, ed., *Hawkins Papers,* 2: 672.

18. Reid and Eaton, *Life of Jackson,* pp. 49–50.

19. David Crockett, *The Life of David Crockett,* facsimile ed. (Knoxville, 1973), pp. 88–90.

20. Reid and Eaton, *Life of Jackson,* p. 50; Jackson to Blount, November 4, 1813, Bassett, ed., *Correspondence of Jackson,* 1: 341; James Parton, *Life of Andrew Jackson,* 3 vols. (Boston, 1887–88), 1: 439.

21. Coffee to his wife, November 4, 1813, John DeWitt, ed., "Letters of General John Coffee to His Wife, 1813–1815," *Tennessee Historical Magazine* 2 (1916): 277.

22. Augustus C. Buell, *A History of Andrew Jackson,* 2 vols. (New York, 1904), 2: 305.

23. Halbert and Ball, *Creek War,* p. 269; Eggleston, *Red Eagle,* p. 161.

24. Call's Journal, quoted in Herbert J. Doherty, Jr., *Richard Keith Call: Southern Unionist* (Gainesville, Fla., 1961), p. 6; Eggleston, *Red Eagle,* p. 163.

25. Remini, *Jackson and the Course of American Empire,* p. 194. James, *Andrew Jackson,* pp. 159–61, also places Weatherford at Talladega.

286 Notes to Pages 120–125

26. Rowland, *Andrew Jackson's Campaign*, p. 160; Remini, *Jackson and the Course of American Empire*, p. 196.

27. Crockett, *Life of David Crockett*, p. 90; James, *Andrew Jackson*, p. 160.

28. Jackson to Governor Blount, November 11, 1813, Brannan, ed., *Official Letters*, p. 265; see also Reid and Eaton, *Life of Jackson*, p. 55.

29. Crockett, *Life of David Crockett*, pp. 92–93.

30. Remini, *Jackson and the Course of American Empire*, p. 197; Reid and Eaton, *Life of Jackson*, pp. 56–57; Mahon, *War of 1812*, p. 237.

31. Rowland, *Andrew Jackson's Campaign*, p. 161.

32. Jackson to Blount, November 12, 1813, Brannan, ed., *Official Letters*, p. 265; the figure of seventeen is confirmed by Crockett, *Life of David Crockett*, p. 93.

33. Reid and Eaton, *Life of Jackson*, p. 57; Rogin, *Fathers and Children*, p. 151; Coffee to his wife, November 12, 1813, Dewitt, ed., "Letters of Coffee," p. 278.

34. Richard H. Faust, "Another Look at General Jackson and the Indians of the Mississippi Territory," *Alabama Review* 28 (1975): 210.

35. Pickett, *History of Alabama*, p. 548n.; Coffee to his wife, October 25, 1813, DeWitt, ed., "Letters of Coffee," 276; Remini, *Jackson and the Course of American Empire*, pp. 191 and 450, n. 18.

36. Reid and Eaton, *Life of Jackson*, p. 60; James, *Andrew Jackson*, p. 162.

37. Reid and Eaton, *Life of Jackson*, pp. 71–72n.; Halbert and Ball, *Creek War*, pp. 271–72; Rowland, *Andrew Jackson's Campaign*, pp. 163–64; Pickett, *History of Alabama*, pp. 556–57.

38. Letters from friendly chiefs to General Floyd, November 18, 1813; Floyd to Governor Early, November 16, 1813, both in Floyd Papers, Georgia Archives; John Floyd to Mary Floyd, November 18, 1813, "Letters of John Floyd, 1813–1838," *Georgia Historical Quarterly* 33 (1949): 234; Peter A. Brannon, ed., "Journal of James A. Tait for the Year 1813," *Georgia Historical Quarterly* 8 (1924): 231–32.

39. Brannon, ed., "Journal of Tait," p. 231.

40. Hawkins to secretary of war, October 25, 1813, *ASP, IA*, 1: 847; Pickett, *History of Alabama*, pp. 557–59, 469–70.

41. John Floyd to Mary Floyd, December 5, 1813, "Letters of Floyd," p. 235.

42. Ibid.

43. Pickett, *History of Alabama*, p. 558; Brannon, ed., "Journal of Tait," pp. 234–35.

44. Floyd to Mary Floyd, December 5, 1813, p. 236.

45. Ibid.; Tait wrote, "Never before did the limpid waters receive the tinge of human blood" (Brannon, ed., "Journal of Tait," p. 234).

46. Brannon, ed., "Journal of Tait," p. 234; Coffee to his wife, December 27, 1813, DeWitt, ed., "Letters of Coffee," p. 279; Pickett, *History of Alabama*, p. 559.

47. Floyd to Mary Floyd, December 5, 1813, p. 236; Brannon, ed., "Journal of Tait," pp. 234–35; Pickett, *History of Alabama*, p. 559.

48. Floyd to Mary Floyd, December 5, 1813, p. 236.

49. Pickett, *History of Alabama*, p. 559.

50. Rowland, *Andrew Jackson's Campaign*, p. 169; Halbert and Ball, *Creek War*, pp. 246–48.

51. Halbert and Ball, *Creek War*, p. 241.

52. John Francis Hamtramck Claiborne, *Mississippi as a Province, Territory and State with Biographical Notices of Eminent Citizens* (1880; rpt. Baton Rouge, 1964), p. 338.

53. Pickett, *History of Alabama*, p. 572; Cotterill, *Southern Indians*, p. 185; Claiborne, *Sam Dale*, p. 133; Claiborne, *Mississippi*, p. 328.

54. Pickett, *History of Alabama*, p. 572; Claiborne, *Sam Dale*, pp. 135–36, 140; Claiborne, *Mississippi*, pp. 338, 328–29.

55. Claiborne, *Sam Dale*, p. 140; Halbert and Ball, *Creek War*, pp. 246–69.

56. Stiggins, Narrative, pp. 169–72.

57. Halbert and Ball, *Creek War*, pp. 251–53.

58. Driesback, "Weatherford," n.p. Driesback, a relative of Weatherford's, talked to many members of the family and to William Hollinger, who said he got this account firsthand from Weatherford. Hollinger told Driesback that "these are facts, for Weatherford related them to me, and he never lied."

59. Woodward, *Reminiscences*, pp. 100–101; Halbert and Ball, *Creek War*, pp. 255–56; Claiborne, *Sam Dale*, pp. 140–41; Stiggins, Narrative, pp. 171–72; Pickett, *History of Alabama*, p. 576n. Paul Ghioto, former ranger-historian at Horseshoe Bend National Military Park, says such a bluff no longer exists.

60. Halbert and Ball, *Creek War*, pp. 256–58.

61. Claiborne, *Sam Dale*, p. 141; Claiborne, *Mississippi*, p. 340.

62. Claiborne, *Mississippi*, p. 340; Claiborne, *Sam Dale*, pp. 141–42.

63. Halbert and Ball, *Creek War*, pp. 262–63.

10: The Demise of the Red Sticks: Horseshoe Bend and Weatherford's Surrender

1. Brannon, ed., "Journal of Tait," pp. 235–36; Pickett, *History of Alabama*, p. 584.

2. Stiggins, Narrative, pp. 295–96.

3. Ibid., pp. 296–97.

4. Woodward, *Reminiscences*, pp. 101–102.

5. Rowland, *Andrew Jackson's Campaign*, p. 117; Pickett, *History of Alabama*, pp. 584–85.

6. Brannon, "Journal of Tait," p. 237, estimates fifty Indians lost; but Pickett, *History of Alabama*, p. 585, says "the loss of the enemy must have been considerable"; Stiggins, Narrative, p. 297.

7. Brannon, "Journal of Tait," p. 237, and Pickett, *History of Alabama*, p. 585, give the same statistics.

8. Brannon, "Journal of Tait," pp. 237–38.

9. Stiggins, Narrative, p. 298; Ross Hassig, "Internal Conflict in the Creek War of 1813–1814," *Ethnohistory* 21 (1974): 263; Hawkins to Armstrong, July 13, 1813, Grant, ed., *Hawkins Papers*, 2: 646.

10. Stiggins, Narrative, pp. 297–99.

11. General John Floyd's will, "Letters of Floyd," p. 267.

12. Reid and Eaton, *Life of Jackson*, p. 126.

13. Marion Elisha Tarvin, "The Muscogees or Creek Indians from 1517 to 1893," *Baldwin County Historical Society Quarterly* 8 (1980): 19. Tarvin wrote this account in 1893 and interviewed members of Weatherford's family and old soldiers, who placed Red Eagle at the Battle of Emuckfau. See also John Sugden, "The Southern Indians in the War of 1812: The Closing Phase," *Florida Historical Quarterly* 60 (1982): 279.

14. Reid and Eaton, *Life of Jackson*, pp. 126–27.

15. Ibid., pp. 127–28.

16. DeWitt, ed., "Letters of Coffee, to His Wife," pp. 280–81; see also Jackson's letter to Rachel, February 21, 1814, Jackson Papers, Missouri Historical Society, St. Louis: "It was the fate of our brave nephew Alexander Donelson to fall, but he fell like a hero."

17. Reid and Eaton, *Life of Jackson*, pp. 128–29.

18. Pickett, *History of Alabama*, p. 581.

19. Reid and Eaton, *Life of Jackson*, pp. 129–30.

20. Ibid., pp. 131–32.

21. Ibid., pp. 133–34.

22. Pickett, *History of Alabama*, p. 582; Reid and Eaton, *Life of Jackson*, p. 133–34.

23. Reid and Eaton, *Life of Jackson*, pp. 135–36.

24. Ibid., pp. 136–37.

25. Remini, *Jackson and the Course of American Empire*, pp. 209–10; Pickett, *History of Alabama*, p. 583; Parton, *Life of Jackson*, 1: 499–500.

26. Pickett, *History of Alabama*, p. 586; Reid and Eaton, *Life of Jackson*, pp. 139, 141.

27. Rowland, *Andrew Jackson's Campaign*, p. 197.

28. Jackson to Pinckney, March 22, 1814, Bassett, ed., *Correspondence of Jackson*, 1: 484.

29. General Orders, March 24, 1814, ibid., pp. 486–88.

30. Jackson to Blount, March 31, 1814, ibid., p. 490.

31. Coffee to Jackson, April 11, 1814, John Coffee Papers, Dyas Collection, Tennessee State Library and Archives, Nashville.

32. Jackson to Mrs. Jackson, April 1, 1814, Bassett, ed., *Correspondence of Jackson*, 1: 493.

33. Reid and Eaton, *Life of Jackson*, p. 153.

34. Jackson to Pinckney, March 28, 1815. In the complete letter, printed in the *National Daily Intelligencer* (Washingon, D.C.), April 18, 1814, Jackson wrote: "Major McIntosh, who joined the army with part of his tribe, greatly distinguished himself. When I get an hour's leisure I will send you a more detailed account." Although not specified, it is probably this action to which Jackson refers, for no other feat by the friendly Indians was as important.

35. Morgan to Blount, April 1, 1814, *Clarion and Tennessee State Gazette* (Nashville), April 12, 1814.

36. Jackson to Pinckney, March 28, 1814, Bassett, ed., *Correspondence of Jackson*, 1: 489; Jackson to Blount, March 31, 1814, ibid., p. 491.

37. Reid and Eaton, *Life of Jackson*, p. 150.

38. Ibid., pp. 150–53.

39. Jackson to Blount, March 31, 1814, p. 491.

40. Donald Day and Harry Herbert Ullom, eds., *The Autobiography of Sam Houston* (Norman, Okla., 1954), p. 12; Houston to President Monroe, March 1, 1815, Amelia W. Williams and Eugene C. Barkers, eds., *The Writings of Sam Houston, 1813–1863*, 8 vols. (Austin, Texas, 1938–43), 1: 3.

41. McKenney and Hall, *Indian Tribes of North America*, 2: 178–94.

42. Halbert and Ball, *Creek War,* p. 277. The authority for the statement was "an aged man, Mr. Evans, of Neshoba County, Mississippi."

43. Jackson to Blount, March 31, 1814, p. 491; joint statement by three of Coffee's officers, Hammond, Bean, and Russell, in Jackson Papers, Library of Congress, Washington, D.C.

44. Jackson to Blount, March 31, 1814, pp. 491–92.

45. Jackson to Col. Perkins, April 1, 1814, in *Nashville Whig,* April 27, 1814; Owsley, *Struggle for the Gulf Borderlands*, pp. 81–82.

46. Reid and Eaton, *Life of Jackson,* p. 155; Jackson to Rachel, April 14, 1814, Jackson Papers, Library of Congress; Remini, *Jackson and the Course of American Empire*, p. 216.

47. Reid and Eaton, *Life of Jackson*, pp. 157–58.

48. Marie Bankhead Owen, ed., "Indian Tribes and Towns in Alabama," *Alabama Historical Quarterly* 32 (1950): 170.

49. Jackson to Pinckney, April 14, 1812, Bassett, ed., *Correspondence of Jackson*, 1: 500.

50. Pinckney to Jackson, April 7, 1814, ibid., pp. 496–97.

51. Reid and Eaton, *Life of Jackson*, p. 165.

52. Pickett, *History of Alabama*, pp. 593–94; James, *Andrew Jackson*, p. 172; Reid and Eaton, *Life of Jackson*, p. 165.

53. Undated fragment in Reid's handwriting (John Reid Papers, Tennessee State Library and Archives), reprinted in James, *Andrew Jackson*, p. 172.

54. Reid and Eaton, *Life of Jackson*, p. 165.

55. Pickett, *History of Alabama*, p. 594.

56. Reid and Eaton, *Life of Jackson*, p. 166.

57. Ibid., pp. 166–67.

58. Pickett, *History of Alabama*, pp. 594–95.

59. Eggleston, *Red Eagle*, p. 340.

60. Reid and Eaton, *Life of Jackson*, p. 167; Pickett, *History of Alabama*, p. 595.

61. Henry Sale Halbert, "Creek War Incidents," *Alabama Historical Society Transactions* 2 (1897–98): 101–102.

62. Pickett, *History of Alabama*, p. 595.

63. Eggleston, *Red Eagle*, p. 342.

64. Woodward, *Reminiscences*, pp. 43, 102; Driesback, "Weatherford," n.p.

11: The Treaty of Fort Jackson and the Rising Career of William McIntosh

1. Reid and Eaton, *Life of Jackson*, pp. 173–74.

2. Parton, *Life of Jackson*, 1: 542.

3. Armstrong to Jackson, May 22, 1814, Jackson Papers, Library of Congress, Washington, D.C.

4. Remini, *Jackson and the Course of American Empire*, p. 222.

5. Armstrong to Jackson, May 24, 1814, *American State Papers, Military Affairs* (Washington, D.C., 1834), 3: 785; hereinafter *ASP, MA*.

6. Pinckney to Hawkins, April 23, 1814, *ASP, IA*, 1: 857–58.

7. Jackson to Pinckney, May 18, 1814, Bassett, ed., *Correspondence of Jackson*, 2: 3.

8. Hawkins report, June 14, 1814, Cuyler Collection, quoted in Pound, *Benjamin Hawkins*, p. 236.

9. Jackson to Hawkins, July 11, 1814, Bassett, ed., *Correspondence of Jackson*, 2: 15; Jackson to Coffee, July 17, 1814, ibid., p. 16.

10. Reid and Eaton, *Life of Jackson*, pp. 186–87.

11. Remini, *Jackson and the Course of American Empire*, p. 226.

12. Treaty with the Creeks, 1814, in Kappler, *Indian Affairs*, 2: 108.

13. See Remini, *Jackson and the Course of American Empire*, p. 227.

14. Reid and Eaton, *Life of Jackson*, p. 187.

15. Kappler, *Indian Affairs*, 2: 25.

16. Reid and Eaton, *Life of Jackson*, pp. 187–89.

17. Ibid., pp. 189–90.

18. Ibid., pp. 190–91.

19. Pinckney to Hawkins, April 23, 1814, *ASP, IA*, 1: 858; Jackson to Blount, August 9, 1814, Bassett, ed., *Correspondence of Jackson*, 2: 24.

20. Pound, *Benjamin Hawkins*, p. 237; Reid and Eaton, *Life of Jackson*, pp. 184–85.

21. Pickett, *History of Alabama*, pp. 599–600.

22. Parton, *Life of Jackson*, 1: 557.

23. Untitled paper, August 8, 1814, *ASP, IA*, 1: 837.

24. Kappler, *Indian Affairs*, 2: 109.

25. Remini, *Jackson and the Course of American Empire*, p. 231.

26. Jackson to Armstrong, August 10, 1814, Bassett, ed., *Correspondence of Jackson*, 2: 25–26.

27. Ibid.

28. Jackson to Manrique, August 24, 1814, ibid., pp. 28–29.

29. Claiborne to Jackson, August 27, 1814, ibid., p. 36; Reid and Eaton, *Life of Jackson*, p. 195; Bassett, ed., *Correspondence of Jackson*, 2: 36, n. 1.

30. Hawkins to Tustunnuggee Hopoie and Tustunnuggee Thlucco, enclosure to Jackson, August 30, 1814, Grant, ed., *Hawkins Papers*, 2: 694; ibid., p. 695, n. 1; Hawkins to Monroe, October 5, 1814, ibid., p. 696; Jackson to Hawkins, October 19, 1814, *ASP, IA*, 1: 861.

31. Hawkins to Monroe, October 12, 1814, Grant, ed., *Hawkins Papers*, 2: 696; Jackson to Monroe, October 31, 1814, Bassett, ed., *Correspondence of Jackson*, 2: 85.

32. Hawkins to Monroe, October 5, 1814, p. 696.

33. Hawkins to Graham, August 1, 1815, *ASP, IA*, 2: 493; see treaty in Kappler, *Indian Affairs*, 2: 109.

34. Cotterill, *Southern Indians*, p. 193.

35. Bassett, *Correspondence of Jackson*, 2: 210, n. 2; Cotterill, *Southern Indians*, p. 194.

36. Bassett, *Correspondence of Jackson*, 2: 211, n. 3.

37. Jackson to Hawkins, August 14, 1815, ibid., p. 214.

38. Ibid.; Pound, *Benjamin Hawkins*, p. 239.

39. Cotterill, *Southern Indians*, p. 195.

40. Gordon T. Chappell, "John Coffee: Surveyor and Land Agent," *Alabama Review* 14 (1961): 189–90; Crawford to Jackson, March 8, 1816, Bassett, *Correspondence of Jackson*, 2: 235.

41. A Memorial by a Committee of Five Citizens of Davidson County, no date, *ASP, IA*, 2: 91; secretary of war to commissioners, April 16, 1816, ibid., p. 109.

42. Jackson to Crawford, June 10, 1816, ibid., pp. 110–11; Crawford to Jackson, July 1, 1816, ibid., p. 113.

43. Oliver H. Prince, *A Digest of the Laws of the State of Georgia* (Milledgeville, 1822), pp. 529–30.

44. Cotterill, *Southern Indians*, pp. 231–32; Daniel L. Littlefield, Jr., *Africans and Seminoles: From Removal to Emancipation* (Westport, Conn., 1977), p. 3.

45. Correspondence between Hawkins and Nicholls, March 19–April 28, 1815, *Niles' Weekly Register*, June 10, 1815.

46. Report from Nicholls to Admiral Cochrane, cited in Mahon, *War of 1812*, p. 347–48.

47. Owsley, "Prophet of War," pp. 283–85.

48. Jackson's talk to the Creeks, September 4, 1815, Bassett, ed., *Correspondence of Jackson*, 2: 216.

49. Owsley, *Struggle for the Gulf Borderlands*, p. 183.

50. Address to the king of England from the Indians, March 10, 1815, *American State Papers, Foreign Relations,* 6 vols. (Washington, D.C., 1824), 4: 552–53; hereinafter *ASP, FR.*

51. Ibid.

52. Hawkins to Nicholls, May 28, 1815, *ASP, FR,* 4: 550.

53. Owsley, *Struggle for the Gulf Borderlands,* pp. 180–82; see also Owsley, "Prophet of War," pp. 286–87.

12: "The Gallant Major McIntosh" Becomes a General in the Seminole War

1. Jackson to governor of Pensacola, April 23, 1816, *ASP, FR,* 4: 499; Report of Captain Amelung to General Jackson, June 4, 1816, and Jackson to Crawford, June 15, 1816, ibid., p. 557; Kenneth W. Porter, *The Negro on the American Frontier* (New York, 1971), p. 217.

2. Gaines to Crawford, April 30, 1816, with enclosures from Little Prince, *ASP, FR,* 4: 557–58.

3. Gaines to Clinch, May 23, 1816, ibid., p. 558; A Soldier, "Gen. Clinch and the Indians," *Army and Navy Chronicle,* 13 vols. in 12 (Washington, D.C., 1835–42), 2: 114.

4. J. Loomis to Patterson, August 13, 1816, *ASP, FR,* 4: 560; Porter, *Negro on the American Frontier,* p. 217.

5. Gaines to Commodore Patterson, May 22, 1816, *ASP, FR,* 4: 558–59; Gaines to Clinch, May 23, 1816, ibid., p. 558.

6. Report of Jairus Loomis to Commodore Patterson, August 13, 1816, ibid., pp. 559–60.

7. "Gen. Clinch and the Indians," *Army and Navy Chronicle,* 2: 114–15; Porter, *Negro on the American Frontier,* p. 219.

8. "Gen. Clinch and the Indians," *Army and Navy Chronicle,* 2: 115.

9. Report of Jairus Loomis to Commodore Patterson, *ASP, FR,* 4: 559–60; report of Patterson to Secretary of Navy Crowninshield, ibid., p. 561; Porter, *Negro on the American Frontier,* p. 219.

10. Frank L. Owsley, Jr., "Ambrister and Arbuthnot: Adventurers or Martyrs for British Honor?" *Journal of the Early Republic* 5 (1985): 292–93.

11. "Gen. Clinch and the Indians," *Army and Navy Chronicle,* 2: 116.

12. Ibid., pp. 115–16.

13. Ibid.

14. Ibid., p. 114; Woodward, *Reminiscences,* pp. 114, 116.

15. Edwin C. McReynolds, *The Seminoles* (Norman, Okla., 1957), p. 78; Parton, *Life of Jackson,* 2: 399, 407.

16. Perryman to Lieutenant Sands, February 24, 1817, *ASP, IA,* 2: 155.

17. Remini, *Jackson and the Course of American Empire,* pp. 332–33; Jackson to Butler, June 21, 1817, Bassett, ed., *Correspondence of Jackson,* 2: 299.

18. Creek deputation to President Madison, January 15, 1817, NA Microfilm M-271, reel 2, 48–49.

19. Claims of the friendly Indians for losses sustained by them in their civil war, April 1, 1816, ibid., reel 1, 1122.

20. Creek deputation to Graham, March 8, 1817, ibid., reel 2, 52–56.

21. Kappler, *Indian Affairs*, 2: 86; Creek deputation to Graham, March 8, 1817, NA Microfilm M-271, reel 2, 56.

22. Creek deputation to Graham, March 10, 1817, ibid., reel 2, 57–60; Creek deputation to Graham, March 15, 1817, ibid., reel 2, 61.

23. Graham to Jackson, May 16, 1817, *ASP, IA*, 2: 141–42.

24. Commissioners to Graham, July 8, 1817, Bassett, ed., *Correspondence of Jackson*, 2: 300–301.

25. Chiefs and headmen to commissioners, July 2, 1817, *ASP, IA*, 2: 143.

26. Instructions to a deputation of our warriors, September 19, 1817, ibid., p. 145.

27. Treaty with the Cherokees, July 8, 1817, ibid., p. 130.

28. Jackson to Coffee, July 13, 1817, Bassett, ed., *Correspondence of Jackson*, 2: 307.

29. Charles H. Coe, *Red Patriots: The Story of the Seminoles* (Cincinnati, 1898), pp. 14–15.

30. John K. Mahon, *History of the Second Seminole War, 1835–1842* (Gainesville, Fla., 1967), p. 20.

31. Gaines to secretary of war, October 1, 1817, *ASP, MA*, 1: 685.

32. Gaines to Jackson, November 21, 1817, *ASP, IA*, 2: 160; A. Culloh to Gaines, April 3, 1817, *ASP, MA*, 1: 683.

33. Mitchell to Graham, December 14, 1817, *ASP, MA*, 1: 688; Gaines to Jackson, November 21, 1817, p. 160.

34. Remini, *Jackson and the Course of American Empire*, p. 346; McReynolds, *Seminoles*, p. 81; James W. Silver, *Edmund Pendleton Gaines, Frontier General* (Baton Rouge, 1949), p. 72; Woodward, *Reminiscences*, p. 53.

35. Silver, *Gaines*, p. 73; Gaines to Calhoun, December 15, 1817, *ASP, MA*, 1: 689.

36. Mitchell to Bibb, December 15, 1817, Carter, ed., *Territorial Papers*, 18: 215–16; Irvin to Arbuckle, December 23, 1817, *ASP, MA*, 1: 692; Mitchell to secretary of war, February 3, 1818, Carter, ed., *Territorial Papers*, 18: 244; Mitchell to Graham, December 14, 1817, *ASP, MA*, 1: 688.

37. Calhoun to Gaines, December 16, 1817, *ASP, MA*, 1: 689; Calhoun to Jackson, December 26, 1817, ibid., p. 690.

38. "Troops Raised without Consent of Congress," Committee Report, ibid., 2: 101.

39. Gaines to Brearly, January 11, 1818, ibid., 2: 103.

40. "Troops Raised without Consent of Congress," ibid., p. 99.

41. Ibid., pp. 99–101.

42. Thomas Hart Benton, *Thirty Years' View; or a History of the Working of the American Government for Thirty Years, from 1820 to 1850*, 2 vols. (New York, 1854), 1: 170.

43. Calhoun to Jackson, February 6, 1818, *ASP, MA*, 1: 697.

44. Jackson to Calhoun, March 25, 1818, ibid., pp. 698–99.

45. Ibid., p. 699.

46. Jackson to Calhoun, April 8, 1818, ibid., pp. 699–700; Jackson to the commanding officer, St. Marks, April 6, 1818, ibid., p. 704.

47. Robert Butler, adjutant general, to Brigadier General Daniel Parker, May 3, 1818, ibid., pp. 703–704.

48. Jackson to Calhoun, April 20, 1818, ibid., p. 700.

49. Ibid.; also Butler to Parker, May 3, 1818, ibid., p. 703.

50. Woodward, *Reminiscences*, pp. 54–55; Muster-roll of the general, field, and staff officers of General W. McIntosh's brigade of Indian warriors, *ASP, MA*, 2: 119.

51. Butler to Parker, May 3, 1818, p. 704.

52. Ibid.; An Officer Attached to the Expedition, *A Concise Narrative of the Seminole Campaign* (Nashville, 1819), pp. 30–31.

53. Arrest of Captain Obed Wright, House Report, December 14, 1818, *ASP, MA*, 1: 774–78.

54. Glasscock to Jackson, April 30, 1818, ibid., p. 776.

55. Jackson to chiefs and warriors of the Chehaw village, May 7, 1818, ibid., p. 776; Jackson to Rabun, May 7, 1818, ibid., p. 777.

56. Rabun to Calhoun, June 1, 1818, ibid., p. 774.

57. Secretary of war to Mitchell, July 13, 1818, Carter, ed., *Territorial Papers*, 18: 374.

58. Jackson to Calhoun, June 2, 1818, *ASP, MA*, 1: 708.

13: McIntosh and Mitchell: An Unholy Alliance

1. Antonio J. Waring, ed., Introduction, *Laws of the Creek Nation* (Athens, Ga., 1960), pp. 2–3.

2. U.S. Congress, *Report on Messages of the President, Select Committee, House Report*, No. 98, 19th Cong. 2d sess., vol. 3, *The Georgia Indian Controversy*, March 3, 1827, p. 449; hereinafter cited as HR 98, 19/2 (161).

3. William Baldwin to William Darlington, April 19, 1817, William Darlington, comp., *Relinquiae Baldwinianae: Selections from the Correspondence of the Late William Baldwin, M.D.* (Philadelphia, 1843), pp. 216–17.

4. John Clarke, *Considerations on the Purity of the Principles of William H. Crawford . . .* (Augusta, 1819), p. 131.

5. "Slaves Imported by the Indian Agent Contrary to Law, Report of the United States Attorney-General, January 21, 1821," communicated by the president to the Senate, May 4, 1822, *American State Papers, Miscellaneous* (Washington, D.C., 1832–61), 2: 958–60; hereinafter Wirt Report, *ASP Misc.*

6. Gaines to Calhoun, October 17, 1819, *ASP, MA*, 2: 130.

7. Wirt Report, *ASP Misc.*, 2: 958–60.

8. Ibid., p. 961.

9. Ibid., pp. 965, 975.

10. Cotterill, *Southern Indians*, p. 214.

11. Jackson to Calhoun, February 14, 1818, Bassett, ed., *Correspondence of Jackson*, 2: 355.

12. Bonner, "William McIntosh," p. 130; Affidavit of Colonel William Hambly, HR 98, 19/2 (161), p. 397.

13. Mitchell to Secretary Calhoun, March 25, 1818, NA Microfilm, M-271, reel 2, 758; Mitchell to Secretary Calhoun, February 3, 1818, Carter, ed., *Territorial Papers*, 18: 244; Bonner, "William McIntosh," p. 130.

14. Cotterill, *Southern Indians*, p. 209.

15. Questions put to the chiefs, headmen, and warriors of the Creek Nation, June 29, 1825, HR 98, 19/2 (161), pp. 397, 449.

16. Mitchell to Secretary Calhoun, June 17, 1818, Carter, ed., *Territorial Papers*, 18: 352.

17. Ibid., p. 353.

18. McIntosh to Mitchell, agent, a Code of Laws for the Creek Nation, NA Microfilm M-271, reel 2, 772–75; Waring, ed., *Laws of the Creek Nation*, pp. 11–12.

19. Green, *Politics of Indian Removal*, p. 52; Green's conclusion is based on Ulrich B. Phillips, *Georgia and States Rights* (1901; rpt. Yellow Springs, Ohio, 1968), chap. 4.

20. Calhoun to Pickens and Flournoy, August 8, 1820, *ASP, IA*, 2: 249–50.

21. Mitchell to Calhoun, January 22, 1819, Carter, ed., *Territorial Papers*, 18: 543; Big Warrior to Monroe, January 22, 1819, NA Microfilm M-271, reel 2, 1141.

22. McIntosh to Calhoun, February 14, 1819, NA Microfilm M-271, reel 2, 1235; McIntosh to Calhoun, February 23, 1819, ibid., 1237–40.

23. McIntosh to Calhoun, March 9, 1819, ibid., 1242–45.

24. Cotterill, *Southern Indians*, p. 210; Mitchell to Calhoun, August 8, 1819, NA Microfilm M-271, reel 2, 1496–97.

25. Calhoun to Cherokees, February 11, 1819, *ASP, IA*, 2: 190.

26. Big Warrior and chiefs to Calhoun, November 21, 1819, NA Microfilm, M-271, reel 2, 1142; McIntosh to Calhoun, December 31, 1819, ibid., reel 3, 423–24.

27. Calhoun to Pickens and Flournoy, August 8, 1820, *ASP, IA*, 2: 249–50.

28. Forney and Meriwether to Calhoun, January 9, 1821, ibid., p. 254.

29. Talk delivered by U.S. commissioners, undated, ibid., p. 252; Talk by the Georgia commissioners, December 27, 1820, ibid., p. 252; Talk by the Georgia commissioners, December 28, 1820, ibid.

30. Answer of the chiefs to the talk of the Georgia commissioners, delivered by General McIntosh, ibid., pp. 252–53.

31. Talk delivered by the Georgia commissioners to the Creek Indians, December 29, 1820, ibid., p. 253.

32. Forney and Meriwether to Calhoun, January 9, 1821, ibid., p. 254.

33. Samuel Gardner Drake, *The Aboriginal Races of North America: Comprising Biographical Sketches of Eminent Individuals* (Philadelphia, 1860), p. 392.

34. Holmes to Calhoun, February 3, 1821, *ASP, IA*, 2: 257.

35. Forney and Meriwether to Calhoun, January 9, 1821, ibid., 2: 254; Kappler, *Indian Affairs*, 2: 195–96.

36. Forney and Meriwether to Calhoun, January 9, 1821, *ASP, IA*, 2: 254.

37. Calhoun to Campbell and Meriwether, July 16, 1824, ibid., p. 565.

38. Angie Debo, *The Road to Disappearance* (Norman, Okla., 1941), pp. 86–87.

39. Thomas L. McKenney to Senate, December 27, 1821, *ASP, IA*, 2: 261.

40. Green, *Politics of Indian Removal*, pp. 74–75.

41. Waring, ed., *Laws of the Creek Nation*, p. 5.

42. Affidavit of William Scott, HR 98, 19/2 (161), p. 404; Affidavit of John Winslett, ibid., p. 415.

14. McIntosh and Crowell: Foes in the Deadly Game of Land Cessions

1. Cotterill, *Southern Indians*, p. 214; Crowell to Calhoun, August 20, 1821, NA Microfilm M-271, reel 3, 909.

2. Capers to Calhoun, January 8, 1824, HR 98, 19/2 (161), p. 24; A. Hamil to Capers, March 25, 1823, ibid., p. 43.

3. Extract of talk held by General Jackson, September 18, 1821, *ASP, IA*, 2: 413.

4. Unratified treaty between Creeks and Cherokees, December 11, 1821, Records of the Bureau of Indian Affairs, Documents Relating to the Negotiation of Ratified and Unratified Treaties with Various Tribes of Indians, 1801–69, NA Microfilm T-494, reel 8, 28.

5. Ibid., 29; Agreement between Creeks and Cherokees, October 30, 1822, ibid., 37–40.

6. Hicks to Calhoun, January 10, 1822, NA Microfilm M-271, reel 4, 132–33.

7. Cherokee chiefs to Big Warrior and Little Prince, October 24, 1823, HR 98 19/2 (161), p. 451; McIntosh to Ross, October 21, 1823, ibid., pp. 638–39.

8. Samuel Carter III, *Cherokee Sunset: A Nation Betrayed* (Garden City, N.Y., 1976), p. 57.

9. Cherokee chiefs to Big Warrior and Little Prince, October 24, 1823, HR 98 19/2, (161), p. 452.

10. Campbell to secretary of war, November 28, 1823, quoted in Major Andrews, report, ibid., p. 308; Cherokee chiefs to Big Warrior and Little Prince, ibid., p. 451.

11. Captain Thomas Triplett's testimony, ibid., pp. 390, 389.

12. Samuel Hawkins to Governor Troup, April 12, 1825, ibid., pp. 373–74; Questions put to the chiefs, headmen, and warriors of the Creek Nation by Gaines, June 29, 1825, ibid., p. 449.

13. Crowell to Hambly, August 22, 1823, ibid., p. 163.

14. Chilly McIntosh to Barbour, May 17, 1825, ibid., p. 154; Judge Cuyler to Crowell, July 14, 1825, ibid., p. 388; Major Andrews, report to the secretary of war, August 1, 1825, ibid., p. 336.

15. Cherokee chiefs to Big Warrior and Little Prince, October 24, 1823, HR 98 19/2 (161), p. 452.

16. Tuckabatchee talk, May 24, 1824, in *Niles' Weekly Register*, December 4, 1824.

17. Answers of Elijah M. Amos, HR 98, 19/2 (161), p. 209.

18. Campbell to Calhoun, January 8, 1825, *ASP, IA*, 2: 574; Campbell to secretary of war, November 28, 1823, quoted in Major Andrews, report, HR 98, 19/2 (161), p. 308.

19. Answers of Joel Bailey, ibid., p. 546; Campbell to Troup, December 14, 1824, *ASP, IA*, 2: 572.

20. Affidavit of William Lott, HR 98, 19/2 (161), p. 432; Affidavit of Andrew Berryhill, ibid., pp. 427–28.

21. Campbell to Crowell, October 13, 1824, *ASP, IA*, 2: 567.

22. Contract with Broadnax, November 8, 1824, ibid., p. 567; Campbell to Broadnax, December 4, 1824, ibid., 568.

23. Address to Creek Council, December 7, 1824, ibid., p. 568.

24. Reply by the chiefs, December 8, 1824, ibid., p. 569.

25. Commissioners to Creek Council, December 9, 1824, ibid., pp. 569–70.

26. Ibid., p. 570.

27. Ibid.

28. Note by Chilly McIntosh, clerk of National Council, HR 98, 19/2 (161), p. 457.

29. Chiefs to commissioners, December 11, 1824, *ASP, IA*, 2: 571.

30. Ibid.

31. Affidavit of Luther Blake, HR 98, 19/2 (161), p. 408; Affidavit of Nimrod Doyell, ibid., p. 418; Affidavit of Solomon Belton, ibid., p. 447; Affidavit of Samuel Srells, ibid., p. 429; Campbell to Calhoun, January 8, 1825, *ASP, IA*, 2: 575.

32. Commissioners' report, December 14, 1824, *ASP, IA*, 2: 572.

33. Commissioners' report, December 16, 1824, ibid., p. 573; Commissioners' report, December 18, 1824, ibid.

34. Commissioners' report, December 18, 1824, ibid.

35. Campbell to Calhoun, January 8, 1825, ibid., pp. 574–75.

36. Bonner, "William McIntosh," p. 136.

37. Allen M. Prior's certificate, August 26, 1825, HR 98, 19/2 (161), p. 633.

38. Deposition of Joel Bailey, October 4, 1826, McIntosh Papers, Thomas Gilcrease Museum, Tulsa, Oklahoma.

39. Corbin, *History and Genealogy of McIntosh*, p. 25.

40. Hodgson, *Remarks during a Journey through North America*, p. 197.

15: Betrayal at Indian Springs and the Deaths of McIntosh and Weatherford

1. Campbell to Calhoun, January 8, 1825, *ASP, IA*, 2: 574–75.

2. Ibid.; Campbell to Calhoun, January 11, 1825, ibid., p. 575; Campbell to Crowell, January 12, 1825, ibid., p. 576; Campbell to chiefs of Creek Nation, January 12, 1825, ibid.

3. Calhoun to Campbell, January 18, 1825, ibid., p. 578.

4. Calhoun to Crowell, January 18, 1825, ibid.

5. Georgia congressional delegation to Cocke, February 4, 1825, HR 98, 19/2 (161), p. 125.

6. Creek chiefs to President Monroe, January 25, 1825, *ASP, IA*, 2: 579; Testimony of William Barnard, HR 98 19/2 (161), p. 224.

7. Creek chiefs to President Monroe, January 25, 1825, *ASP, IA*, 2: 579.

8. Affidavit of Major J. H. Broadnax, HR 98, 19/2 (161), p. 440.

9. Ibid.; Crowell to commissioners, February 7, 1825, *ASP, IA*, 2: 581.

10. Commissioners' report, February 10, 1825, ibid., p. 582.

11. Commissioners' report, February 11, 1825, ibid.

12. Commissioners' report, February 12, 1825, ibid.

13. Answers by Duncan Campbell, July 24, 1825, HR 98, 19/2 (161), pp. 534–35.

14. Captain Thomas Triplett's testimony, July 20, 1825, ibid., p. 392.

15. Answers by Duncan Campbell, July 24, 1825, ibid., p. 535.

16. Kappler, *Indian Affairs*, 2: 215.

17. Crowell to secretary of war, February 13, 1825, HR 98, 19/2 (161), p. 132.

18. List of signees to the treaty at Indian Springs, ibid., pp. 254–56.

19. Kappler, *Indian Affairs*, 2: 216.

20. Creek chiefs to the president, February 21, 1825, HR 98, 19/2 (161), pp. 133–34.

21. Exposition of the United States commissioners, November 12, 1825, ibid., p. 825; Governor Troup to Georgia congressional delegation, February 17, 1825, Edward J. Harden, *Life of George M. Troup* (Savannah, 1859), pp. 261–62.

22. Campbell and Meriwether to Governor Troup, February 13, 1825, Harden, *Life of Troup*, p. 260; Captain Thomas Triplett's testimony, July 20, 1825, HR 98, 19/2 (161), p. 392.

23. Address of friendly chiefs to Troup, February 17, 1825, Harden, *Life of Troup*, pp. 263–64.

24. Executive Journal, February 19, 1825; Troup to hostile Indians, February 26, 1825, ibid., pp. 265–67.

25. Ibid., p. 267.

26. Lamar to Troup, March 10, 1825, HR 98, 19/2 (161), p. 372.

27. Ibid., pp. 369, 371.

28. Chilly McIntosh to Governor Troup, March 3, 1825; Governor Troup to Chilly McIntosh, March 5, 1825, Harden, *Life of Troup*, pp. 269–70.

29. Crowell to secretary of war, March 12, 1825, HR 98, 19/2 (161), p. 137.

30. McIntosh to Troup, March 29, 1825, *ASP, IA,* 2: 757.

31. Troup to McIntosh, April 4, 1825, ibid., p. 758.

32. McIntosh to Troup, April 12, 1825, ibid., p. 759.

33. McIntosh and other chiefs to the Georgia legislature, April 12, 1825, ibid., pp. 759–60.

34. McIntosh to Troup, April 12, 1825, ibid., p. 759.

35. Ibid.

36. Harden, *Life of Troup,* p. 276.

37. Interrogatories and answers from Jesse Cox, May 28, 1825, HR 98, 19/2 (161), p. 205.

38. Crowell to Barbour, April 27, 1825, ibid., p. 140.

39. Interrogatories and answers from Abram Miles, June 4, 1825, ibid., p. 207.

40. Affidavit of Francis Flournoy, May 16, 1825, ibid., p. 150.

41. Governor Troup to President Adams, May 3, 1825, Harden, *Life of Troup,* p. 278.

42. Peggy and Susannah McIntosh to U.S. commissioners, May 3, 1825, HR 98, 19/2 (161), p. 376.

43. Affidavit of Francis Flournoy, May 16, 1825, ibid., p. 151; Corbin, *History and Genealogy of McIntosh,* p. 36.

44. Affidavit of Francis Flournoy, HR 98, 19/2 (161), p. 151.

45. Major Andrews' report to the secretary of war, August 1, 1825, ibid., pp. 323–24, 339; Affidavit of Francis Flournoy, May 16, 1825, ibid., p. 151.

46. Harden, *Life of Troup,* p. 344.

47. Jane Hawkins to commissioners, May 3, 1825, *ASP, IA,* 2: 768–69.

48. Mrs. M. Davis Hahn, ed., "Act for the Relief of John Randon," *Baldwin County Historical Quarterly* 7 (1980): 27.

49. Pickett, *History of Alabama,* pp. 596–97; Driesback, "Weatherford," n.p.

50. Rowland, *Andrew Jackson's Campaign,* pp. 111–112.

51. Driesback, "Weatherford," n.p.

52. See Benjamin W. Griffith, Jr., "Lt. David Moniac, Creek Indian: First Minority Graduate of West Point," *Alabama Historical Quarterly* 43 (1981): 99–110.

53. Claiborne, *Sam Dale,* p. 129.

54. I am grateful to Paul Ghioto, ranger-historian, formerly at the Horseshoe Bend National Military Park, for these inscriptions.

16: The Bitter Aftermath

1. General Ware to Governor Troup, May 1, 1825, HR 98, 19/2 (161), p. 147.

2. Troup to President Adams, May 3, 1825, Harden, *Life of Troup,* pp. 277–78; Troup to Marshall, HR 98, 19/2 (161), p. 145.

3. Affidavit of Dr. Bartlett, June 14, 1825, HR 98, 19/2 (161), pp. 405–406; Affidavit of Solomon Belton, June 22, 1825, ibid., pp. 446–47.

4. Troup to the president, May 3, 1825, Harden, *Life of Troup,* p. 278; Chilly McIntosh et al. to Barbour, May 17, 1825, Green, *Politics of Indian Removal,* p. 99.

5. General Orders, May 5, 1825, Harden, *Life of Troup,* p. 279; Campbell to secretary of war, May 4, 1825, HR 98, 19/2 (161), p. 145.

6. Grand Jury Presentments, Milledgeville, Ga., May term, 1825, *ASP, IA,* 2: 771–72.

7. Crowell to secretary of war, May 8, 1825, HR 98, 19/2 (161), p. 146.

8. Address from friendly Creeks, May 18, 1825, ibid., p. 165; McDonald to Troup, May 6, 1825, ibid., p. 149.

9. Governor Troup's message to Georgia General Assembly, May 23, 1825, Harden, *Life of Troup,* pp. 293, 296; Secretary of war to Troup, May 18, 1825, HR 98, 19/2 (161), p. 155.

10. Troup to Andrews, May 31, 1825, HR 98, 19/2 (161), p. 175.

11. Harden, *Life of Troup,* p. 336.

12. Andrews to Barbour, June 2, 1825, HR 98, 19/2 (161), pp. 171–73.

13. Andrews to Barbour, June 7, 1825, ibid., p. 178; Andrews to Barbour, June 12, 1825, ibid., p. 183.

14. Report and resolutions on Crowell, Georgia legislature, June 10, 1825, ibid., pp. 188–95.

15. Andrews to Crowell, June 21, 1825, ibid., p. 241; Troup to Andrews, June 28, 1825, ibid., p. 249; Andrews to Troup, July 4, 1825, ibid., p. 268.

16. Gaines to Troup, July 1, 1825, Harden, *Life of Troup,* p. 357; Troup to Gaines, July 4, 1825, Harden, *Life of Troup,* pp. 357–58.

17. Gaines to Troup, July 10, 1825, HR 98, 19/2 (161), pp. 280–81; Certificate of Edwards and Marshall, July 9, 1825, ibid., p. 275.

18. Troup to Gaines, July 16, 1825, *ASP, IA,* 2: 801.

19. Gaines to Troup, July 28, 1825, ibid., pp. 801–802.

20. Barbour to Troup, July 21, 1825, ibid., p. 809; Troup to Barbour, August 15, 1825, ibid., p. 811.

21. Troup to General Assembly, November 8, 1825, ibid., p. 780.

22. Harden, *Life of Troup,* pp. 423–24.

23. President Adams to Senate, January 31, 1826, *ASP, IA,* 2: 611–12.

24. Troup to General Assembly, November 8, 1825, ibid., p. 779; Andrews's report to secretary of war, August 1, 1825, HR 98, 19/2 (161), p. 324; Troup to President Adams, July 26, 1825, ibid., p. 302.

25. Andrews's report, August 1, 1825, pp. 315–16, 347.

26. Kappler, *Indian Affairs*, 2: 264, 268.

27. James C. Bonner, *Georgia's Last Frontier: The Development of Carroll County* (Athens, Ga., 1971), p. 16.

28. Interview between secretary of war and delegation of Creeks, Opothle Yoholo, speaker, November 30, 1825, NA Microfilm T-494, reel 1, p. 769.

29. President Adams to Senate, January 31, 1826, *ASP, IA*, 2: 611–12.

30. Kappler, *Indian Affairs*, 2: 266.

31. Troup to Adams, February 11, 1826, Harden, *Life of Troup*, p. 434.

32. Berrien to Troup, May 30, 1826, ibid., p. 442.

33. Statement by Chilly McIntosh in *Tuscumbia Patriot*, November 30, 1827; see Grant Foreman, *Indians and Pioneers: The Story of the American Southwest before 1830* (Norman, Okla., 1936), p. 256.

34. Grant Foreman, *Indian Removal: The Emigration of the Five Civilized Tribes* (Norman, Okla., 1953), p. 29, n. 21.

35. McKenney and Hall, *Indian Tribes of North America*, 1: 267–68.

36. Ibid., p. 20, n. 2, from *Cherokee Advocate*, March 6, 1846, p. 3.

37. Hodgson, *Remarks during a Journey through North America*, pp. 267–69; James D. Horan, *The McKenney-Hall Portrait Gallery of American Indians* (New York, 1986), p. 134.

38. George Bird Grinnell, "Tenure of Land among the Indians," *American Anthropologist* 9 (1907): 2; Talk of President Jefferson and Creek Indians, November 3, 1805, NA Microfilm M-15, reel 2, 75–76.

Bibliography

— • —

Primary Sources

Manuscript Collections

Bacon, Edmund. Letters. Department of Archives and Manuscripts, Louisiana State University, Baton Rouge.

Coffee, John. Papers. Dyas Collection, Tennessee Historical Society, Tennessee State Library and Archives, Nashville.

Creek Indian Letters, Talks, and Treaties, 1705–1829. Georgia Department of Archives and History, Atlanta.

Floyd, John. Papers. Georgia Department of Archives and History, Atlanta.

General Records of the Department of State: "War of 1812 Papers" of the Department of State, 1789–1815. National Archives, Washington, D.C. Microfilm M-588, 7 reels.

Governors' Letterbooks. Georgia Department of Archives and History, Atlanta.

Hawkins Papers. Georgia Department of Archives and History, Atlanta.

Hays, Louise Frederick, ed. "Letters of Benjamin Hawkins, 1797–1815." Typescript. 1939. Georgia Department of Archives and History, Atlanta.

——. "Unpublished Letters of Timothy Barnard." Typescript. 1939. Georgia Department of Archives and History, Atlanta.

Jackson Papers. Huntington Library, San Marino, California.

Jackson Papers. Library of Congress, Washington, D.C.

McIntosh Papers. Thomas Gilcrease Museum, Tulsa, Oklahoma.

Pickett, Albert James. Manuscripts. Alabama State Archives, Montgomery.

Records of the Bureau of Indian Affairs: Documents Relating to the Negotiation of Ratified and Unratified Treaties with Various Tribes of Indians, 1801–69. National Archives, Washington, D.C. Microfilm T-494, 10 reels.

Records of the Bureau of Indian Affairs: Letterbook of Creek Trading House, 1795–1816. National Archives, Washington, D.C. Microfilm M-4, 1 reel.

Records of the Bureau of Indian Affairs: Letters Received by the Office of the Secretary of War Relating to Indian Affairs, 1800–1823. National Archives, Washington, D.C. Microfilm M-271, 4 reels.

Records of the Bureau of Indian Affairs: Letters Received by the Superintendent of Indian Trade, 1806–24. National Archives, Washington, D.C. Microfilm T-58, 1 reel.

Records of the Bureau of Indian Affairs: Letters Sent by the Office of Indian
Affairs, 1824–81. National Archives, Washington, D.C. Microfilm M-21, 166
reels.

Records of the Bureau of Indian Affairs: Letters Sent by the Secretary of War
Relating to Indian Affairs, 1800–1824. National Archives, Washington, D.C.
Microfilm M-15, 6 reels.

Records of the Bureau of Indian Affairs: Letters Sent by the Superintendent of
Indian Trade, 1807–23. National Archives, Washington, D.C. Microfilm
M-16, 6 reels.

Records of the Bureau of Indian Affairs: Special Files of the Office of Indian
Affairs, 1807–1904. National Archives, Washington, D.C. Microfilm M-574,
85 reels.

Records of the Office of Indian Affairs: Registers of Letters Received, 1824–80.
National Archives, Washington, D.C. Microfilm M-18, 126 reels.

Records of the Office of the Secretary of War: Confidential and Unofficial
Letters Sent, 1814–47. National Archives, Washington, D.C. Microfilm
M-7, 2 reels.

Records of the Office of the Secretary of War: Letters Received, Main Series,
1801–70. National Archives, Washington, D.C. Microfilm M-221, 317 reels.

Records of the Office of the Secretary of War: Letters Received, Unregistered
Series, 1789–1861. National Archives, Washington, D.C. Microfilm M-222,
34 reels.

Records of the Office of the Secretary of War: Letters Sent Relating to Military
Affairs, 1800–1889. National Archives, Washington, D.C. Microfilm M-6,
110 reels.

Records of the Office of the Secretary of War: Registers of Letters Received,
Main Series, 1800–1870. National Archives, Washington, D.C. Microfilm
M-22, 134 reels.

Southeastern Indian Papers. Department of Archives and Manuscripts, Louisiana State University, Baton Rouge.

Tunstall, Tom Tate. "David Moniac, Civil History." Manuscript. U.S. Military
Academy Archives, West Point, New York.

Wilson, Henry. Papers. Department of Archives and Manuscripts, Louisiana
State University, Baton Rouge.

Published Sources

*American State Papers, Documents, Legislative and Executive, of the Congress of the
United States.* 38 vols. Washington, D.C.: Gale and Seaton, 1832–61.

Annals of Congress, 1789–1824. 42 vols. Washington, D.C.: Gale and Seaton,
1834–56.

Baldwin, William. *Relinquiae Baldwinianae: Selections from the Correspondence of the Late William Baldwin, M.D.* William Darlington, comp. Philadelphia: Kimber and Sharpless, 1843.

Bartram, William. "Observations on the Creek and Cherokee Indians." (1789). *Transactions of the American Ethnological Society,* 3, pt. 1 (1953): 1–81.

———. *Travels through North and South Carolina, Georgia, East and West Florida.* Facsimile of 1792 edition. Savannah: Beehive Press, 1973.

Bassett, John Spencer, ed. *Correspondence of Andrew Jackson.* 7 vols. Washington, D.C.: Carnegie Institution, 1926–35.

Bonner, James C., ed. "James R. Vinton, 'Journal of My Excursion to Georgia, and the Creek Nation—1827.'" *Georgia Historical Quarterly* 44 (1960): 74–84.

Bossu, Jean Bernard. *Travels in the Interior of North America, 1751–62.* 1768. Reprint. Translated by Seymour Feiler. Norman: University of Oklahoma Press, 1926.

Brannan, John, ed. *Official Letters of the Military and Naval Officers of the United States during the War with Great Britain in the Years 1812, '13, '14, and '15.* Washington, D.C.: Way and Gideon, 1823.

Brannon, Peter A., ed. "Journal of James A. Tait for the Year 1813." *Georgia Historical Quarterly* 8 (1924): 229–39.

Carter, Clarence E., ed. *Territorial Papers of the United States: Territory South of the River Ohio, and Mississippi Territory.* 22 vols. Washington, D.C.: U.S. Government Printing Office, 1934.

Crevecoeur, Michel Guillaume St. Jean de. *Letters from an American Farmer.* London: Davies, 1782.

Crockett, David. *The Life of David Crockett.* Facsimile ed. Knoxville: University of Tennessee Press, 1973.

Day, Donald, and Harry Herbert Ullom, eds. *The Autobiography of Sam Houston.* Norman: University of Oklahoma Press, 1954.

DeWitt, John, ed. "Letters of General John Coffee to His Wife, 1813–1815." *Tennessee Historical Magazine* 2 (1916): 274–85.

Ellicott, Andrew. *The Journal of Andrew Ellicott.* Philadelphia: Budd & Bertram, 1803.

Forbes, John. "A Journal of John Forbes, May, 1803: The Seizure of William Augustus Bowles." Transcribed by Mrs. J. W. Greenslade. *Florida Historical Society Quarterly* 9 (1931): 279–89.

Foster, Sir Augustus John. *Jeffersonian America: Notes on the United States of America, Collected in the Years 1805–6–7 and 11–12.* Edited by Richard Beale Davis. San Marino, Calif.: Huntington Library, 1954.

Grant, C. L., ed. *Letters, Journals and Writings of Benjamin Hawkins,* 2 vols. Savannah: Beehive Press, 1980.

Harden, Edward J. *Life of George M. Troup.* Savannah: E. J. Purse, 1859.

Hawkins, Benjamin. *Letters of Benjamin Hawkins, 1796–1806 . . .* In *Collections of the Georgia Historical Society* 9 (1916). Reprint. Spartanburg, S.C.: Reprint Co., 1974.

————. *A Sketch of the Creek Country in the Years 1798 and 1799.* In *Collections of the Georgia Historical Society* 3, pt. 2 (1848). Reprint. Spartanburg, S.C.: Reprint Co., 1974.

Hodgson, Adam. *Remarks during a Journey through North America in the Years 1819, 1820, and 1821.* New York: Samuel Whiting, 1823.

Janson, Charles William. *The Stranger in America: Containing Observations Made during a Long Residence in That Country.* London: J. Cundee, 1807.

Kappler, Charles J. *Indian Affairs, Laws and Treaties.* 3 vols. Washington, D.C.: U.S. Government Printing Office, 1892–1913.

"Letters of John Floyd, 1813–1838." *Georgia Historical Quarterly* 33 (1949): 228–69.

Mauelshagen, Carl, and Gerald H. Davis, ed. and trans. *Partners in the Lord's Work: The Diary of Two Moravian Missionaries in the Creek Indian Country, 1807–1813.* Research Paper 21. Georgia State College, Atlanta, 1969.

Milfort, Louis LeClerc. *Memoirs, or a Quick Glance at My Various Travels and My Sojourn in the Creek Nation.* 1802. Translated and edited by Ben C. McCary. Savannah: Beehive Press, 1959.

Motte, Jacob Rhett. *Journey into Wilderness: An Army Surgeon's Account of Life in Camp and Field during the Creek and Seminole Wars, 1836–1838.* Edited by James F. Sunderman. Gainesville: University of Florida Press, 1953.

Pope, John. *A Tour through the Southern and Western Territories of the United States of North America; the Spanish Dominions on the River Mississippi, and the Floridas; the Countries of the Creek Nations; and Many Uninhabited Parts.* Richmond: J. Dixon, 1792.

Reid, John, and John Henry Eaton. *The Life of Andrew Jackson.* 1817. Reprint, edited by Frank L. Owsley, Jr. University, Ala.: University of Alabama Press, 1974.

A Report of the Committee of the State of the Republic to Whom Was Referred So Much of the Governor's Message at the Opening of the Extra Session of the General Assembly of the State of Georgia, as Relates to the Murder of McIntosh and His Friends and the Troubles Which Have Arisen in the Indian Country. Milledgeville, Ga.: Camak & Ragland Printers, 1825.

Royce, C. C. "Indian Land Cessions in the United States." In *Eighteenth Annual Report of the Bureau of American Ethnology,* pp. 527–964. Washington, D.C.: U.S. Government Printing Office, 1899.

Smith, Sam B., and Harriet Chappell Owsley. *The Papers of Andrew Jackson.* Knoxville: University of Tennessee Press, 1980.

Stiggins, George. "A Historical Narration of the Genealogy, Traditions, and Downfall of the Ispocaga or Creek Tribe of Indians, Written by One of the Tribe." Draper Manuscripts, vol. 5, Georgia, Alabama, and South Carolina

Papers, in Wisconsin Historical Society. Edited by Theron A. Nunez, Jr. *Ethnohistory* 5 (1958): 69–72, 131–75, 292–301.

U.S. Congress. *Report on Messages of the President, Select Committee, House Report*, No. 98, 19th Cong., 2d sess., Vol. 3, *The Georgia Indian Controversy*, March 3, 1827. Washington, D.C.: U.S. Government Printing Office, 1837.

West, Elizabeth Howard. "A Prelude to the Creek War of 1813–1814, in a Letter of John Innerarity to James Innerarity." *Florida Historical Quarterly* 18 (1940): 247–66.

Williams, Amelia W., and Eugene C. Barker, eds. *The Writings of Sam Houston, 1813–1863.* 8 vols. Austin: University of Texas Press, 1938–43.

Woodward, Thomas S. *Reminiscences of the Creek, or Muscogee Indians, Contained in Letters to Friends in Georgia and Alabama.* 1859. Reprint. Tuscaloosa, Ala.: Alabama Book Store, 1939.

Newspapers

Augusta Chronicle, July 25, 1803; October 10, 12, 1805.
Augusta Herald, July 9, 1812; August 27, 1812.
Baldwin (Alabama) *Times*, June 25, 1968.
Clarion and Tennessee State Gazette (Nashville), April 12, 1814.
Columbian Museum & Savannah Advertiser, January 21, 1800.
Milledgeville (Georgia) *Southern Recorder*, April 4, 18, 1820; May 3, 1825.
Mississippi Republican, March 25, 1814.
Nashville Whig, April 27, 1814.
National Daily Intelligencer (Washington, D.C.), April 18, 1814.
Niles' Weekly Register, June 10, 1815; November 7, 1818; December 4, 1824; May 3, 1825.
Tuscumbia (Alabama) *Patriot*, November 30, 1827.

Secondary Sources

Books

Abernethy, Thomas P. *The Formative Years in Alabama, 1815–1828.* 2d ed. University, Ala.: University of Alabama Press, 1965.

———. *The South in the New Nation, 1789–1819.* Baton Rouge: Louisiana State University Press, 1961.

Adair, James. *History of the American Indians.* 1775. Reprint. Edited by Samuel Cole Williams. New York: Promontory Press, 1930.

Adams, Henry. *History of the United States of America during the Jefferson and Madison Administrations.* 9 vols. New York: Scribner's, 1921.

Benton, Thomas Hart. *Thirty Years' View; or, a History of the Working of the American Government for Thirty Years, from 1820 to 1850.* 2 vols. New York: D. Appleton, 1854.

Berkhofer, Robert F., Jr. *Salvation and the Savage: An Analysis of Protestant Missions and American Indian Responses, 1787–1862.* St. Louis: Concordia, 1966.

Bonner, James C. *Georgia's Last Frontier: The Development of Carroll County.* Athens: University of Georgia Press, 1971.

Buell, Augustus C. *A History of Andrew Jackson.* 2 vols. New York: Charles Scribner's Sons, 1904.

Carter, Samuel Carter III. *Cherokee Sunset: A Nation Betrayed.* Garden City, N.Y.: Doubleday, 1976.

Catlin, George. *North American Indians.* 2 vols. Edinburgh: John Grant, 1926.

Caughey, John Walton. *McGillivray of the Creeks.* Norman: University of Oklahoma Press, 1938.

Claiborne, John Francis Hamtramck. *Life and Times of Gen. Sam Dale, the Mississippi Partisan.* New York: Harper and Brothers, 1860.

———. *Mississippi as a Province, Territory and State with Biographical Notices of Eminent Citizens.* 1880. Reprint. Baton Rouge: Louisiana State University Press, 1964.

Claiborne, Nathaniel Herbert. *Notes on the War in the South; With Biographical Sketches of the Lives of Montgomery, Jackson, Sevier, the Late Governor Claiborne, and Others.* Richmond: Wiliam Ramsey, 1819.

Clarke, John. *Considerations on the Purity of the Principles of William H. Crawford, Esq., Deducible from His Conduct, in Connexion With That of Charles Tait, Esq., toward the Author of This Publication.* Augusta: Georgia Advertiser Office, 1819.

Coe, Charles H. *Red Patriots: The Story of the Seminoles.* Cincinnati: Editor Publishing Co., 1898.

Cohen, Felix S. *Handbook of Federal Indian Law.* Washington, D.C.: U.S. Government Printing Office, 1945.

Corbin, Harriet Turner (Porter). *A History and Genealogy of Chief William McIntosh, Jr.* Long Beach, Calif.: Privately printed, 1967.

Corkran, David H. *The Creek Frontier, 1540–1783.* Norman: University of Oklahoma Press, 1967.

Cotterill, Robert S. *The Southern Indians: The Story of the Civilized Tribes before Removal.* Norman: University of Oklahoma Press, 1954.

Coulter, E. Merton, and Albert B. Saye. *A List of Early Settlers of Georgia.* Athens: University of Georgia Press, 1949.

Debo, Angie. *The Road to Disappearance.* Norman: University of Oklahoma Press, 1941.

Doherty, Herbert J., Jr. *Richard Keith Call: Southern Unionist.* Gainesville: University of Florida Press, 1961.

Deloria, Vine, Jr. *God Is Red.* New York: Dell, 1973.

Doster, James F. *The Creek Indians and Their Florida Lands, 1740–1823.* 2 vols. New York: Garland, 1974.

Drake, Benjamin. *Life of Tecumseh and His Brother the Prophet.* Cincinnati: E. Morgan, 1841.

Drake, Samuel Gardner. *The Aboriginal Races of North America: Comprising Biographical Sketches of Eminent Individuals*. Philadelphia: C. DeSilver, 1860.

Driver, Harold Edson. *Indians of North America*. Chicago: University of Chicago Press, 1961.

Dunbar, Seymour. *A History of Travel in America*. New York: Tudor, 1937.

Edmunds, R. David. *The Shawnee Prophet*. Lincoln: University of Nebraska Press, 1983.

――――. *Tecumseh and the Quest for Indian Leadership*. Boston: Little, Brown, 1984.

Eggan, Frederick Russell. *The American Indian: Perspective for the Study of Social Changes*. Chicago: Aldine, 1966.

――――. *Social Anthropology of North American Tribes*. Chicago: University of Chicago Press, 1955.

Eggleston, George Cary. *Red Eagle and the Wars with the Creek Indians of Alabama*. New York: Dodd, Mead, 1878.

Farb, Peter. *Man's Rise to Civilization: The Cultural Ascent of the Indians of North America*. 2d ed., rev. New York: Dutton, 1978.

Foreman, Grant. *The Five Civilized Tribes*. Norman: University of Oklahoma Press, 1934.

――――. *Indian Removal: The Emigration of the Five Civilized Tribes*. Norman: University of Oklahoma Press, 1953.

――――. *Indians and Pioneers: The Story of the American Southwest before 1830*. Norman: University of Oklahoma Press, 1936.

French, Benjamin Franklin. *Historical Collections of Louisiana and Florida*. 2d ser. New York: A. Mason, 1875.

Fundaburk, Emma Lila, ed. *Southeastern Indians: Life Portraits*. Metuchen, N.J.: Scarecrow Reprint Corp., 1969.

Gatschet, Albert S. *A Migration Legend of the Creek Indians, with a Linguistic, Historic, and Ethnographic Introduction*. 2 vols. Philadelphia: Daniel G. Brinton, 1884.

Gilmer, George R. *Sketches of Some of the First Settlers of Upper Georgia of the Cherokees, and of the Author*. New York: D. Appleton, 1855.

Green, Michael D. *The Politics of Indian Removal: Creek Government and Society in Crisis*. Lincoln: University of Nebraska Press, 1982.

Griffith, Lucille. *Alabama: A Documentary History to 1900*. Rev. ed. University, Ala.: University of Alabama Press, 1972.

Halbert, H. S., and T. H. Ball. *The Creek War of 1813 and 1814*. 1895. Reprint. Edited by Frank L. Owsley, Jr. University, Ala.: University of Alabama Press, 1969.

Harris, W. Stuart. *Dead Towns of Alabama*. University, Ala.: University of Alabama Press, 1977.

Hays, Louise Frederick. *Hero of Hornet's Nest: A Biography of Elijah Clark, 1733–1799*. New York: Stratford House, 1946.

Heath, Milton S. *Constructive Liberalism: The Role of the State in Economic Development in Georgia to 1860.* Cambridge, Mass.: Harvard University Press, 1954.

Henri, Florette. *The Southern Indians and Benjamin Hawkins.* Norman: University of Oklahoma Press, 1986.

Holland, James W. *Andrew Jackson and the Creek War: Victory at the Horseshoe.* University, Ala.: University of Alabama Press, 1968.

Horan, James D. *The McKenney-Hall Portrait Gallery of American Indians.* New York: Bramhall House, 1986.

Hudson, Charles M., ed. *Black Drink: A Native American Tea.* Athens: University of Georgia Press, 1979.

————. *The Southeastern Indians.* Knoxville: University of Tennessee Press, 1976.

Jahoda, Gloria. *The Trail of Tears: The Story of the American Indian Removal, 1813–1855.* New York: Holt, 1975.

James, Marquis. *The Life of Andrew Jackson.* New York: Bobbs-Merrill, 1938.

Littlefield, Daniel F., Jr. *Africans and Seminoles: From Removal to Emancipation.* Westport, Conn.: Greenwood Press, 1977.

MacGill, Caroline E., et al., *History of Transportation in the United States before 1860.* New York: P. Smith, 1948.

McKenney, Thomas Loraine, and James Hall. *History of the Indian Tribes of North America, with Biographical Sketches and Anecdotes of the Principal Chiefs. Embellished with One Hundred and Twenty Portraits, from the Indian Gallery in the Department of War, at Washington.* 3 vols. Vol. 1, Philadelphia: E. C. Biddle, 1836; vol. 2, Philadelphia: F. W. Greenough, 1838; vol. 3, Philadelphia: D. Rice and G. Clark, 1844.

McKenney, Thomas Loraine, and James Hall. *The Indian Tribes of North America.* Edited by Frederick Webb Hodge. 2 vols. Edinburgh: J. Grant, 1933.

Macleod, William Christie. *The American Indian Frontier.* New York: Knopf, 1928.

McReynolds, Edwin C. *The Seminoles.* Norman: University of Oklahoma Press, 1957.

Mahon, John K. *History of the Second Seminole War, 1835–1842.* Gainesville: University of Florida Press, 1967.

————. *The War of 1812.* Gainesville: University of Florida Press, 1972.

Malone, Henry T. *Cherokees of the Old South: A People in Transition.* Athens: University of Georgia Press, 1956.

Meek, Alexander R. *The Red Eagle.* Montgomery, Ala.: Paragon Press, 1914.

Mereness, Newton Dennison, ed. *Travels in the American Colonies.* New York: Macmillan, 1916.

Merk, Frederick. *History of the Western Movement.* New York: Knopf, 1978.

Moore, William V. *Indian Wars of the United States.* Philadelphia: J. B. Smith, 1858.

Myer, William E. *Indian Trails of the Southeast.* U.S. Bureau of Ethnology, Annual Report 42. Washington, D.C.: U.S. Government Printing Office, 1924–25.

Nammack, Georgiana C. *Fraud, Politics, and the Dispossession of Indians.* Norman: University of Oklahoma Press, 1969.

O'Donnell, James H. III. *Southern Indians in the American Revolution.* Knoxville: University of Tennessee Press, 1973.

An Officer Attached to the Expedition. *A Concise Narrative of the Seminole Campaign.* Nashville: M'Lean and Tunstall, 1819.

Owsley, Frank L., Jr. *Struggle for the Gulf Borderlands: The Creek War and the Battle of New Orleans, 1812–1815.* Gainesville: University of Florida Press, 1981.

Parton, James. *Life of Andrew Jackson.* 3 vols. Boston: Houghton Mifflin, 1887–88.

Peake, Ora Brooks. *A History of the United States Indian Factory System, 1795–1822.* Denver: Sage Books, 1954.

Perdue, Theda. *Slavery and the Evolution of Cherokee Society, 1540–1866.* Knoxville: University of Tennessee Press, 1979.

Phillips, Ulrich B. *Georgia and States Rights.* 1901. Reprint. Yellow Springs, Ohio: Antioch Press, 1968.

Pickett, Albert James. *History of Alabama.* 1851. Reprint. Birmingham, Ala.: Birmingham Book and Magazine Co., 1962.

Porter, Kenneth Wiggins. *The Negro on the American Frontier.* New York: Arno Press, 1971.

Pound, Merritt. *Benjamin Hawkins: Indian Agent.* Athens: University of Georgia Press, 1951.

Prince, Oliver Hillhouse. *A Digest of the Laws of the State of Georgia.* Milledgeville, Ga.: Grantland & Orme, 1822.

Prucha, Francis Paul. *American Indian Policy in the Formative Years: The Indian Trade and Intercourse Acts, 1790–1834.* Cambridge, Mass.: Harvard University Press, 1962.

Quincy, Josiah. *Figures of the Past: From the Leaves of Old Journals.* Boston: Roberts Brothers, 1883.

Reid, John Phillip. *A Law of Blood: The Primitive Law of the Cherokee Nation.* New York: New York University Press, 1970.

Remini, Robert V. *Andrew Jackson and the Course of American Empire, 1767–1821.* New York: Harper & Row, 1977.

————. *Andrew Jackson and the Course of American Freedom, 1822–1832.* New York: Harper & Row, 1981.

Riley, Benjamin Franklin. *Makers and Romance of Alabama History.* N.p.: N.p., 1915.

Ringwalt, John Luther. *Development of Transportation Systems in the United States.* Philadelphia: Railway World Office, 1888.

Rogin, Michael Paul. *Fathers and Children: Andrew Jackson and the Subjugation of the American Indian*. New York: Knopf, 1975.

Rowland, Mrs. Dunbar. *Andrew Jackson's Campaign against the British, or the Mississippi Territory in the War of 1812*. New York: Macmillan, 1926.

Schoolcraft, Henry Rowe. *The American Indians*. Rochester, N.Y.: Wanzer, Foot, and Co., 1851.

———, ed. *Historical and Statistical Information, Respecting the History, Conditions and Prospects of the Indian Tribes of the United States*. 6 vols. Philadelphia: Lippincott, 1851–57.

Shaw, Helen Louise. *British Administration of the Southern Indians, 1756–1783*. Lancaster, Pa.: Lancaster Press, 1931.

Silver, James W. *Edmund Pendleton Gaines, Frontier General*. Baton Rouge: Louisiana State University Press, 1949.

Smith, Mrs. Margaret (Bayard). *The First Forty Years of Washington Society*. Edited by Gaillard Hunt. New York: Charles Scribner's, 1906.

Sprague, John T. *The Origin, Progress, and Conclusion of the Florida War*. Facsimile of the 1848 edition. Gainesville: University of Florida Press, 1964.

Swanton, John R. *Early History of the Creek Indians and Their Neighbors*. Bureau of American Ethnology, 73d Bulletin. Washington, D.C.: U.S. Government Printing Office, 1922.

———. *Social Organizations and Social Usages of the Indians of the Creek Confederacy*. 1928. Reprint. New York: Johnson Reprint Corp., 1970.

Viola, Herman J. *Thomas L. McKenney, Architect of America's Early Indian Policy, 1816–1830*. Chicago: Swallow Press, 1974.

Waldo, Samuel Putnam. *Memoirs of Andrew Jackson*. 5th ed. Hartford: J. W. Russell, 1820.

Waring, Antonio J., ed. *Laws of the Creek Nation*. Athens: University of Georgia Press, 1960.

White, George. *Historical Collections of Georgia*. New York: Rudney & Russell, 1854.

Wilkins, Thurman. *Cherokee Tragedy: The Story of the Ridge Family and the Decimation of a People*. New York: Macmillan, 1970.

Woodward, Grace S. *The Cherokees*. Norman: University of Oklahoma Press, 1963.

Wright, J. Leitch, Jr. *Britain and the American Frontier, 1783–1815*. Athens: University of Georgia Press, 1975.

———. *The Only Land They Knew: The Tragic Story of the American Indians in the Old South*. New York: Free Press, 1981.

———. *William Augustus Bowles: Director General of the Creek Nation*. Athens: University of Georgia Press, 1967.

Wrone, David R., and Russell S. Nelson, Jr. *Who's the Savage?* Greenwich, Conn.: Fawcett, 1973.

Young, Mary E. *Redskins, Ruffleshirts, and Rednecks: Indian Allotments in Alabama and Mississippi, 1830–1860*. Norman: University of Oklahoma Press, 1961.

Articles

Bast, Homer. "Creek Indian Affairs, 1775–1778." *Georgia Historical Quarterly* 33 (1949): 1–25.

Bonner, James C. "Tustunugee Hutkee and Creek Factionalism on the Georgia-Alabama Frontier." *Alabama Review* 10 (1957): 111–25.

————. "William McIntosh." In Horace Montgomery, ed., *Georgians in Profile: Historical Essays in Honor of Ellis Merton Coulter*, pp. 114–43. Athens: University of Georgia Press, 1958.

Brannon, Peter A. "Fort Bainbridge." *Arrow Points* 5 (1922): 24–26.

————. "Pole Cat Springs Agency." *Arrow Points* 10 (1925): 24–26.

————. "Tuckabahchi Chiefs." *Arrow Points* 14 (1929): 33.

————. "Tuckabahchi Sons-in-law." *Arrow Points* 14 (1929): 43.

Bryars, Tunstall. "Chart of the Family of Sehoy and Col. Marchand." *Baldwin County Historical Society Quarterly* 6 (1979): 50.

Chappell, Gordon T. "John Coffee: Surveyor and Land Agent." *Alabama Review* 14 (1961): 189–90.

Clay, Mrs. Clement. "Recollections of Opothleyoholo." *Arrow Points* 4 (1922): 35–36.

Coley, C. J. "Creek Treaties, 1790–1832." *Alabama Review* 11 (1958): 163–76.

Cotterill, R. S. "Federal Indian Management in the South, 1790–1825." *Journal of American History* 20 (1933): 335–47.

Coulter, E. Merton. "Mary Musgrove, 'Queen of the Creeks': A Chapter of Early Georgia Troubles." *Georgia Historical Quarterly* 11 (1927): 1–30.

Crane, Verner W. "The Origins of the Name of the Creek Indians." *Journal of American History* 5 (1918): 339–42.

Dobyns, Henry F. "Estimating Aboriginal American Population: An Appraisal of Techniques with a New Hemispheric Estimate." *Current Anthropology* 7 (1966): 414.

Downes, Randolph C. "Creek-American Relations, 1782–1790." *Georgia Historical Quarterly* 21 (1937): 142–84.

Driesback, J. D. "Weatherford—'The Red Eagle.'" *Alabama Historical Reporter* 2 (1884): 20 unnumbered pages.

Faust, Richard H. "Another Look at General Jackson and the Indians of the Mississippi Territory." *Alabama Review* 28 (1975): 201–17.

Gallaher, Ruth A. "The Indian Agent in the United States before 1850." *Iowa Journal of History and Politics* 14 (1916): 3–32.

Goff, John H. "The Path to Oakfuskee, Upper Creek Route in Georgia to the Creek Indians." *Georgia Historical Quarterly* 39 (1955): 1–36.

Green, Michael D. "Alexander McGillivray." In *American Indian Leaders*, edited by R. David Edmunds. Lincoln: University of Nebraska Press, 1980.

Griffith, Benjamin W., Jr. "Lt. David Moniac, Creek Indian: First Minority Graduate of West Point." *Alabama Historical Quarterly* 43 (1981): 99–110.

Grinnell, George Bird. "Tenure of Land among the Indians." *American Anthropologist* 9 (1907): 1–11.

Haas, Mary R. "Creek Inter-town Relations." *American Anthropologist* 42 (1940): 479–83.

Hahn, Mrs. M. Davis, ed. "Act for the Relief of John Randon." *Baldwin County Historical Quarterly* 7 (1980): 27.

Halbert, Henry Sale. "Creek War Incidents." *Alabama Historical Society Transactions* 2 (1897–98): 101–102.

Hall, Arthur N. "The Red Stick War: Creek Indian Affairs during the War of 1812." *Chronicles of Oklahoma* 12 (1934): 264–93.

Hassig, Ross. "Internal Conflict in the Creek War of 1813–1814." *Enthnohistory* 21 (1974): 251–71.

Hemperley, Marion. "Benjamin Hawkins' Trip across Georgia in 1796." *Georgia Historical Quarterly* 14 (1971): 114–36.

Hewitt, J. N. B. "Notes on the Creek Indians." *Bureau of American Ethnology Bulletin 123.* Washington, D.C.: U.S. Government Printing Office, 1939.

Hryniewicki, Richard J. "The Creek Treaty of Washington, 1826." *Georgia Historical Quarterly* 48 (1964): 425–41.

Lurie, Nancy O. "Indian Cultural Adjustment to European Civilization." In *Seventeenth-Century America: Essays in Colonial History,* edited by James Morton Smith, pp. 33–60. Chapel Hill: University of North Carolina Press, 1959.

McCluggage, Robert W. "The Senate and Indian Land Titles, 1800–1825." *Western Historical Quarterly* 1 (1970): 415–25.

Mason, Carol I. "Eighteenth Century Culture Change among the Lower Creeks." *Florida Anthropologist* 16 (1963): 65–80.

Nunez, Theron A., Jr. "Creek Nativism and the Creek War of 1813–1814." *Ethnohistory* 5 (1958): 1–17.

O'Donnell, James H. III. "Alexander McGillivray: Training for Leadership, 1777–1783." *Georgia Historical Quarterly* 49 (1965): 172–86.

Orr, William Gates. "Surrender of Weatherford." *Transactions of the Alabama Historical Society, 1897–1898* 2 (1898): 57–78.

Owen, Marie Bankhead. "Indian Chiefs." *Alabama Historical Quarterly* 33 (1951): 81–83.

————, ed. "Indian Tribes and Towns in Alabama." *Alabama Historical Quarterly* 32 (1950): 169–71.

Owsley, Frank L., Jr. "Ambrister and Arbuthnot: Adventurers or Martyrs for British Honor?" *Journal of the Early Republic* 5 (1985): 290–308.

————. "British and Indian Activities in Spanish West Florida during the War of 1812." *Florida Historical Quarterly* 46 (1967): 111–23.

————. "The Fort Mims Massacre." *Alabama Review* 24 (1971): 192–204.

————. "Prophet of War: Josiah Francis and the Creek War." *American Indian Quarterly* 11 (1985): 273–93.

Parsons, Lynn Hudson. "'A Perpetual Harrow Upon My Feelings': John Quincy Adams and the American Indian." *New England Quarterly* 46 (1973): 339–79.

Payne, John Howard. "The Green Corn Dance." Edited by John R. Swanton. *Chronicles of Oklahoma* 10 (1932): 170–95.

Pickett, Andrew J. "The Death of McIntosh, 1825." *Arrow Points* 10 (1925): 31–32.

Powell, B. E. "Was Tecumseh's 'Arm of Fire' the Comet of 1811?" *Georgia Journal of Science* 39 (1981): 87.

Prucha, Francis Paul. "Andrew Jackson's Indian Policy: A Reassessment." *Journal of American History* 56 (1969): 527–39.

Silver, James W. "A Counter-Proposal to the Indian Removal Policy of Andrew Jackson." *Journal of Mississippi History* 4 (1942): 207–15.

————. "General Gaines Meets Governor Troup: A State-Federal Clash in 1825." *Georgia Historical Quarterly* 27 (1943): 248–70.

A Soldier. "Gov. Clinch and the Indians." *Army and Navy Chronicle* 2 (1836): 114–16.

Speck, Frank G. "The Creek Indians of Taskigi Town." *American Anthropological Association Memoirs* 2 (1907): 116–17.

Sugden, John. "The Southern Indians in the War of 1812: The Closing Phase." *Florida Historical Quarterly* 60 (1982): 279.

Swan, Caleb. "Position and State of Manners and Arts in the Creek, or Muscogee Nation in 1791." In Henry Rowe Schoolcraft, *Historical and Statistical Information, Respecting the History, Condition, and Prospects of the Indian Tribes of the United States,* 5: 251–83. Philadelphia: Lippincott, 1855.

Swanton, John R. "Notes on the Mental Assimilation of the Races." *Journal of the Washington Academy of Sciences* 16 (1926): 493–502.

Tarvin, Marion Elisha. "The Muscogees or Creek Indians from 1517 to 1893." *Baldwin County Historical Society Quarterly* 8 (1980): 8–21.

Thomason, Hugh M. "Governor Peter Early and the Creek Indian Frontier, 1813–1815." *Georgia Historical Quarterly* 45 (1961): 223–37.

Tunstall, Tom Tate. "Tom Tate Tunstall Defends the Name of Weatherford." *Arrow Points* 9 (1924): 6–8.

Way, Royal B. "The United States Factory System for Trading with the Indians, 1796–1822." *Journal of American History* 6 (1919): 220–35.

Wesley, Edgar B. "The Government Factory System among the Indians, 1795–1822." *Journal of Economic and Business History* 4 (1932): 487–511.

West, Elizabeth Howard, ed. "A Prelude to the Creek War of 1813–14: In a Letter of John Innerarity to James Innerarity." *Florida Historical Quarterly* 18 (1940): 247–66.

Whitaker, Arthur P. "Alexander McGillivray, 1783–1789." *North Carolina Historical Review* 4 (1928): 181–203.

Willis, William S. "Patrilineal Institutions in Southeastern North America." *Ethnohistory* 10 (1963): 250–69.

Wright, J. Leitch, Jr. "Creek-American Treaty of 1790: Alexander McGillivray and the Diplomacy of the Old Southwest." *Georgia Historical Quarterly* 51 (1967): 379–400.

Index

———— • ————